Major To Minor

Printed in the United Kingdom by Biddles Ltd, Surrey

Published by Sanctuary Publishing Limited, Sanctuary House, 45-53 Sinclair Road, London W14 0NS, United Kingdom

www.sanctuarypublishing.com

Copyright: Mike Read, 2000

Cover photograph: © Steven Goldman. Author photograph: © Classic FM

All rights reserved. No part of this book may be reproduced in any form or by any electronic or mechanical means, including information storage or retrieval systems, without permission in writing from the publisher, except by a reviewer, who may quote brief passages.

While the publishers have made every reasonable effort to trace the copyright owners for any or all of the photographs in this book, there may be some omissions of credits for which we apologise.

ISBN: 1-86074-316-1

Major To Minor
The Rise And Fall Of The Songwriter

Mike Read

About The Author

Mike Read has been a household name in Britain for 20 years, winning ten National Broadcaster Of The Year awards during his time with Radio 1 and Classic FM. He now presents a daily breakfast show for Jazz FM. His top-rated television programmes include *Saturday Superstore*, *Pop Quiz* and *Top Of The Pops*.

During the '90s he wrote seven successful stage musicals and three screenplays. Dozens of artists have recorded his songs, including Cliff Richard, David Essex, Leo Sayer, Marc Almond, Gene Pitney, Colin Blunstone, Justin Hayward, King's College Choir, The Eton College Choir and HM Band Of The Royal Marines. Mike is a poet of some note, chairman of the Rupert Brooke Society and a keen tennis player. This is his 29th book.

Acknowledgements

Thanks to Jeff Hudson at Sanctuary for convincing me to write the book; the songwriters featured in this book, who have given me a lot of their time; the songwriters with whom I've collaborated; the artists who have recorded my songs; and to the writers whose songs have been an enormous inspiration.

Contents

	Foreword	9
	Introduction	11
1	America's First Songwriter	23
2	Music Halls To Musicals	44
3	The Songwriters Go To War	56
4	Rags To Riches	85
5	East Meets West	91
6	The Golden Years	104
7	The Child Is Father To The Man	130
8	I Write The Songs (US)	139
9	I Write The Songs (UK)	158
10	Change Partners	196
11	Let's Work Together	202
12	Absolutely Brill	230
13	Writing From Within	252
14	Pop Into The Theatre	272
15	The Stories Behind The Songs	287
16	Personal Experiences	301
17	Where Do We Go From Here?	315
	Bibliography	325
	Index	326

Foreword

Songs are the most important ingredients of the popular music industry. Always have been, always will be. I would say that wouldn't I? But songs – the good ones, anyway – survive through the ages, move on through generations and carry a timeless message, even though their interpreters, orchestrators and producers and the methods by which they are recorded may alter drastically over the decades. The songs live on.

Even the greatest of stars – the Presleys, the Beatles and the Sinatras – can only peak once (although in some cases it's a long peak, a kind of Table Mountain summit) before they move gently into a different plane, often recalled, frequently replayed, but nevertheless history. John Lennon's songs have, sadly, long outlived him, and so will Paul McCartney's.

Yet, paradoxically, the songwriter – unless he or she is a performer as well – is often little more than a name to the millions who derive such pleasure from the songs. Mike Read, no mean songwriter himself, has within these pages boldly attempted to put this right. By adding flesh and blood to many of the enigmatic handles, he has paid great tribute to the vital art of the popular songwriter, at least in its American and British forms, in which guises it has known no equal. From Stephen Foster to Diane Warren, much has changed and much has remained the same, but a great song is still king.

Perhaps great songs seem rarer now; certainly many more records are successful these days without the assistance of anything that resembles the notion of what would have been considered a memorable tune or an intelligent lyric as recently as 20 years ago. But much the same thing was said about rock 'n' roll's first batch of hits back in the '50s, and many of the songs of, say, Buddy Holly, the Bryants, Lieber and Stoller, Pomus and Shuman and Chuck Berry are now indisputable standards, showing no more inclination to go away than 'Smoke Gets In Your Eyes' or 'Stardust'.

Songwriters are sensitive, astute people, and Mike Read's book gives

Major To Minor

this view a certain amount of credence and proves beyond doubt that the world would be a poorer and the music world a non-existent place one without the bright sparks who are able to touch so many lives with such short bursts of inspiration.

Tim Rice

Introduction

Words and melodies have always been a powerful and all-consuming passion of mine, even before I had any real grasp of the English language. I have instant recall over where I first heard them, my emotions on hearing them and how deeply they affected me. I wasn't really aware of the songwriters, although I suppose that I was vaguely aware that somebody must have written them. I do know that I felt that some of the songs had always existed. They hadn't, of course, but then I felt the same about myself, and I hadn't either, as far as I knew.

I imagined that the songs that I heard my mother singing snatches of around the house all came from the same period, as they were – rather obviously – new to me. People humming and whistling songs as they went about their business was once a part and parcel of daily life that carried these tunes down through the decades, passing them on from generation to generation.

For me, there were several factors that made songs sound haunting, exhilarating, or laden with an inordinate sadness, but to put those down in words would be to try and earth something that has to remain mystical, and firmly rooted in the realm of metaphysics, if that's not too paradoxical.

On those golden summer pre-school days that last forever, I'd trail my mother around the vegetable garden, prior to pea-shelling duties, and catch strains of 'Me And Jane In A Plane', 'Mairzy Doats' or 'Papa Piccolino'. This was wonderful stuff! Little did I know that, some 35 years later, the writer of the latter song, Bob Musel, would take a great interest in my career, and would often relate tales of the great songsmiths of yesteryear over a slap-up lunch. He roared with surprised and delighted laughter when I launched into 'Papa Piccolino', one of the first songs I remembered hearing. Neither, at the time, would I have dreamed that, in the year 2000, I'd be discussing the origins of 'Mairzy Doats' with the song's 87-year-old writer, Milton Drake.

My maternal grandmother had a pretty good singing voice, so a lot of her favourites also embedded themselves in my ever-growing reservoir of words and tunes. Again, for all I knew, these could have been brand-new songs. Nobody told me otherwise. Somehow, though, I was aware that they weren't. They seemed full of nostalgia, and oozed sentimentality. I loved them. 'Lily Of Laguna' sounded wonderful. I didn't know who Lily was, or where Laguna was located, but it hardly mattered. If I had any idea where it might be geographically, I suppose that I thought that it must be somewhere near the little wooden hut of another song she sang, 'I Wouldn't Leave My Little Wooden Hut For You'. I'm not sure that I ever heard her sing a song all the way through, but the repertoire did contain fragments of many songs, from the plaintive 'If You Were The Only Girl In The World' (surely her favourite) to the more rumbustious 'Has Anybody Here Seen Kelly?'. Much later, I realised that some of these were songs not only from her teenage years but also from those of my great-grandmother.

My grandparents always had piles of sheet music lying around, which is where I first discovered Stephen Foster's songs, long before I was aware that he'd written them. I loved 'Some Folks', and 'The Old Folks At Home', for which I felt an unbidden bond, but rather curiously got another favourite, 'On The 'Gin, 'Gin 'Ginny Shore', inextricably tangled up with the Surrey beauty spot Virginia Water, and the tune to 'Davy Crockett'. I used words that I imagined I'd heard to a distorted version of another song. I think I discovered plagiarism and songwriting at the same time.

The places sung about in these songs could have been real or imaginary; I was happy with either. 'The Lincolnshire Poacher' – which I adored but again confused the words slightly, fondly imagining it to be about boy scouts – I knew to be a real place; but I wasn't so sure about Carolina, as in "nothing could be finer than to be in Carolina". Only much later would I discover that the composer of 'Carolina', Walter Donaldson, was also responsible for 'On The 'Gin, 'Gin 'Ginny Shore'. If I'd known that these songwriters were subliminally shaping my future (I know, then it wouldn't have been subliminal) then I'd have paid more attention, asked more questions, found out who they were and, most importantly, tried to discover why they'd picked on me!

My grandfather had clearly been an enthusiastic listener to the radio detective series *Paul Temple*, and although I had little interest in whatever dialogue was taking place, the theme tune had me in a vice-like grip. This was a mighty, mighty melody. Was it really possible for a human being to create something like this? The position of that particular radio set, at my grandparents home in Lancashire, meant that I stood at the window, where I was able to take in a panoramic view of the Pennines, with romantic ribbons of steam emitting from distant railway locomotives. Why, out of all the music on the radio that held me spellbound, I should link the *Paul Temple* theme – a piece of music written, unbeknownst to me, about a train called the *Coronation Scot* – with those distant engines is beyond me. I later determined the reason to be Vivian Ellis' brilliant musical encapsulation, which I mumbled to him rather feebly when placed next to him at a Performing Rights Society bash at London's Savoy Hotel. So much to say to him, so little said.

The first time I attempted to perform for my family exposed my inability to hold a note. In my enthusiasm, I always expel too quickly, rather than controlling my breath, clearly going for volume rather than quality. This appears to remain the weakest point in my vocal armoury, as my sterner critics have frequently noted. Bitterly hurt at the tears of mirth that my efforts elicited, of what I believed to be a soul-stirring rendition of 'Roll The Cotton Down', I let myself be guided towards something with a lyric that I could grasp more easily. My cotton-rolling period gave way to the more English 'Out Of Town'. I have to confess that, although I grew to love it, it was suggested by "Auntie" Joan, my tap-dancing teacher. I was one of her "tinies". Tinies were, I later realised, guaranteed to make parents simper at stage shows, whilst not possessing the real talent of the older children in her class. I was happy with that. For a while I was rather proud to be thought of as being tone deaf, but as soon as I realised that this meant that I couldn't get to grips with the songs that I loved I stopped being lazy and began to hit the right notes, more or less.

My absolute fascination with words and music must have helped me to absorb the words to 'Out Of Town' while simultaneously tapping my tap shoes and trying in vain to click my fingers like the older children could. In as late as 1998, not having performed it since the age of six, I was able to sing every word and note in an impromptu rendition for Auntie Joan a short while before she died. Her pianist for my appalling attempts at dancing was her sister, Barbara Andrews, whose daughter Julie was already a highly-successful actress and singer. Auntie Barbara would later be incredibly supportive of my early attempts at writing songs. She was both encouraging and influential, and I remain indebted.

Another hitherto-unknown style of music invaded my senses as a boy. The Sea Scouts (to whom I nursed a not-very-secret desire to belong) held their annual fête in the garden, which always meant exciting stalls such as "Ye Olde Wishing Well", a fortune teller, and "Pick A Straw". There were also numerous other delights, including one year a bunch of big blokes with musical instruments. I wasn't quite sure what they were doing with them, but the energy was enormous. I found one song in particular, 'Party Doll', a little baffling. Why were these big guys – who, it has to be said, weren't dressed like everybody else – singing about dolls? I couldn't imagine, nor dared ask. It took me a few years to catch on, but I got there in the end.

This music, too, like hymns, traditional songs and the old sentimental stuff, went down a storm in my book.

Many traditional songs also stirred some ancient Celtic blood in me. 'Westering Home' I thought was magical, and still do, while the way the notes fell in 'Sweet Polly Oliver' and 'The Ash Grove' absolutely mesmerised me. The stirring Celtic melody of 'The Minstrel Boy', with words by Thomas Moore, left me wondering how it was possible to conceive such a beautiful tune.

I found hymns equally moving. The innate majesty of 'Hills Of The North Rejoice' can still reduce me to tears, and the dazzlingly simplistic 'Glad That I Live Am I', with words by Geoffrey Shaw set to a melody by Lizette Reese, is a perfect distillation of human existence:

> Glad that I live am I;
> That the sky is blue;
> Glad for the country lanes,
> And the fall of dew.
> After the sun the rain,
> After the rain the sun;
> This is the way of life,
> Till the work be done.
> All that we need to do,
> Be we low or high,
> Is to see that we grow
> Nearer the sky.

No diatribe of stylistic felicities could better explain life on Earth.

INTRODUCTION

Many other classic pieces of hymnody were almost as gripping. Blake's powerful 'Jerusalem', with the later addition of Parry's emotive melody, is probably the most obvious example of the perfect marriage of words and music. Less obvious but equally potent are the 17th-century Scottish psalter 'Pray That Jerusalem...' and 'Non Nobis Domine', which Rudyard Kipling wrote for the Pageant Of Parliament in 1934

In some instances it was the melodies that drove home, while in others – like this hymn, with words by Thomas Carlyle, on a not entirely dissimilar theme to 'Glad That I Live Am I' – it was the lyric:

> So here hath been dawning
> Another blue day:
> Think, wilt thou let it slip useless away?
> Out of eternity this new day is born
> Into eternity, at night, will return.

My father's repertoire also had a profound effect on my musical dawn. It ranged from novelty numbers such as 'Ginger, You're Barmy', and a nonsense song that began, "Aura chickerau chickeracka roona" (I learned to sing it but not to spell it), to a magical melody that I later discovered was written by Frenchman Georges Auric: the theme to 'Moulin Rouge.' The latter was never sung, always whistled. My father was an habitual and not unimpressive whistler, undoubtedly borne out of years of playing the harmonica.

The magical world of music and words that was continually in my head often led to periods of deep nostalgia (which I'd had no time to accrue, so heaven knows where it came from) and troughs of self-inflicted loneliness, when I'd let an overwhelming sadness wash over me. These would be accompanied by an almost mantra-like but slightly pathetic chanting of songs that seemed poignant at the time, like 'Where Oh Where Has My Little Dog Gone?', which appeared on my musical box, and 'Home, Home On The Range'. 'Little Dog' was, by then, getting on for 100 years old, but I neither knew nor cared; it moved me emotionally, and that was all that mattered. Bizarrely, I can remember not only the exact locations in the garden or the house where I sang these, but also the atmosphere, the emotions and often what I was wearing. I had to dress in certain clothes for certain songs.

MAJOR TO MINOR

When the theme tune to *Riders Of The Range* came on the radio and riveted me to the spot, I was staring over the laurel hedge to the white house opposite, the home of a little girl called Kay, imagining that these cowboy chaps (no clothing pun intended!) were not too far beyond her garden. I don't remember listening to or understanding any of the stories, but that theme song...!

I became aware of America and American songs through the two boys who lived next door, Robert and Michael Sherwell, who taught me endless verses of 'Ten Little Indians' and 'Davy Crockett'. The boys were, of course, Americans. Both once left a children's Christmas party, which my parents had organised, in high dudgeon because my apparently unworldly English friends didn't know all 17 verses of their beloved 'Davy Crockett'. Yes, Robert and Michael knew them all! This was harsh treatment, I thought. The hero of the Alamo was hardly part of the cultural experience of a bunch of English kids who'd barely started school.

It was good to have them as neighbours, though, for, as well as giving masterclasses in lengthy songs from the New World, they were a conduit to important aspects of life that until then had had no place in mine, like smashing American bicycles, waffles with maple syrup, a father with a Dodge automobile and Dell comics. They also had an American nanny, who was pretty and also sang like a dream. For a long time, I assumed that the song ever-present on her lips, the refrain from which would waft over whenever she was in the orchard, was written for her. It might well have been, as her rendition of 'Don't Let The Stars Get In Your Eyes' remains the most abiding version with me.

Apart from pointing the finger at groups and singers too numerous to mention, I feel that at least some of the blame for a major musical sea change must fall on the shoulders of Ian Gibb. He was the one, after all, who always had the *New Musical Express* at school. I'd never seen it before. I didn't even know that there was a paper devoted entirely to music. I'd heard the songs on the radio, of course, and avidly watched *Juke Box Jury* and *Thank Your Lucky Stars*, but as soon as I had a periodical in my hands from which I could absorb everything about the artists, songs and songwriters I was lost.

My grandfather bought me my first guitar, although I wasn't exactly sure what to do with it. I soon took on the characteristic of a piece of musical blotting paper, avidly learning chords from anyone who could be bothered to show me. Unlike other kids, I had no desire to be a lead guitarist. As long as I was able to play a few chords, I could embark upon the more important business of writing songs. To an impressionable lad, there were so many magical songs pouring out of the radio that it would be impossible to begin a roll of honour, but the bewitching songs of Lennon and McCartney, the blues-based energy and swagger of compositions by Jagger and Richards, the flawless interpretations that The Everly Brothers brought to their own and other people's songs, and the pure simplicity of Buddy Holly's canon (which I tardily discovered some while after his demise) must rate a special mention.

My earliest attempts at writing reveal a very diverse approach to a wide variety of subjects. I wrote songs about Charles Dickens, patron of the arts Edward James, a friend's psychedelic roadshow, Gilbert and Sullivan's *Iolanthe*, and regularly attempted to emulate Bob Dylan with "stream-of-consciousness" songs. "Don't get caught in the spider's web of uniformity," I drawled, and certainly meant it, even though Dylan had probably already drawled something very similar, and executed it with more conviction.

It was while having tea at an uncle and aunt's house that I scribbled down the germ of an idea which was to become my first published song. I know it sounds like a flight of fancy, but it was genuinely written on the back of an envelope.

Having had the gall to walk with the song into the offices of Carlin Music, at 17 Savile Row, London, I was rewarded for my brazen attitude – with what I later perceived to more encouragement than conviction – by publisher Dave Most (another person whom I later came to know well), who offered to take the song. He muttered something about it possibly being suitable for Herman's Hermits...or maybe it was "not suitable for Herman's Hermits"? When I tell the story, it's always the former version. I think that it has a little more showbiz zest.

It was easier to get it published than it was to convince my father to sign the contract. In my mind, I was already a published writer; it was now surely a short step to writing for Cream or John Mayall's Bluesbreakers, and possibly American artists, too. I was certain that I could even knock up something pretty reasonable for The Byrds or The Lovin' Spoonful. In the eyes of the law, though, I was still a minor, and embarrassingly needed a parental signature for the dream to become reality.

Although he was convinced that I was signing away any paltry goods and chattels that I might have possessed, I succeeded in breaking down my father's resistance. After a week of breathing in the rarefied atmosphere reserved for us songwriting legends, I returned to the land of mortals. I never heard another word about 'Evening Paper', a classic song about the world of a classified ads, where our hero places an advertisement offering "Happiness For Hire". In retrospect, a rather arrogant action. In retrospect, not an earth-shattering song.

There's so much more than I could write in an introduction to the fascinating and beguiling world of the songwriters and their creations, of which I've been lucky enough to have played a small part. It would be foolish and uncharacteristically coy to omit at least a passing mention of the first single with my name on the writing credit. 'February's Child', written for my first girlfriend, Valerie Edge, has bizarrely enough (for me) become a collector's item. Valued at anywhere between £125 and £140, I now regret pressing the hundreds of free copies into the hands of unwilling friends and relations. I often think about asking for them back. The single featured vocals by me, rather uninterestingly, and somewhat more interestingly the backing vocals of one of the century's finest and most adventurous lyricists, Tim Rice. I'm still puzzled as to why he was given a knighthood for these few paltry harmonies. Obviously, they must have had a hidden depth and quality invisible to the rest of the group.

At about the same time, and owing to the absence of any real talent, I was inveigled into singing backing vocals on some demos for Tim and Andrew's musical about Richard The Lionheart. One of the tracks limped out as a single, but the obligatory backing vocalist's knighthood was nowhere to be seen. It was either my lack of timbre or talent.

TMB Rice also springs to mind when I recall the strangest conversation I had for this book. Interviewing Leiber and Stoller about the songs that they wrote for Elvis Presley, while dressed and made up as Pharaoh (in the guise of Elvis) during rehearsals for the part in Tim and Andrew's *Joseph* and sitting on the cricket pitch of an English public school, will remain forever etched in my memory.

Another guy who was very helpful to a budding songwriter was Barry Mason, when he clearly had more important things to do, like write hit songs. Clutching a tape of some of my songs, I knocked, unannounced on the door of his house in Esher, not quite knowing what response I'd get, if any. However, he not only invited me in but also actually listened to the songs there and then, made a few constructive suggestions and, best of all, he was also pretty complimentary about them. He said that he felt sure that I was "going to make it". It was a real thrill, and an emotional experience to be able to invite him onto my TV series *Pop Quiz* a few years later.

I first heard what was to become one of my favourite phrases in John Lennon's enchanting song 'Beautiful Boy': "Life is what happens to you while you're busy making other plans." I'm not quite sure whether he wrote it or borrowed it, but either way it's popped its head up on a number of unexpected occasions in my life, notably propelling my move into radio and television, a twist on my life that I hadn't allowed for. The whirligig of fun, music and good times that followed (hooray!) left little time for sleep, let alone writing songs, but I managed to sneak out the odd single, some self-penned and some covers. For these forays into the world of vinyl, I hid – not too successfully – behind a series of bewildering pseudonyms: The Trainspotters, The Ghosts, The Rock-olas and The Grasshoppers. I chose the latter, rather obviously, for my version of The Crickets' 'Teardrops Fall Like Rain', a great song co-written by Crickets Jerry Allison and Glen D Hardin.

I'd interviewed Jerry (known as "JI") and the other Crickets on one or two of their UK visits, and found them charming, courteous and delightful, but wondered how far JI's charm was being stretched when he complimented me on my version of his song. Come to think of it, what a hell of a shrewd judge!

When I covered 'Language Of Love', one of many great songs written by the gifted John D Loudermilk, he didn't pass comment, although he did invite me to perform it with him onstage at the Country Music Festival at Wembley. He couldn't possibly have imagined that I could add anything to his own delivery, so I presume that he meant it to be a masterclass: "Follow me boy, and I'll show you how you should play it!" I did, and he did, but the most fascinating aspect of the performance was John's wife acting out the lyrics in Indian sign language. That was the show stealer. I was just happy to be on stage, performing with one of the songwriting greats.

I consider myself lucky to have such a genuinely broad taste in music. I can get as excited by Robert Johnson as I can by Elgar. Doo-wop sends me into the same paroxysms as punk – bring on The Orioles or The Clash. I get as much of a buzz listening to current stuff from Travis and Lena Marlin as I do from Stephen Foster's canon from the mid 1800s, late-'60s Soft Machine or '80s acts The Proclaimers and The Icicle Works. I get the same kick playing Thane Russal's electrifying mid-'60s version of 'Security' as I do playing his father, Carrol Gibbons', song 'Gardens In The Rain'. I can identify equally with Scott Walker and Nick Drake, and can recall the excitement of great songs being played live by Rory Gallagher and The Jam.

I still get a thrill when I hear my songs in musicals, or performed by a choir, but for any writer gripped by Top 40 fever from an early age the biggest kick must be seeing one of your songs in the chart, the same chart that your childhood heroes once haunted. I've been fortunate to have two of these, a paltry number compared to legendary writers but, nevertheless, a thrill that remains undimmed. I'm delighted that both Cliff Richard and David Essex were rash enough to take the plunge, and I'm relieved that their careers remain unaffected. Maybe here is an appropriate place to thank some of the other great artists who have also recorded my songs, including Gene Pitney, Leo Sayer, Marc Almond, Colin Blunstone, Donovan, Justin Hayward, Jon Anderson, Steve Harley, Don McLean, Alvin Stardust, Captain Sensible, the late Paul Young, The Kings College Choir, The Eton College Choir and HM Band Of The Royal Marines. Bless you all!

I've also had the pleasure of writing the occasional song with talented composers such as Simon May, Albert Hammond, Geoff Goddard, Andrew Lloyd Webber, Michael Reed, Chris Eaton and Guy Fletcher, as well as working with the words of two of this century's finest poets, Sir John Betjeman and Rupert Brooke.

Of all the music business functions – awards ceremonies and the like – I still get the greatest thrill from being at a gathering of songwriters. The Ivor Novello Awards is always a moving ceremony, where songwriters of all ages gather to pay tribute to their fellow tradesmen, with genuine admiration and respect. At this event, more than any other music business awards dinner, I am aware of belonging to an extended and rather special family, who are the creative engine room of the industry.

Or at least, they were. I find it extraordinary that the role of the truly independent songwriter has been allowed to expire quietly and without protest. Bringing them back into the arena would certainly improve the prospects of reviving the United Kingdom's musical exports. Classical composers are virtually canonised, while professional songwriters (with the exception of artists who write their own material) live in relative obscurity.

The names of most independent and/or non-performing songwriters are completely unknown, not only to the general public but also to people in the music industry, and sometimes even to the artists themselves.

Introduction

It would be impossible to include every songwriter in this book, or it would become a ten-volume epic, so I've decided to investigate in more depth the early innovators, who helped in some way to change, create and shape the future for others in the profession. In some instances I've let just one or two voices speak for their era, while other periods are bursting with so much talent and vision that it would be imprudent not give some sort of representation to several composers and lyricists. To list everybody would be to fill the book with names alone. If you're not here, it's no reflection on your standing in the industry, talent, charm or the size of your PRS return. It would have been a lifetime's work to talk to and include everybody.

A post-WWI potted overview would be that, during the 1920s, the advent of radio stations carried the songwriters' wares into millions of homes, while the first talking films that appeared later in the decade opened even more doors for lyricists and composers alike. 1932 saw the release of the first musical film, after which the wise men at Warner Bros intelligently formed a publishing company. During the '30s and '40s, songwriters' royalties were becoming big business, as composers and lyricists then had the extra areas of film and radio in which to work, with television expanding rapidly.

From the late '40s onwards, life was healthy for the independent songwriter. There were more record companies, more radio and television outlets and more new artists to write for and printed charts of record sales became a tangible barometer for success. Hardly any artists wrote their own songs, and having a song recorded by one singer could easily result in several cover versions. From the mid '50s onwards, the Tin Pan Alleys in both the US and the UK were adding rock 'n' roll to their traditional diet and many new songwriters emerged, encouraged by the possibility of writing hit songs around a basic three- or four-chord structure. Although in terms of longevity it helped to be good at your craft, more writers were discovering that you didn't have to be a trained musician, or in some cases even a musician at all, in order to be able to write hits in the modern idiom.

The coming of The Beatles, for whom Lennon and McCartney wrote the majority of the songs, heralded the beginning of the end for the independent songwriter, and inspired confidence in groups and artists to write their own material. However, this was a long, slow death. Over that drawn-out period, artists began to write songs that suited their voices and vocal ranges, and were able to tailor lyrics to their own requirements and feelings, rather than singing someone else's words.

In many cases, artists writing their own songs had short-lived strength but no length. America still has a healthy and flourishing songwriting scene in Nashville, but the climate for would-be writers in Britain is currently unhealthy. Our composers and lyricists are suffering from the worst chart drought in America since the early '60s.

Although it can be subjective, I've tried to keep within the guidelines of the mainstream "popular songwriter", without wading into too many tributaries or straying into the equally worthy world of classical music or opera and other musical areas.

This book is not intended to be a definitive or even comprehensive take on songwriting and songwriters, but instead plots the course of the popular song through the lives and works of their creators, from the first songwriter saying, "Wait a minute, I could make a living doing this" to the death of the independent songwriter in Britain.

As an increasing number of artists write their own material, another criterion had to be the virtual exclusion of non-dedicated songwriters, ie those who are known primarily as performers. There are of course writers here who are known equally as performers and creators, such as Lennon and McCartney, Jagger and Richards, Buddy Holly, Paul Simon, Chuck Berry and Neil Sedaka, but history will almost certainly judge them more on their writing skills than on their live performances, which will inevitably fade from living memory.

Generally, popular songs have always been associated more with the interpreter than with the writer, while the names of classical composers are often welded to the piece of music concerned, ie Beethoven's Fifth, Rachmaninov's Piano Concerto Number Two in C minor, Handel's Water Music, or Elgar's Pomp And Circumstance Marches. Apart from aficionados, a majority of 20th-century songs are identified with the artist who had most success with them, with only the most eminent composers and lyricists permeating the psyche of the populace.

Songwriters unwittingly help to chart our lives, their songs conjuring up a whole spectrum of human emotions: pleasure, pain, love, romance, grief, despair, angst, loneliness and optimism – the list is endless. So is the talent of the great writers, who seem to pluck magic out of the air, create something from nothing, and touch the lives of millions of people whom they'll never meet. This is their story.

1 *America's First Songwriter*

The first person to make a living solely as a professional songwriter was Stephen Foster, the son of once-prosperous parents living in Pittsburgh, Pennsylvania. His father, Colonel William Barclay Foster, served three terms in the State Legislature, was twice mayor of Allegheny City, and married Eliza Clayland Tomlinson in 1807. Stephen, born in 1826, arrived rather patriotically on 4 July, within hours of the death of John Adams, the second president of the USA, and also that of Thomas Jefferson, his successor and founder of the Democratic Republican Party.

The American Jubilee Day baby was the youngest surviving member of the Foster siblings (including a half-brother), and from an early age began to pick out melodies and harmonies on his sister Ann's guitar. By this time, the Foster family had been in America for almost exactly 100 years, since Stephen's great-grandfather, Alexander Foster, had left Londonderry in 1725. Whether he was disillusioned by the recent statute enabling the English Parliament to legislate for Ireland, or enticed by the promise of prosperity in the New World, he left the Emerald Isle, eventually settling in Pennsylvania. Stephen's maternal roots were also English; the Reverend James Clayland, an ancestor on his mother's side, had arrived in Maryland in around the early 1670s, at the time when the Royal African Company had been granted rights (under the English flag) to collect slaves from West Africa and supply them to Jamaica, Barbados and Virginia.

As yet, science isn't able to explore with absolute certainty the likelihood that creative influences could lay dormant in a family's genes, or the possibility that they could be triggered in a descendant at a future date by an indeterminate catalyst. Until we have a cogitable handle on those areas of genetics, and later biographers reveal that Foster was influenced by John Dryden, Britain's poet laureate during Clayland's life, and by Irish songs sung by Alexander Foster on the banks of the River Foyle, the more palpable influences must suffice!

From early boyhood, Foster had been exposed to an eclectic mix of music, including sentimental parlour ballads, black minstrelsy, Celtic songs, rallying choruses written in the Civil War, comic narratives and classical music. As a boy, the works of Beethoven (who died the year after Foster was born) and Schubert (who died in the following year) were popular, and during those years the creative juices of the young Pennsylvanian started to flow. The "high Romantics" – Mendelssohn, Verdi, Liszt, Gounod, Wagner and Berlioz – were writing music to which he would have certainly been subjected, through essentially amateur interpretations. A quote from Berlioz would certainly prove apposite to Foster's life: "Time is a great teacher, but unfortunately it kills all of its pupils."

Thomas Moore's Irish ballads also played an important part in the formation of Foster's more nostalgic compositions. Born in Dublin in 1779, Moore was a gifted writer of verse. The mutinous winds that fanned the flames of the French Revolution, which had raged during his school years, also rekindled the unrest in the hearts of many Irish Catholics.

Strangely reflecting another area of oppression that was also to have a profound effect on Fosters songwriting, Moore declared: "Born of Catholic parents I had come into the world with the slave's yoke around my neck..." In 1793, an Act was passed by the Irish Parliament which, amongst other provisions, allowed Catholics to enrol at Dublin's Trinity College. Moore was one of the first to go up, studying there from 1794-99, making a name for himself as an exceptional versifier, London society eulogising his talent, and his name swiftly reaching leonine proportions in the literary world. His words appeared to catch the spirit of the time, as Foster's would half a century later. After briefly working for the Admiralty Court Of The Bermudas in 1804, Moore then toured America, where he was disgusted by "the baser side of Democracy, which has nowhere, and at no time, found such blatant expression as in the United States of America". His *Odes And Epistles* was published there in 1806, and contained many of his 'Poems Relating To America', which he'd written during his travels in the still-young country. He penned verses in Norfolk, Virginia, the city of Washington, Philadelphia and Buffalo; but the anti-American tone in the preface to these poems, in which he refers to "the rude familiarity of the lower orders" and "the unpolished state of society in general", and points up the reasons that will "repress every sanguine hope of the future energy and greatness of America", resulted in harsh treatment from critics on both sides of the Atlantic.

The idea of putting words to old Irish melodies had originally been planted in Moore's head in 1797, when he was 18, but it wasn't until 1807 that he began to explore this device in earnest. Over the next 20 years he worked with many old Irish, English, Scottish, Welsh, Portuguese, German, French and Italian airs in this manner, initially with Sir John Stevenson undertaking the musical arrangements. Moore became incredibly popular in America and Britain, with three of his songs featuring in what could well have been one of the first retrospective popular music charts, a Top 44 of the most popular songs in America between 1801 and 1825, compiled by musicologist Charles Hamm. The rise in popularity of the piano, which was manufactured in America from 1813, did much to spread the wares of the songsmiths, although unsurprisingly there were few Americans practising the art until the 1830s.

Until the mid 1830s, most of the songsheets contained only lyrics, and more often than not failed to provide any reference to the music. Books of these sheets would invariably feature the words of writers such as Robert Burns, Charles Dibden, Walter Scott and Thomas Moore. Moore's songs caught the imagination of Foster's sister Charlotte, who included several of them in her repertoire, including 'Flow On, Thou Shining River', 'Come Rest In This Bosom' and 'There's Nothing True But Heaven'. The latter was set to music by Oliver Shaw, the first American-born songwriter to achieve major commercial success. Unlike Foster three decades later, however, Shaw was not only a songwriter, but he also worked as a music teacher and publisher.

Other classics from Moore's pen that seemed to have influenced Foster are 'The Harp That Once Through Tara's Halls', ''Tis The Last Rose Of Summer' and 'When Cold In The Ground'. Foster may well have had the latter in mind when conceiving his 'Massa's In De Cold Ground', while 'Ah! May The Red Rose Live Always' owes more than a passing nod to the Dublin poet. Moore's influence was far reaching.

The words for Stephen Foster's first published song, 'Open Thy Lattice Love', had been written in the previous year by George P Morris , already a composer and author of some ten years' standing, and could have been inspired by one of the songs in Moore's 'The Summer Fête': "In my lattice is gleaming/The watch-light for thee." Morris uses the same metre as Moore, and could conceivably have been moved to expand the latter's mention of the sea. Morris had also been the wordsmith for Henry Russell's

'Woodman! Spare That Tree!', published in 1837, a live performance of which was witnessed by the young Stephen at the age of six. Before Foster's songs became popular, Russell was certainly one of the most prolific and successful songwriters in America, through compositions such as 'Woodman! Spare That Tree!', 'The Ship On Fire' and 'The Maniac'.

While the Celtic area in which Thomas Moore worked influenced Foster's sentimental ballads, the songs that brought him more commercial recognition had more complex roots.

Slavery has reared its head in many forms, as far back as ancient Greece and Rome, and in the practice of villeinage and vassalage in the feudal ages, when serfs would be beholden to the lord of the manor. As early explorers discovered, slavery even existed within black African communities. It was from these existing labour structures that the expanding Portuguese and Spanish sugar cane industry drew their workforce in Brazil and the Caribbean. There had been African slaves in the English colony of Virginia since 1619, although most of the manual labour throughout the ensuing decades was undertaken by Europeans or the native Americans. This situation had changed radically by 1690, by which time England was shipping huge numbers of slaves to the colonies in the New World to work on the vast sugar plantations. During the Atlantic slave trade, more than eleven million Africans were transported to the Americas, 70 per cent of whom initially worked on the sugar plantations.

Slavery was eventually abolished in England by 1775, and was declared illegal by America's northern states at the time of the American War Of Independence, with the Atlantic slave trade ceasing in 1807. The southern states, however, virtually ignored these decrees, because the livelihood of the southern planters depended upon it, even going as far as intensifying the breeding of slaves, creating what were tantamount to stud farms, in order to produce an ongoing workforce. Slavery was brought to an end in all British colonies by 1834, following the 1833 Act Of Emancipation. America didn't rid themselves of this travesty of human rights until the early 1860s, after the outcome of the Civil War, before which only ten per cent of the black community in America were free.

Cutting cotton, sugar and tobacco for a pittance is a hard enough life, but this was frequently exacerbated by the unnecessarily brutal treatment meted out by the slave owners, who branded their charges and split up families and tribes. To attempt an escape could mean death; to stay could mean death – an unhealthy choice, offering only a brace of unenviable options. To survive these deplorable conditions, they dug deep into one of the oldest resources known to man, and sang to keep their spirits up.

The English settlers took ballads and folk music from the British Isles to the New World, comforting and friendly songs from home, which not only helped them through turbulent nights in the Atlantic but also helped to allay homesickness in a strange new world. In the same way, many of the transported Africans used the native rhythms and chants inherent in them to see them through the hardest work, often accentuating certain syllables and increasing the volume when necessary, much like a modern tennis player grunts at the moment of impact between racquet and ball. This also created a glimmer of security in a seemingly hopeless situation. The futility of their lives, yoked to their fear of the slave owners, created a deep sense of collective spirit among the plantation communities, a spirit often absent in their English "massas".

Long an unconquered nation, the English middle and upper classes held an inbred arrogance and an unquestionable ability to organise, but their aloofness and apparent self-sufficiency rarely allowed them to display warmth or genuine love for their fellow countrymen. Although the slaves looked after the sick, aged and infirm in their own communities, many would be turned out when there was no further use for them, the tribes and families would be divided, and the women sexually assaulted. They were even banned from beating drums, as it was thought that they might use them to communicate and start a riot.

George Pinckard wrote an eye-witness account of slaves in Savannah, Georgia, in 1816: "We saw them dance, and heard them sing. In dancing, they scarcely moved their feet, but threw about their arms, and twisted and writhed their bodies into a multitude of disgusting and indecent attitudes. Their was a wild yell devoid of all softness and harmony, and loudly chanted in harsh harmony."

The Church had long thought the Africans to be beyond redemption, that they displayed a total ignorance of God and the Christian faith, were incapable of realising the errors of their ways and were intransigent upon the subject. In all probability, their teaching methods were offensive, and therefore ineffective.

In spite of these misgivings, things began to evolve spiritually in their own mysterious way. As prospects in this life didn't look too rosy, many began to turn their attention to the afterlife. Maybe there were better times ahead. Many heard the word of Christianity for the first time and joined in with shout-and-response hymns, where the preacher would throw the congregation a line and they would repeat it. Despite being practised in England, this style of singing would not have been unfamiliar to them in their homeland, and it gave them another outlet for their frustration.

For some reason, they avidly latched onto the hymns of Dr Isaac Watts, a non-conformist minister from Southampton, England. His words possibly touched a chord. In 'Jesus Shall Reign Where'er The Sun', the son of God is offered to "people and realms of every tongue". Here was a man – albeit in Heaven – who could love everyone, no matter who they were. They must have thought that this place sounded a hell of a lot better than the one in which they were living. They were also offered hope in another of Watts' hymns:

> There is a land of pure delight,
> Where Saints immortal reign;
> Infinite day excludes the night,
> And pleasures banish pain.

Two of his most popular songs with this new-found audience were 'When Can I Read My Title Clear?' and 'When I Survey The Wondrous Cross'. The Africans gradually infused Watts' hymns and spirituals with their natural African rhythms and fervour. This music and these words were certainly more uplifting than the psalms that they'd previously had to sing, with their rather solemn pace.

Thus the African rhythms – which had gradually been suppressed for half a century and supplanted by funereal psalms – had found a voice again through a conduit unwittingly supplied by Isaac Watts, "the father of English hymnody". They may also have heeded some of his words of wisdom to help them to shut out the pain when life became too unbearable: "Acquire a government over your ideas, that they may come down when they are called, and depart when they are bidden."

Charles Wesley, 33 years Watts' junior, also wrote hymns with which the African-Americans identified:

> Let us each for other care
> Each the other's burden bear.

This hymn was built around an old Irish air, while for the hymn below, with its even more poignant words, he used an old Scots melody:

> Help us to help each other, Lord,
> Each other's cross to bear,
> Let each his friendly aid afford
> And feel his brother's care.

The negro spiritual had begun its journey, but the downside for the plantation communities was the songs of the blackface genre. These were songs that were written and sung by white performers about black people. The first blackface performer may well have been Micah Hawkins, who put the words of a comic song about the Battle Of Plattsburg into the mouth of a black sailor. 'Backside Albany' used a jokey black dialect that opened up a new area of parodic songwriting for performers, and led to Stephen Foster liberally employing it on his blackface songs. He'd surely never have dreamt of using terms like "ribber", "nebber" and "de", had it not been a current fad.

The baton for these songs of racial caricature, which became known as *Ethiopian delineation*, was picked up by George Washington Dixon, who popularised 'Coal Black Rose', songs about black northern dandy 'Zip Coon', and 'Long Tail Blue'. The chorus of 'Zip Coon', "O zip a duden duden duden zip a duden day", proved durable enough to reverberate through the decades and claim ancestry to Ray Gilbert and Allie Wrubell's 'Zip-A-Dee Doo-Dah', which appeared on the soundtrack of the 1946 film *Song Of The South*. Maybe the "doo-dah" was borrowed from the lyric of Foster's 'Camptown Races'.

Another purveyor of blackface was Thomas Dartmouth "Daddy" Rice, whose song 'Jim Crow' and its accompanying dance, in which he gyrated, twisted and jerked, caught the imagination of the public. If moving pictures had been invented, surely Rice would have pre-dated the small-screen imposition placed on Elvis Presley by over a century, and would only have been shot from the waist up. Although Foster was only a boy at the time, 'Jim Crow' was inescapable. A friend of his later revealed that "clerks hummed it...artisans thundered it...boys whistled it in the streets, ladies warbled it in parlours and house-maids repeated it to the clink of crockery in kitchens". A hit, then! The music appealed to the male section of the population, who had never felt comfortable with genteel piano recitals and who now found a united voice in blackface, which they felt proved that they were all-American boys. This display of passive xenophobia acted as a bond in a country that was still searching for an identity, that had imported Africans against their will, and that was now, in effect, being forced to accommodate them. It provided a convenient theatrical mask for a subconscious culpability.

The older generation deplored the new sound that began to sweep the country, venting its spleen in periodicals like *National Intelligence* magazine: "Listen to that disease called a popular song...why, the thing is more contagious than cholera."

The acrimonious invective of dissenters has never succeeded in arresting the inevitability of a new musical craze, so in an attempt to satiate the musical hunger of the populace during the 1840s, minstrel shows were born. These shows comprised a group of white performers purveying music, comedy and dance using a combination of banjo, fiddle, bones and any other instruments that came to hand. It heralded the line-up of the self-contained small unit that has survived into the 21st century.

The Virginia Minstrels were the first to make the breakthrough, even though they were only in existence for six months. They were an instant hit, touring America and England and inspiring a host of other minstrel groups, just as Lonnie Donegan would later spearhead the skiffle craze, and The Beatles the beat boom over a century later.

One of the most successful of the new wave of minstrel outfits was Christy's Original Band Of Virginia Minstrels, who rather cheekily purloined the defunct unit's name. They were formed by Edwin Pearce Christy and his stepson, George, who had forsaken his own name of Harrington and adopted his stepfather's surname. Not only did Christy's minstrels prove enduring (they played for four years in Pittsburgh and Cincinatti and in New York from 1846-56) but they also revolutionised blackface by using four-part harmony onstage, and were to play their part in the fortunes of Stephen Foster.

Other musicians who influenced him included blackface singer and circus performer Dan Rice (Daniel McLaren), a New Yorker who had worked for Barnum's American Museum before arriving in Pittsburgh and with whom Foster became friends in the early 1840s. He was also influenced by the work of Henry Kleber, a German émigré, music teacher, composer, church organist and member of the Pittsburgh Philharmonic Society. Kleber appealed to the more traditional and serious side of Foster's nature, while Rice's stage persona put him in the frame of mind for writing for Ethiopian delineators.

Many of the musical characters that crossed Foster's path had more than one string to their bows, whereas his own ambition lay exclusively in songwriting. They often performed, composed, published, copyrighted, acted as agents and impresarios and performed any function where there was a dollar or two to be made, while Foster had no aspirations to be any further immersed in the entertainment industry than writing songs. Songwriting was an occupation that had never existed in America until Foster declared his intent to travel that untrodden path.

He began his musical education on the clarinet, which he played in a band in the nearby town of Towanda and started composing at the age of 13, while at school. However, he didn't seem too enamoured with the schools he attended, much to the chagrin of his parents. On finishing his education, he sang in a group with friends as The Five Nice Young Men, and wrote his first blackface songs, 'Lou'siana Belle' and 'Uncle Ned'. The abolitionists, who were working to bring about the eradication of slavery, had a powerful voice in Pittsburgh, and while Foster counted several of them amongst his friends, he appeared ambivalent about the racial situation. Many people have no burning desire to be a protagonist, and grow up accepting things as they stand. They come into it, observe it, accept it, and get on with their lives. After all, blackface was the current trend. It was cool; it was happening.

As the years passed, though, he became increasingly compassionate about the plight of the plantation communities and would insist that The Christy Minstrels performed his songs in that vein, with pathos, and should not treat them as comedic. Before they performed Foster's 'Oh! Boys, Carry Me 'Long', he gave them his instructions: "I hope you will preserve the harmony in the chorus just as I have written it, and practise the song well before you bring it out...Remember it should be sung in a pathetic, not a comic style."

Foster was also insistent that white singers performing his blackface songs were not to mock the slaves but should elicit compassion from the audience, and that they should "build up taste...among refined people by making words suitable to their taste, instead of the trashy and really offensive words which belong to some songs of that order".

Without any form of cohesion or focus, he tended to hand his songs out to performers in a rather haphazard manner, making it difficult for him to keep tabs on them and in many cases finding that other people had illegally copyrighted them. After all, this is what writers had been used to doing. Songs were a living, breathing entity. You heard somebody's composition, learned it and sometimes added your own verses. Many writers used other people's tunes to which they would add new lyrics. This had certainly been the way for centuries in Britain, where songs would be handed down, passed on, rearranged, misheard and often wrongly copied. Songs were made up, sung and given freely to any who wished to sing them.

The Industrial Revolution in Britain and America changed that *laissez-faire* way of life forever. Commercialism was upon the Western world, rolling over it like an unstoppable tank and the gentle art of songwriting fell in step, along with every other trade that could lead to a fast buck. For the sharp practitioners, exploitation became the name of the game, often at the expense of the creatives. Initially naïve in this area, Foster would soon wise up; but with no national system to help songwriters, he had to throw in his lot with the slightly chaotic structures already in place. There was no network of outlets to facilitate a simple method of distribution for publishers or agents and no performing right fees legally due to songwriters or publishers when their songs were performed in public venues. The only way to guarantee monies was to sell them to a publisher and/or be given a small royalty. Even so, there was no way of determining whether the person to whom a song was sold would behave honourably with regard to its copyright.

Another major concern for writers was the ability of any publisher to pirate a song without fear of reprehension. It was akin to carrying a golden goose through a minefield. The increasing and widespread popularity of the modern song meant that those wishing to capitalise on their successes were on a major learning curve.

America's first copyright law, drafted in 1790, extended only to maps, charts and books. Music could not be copyrighted until 1831, when the composer was given exclusive rights to "printing, reprinting, publishing and vending".

Although US copyright law included musical compositions from 1831, it was the French who first introduced a support system to protect composers' rights, in as early as 1851, with SACEM (Societé Des Auteurs,

Compositeurs Et Editeurs De Musique). Britain and America wouldn't get themselves properly organised until the next century, even lagging behind Italy, Austria, Spain and Germany. However, a reciprocal agreement between America and Britain would be in place by 1891, extending the composers' rights to include "completing, copying, executing and finishing", before which they could "borrow" songs from the other country without fear of reprisal. The lack of a supportive body didn't deter Foster. Young songwriters write songs and assume that everything else will look after itself, although disillusionment can set in when success and popularity fail to convert sales into royalties.

By the 1840s, his father's fortunes were very much on the wane and in many respects he was a broken man, shored up by the fortitude of his wife and the support of his family. Although Stephen was stepping up his songwriting activities, he still needed to earn a living, and to this end took work as a book-keeper in early 1847, in Cincinatti, where he started to sell songs to a local music publisher.

Cincinnati boasted a more multiracial society than Pittsburgh, including a large German community, many African-Americans and Jews. Not surprisingly, racial tension ran high, often boiling over and leading to mob rule, which the authorities – who insisted on segregation – found it difficult to contain.

From his office window, Foster could see the Ohio River, with its great steamers plying back and forth to St Louis, New Orleans and Memphis in the deep south and could hear at first hand the enslaved deck-hands singing work songs.

Back in Pittsburgh, Foster's brother Morrison – always a champion of his younger sibling's music – organised for some of his songs to be performed at a local ice cream parlour, which had begun to use live music as a way of attracting customers. One of the his brother's songs that Morrison put forward was 'Away Down South', which became one of 35 entries in the Eagle Ice-cream Saloon songwriting competition. The proprietor offered a "premium for the best melody" to be set to music, to be awarded by the music director, Nelson Kneass, with a silver cup going to the author of the best "original words of an Ethiopian melody or extravaganzas". The winners were decided according to the enthusiasm of the customers, so presumably the more of their mates the participants packed into the place the better. Foster was not present for the competition, so was unable even to assist in the applause for his own song. Not only did it not win, but several of those present tried to copyright it themselves the following day, even though it wasn't the world's most challenging lyric:

> My lub she hab a very large mouf,
> One corner in de Norf,
> Tudder corner in de Souf.

It was a theme which was still drawing breath over 100 years later, when Tommy Steele had a British top ten hit with 'What A Mouth (What A North And South)' in 1960.

Another of Foster's songs that Morrison submitted was 'Oh! Susanna', which received its first live airing there on Saturday 11 September 1847. Many consider this to be the birth of popular music in the form that we know it today. The song, which trumpets the new technology of the time – the telegraph, steam locomotives and steamboats – also contains an element of racism, the perceived romance of the deep south, nostalgia and home-spun sentiments:

> I come from Alabama
> With my Banjo on my knee
> I'se gwine to Lou'siana
> My true lub for to see.

Surely and steadily, the song gathered momentum, until it raged like a forest fire through the concert halls of New York and the gold-mining communities of California to the thoroughfares of the big towns and cities and along the Ohio and Mississippi Rivers. It's incredible that, for an era in which communication was still comparatively primitive (there was no television, radio or cinema, and the invention of sound recording was another 30 years away), 'Oh! Susanna's popularity was so far reaching. Between 1848 and 1850, there were no less than 30 different arrangements of the song and 16 different publishers.

WC Peters, the publisher who had the most legitimate claim to it, made a lot of money from 'Oh! Susanna' and other Foster songs, as did several more purveyors of sheet music and song books, but the writer himself saw very little return for his global hit, or for his other successes, like 'Uncle

Ned'. On the positive side, he realised the power and earning potential of the popular song. If he could write such potent material, there had to be a living to be made from it, provided that he had a contract that guaranteed him his rightful share. Certainly the pernicious nature of some of the more machiavellian publishers tended to – and would, for the next century – tar them all with the same brush, in the eyes of some songwriters. Many, though, were simply opportunists with good business brains. After all, not too many young songwriters had the wherewithal to back their own talent.

Having taken the plunge to write full time, he struck a publishing deal in Baltimore with the writer of the enduring 1845 song 'Jim Crack Corn (De Blue Tail Fly)', FD Benteen, and another with Firth, Pond And Co in New York. His sheet music would sell for 25¢, of which he would receive 2¢. Not a world-beating deal, but at least it was properly structured. Early in 1850, he left his job in Cincinatti and returned to Pittsburgh, where, in July of that year, he married Jane McDowell, who would later be his inspiration for 'Jeannie With The Light-Brown Hair'. Increasingly prolific, his reputation was growing and he was writing strong songs, including what proved to be one of his most durable classics, 'Camptown Races'. The most likely inspiration for this setting seems to have been the town of Campton, Pennsylvania, just 14 miles from where Foster went to school at one time and where a five-mile-long horse race was regularly run. The clue is in the fourth verse:

> 'See dem flyin' on a ten-mile heat,
> Doo-dah! Doo-dah!
> Round de race-track den repeat,
> Doo-dah! Doo-dah day!'

Foster then came up with possibly his most enduring and endearing song, 'The Old Folks At Home.' The song sold itself back to the black slaves that had been its inspiration. They adopted it as their own, proving once again that songs often have the power to cross, and sometimes break down, social barriers. A century later, the civil rights movement would condemn this and other Foster songs as presenting negative ethnic images, declaring that they should be eradicated from all songbooks. Even in 1851, negro leader Frederick Douglass put pressure on the country's leaders, calling for the abolition of slavery. It wasn't a new theme, but there was a top-level debate about whether to split the country in two, with the southern states retaining slaves. Some spoke of the possibility of civil war.

Keen to move into areas other than blackface, Foster made a conscious decision to omit his name from songs in that vein, on one occasion agreeing only that the name of the performer, Christy, appeared on the music. The song was such a runaway success around the world that Foster realised the error of his ways, and attempted to perform a U-turn. He wrote to Christy: "I have concluded to reinstate my name on my songs and to pursue the Ethiopian business without fear or shame…but I am not encouraged in undertaking this so long as 'The Old Folks At Home' stares me in the face with another's name on it…I find I cannot write at all unless I write for the public approbation and get credit for what I write." Foster's name wasn't reinstated on the song until 15 years after his death.

Here was a song that combined two of his influences from opposite ends of the spectrum, a lilting, emotive Celtic melody with blackface lyrics. The B section of the song, where it veers upwards after the verse, is particularly in the Celtic vein. His original verse ran:

> Way down upon the Pedee Ribber
> Far, far away
> Dat's where my heart is turning ebber
> Dere's wha my brudders play

During one of many reworkings of the song, he jettisoned South Carolina's Pedee River and substituted North Florida's Suwanee River, which soon became Swanee for reasons of scansion, and this proved to be another extraordinarily popular song, permeating the far corners of the Earth. One small example presented here is testimony to this. Michael Blann, a singing shepherd who from 1852 spent his life watching the sheep on the remote South Downs in England, had handwritten 'The Old Folks At Home' in his personal songbook, alongside his favourite English folk songs. The sentiments undoubtedly appealed to the masses from so many different countries, cultures and creeds.

In 1852, Foster wrote (amongst other songs) two more highly-acclaimed numbers, 'Massa's In De Cold Ground' and 'My Old Kentucky Home Good-night', the latter including a line that our ever-changing language now renders doubly dubious: "the darkies are gay". No writer can possibly guess at how the language will shift over the years, or whether it will turn their contemporary turns of phrase into anachronistic peccadilloes. After all, songwriter and music publisher Noel Gay's strap line was initially the fairly innocuous "make every song a gay song", while Marc Bolan's T Rex number 'Get It On' had to have its title changed in the States to 'Bang A Gong'. It was fine in Britain, as at that point in time the phrase "get it on" didn't have the same sexual connotations. In the late '50s, Floyd Robinson's 'Makin' Love' didn't cause a single eyelid to bat, as the phrase hadn't inherited its later implications.

On the positive side, his realisation that black people had dignity, too, led Foster to write his first song of this ilk without the use of dialect. The words notwithstanding, 'My Old Kentucky Home Good-night' was duly adopted as the Kentucky state song, and the modern, revised version was adopted by the state's House Of Representatives in 1986.

It has been pointed out that, either deliberately or subconsciously, Foster used the phrase "no more" as a recurring theme. It certainly has a sentimental and nostalgic ring to it that has always had mass appeal, and Foster used it in his verses to rail against work, to mourn a loved one, to proclaim joy at dying, the promise of commitment and the passing of youth. Over a century later, John Lennon and Paul McCartney would latch onto the use of personal pronouns in order to give their early songs broad appeal. 'From Me To You', 'I'll Get You', 'She Loves You', 'PS I Love You' and 'I Wanna Hold Your Hand' all employed a basic but compelling technique and, like Foster's songs, made use of the vernacular of the time. Kids in the street said "yeah", so why not use it in songs, for easier identification, essentially branding your product and selling youth their own lifestyle, or at least the lifestyle to which they aspired? Ira Gershwin successfully incorporated the New York slang of the '20s and '30s into many of his lyrics, like these lines from 'You're A Builder-Upper':

> You're a builder-upper,
> A breaker-downer,
> A holder-outer,
> And I'm a giver-inner.

And from 'I Don't Think I'll Fall In Love Today', the song inspired by GK Chesterton's poem 'A Ballade Of Suicide':

> If I should get a gun and bump this chump off
> Oh, I suppose you'd ask, "What causes that?"

In the song 'Swing Trot', he uses "slightly screwy", a slang phrase that's commonplace today, and in 'Modernistic Moe', he writes:

> I used to work in a nightclub
> For 60 bucks a week
> To please the chumps.

Songwriter, playwright and theatrical producer George M Cohan used turn-of-the-century colloquialisms to great effect, writing as the people with whom he mixed actually spoke, as opposed to how they were perceived to speak. In his 1903 musical *Running For Office*, he used the word "bird" for girl, "coco" (as in coconut) for head, and "getting loaded" for getting drunk. As one would expect, the critics loathed the expressions, dismissing them as a cheap and blatant attempt at appealing to the masses. Of course, this is exactly what happened, and the public took Cohan's use of words to their hearts while the critics were left in his wake.

To an extent, this is what Foster did this with his blackface songs. The American ear perceived the way in which the African slaves had modified English words as colloquial but fascinating. Foster, however, differed from many other songwriters in that there was no sexuality in his lyrics; they were asexual to the extent that women were idealised, mourned or worshipped, but never the objects of lust or physical desire.

At the end of 1854, against a background of dock strikes and a an epidemic of cholera, he wrote the unwittingly ironic 'Hard Times Come Again No More'. More in keeping would have been a song from Noël Coward's 1952 *Globe Revue*, 'There Are Bad Times Just Around The Corner'.

In 1855, Foster suffered the traumatic experience of losing both his parents and his home, forcing him to move across the river to Pittsburgh and into lodgings with his young family. In 1856 and 1857, he was a professional songwriter who had stopped writing commercial songs. His last profitable venture in that area had been 'Some Folks', penned in 1855. Instead, he invested his creativity into campaign songs for the democrats, led by James Buchanan, whose brother had married Foster's sister, Ann.

However, it was more his father's politics that lingered in him rather than any strong feelings of racism. One of the country's fiercest abolitionists was John Brown, from Connecticut, who used guerrilla tactics to stop Kansas from becoming a slave state and attempted to create a republic of former slaves. Brown's attempts were thwarted in 1859, when he was captured by the forces of Colonel Robert E Lee and hanged. Both captive and captor became immortalised in song, the latter in L Wolfe Gilbert's and Lewis Muir's number included in the stage musical *Come Over Here*, 'Waiting For The Robert E Lee' (the paddle steamer named after the colonel); the former achieving musical immortality in 'John Brown's Body'. The abolitionists, who in June 1856 had just nominated the first republican presidential candidate, ironically set their own political lyrics to several of Foster's songs, including 'My Old Kentucky Home' and 'Camptown Races'. By dint of the popularity of his work, he was writing for both sides.

On 20 December 1860, having fought an anti-slavery campaign, Abraham Lincoln was elected the 16th president of the United States. They weren't to remain united for long, though, as the outraged southern states joined South Carolina – who had already seceded from the Union – in the Confederacy. Within months, the Confederate States Of America, led by Jefferson Davis, were plunged into a civil war with the Union. The enslaved Africans were counting on Lincoln to carry the day, as the words of 'Go Down Moses' testify:

> Go down, Abraham, way down in Dixie's land,
> Tell Jeff Davis to let my people go.

The rallying songs of the Union included 'Battle Hymn Of The Republic', 'John Brown's Body', Thomas Moore's 'The Minstrel Boy', 'Marching Through Georgia' and 'When Johnny Comes Marching Home Again', while the Confederates also adopted the latter song, as well as 'The Yellow Rose Of Texas', 'Dixie's Land' and 'God Save The South'. Music certainly played its part in the American Civil War, as is borne out in this observation on the Lower Peninsula Campaign of 1862:

> Heintzleman joined the desperate struggle to close the broken ranks. He hit on the novel idea of rallying them with music.

Major To Minor

Finding several regimental bands standing by, bewildered as the battle closed in, Heintzleman ordered them to take up their instruments. "Play! Play! It's all you're good for," he shouted. "Play, damn it! Play some marching tune! Play 'Yankee Doodle!' Or any doodle you can think of, only play something!" Before long, over the roar of the guns, came the incongruous sound of 'Yankee Doodle', and then 'Three Cheers For The Red, White And Blue'. One of [General Joseph] Hooke's men thought the music was worth a thousand men. "It saved the battle."

There were many such instances of music firing both sides with resolve and fervour.

Away from the fields of conflict, other popular songs of the day were John Howard Payne and Henry Rowley Bishop's 'Home, Sweet Home', with it's thatched-cottage sentimentality, and 'Polly Wolly Doodle', with it's nonsense lyrics:

> Oh, a grasshopper sat on a railroad track
> Singin' "Polly Wolly Doodle" all the day,
> Was a-pickin' his teeth with a carpet tack
> Singin' "Polly Wolly Doodle" all the day.

While 'John Brown's Body' was breathing fire into the bellicose bellies of the Confederate and Unionist armies in America, England was cheerily chirping the smash of 1862, the rather jolly 'Blaydon Races'.

Forsaking the commercial side of songwriting when there's nothing in the bank has always been a recipe for disaster. Songwriters live with the thought that the real runaway hit is just around the corner, and one of the exciting intangibles about writing songs is that it just might be! Today might be the day! This might be the song! In Foster's case, however, it wasn't to be. Before his death, he would pen only one more notable song. When the chips are down, in the areas of music in which they've chosen to work, songwriters will inevitably – if reluctantly – return to the arena of their commercial success. Unwilling, but impecunious, he went back to blackface.

Foster's financial state had reached the crisis point at which many songwriters would go back to the day job. Instead of succumbing, however, he applied common sense to the situation. Aware of what we'd now refer to as "intellectual properties", he systematically drew up a list of all his published songs, the amount each one had earned to that date, and calculated the likely future earnings of his copyrights. His biggest money-spinners were 'Old Folks At Home', 'My Old Kentucky Home Goodnight', 'Old Dog Tray' and 'Massa's In De Cold Ground'. The 36 songs that Firth, Pond And Co published he assessed as being worth $2,786.77, and offered to sell them the rights for that amount, but eventually settling for $1,500. To the publisher Stephen Benteen, he sold his future rights to a further 16 songs for a paltry $200.

In the following year, he struck up a new deal with Firth, Pond And Co which tied him exclusively to the company for two and a half years, giving him a ten per cent royalty and an advance of $100 for each song, with the publishers requiring twelve songs a year. During the term of the agreement, they published only 16 of his songs, which accrued royalties of just $1,700. In their debt, and eager to regain his former glory, he moved to New York in 1860, finding lodgings at 113 Greene Street and entering into yet another contract. This time they offered him a salary of $800 for twelve songs a year, while Philadelphia publishers Lee And Walker paid him $400 for six songs.

He was now on a minimum of $1,200 a year, and trading heavily on his previous success. In fact, the only big song he wrote after moving to New York was 'Old Black Joe'. Foster's granddaughter, Jessie Welsh Rose, was later able to describe the circumstances relating to the character who inspired the song. Joe worked for Foster's in-laws, and was "an old coloured man who drove for Dr McDowell for many years. He also had some household duties, such as admitting visitors in the evenings. All through the sweetheart days Joe watched Foster come and go, presenting to 'Miss Jenny' with much shuffling of feet and many broad grins...'Someday I'm going to put you in a song,' he told Joe...The old man was gone when the day of inspiration came." Maybe the melancholic spirituality of the song was born out of Joe's death.

During the last four years of his life, Stephen Foster's wrote 100 pieces of music, often collaborations, including many with George Cooper, who was responsible for the lyrics to his Civil War songs. However potent the songs they wrote for the democrats, the abolitionists eventually carried the day. On 1 January 1863, President Abraham Lincoln signed the Emancipation Proclamation that gave all slaves in the Confederate states their freedom. In his address at Gettysburg, five months after the Confederates were routed there, Lincoln decreed that "The old south must be destroyed and replaced by new propositions and ideas." His speech also referred to the creed of the original settlers: "Four score and seven years ago, our fathers brought forth upon this continent a new nation, conceived in liberty and dedicated to the proposition that all men are created equal."

In April 1865, the Confederate Army surrendered and the war was over, although it was soured for the Unionists by the assassination of Lincoln in the following week. Despite being the realisation of a dream for those who'd spent their lives in bondage and the granting of their civil rights in the following year, an undercurrent of prejudice continued in the former rebel states as the Ku Klux Klan pursued their goal of white supremacy. That prejudice still burns in some areas of the south in the present day.

Meanwhile, as a new dawn was breaking for some, the sun was setting on Stephen Foster. Increasingly dependent an alcohol to keep the spectre of failure at bay, his wife, Jane, decamped for a lengthy spell to Pennsylvania, and tried to encourage her husband to do the same. In early 1864, he developed a fever and possible symptoms of tuberculosis in the North American Hotel in New York's Bowery area. He fell – apparently – in the hotel bedroom, severing his jugular vein. Family and friends have always strongly refuted the idea of suicide, and the real story of what happened in his hotel bedroom will probably never be known. Whatever the cause of his demise, America's first professional songwriter died in hospital three days later. All that he had on him was 38¢ and a scrap of paper, on which he'd written five words, which could have been anything from a new song title to a suicide note: "Dear hearts and gentle people."

Foster's influence was such that, 86 years later, those few enigmatic words would inspire songwriter Bob Hilliard to write a lyric entitled 'Dear Hearts And Gentle People', to the music of Sammy Fain. Recorded by Bing Crosby in Los Angeles on 26 October 1949, it became his 20th million-seller.

During Foster's lifetime, his total earnings from his entire canon were just $15,091. After his death, the total crept up to $19,290. Surely no other songwriter has been fêted and remembered in so many diverse ways over such a long period of time.

The first of several public monuments to his memory was Guiseppe Moretti's sculpture in Pittsburgh's Highland Park, which was erected in 1900. On the 50th anniversary of Foster's death, the *Chicago Evening Post* commented: "Today was devoted to the memory of Stephen Foster, whose simple words set to music made Foster's name a household word throughout the world." In July 1926, centennial celebrations were held in Pittsburgh, at the biggest open-air concert they had ever staged, with an audience of 12,000 people. The 90-strong Pittsburgh Orchestra was broadcast on the infant medium of radio, and the whole event was filmed for posterity.

There were also celebrations in Kentucky, where a quartet and the Louisville military band honoured his memory, in the presence of five former governors. Even New York, which had chewed him up and spat him out, paid tribute with a programme of Foster's songs.

His name lives on in music, statues, a memorial home, a public school, societies and a 1939 biopic, directed by Darryl Zanuck and starring Al Jolson as EP Christy of The Christy Minstrels. His songs have spawned hundreds of cover versions over the years, with 'Beautiful Dreamer' being covered by such diverse artists as Roy Orbison, Natalie Cole, Billy J Kramer and Marty Robbins. Glenn Miller recorded 'Jeannie With The Light-Brown Hair'; Harry James And The Mills Brothers covered 'The Old Folks At Home'; James Last, James Taylor and The Byrds cut 'Oh! Susanna'; and Gene Krupa, Lawrence Welk and Randy Newman did their own versions of 'My Old Kentucky Home'. Not bad for a man who died young and alone, with just 38¢ in his pocket.

2 Music Halls To Musicals

The enormous popularity of Stephen Foster's songs encouraged many others to tread the same path, with varying degrees of success.

James A Bland was born in New York on 22 October 1854, into what was considered a good negro family. His father, an examiner for the US Patent Office, encouraged his son to study Law, which he later forsook for a career as a songwriter and singer. At the age of 21, he joined Callender's Original Georgia Minstrels, who toured the United States and Europe for the next 25 years, to great acclaim. Bland himself later resided in Britain for several years, and performed for Queen Victoria and Edward, Prince Of Wales.

Like many songwriters, Bland's ability to manage his money was poor, and despite his legal training he neglected to keep tabs on his potential earnings. Known as "the prince of the negro songwriters", he penned over 700 songs, 37 of which are in the American Library Of Congress and one of which is prestigiously being adopted as the state song for Virginia:

> Carry me back to old Virginny.
> That's where the cotton and the corn and the taters grow.
> There's where the birds warble sweet in the springtime.
> There's where the old darkey's heart am long'd to go.

Amazingly, these are the words of an educated black New Yorker, writing in a manner influenced by blackface!

Written in 1875, 'Carry Me Back To Old Virginny' was made the official state song of the Old Dominion by the Virginian Legislature 65 years later, in 1940. By 1970, the song was deemed by some to contain racially unacceptable lyrics, portraying slavery as a comfortable and harmonious way of life. Despite the words having been written by a black writer, the ensuing debate resulted in State Senator Doug Wilder trying to get it replaced with something more appropriate. Six years later, an attempt to supplant it with 'The Old Dominion' failed, and in as late as 1996 delegate Jay De Boer suggested setting more acceptable words to the song. When the General Assembly vetoed the idea, he put forward his second suggestion for a State song: the 1960s punk classic 'Louie Louie'!

In 1997, 'Virginny' was promoted sideways, and was made state song emeritus, as there were many who felt that the lyrics were too embarrassing to sing in public whilst still being too traditional to lose it altogether. The General Assembly passed a resolution in March 1998 to "establish a sub-committee to make a recommendation for a new state song which, among other things...involves visual images of the historic, natural and scenic beauty that the Commonwealth's citizens celebrate".

They wanted a state song to order, a musical take-away, and sent songwriters of every level scurrying to tailor songs to fit the job description. The competition attracted more than 300 entries, which were judged on their "melody, composition and lyrics...dignity, singability, value as a promotional tool, broad age appeal, adaptability, and visual images of Virginia's historic, natural and scenic beauty". No great constrictions, then! When one of the 59 shortlisted applicants is finally proclaimed the winner, it will surely be followed by a marketing campaign by a sub-sub-committee, whose job it will be to ensure that people take the chosen song to their collective bosom.

Will the investment be sufficient to cultivate an instant passion for their new musical brand leader? Virtually all of the entries to the contest unsurprisingly and, out of necessity, sycophantically trumpet the state's name, in titles such as 'Virginia's My Home', 'Old Virginia', 'Old Virginia, My Home', 'Virginia', 'Virginia, My Virginia', 'Oh, Virginia', and 53 other permutations. One can feel the sub-sub-sub-committee already discussing the forthcoming CD, featuring all 59 entries, entitled *Now That's What I Call Virginia*. We might even have a bonus track, of the well-known seasonal song reworked as 'Yes, Santa Claus, There Is A Virginia'.

Effectively, the demotion of Bland's 125-year-old song has left Virginia without a state song for four years. The question is, will the eventual replacement be considered too bland (no pun intended) by 2025, and compel the General Assembly to insist on something more traditional, like 'Carry Me Back To Old Virginny'?

Other less contentious songs from Bland include 'De Golden Wedding', 'Tell 'Em I'll Be There', 'In The Evening By The Moonlight', and the durable 'Golden Slippers'.

The latter song heralded better times to come. Not in this life, where there was still so much misery and oppression for many black communities, but in the next life, where the sun would shine on everyone and people would wear "dem golden slippers", which were essential footwear for those hoping "to walk de golden street" and ride to the afterlife on "de chariot in de morn". On arrival, there would be friends and family, "Brudder Ben, Sister Luce, Uncle Bacco Juice", all rejoicing in the land "where the rain don't fall, and the wind don't blow".

Like Foster, Bland has not been forgotten, even if 'Virginny' is in the sin bin. He eventually rode that "golden chariot" himself, in 1911, but there were no golden slippers. Instead, he lay in an unmarked grave until 1939, when it was located in Merion, Philadelphia, by ASCAP (the American Society Of Composers, Authors And Publishers) and a headstone was erected. The Lions Club of Virginia also sponsor a contest for schools called the Bland Contest in his honour.

From the middle of the 19th century onwards, Britain had also witnessed an enormous growth in the interest of popular music. Classical works were still considered too highbrow by the working and lower middle classes, whose musical needs led to an increase in the British drinking man's time-honoured propensity for singing in inns and public houses. Even for the middle classes, there was a dearth of British classical composers. Sir John Stainer and, later, Frederick Delius and Charles Villiers Stanford were the best-known of the more prolific composers we could offer during the second half of the 19th century.

Over time, the singing of songs and the telling of musical tales have become a mainstay of the entertainment in British drinking establishments, but by this time it was becoming decidedly more organised, as proprietors began to realise that they could sell the music as well as the alcohol. An industry had begun, which had its critics as well as its supporters.

Any new form of popular musical entertainment is guaranteed to experience a backlash from those more resistant to change, and music halls were no exception. The older generation mourned the loss of the street singers and balladeers, who often brought the news and created their own topical ballads. The halls, however, were a boon to songwriters, giving them a bigger shop window from which to sell their wares.

With the Beer Act of 1830 allowing unrestricted sale of alcohol, almost anybody could turn their house into a beer shop. This proved to be an instant opportunity for many. The trade grew rapidly, and soon threatened the livelihood of many publicans. With their pulling power challenged, many public houses repositioned themselves commercially, bringing in professional or semi-professional artists to entertain their customers in an attempt to keep one jump ahead of their new rivals.

Enticing people onto licensed premises who might otherwise have abstained from alcohol was regarded as creating a potentially serious social dilemma in the eyes of the Temperance Society. In his publication *The Philosophy Of Artificial And Compulsory Drinking Usages In Great Britain And Ireland*, John Dunlop pointed out that "Publicans use all manner of schemes to allure and attract by means of games, music, getting up country wakes...and other entertainments. And the intimate and inseparable connexion in this country between these amusements and drinking is most disastrous and an astonishment to other nations."

The initial areas of growth were London, Birmingham, Yorkshire and Lancashire. The Star, in Bolton, was one of the earliest to open a dedicated concert room. The landlord, Tom Sharples, owned a museum which was attached to the inn, and also owned a music hall, which he advertised in the museum catalogue:

> Then when the shades of evening draw near,
> Again the scene is changed your hearts to cheer;
> Music and mirth inviting bids you stay,
> Softens rough hearts, and makes the sad ones gay.
> Makes old age young, brightens the brow of care,
> Chaseth devils blue, and grim despair.
> The Star of Bolton is the guiding light
> To music-mirth-museum day and night.

Although he wasn't the first to open a music hall, Charles Morton – who converted his public house in the Lambeth area of London before investing £35,000 in the Oxford Music Hall in the West End – had the title "Father Of The Halls" bestowed upon him.

By 1849, 32 public houses were known to have concert rooms, and the number was increasing rapidly. In that year, the *Morning Chronicle* reported that "The attention of the stranger who walks through the streets of Liverpool can scarcely fail to be directed to the great number of placards which invite the public to cheap or free concert-rooms. Of all shapes, and sizes and colours to attract the eye, they cover the walls of the town, and compete with one another in the inducements which they offer to the public to favour with its patronage the houses which they advertise."

Just over 100 years later, Liverpool musical history would repeat itself as jazz venues sprang up in the area, many of which would be converted to beat clubs by the late '50s and early '60s. Certainly, by 1959 the city boasted more than a dozen rock 'n' roll clubs and a veritable plethora of suburban dance halls, which multiplied considerably as The Beatles broke nationally at the end of 1962. Once again, the walls of the town were covered in posters enticing the would-be clientèle to the various establishments, a clientèle who enjoyed songs that dealt with day-to-day life; songs that were racy; songs that were robust, earthy, and reflected the national characteristics of the lower middle and working classes of the period. Like their later counterparts, the music halls in the first flush of the Victorian period attracted an enormous number of young people in their teens and early 20s.

The music halls even began to win out over the theatres, with a contributory factor being the latter's legal inability to sell alcohol. The master of ceremonies for each hall essentially made the difference between *music hall* and *variety*, although his role would eventually be deposed by the widespread use of programmes. Usually seated in an armchair, he would announce the artists and receive good-natured abuse from the audience. Again, there was a parallel situation with the advent of the rock 'n' roll era, when comperes could expect to be subjected to a torrent of defamatory invective. *Plus ça change.*

The mid-Victorian establishment gave a tacet nod of approval to the halls, as they could police the alcohol and the prostitution problems more easily, and the presence of many families helped to keep these problems to a minimum. The tolerance of the authorities led to a major increase in the number of establishments during the 1860s, with London boasting 33 halls by the middle of the decade and major towns possessing at least one hall. In the smaller communities they arrived gradually, over the next two decades, while some of the smaller and less elaborate halls in the big cities began to close, unable to compete with the increasing popularity of the major venues.

Entrepreneurs with a keen eye on the financial potential of the music halls started to organise the business side. In 1858, Ambrose Maynard established the first agency for artists. Two years later, the London Music Hall Owners' Protection Society was formed. In 1865, the Music Hall Provident Society was set up to protect the performers, and in 1866 the first music-hall magazine, *The Magnet*, was published.

By the 1860s, penny songbooks were becoming increasingly popular, helping to spread the fame of the singers and further the opportunities for the songwriters. For the latter, though, there was no protection, and most were forced to peddle their wares to performers at stage doors or bars. If the artist liked what he heard, or the sheet music he was shown, the writer would probably be offered the usual fee of a guinea and sometimes half of the publishing rights. Many lyricists and composers were subjected to the frustration of seeing their songs in print without benefiting from any of the proceeds.

A lack of any form of legal safeguard naturally provides a ideal breeding ground for subversive activities. This became increasingly prevalent in Britain during the last quarter of the 19th century, when the prime exponent of the "where there's a hit there's a writ" scenario appears to have been a certain Thomas Wall of Islington, North London, who set up the prestigious-sounding Copyright And Performing Right Protection Society in 1875. This was not so much to protect musicians as to exploit them. Wall dug up old copyrights, over which he technically didn't have any legal right, and toured the country attempting to extort money for the performance of them out of hapless artists and unwitting music-hall owners, threatening them with legal action for non-compliance.

His thumbscrew tactics worked at all levels of duplicity. The victim either paid the alleged £2 fine or found themselves threatened with court action by Wall, which they were told meant a minimum of a £2 fine plus costs, on which subject he would further lighten their purse – purely as a legal adviser – of half a crown! With somewhere in the region of 20,000 musicians in Britain, he was never short of clients.

Another potential problem for performers and music-hall owners in the capital reared its head in 1878, when the Board Of Works gave London County Council the power to close halls that didn't meet with the required safety regulations. In effect, this meant that halls could have their license terminated for any number of reasons while the authorities hid behind the mask of the new edict. Over the next few years, the London Empire would have had a problem with prostitutes promenading within view of the establishment's clientèle, but in that instance, instead of looking for non-existent safety problems, an agreement was reached whereby the ladies of the night would be screened off from the music-hall customers.

Perhaps protection for the British songwriter was late in coming, as sales of music outweighed the potential amount of performance royalties, and it was perceived to be a waste of time to pursue that route. As far as global royalties were concerned, the powerful players in a country like Great Britain, steeped in imperialism, were probably so impervious to the potential of collecting performance earnings from overseas that they treated the growing necessity for world royalty collection with some contempt.

Wall's scam, which had been successful for 13 years, was finally thwarted in 1888, when a law was passed that abolished the £2 penalty for unauthorised performance of a work. Although songwriters and publishers were keen to establish some form of protection, Wall's con-man tactics, carried out under the banner of the ostensibly reliable auspices of the Copyright And Performing Right Protection Society, certainly deterred anyone from forming any organisation with a similar-sounding name. It would take time and the development of technology to erase the stigma and to necessitate the introduction of such an institution.

By the end of the 19th century, the popularity of sheet music was going through the roof, with annual sales estimated at something like 20 million copies, from 40,000 song titles. Pirated copies of the most popular songs were sold openly on the street at a fraction of the normal price, for which neither writer nor publisher would receive a penny. In 1897, one luckless vendor was assaulted by the composer after trying to sell Leslie Stuart a copy of his own song 'Soldiers Of The Queen', a march that had become the anthem for Queen Victoria's Diamond Jubilee. Stuart might have been physically avenged, but the authorities, instead of being sympathetic to his predicament, fined him £2 for his impromptu pugilistic sortie. An incensed Stuart petitioned unsuccessfully for a change in the copyright law. The pressure that he brought to bear at least oiled the mental wheels of like-minded individuals, although nothing permanent would happen for another 17 years, until the Performing Right Society was formed.

Stuart, born Thomas Barrett in Southport, Lancashire, was one of the leading British songwriters of the late Victorian and Edwardian periods, entering into a highly profitable partnership with American singer Eugene Stratton. As a young boy, he fell under the sway of the tales of America's deep south that his father read to him, especially the book *From Peru To San Francisco On Horseback*. He later admitted to the latter's enduring influence: "I might with truth acknowledge that the songs I ultimately wrote for Eugene Stratton were, as far as their subjects were concerned, given birth to in the course of these imaginary travels." On moving to Manchester with his family at the age of eight, he became so proficient on the piano that he was able to deputise at the Slip Inn public house frequented by his father when their pianist dropped dead at the ivories. He wrote his first song for the landlord of the establishment, Mr O'Riley.

At the age of 14, he applied for the post of organist at the Roman Catholic school in Salford, and during the 1880s managed to combine that job with writing songs, dabbling as an impresario and conducting orchestras. His superiors in the church frowned upon his songwriting activities, however, forcing him to adopt a sobriquet and prompting an eventual cessation of his theological work.

His canon of songs to that date included 'Rip Van Winkle', 'Were I A King' and 'Cherished Vows', but his fame spread rapidly outside Lancashire, and by the 1890s his compositions were beginning to filter through to the London music halls. In 1891, Lottie Collins became one of the big stars of the period, mainly through her rendition of 'Ta-Ra-Ra-Boom-De-Ay', inspiring Stuart to write 'The Girl On The Ran Dan Dan' for her.

Bandwagons were boarded with enthusiasm. Frank W Egerton responded with 'Out On The Ran Dan' in the following year, while Harry Castling came up with an answer song to Lottie Collins' hit with his 'I'm The Man Who Buried Ta-Ra-Ra-Boom-De-Ay'. Answer records down the years have often proved amusing, their writers hoping to cash in on the success of the original but rarely doing so. They would become rife in the '50s and '60s.

The music halls were now coming of age. In 1896, the magazine *Home Notes* wrote that Stuart became a full-time songwriter: "Time was when music-hall songs were decried as being vulgar, low, and commonplace. All this is now being considerably altered. Composers for the music-hall are beginning to write genuine music. Mr Leslie Stuart stands first in this movement."

It was in London that Stuart first met American singer Eugene Stratton. Stratton had arrived in the capital with one of the many minstrel shows that were popular with the British audiences, but when the rest of Haverly's Minstrel Show returned to the US he stayed behind to try his luck as a solo performer. His brief foray into singing proved so unsuccessful that he expeditiously reverted to singing blackface, executing the songs provided by Stuart in a variety of set pieces. The partnership prospered. In the various stage cameos devised by Stuart, Stratton delivered songs like 'Susie Ann', 'Cake Walk' and 'The Coon Drum Major', and met with such an overwhelming response that he was soon dubbed "the idol of the halls".

Impresario George Edwardes was to play a major role in providing a platform and the opportunity for many songwriters, including Stuart, via his shows at London's Gaiety Theatre. He had begun to produce musical variety extravaganzas in as early as 1892, and he not only interpolated Stuart's songs into his existing productions – shows such as *The Yashmak*, *The Shop Girl* and *An Artist's Model* – but, in 1899, he asked the composer to write a complete score for a musical comedy. The response from the Lancashire songwriter was *Florodora*, a work set in the south seas and featuring what was to become a hit song, 'Tell Me, Pretty Maiden', the second line of which would still be quoted throughout the next century: "Are there any more at home like you?" Owen Hall wrote the book while Ernest Boyd-Jones and Paul Rubens supplied the lyrics.

The show opened at the Lyric Theatre on 11 November 1899, and as well as 'Tell Me, Pretty Maiden' also featured 'Whistling', 'Galloping', 'Phrenology', 'I've An Inkling' and 'Willie Was A Gay Boy'. *Florodora* would later become a favourite of Edward, Prince Of Wales, and it became one of the first musicals by an English composer to be produced on Broadway, opening in 1900 at the Casino Theatre, New York, with Leslie Stuart having the luxury of conducting the orchestra himself. A testimony to Stuart's influence came from the black pianist Eubie Blake, the composer of 'I'm Just Wild About Harry', who had been impressed by *Florodora* when he saw it as a boy on its US tour at the turn of the century: "I said to myself, 'If only I could write tunes like that.' I couldn't write music then, but I started to write melodies from that day. That man, that Leslie Stuart, I love him in his grave. He is the cause, the direct cause of me becoming a composer."

While Stuart was in the States, Eugene Stratton was performing one of the composer's new works onstage in London. 'Lily Of Laguna' was to become one of Stuart's best-loved songs:

> She is my love, my lady love,
> She's no girl for sitting down to dream,
> She's the only queen Laguna knows.
> I know she likes me, I know she likes me,
> Because she said so, she is my Lily of Laguna,
> She is my Lily and my rose.

It doesn't take too much imagination to see that the melody and phrasing were a possible blueprint for the song that Bud Flanagan would make popular many years later, the sentiment-laden 'Maybe It's Because I'm A Londoner'.

During the Edwardian period, Stuart was responsible for the score of four more successful musicals, including *The Silver Slipper*, which opened at the Lyric in 1901, and *The School Girl*, first produced at the Prince Of Wales two years later. *The Belle Of Mayfair* first saw the light of day at the Vaudeville in 1906, with Charles Brookfield supplying some of the lyrics. Brookfield had already earned his place in history when, in March 1895, he and fellow actor Charles Hawtrey volunteered information to the authorities about the activities of Oscar Wilde, which led to the poet's conviction for "committing indecent acts". On the night that Wilde was sent to gaol for two years, Brookfield joined Hawtry and the Marquess Of Queensberry for a celebration dinner.

Stuart's last real stage success with a new musical was in 1911, when *Peggy* was produced at the Gaiety. The book, on this occasion, had been written by George Grossmith Jr, whose father, George, had acted extensively for Gilbert and Sullivan, and had also co-written the comic novel *Diary Of A Nobody*. There would be revivals of Stuart's musicals, but his heyday was over. He fell out with Eugene Stratton, gambled extensively, and was bankrupt by 1914. He railed against the ragtime craze as being "out of tune" and "out of time", a cry that would echo down the decades as each generation sought to criticise the inexplicably noisy and tuneless genre of music that supplanted its own. After his death in 1928, the *Manchester Guardian* seemed to concur with Stuart's opinion of jazz in the same breath as singing the late composer's praises: "To hear *Florodora* today is to find an oasis in a desert of percussion and syncopation, and to remember him with gratitude."

Many deplored the new sound of ragtime, decrying it as a tuneless cacophony and predicting its early demise. The resident conductor at the Gaiety Theatre raged: "This is not music! It is against all the principles of music!" The music lives on. The critics don't.

Sadly, Stuart didn't live long enough to hear 'Tell Me, Pretty Maiden' being sung in the 1930 film *The Florodora Girl*, produced by Randolph Hearst and with his mistress, screen star Marion Davies, in the lead role.

The passion for writing songs knows no social or educational boundaries, no geographical limitations, and it has a propensity for luring people away from their day jobs. Leslie Stuart had given up his work as a church organist, Stephen Foster had eagerly escaped from his clerical duties, James Bland had forsaken his original legal aspirations, and the intended career of Lionel Monckton (son of Sir John Monckton, town clerk of the city of London) was also knocked out of kilter.

Lionel Monckton had been educated at Charterhouse and Oriel College, Oxford, and was called to the bar in 1885, becoming a member of Lincoln's Inn. An enthusiastic songwriter, he was entranced by musical theatre, and to that end secured himself a job as a theatre critic, initially for the *Pall Mall Gazette*. It was in this guise that he came to know the all-powerful man behind the Gaiety Theatre, George Edwardes, who, aware of Monckton's interest in writing songs, asked him to contribute to *The Shop Girl*, for which Stuart had also supplied songs. After Monckton had provided compositions for several shows, many starring the Edwardian Gaiety star Gertie Millar (whom Monckton married), Edwardes asked him to write an entire musical. Edwardes eventually came up with *The Arcadians*, one of the first integrated musicals, where the songs actually carry the plot forward rather than being little more than frilly icing on the cake. It was Monckton's finest hour, and is still a favourite of amateur dramatic societies almost a century on, with many a local diva trilling "So follow, follow, follow/The merry, merry pipes of Pan."

Another of Monckton's successful numbers was 'Soldiers In The Park', which he was inspired to write during a thunderstorm in Boulogne. Many writers require peace and seclusion in which to compose, but Monckton was motivated by noise: "I find the roar of the traffic, the whirl of a train, the hum of a motor-car often useful." 'Soldiers In The Park' was to become the biggest hit for a Charterhouse boy until Jonathan King's 'Everyone's Gone To The Moon' in 1965.

While Leslie Stuart's collaboration with Charles Brookfield linked him with the last trial of Oscar Wilde, Monckton had even closer connections. On instructions from Messrs CO Humphreys, Son, And Kershaw, he and Mr Edward Besley, QC, were the counsel for Lord Alfred Douglas at the trial of Regina versus Queensberry in April 1895, when Wilde unsuccessfully took the Marquess Of Queensberry to court for libel. When executing legal duties, he used his full name, John Lionel Monckton. In 1914, Monckton suffered a stroke, and died in the following year.

3 The Songwriters Go To War

Many musically-trained songwriters – such as Stephen Foster, James Bland and Leslie Stuart – seemed, for diverse reasons, unable to harness their undoubted talents to any long-term business acumen, while writers such as Victor Herbert were always able to earn a good living through their talents as musicians.

Victor Herbert was one of the great champions of the songwriting fraternity, managing to combine a successful writing career with his classical passion of cello playing and his tireless efforts in fighting the cause of composers and lyricists.

He was born in February 1859 in Dublin, which was also the birthplace of his grandfather, Samuel Lover, an eminent poet, painter, novelist and composer. Herbert's father, a barrister, had died when Victor was just a child, so he worshipped his grandfather in his stead. He spent several holidays at Lover's subsequent home in Sevenoaks, Kent, before his mother married a Dr Wilhelm Schmidt and moved the family to Stuttgart.

By the spring of 1866, Victor and his brother, Willy (who would later rise to fame in German theatre), were ensconced in their new country. Victor initially studied Greek and Latin at the local gymnasium before deciding to carve out a career for himself in music, for which he possessed a natural gift. He took up the cello as his principal instrument after learning the piano, piccolo and flute, and studied under one of the century's greatest cellists, Bernhard Cossman, between 1874 and 1876.

On taking to the road to earn his living as a cellist, he toured Austria, Germany, France, Italy and Switzerland, playing for a year in the orchestra of Eduard Strauss, who had succeeded his brother, Johann, as "king of the waltz". While on the road, he learned to speak fluent French and Italian, as well as the English and German that he already possessed. By now an accomplished soloist, he spent several years studying musical composition. His first major work was a suite for cello and orchestra.

When the young Viennese soprano Therese Forster came to Stuttgart, Herbert fell in love with her, wooed her and married her in Vienna in 1886. The talented young couple soon moved on, eventually settling in America after being recruited by the Metropolitan Opera Company of New York.

Herbert's roots were classical, but he was also to move into the world of musicals and operetta, and would play an important role in the development of the future of popular songwriting.

He joined the faculty of the National Conservatory Of Music Of America, which had been founded in 1885 by the great American music patron and visionary Jeanette Thurber. The aim of the society was to aid deserving and talented students to study every type of musical training to the highest degree. In March 1891, the *New York Evening Post* wrote: "On the same day that the international copyright bill was passed in the Senate, another bill of importance, from an intellectual point of view, was signed, incorporating the National Conservatory Of Music...The last provision is of special importance as, to our knowledge, no American conservatory has hitherto had the power of legally conferring the degree of Doctor Of Music." Herbert, listed with five other eminent musicians as being tied into the project, was already becoming involved in bodies that were concerned about the future of music, and would increasingly be so.

By 1893, restless and bored with the monotony of performing, he conceived the idea of composing operettas. His first produced work was the comic opera *Ananias*, which had its first outing at the Broadway Theatre, New York, and was performed by The Bostonians, while the producers guaranteed to provide an orchestra comprising at least 20 musicians. Herbert received a $500 advance and five per cent on the first $8,000 of the weekly receipts. One critic, while querying the strength of the libretto in keeping with other papers, also admits that "The composer's gift for melody was obvious."

The Bostonians took the show on the road for two years. Its success encouraged librettists to approach him with other work, although one established wordsmith, Harry B Smith, initially wasn't too keen to work with Herbert. Smith was eventually persuaded to acquiesce, and the pair's first collaboration was *The Wizard Of The Nile*, which opened at the Grand Opera House, Pennsylvania, in September 1895. The musical, offering a pre-*Joseph And The Amazing Technicolour Dream Coat* drought in Egypt and a similar "how can we solve this?" scenario, brought Herbert national acclaim. The show's most popular number proved to be 'Star Light, Star Bright', a popular theme that would continue to inspire songwriters for over half a century. (As well as the theme of the libretto, an interesting parallel between Smith's lyrical approach and those of Tim Rice on Joseph over 70 years later is that they both allowed their characters to freely use the jargon of the time and generally indulge in verbal anachronisms.) *The Wizard Of The Nile* ran for ten years, becoming the first American musical to be performed in German-speaking lands in 1896, when it was produced in Austria.

In 1896 Herbert was elected to join another showbusiness body, the Lambs, a society comprising men of the theatre world who would help to shape its development and oversee its wellbeing. He was able to experience what useful functions these societies were able to perform and what benefits (if any) they could bring to their members.

The next Harry B Smith/Victor Herbert collaboration was *The Serenade*, which, after having a try-out in Chicago, opened in New York in March 1897, again in the capable hands of The Bostonians.

Following on from this, *The Idol's Eye* was their next venture, with a story being based on the old Chinese axiom that anyone who saves the life of a would-be suicide assumes full responsibility for that person's actions. It opened in New York in September 1897, and was another success. The press sang Herbert's praises, writing that, "now Suppé is dead, Sullivan 'written out', Strauss practically quiescent, he has no superior in Europe".

During the writing of the musicals, he was also conducting his band, but he still found the time and energy to write new compositions. In 1898, the year in which the publishers M Witmark And Sons closed a deal to publish Herbert's works, he and Smith saw their new musical, *The Fortune Teller*, appear onstage, with the show's London première occurring three years later, in March 1901.

On the whole, his musicals enjoyed a certain degree of success, but his lifestyle wasn't dependent on them. In 1898, in addition to his other work, he was appointed conductor of the Pittsburgh Symphony Orchestra, with an annual salary of $2,000. His conducting responsibilities didn't restrict his composing, however, and he turned out no less than four more musical operettas during 1899: *Cyrano De Bergerac*, *The Singing Girl*, *The Ameer* and *The Viceroy*. The future seemed bright.

In 1901, however, Herbert had reason to feel doubly aggrieved: he fell out with the orchestra manager, George H Wilson, and the *Musical Courier* wrote a most unnecessarily vitriolic article about him, littered with accusations of plagiarism. Herbert successfully sued the newspaper for libel in a case that became national front-page news, and in which the editor, Marc A Blumenburg, was ridiculed and humiliated. It was later revealed that the journal operated what was tantamount to a payola racket – if a musician or composer paid for advertising with them, their work got a good review; if they refused to pay (as Herbert had), they received a bad review. In October 1902, Herbert was awarded $15,000 damages, which on appeal was later reduced to $5,158.40.

He might have won that victory, but two years later his ongoing hostilities with Wilson led to the orchestra manager using political cunning to depose the conductor. As it happened, it was a case of *fortuna meliores sequitur*, as Herbert's career went from strength to strength while the replacement brought in by Wilson was to lead to the orchestra's demise within a few years, and Wilson would die within four.

In October 1903, Herbert's new musical, *Babes In Toyland*, made its stage debut, with libretto by Glen MacDonough and production by Fred R Hamlin and Julian Mitchell, who had just produced the first stage version of *The Wizard Of Oz*.

The prolific Herbert followed *Babes* with *Babette*. The *Evening Post* commented that "Mr Herbert is, like Johann Strauss, a high-class musician who can adapt his style to popular taste without ever becoming vulgar…Babette is really, for New York, an epoch-making production."

1904 marked the debut of the Victor Herbert Orchestra, which included about half of the Pittsburgh musicians whom he'd previously conducted, who had decided that they would rather play under his baton than perform for the new regime in Pennsylvania.

Later in that year, another of his musicals hit the stage, *It Happened In Nordland*. Its theme, that of a female diplomat representing the United States overseas, would be echoed in Irving Berlin's 1950 musical comedy *Call Me Madam*.

In the late summer of 1905 two more of his musicals were performed, *Miss Dolly Dollars* and *Wonderland*. The latter started life as a hybrid of the Lewis Carroll's books *Alice Through The Looking-Glass* and *Alice In Wonderland* but ended up as an entirely different piece, with hardly any of the Alice characters included. (The linear plots of both of the *Alice* books have always created problems for those who have tried to write stage musicals around them. The librettists' usual conclusion is that that they work best as books, and that trying to earth their dream-like quality, whilst retaining the tradition of the original work, is a tough nut to crack.)

Herbert's next two musicals were *Mlle Modiste* and *The Red Mill*, the latter containing a song called 'Good-a-bye John'. He was violently opposed to other composer's songs being interpolated into his musicals, but on this occasion the producers succeeded by subversion, introducing one by suggesting the type of song that they wanted and singing to Herbert a snatch of how this tune might go. Taking on board their ideas, it seems that the unwitting Herbert wrote the music and Henry Blossom the words, unaware that the producers had sung an existing song to them. They therefore became the innocent plagiarists of 'Good-a-bye John', a song from another show, *The Belle Of Avenue A*. This minor setback didn't deter Herbert one iota, however. More musicals followed, and in 1908 he was elected to the National Institute Of Arts And Letters.

Despite his peripatetic existence, he was ever the patriotic Irishman, and was an enthusiastic member of the Society Of Friendly Sons Of St Patrick, an organisation that had been been formed in 1784 by Irish veterans of the American Revolution. For one of their banquets, Herbert provided six Irish folk songs, which drew heavily on Thomas Moore, the Irish poet whose works had earlier influenced Stephen Foster. Among the pieces were 'The Minstrel Boy' and 'The Harp That Once Thro' Tara's Halls'.

During a six-week period in 1908, three more of his musicals went into production, *Algeria*, *Little Nero* and *The Prima Donna*. Meanwhile, he continued to compose more classically-orientated works, and would maintain an interest in the various societies with which he was involved. In the beginning of 1909, he was elected to yet another, when he was co-opted into the élite New York Musicians' Club. He also accepted a vice presidency later in that same year, an office that he would hold until 1915.

For several years Herbert and several other composers had been working on the development of a copyright law that would be of long-term benefit to all composers and lyricists. He was angry that the new phonograph machines and piano rolls were making an increasing amount of money for the manufacturers but none for the composers. He and John Philip Sousa spoke out on behalf of the composers at the various hearings of the copyright bill. At one hearing, in 1906, Herbert stated that "we stand here for many hundreds of poor fellows who have not been able to come here, possibly because they do not have the price...brother composers whose names figure in the advertisement of these companies who have perforated rolls and talking machines, etc, and who have never received a cent...They pay Mr Caruso $3,000 for each song...for each record...and the composer would not receive a cent. I say that can not be just...morally there is only one side to it, and I hope you will see it and recommend the necessary law."

Whilst the Victor Talking Machine Company agreed in principle to the demands, inventor of musical devices G Howlett Davis railed against the idea. He claimed that it was only through the genius of inventors that these writers with a "minor and remote ethical or equity right", were able to have their works heard by more people.

John O'Connell, representing the independent piano roll manufacturers, was also opposed to Herbert's demands and to a futuristic theory put forward by Sousa, that rolls and records should contain some form of writing, which would one day be decipherable directly from that source.

ST Cameron, of the American Gramophone Company, insisted that copyright was paid on the purchase of the sheet music, and that therefore the purchaser could do what they liked with it.

Meanwhile, George W Pound, the counsel for the Rudolph Wurlitzer Company, suggested that, rather than the mechanical devices being subject to copyright, the composer should receive a percentage for the reproduction of their work. Ignored at the time, the idea would be adopted three years later.

As the confrontation dragged on, Herbert remained at the forefront as spokesman for the composers and writers, and as such was later elected president of the Authors' And Composers' Copyright League Of America.

Both sides of the battle became entrenched, pounding the other at assorted hearings and putting over points of view that ranged from the pragmatic to the idiotic. At last, though, through attacking on a variety of fronts, an agreement was reached by which the composers of songs would be paid a royalty. The law stated that the copyright owner alone could give permission to a manufacturer to record his work, but once he had given that permission it gave other manufacturers the right to record it, as long as they paid the agreed royalty. The bill, signed in March 1909, would change the lives of all future songwriters for the better.

With an agreement now reached, Herbert now felt that he could finally record his music. In the spring of 1909, he signed to the label of the phonograph pioneer who'd also devised the electric light bulb (amongst many other inventions), Thomas Alva Edison. Edison himself was delighted to get Herbert's signature on a contract, writing as much to the composer in a letter that ended optimistically: "From now on we ought to reach a still higher standard in the recording of music."

Herbert, in reply, commented: "The capabilities of the phonograph in spreading culture, instilling a sense of appreciation and discrimination of the best in art, and musically educating the people, are beyond conception, and I am eager to do what I can to enlarge the scope of your truly wonderful invention."

Then, as now, technology was progressing in leaps and bounds. Up until 1908, wax cylinders had been able to reproduce approximately two minutes of music, but after 1908 the introduction of a revolutionary method of sound reproduction, the gramophone, allowed twice that amount of playing time.

Herbert continued to write a string of successful musicals, including *Naughty Marietta*, which contained two of his most popular songs, 'I'm Falling In Love With Someone' and 'Ah! Sweet Mystery Of Life'.

Herbert is acknowledged as being the founder of ASCAP (the American Society Of Composers, Authors And Publishers), although at its initial meeting at Luchow's restaurant in February 1914 there were eight others also there, including lawyer Nathan Burkan, who helped Herbert to draw up a constitution for the projected performing rights organisation. It was intended that the society would represent composers, authors and publishers, ensuring that their monies were collected fairly and efficiently.

Encouraged by the forming of such a society, the second and more formal meeting held five months later attracted over 100 people. It was confirmed then that four types of membership would be offered: those of composer, author, publisher and probationary. The game was afoot, and, although Herbert refused the presidency of the society, he agreed to become vice president.

It was never in doubt that, with new technology springing up everywhere, such a society was needed. It would have been impracticable for writers to have attempted to oversee, control the use of and procure the correct revenue for their own songs from an increasingly widespread area.

The use of recorded music in restaurants to attract a certain clientèle was becoming more and more widespread, with the venues often advertising music as the main attraction. This state of affairs drew Herbert into another protracted battle for the rights of his society members and songwriters in general. He alleged that a New York eating house called Shanleys had allowed his song 'Sweethearts' to be performed on the premises without proper authorisation. The defence, however, claimed that the music was incidental to the main business of providing food. In May 1915, Judge Learned Hand ruled that the song had not been performed for profit. Herbert appealed and lost that case, too, at which point someone with less determination might have capitulated. Not so Herbert. He took the case to the United States Supreme Court, where Justice Oliver Wendell Holmes, himself a writer, historically changed the course of songwriting history by overturning the two previous decisions. If songwriters ever offer up a prayer that is for anything other than the usual plea for inspiration, they should give thanks for the persistence of Herbert and the wisdom of Oliver Wendell Holmes. The future of ASCAP would be littered with confrontations, through the arrival of new technology in the form of radio, talking pictures, television and the computer revolution, but the ground rules had been laid down.

Herbert continued to write operettas, conduct, perform and compose, and also wrote music for motion-picture soundtracks, until his death in New York in May 1924. He is commemorated not only in the minds of the songwriters, for whom he fought so vigorously, but also on a plaque at Luchow's restaurant, where the first ASCAP meeting took place. His wife, Therese, died in 1927, and is buried beside her husband at a mausoleum in Woodlawn Cemetery. In the same year, their daughter unveiled a bronze bust of her father in Central Park. A 3¢ memorial stamp was issued in 1940, and three years later a ship bearing his name was launched. But today, who – apart from those working for ASCAP, and possibly a few devotees – remembers the name Victor Herbert?

Another devout champion of the cause of the songwriter was Charles K Harris, who later in his career would satisfy one of his ambitions and work with Victor Herbert. He once commented that, with his publishing hat on, "My one ambition was to sign up Victor Herbert. His name on my catalogue would mean a great deal to me."

Harris could neither read nor write music, and so, just as Lionel Bart and producer Joe Meek would later do with enormous success in the early '60s, he hummed or plucked his tunes to someone who could down jot the notes for him. The achievements of these three writers, and many others in the same situation, proves that you don't have be a trained musician (and, in Meek's case, not even a musician at all) in order to write commercial songs. People often asked Harris how he could write songs without reading music. He replied: "I cannot distinguish one note from another...as soon as a melody occurred to me, I hummed it. Then I would procure the services of a trained musician for the purpose, hum or whistle the melody for him and have him take it down on paper with notes. He would then arrange it for piano."

Over the decades, many arrangers have successfully and unsuccessfully claimed a percentage of the songwriter's royalty for this service, maintaining that it was their enhancement that made the song a hit. It's all very well embellishing an existing thought, but would they have had that inspiration themselves? The other side of that coin is when the arranger's input has resulted in a potentially ordinary song being given a commercial face at the invitation of the writer. Most songwriters look on their melody being changed by an arranger without their consent as a cardinal sin. The magic is in possessing a natural gift for melody, or in being able to conceive an outstanding and original lyric.

Charles Kassell Harris had talent, combined with enthusiasm. As a boy, he became enamoured of minstrel shows, and in an attempt to emulate his heroes he constructed his own banjo from an old oyster can and a piece of wire. His enthusiasm paid off when he was given a banjo by one of the performers he so revered. The actor Bill Carter, who was rehearsing in the yard of a hotel next door to the Harris' household, admired Harris' enthusiasm and encouraged him by swapping the boy's makeshift instrument for a real banjo.

At the age of 14, Harris moved from East Saginaw, Michigan, where he'd grown up, to Milwaukee, Wisconsin, by which time he'd mastered all of the songs in George C Dobson's *Banjo Book*. Having learned to play such familiar Stephen Foster tunes as 'The Old Folks At Home' and 'Massa's In The Cold, Cold Ground', he decided to teach others the skill. Still in his mid teens, the confident youngster hung a sign outside the house which read: "Prof Charles K Harris, Banjo Teacher". He first began writing songs for the local Phoenix Club, but had his sights set on wider horizons.

Harris noticed that most musical shows always featured songs that didn't suit the plot, but were included for their popularity alone. During the 1880s, he came up with the idea of tailoring songs to suit the situation, thereby supplanting the insignificant material with something more apposite. His first "situation song" was a collaboration with his friend and peer Charles Horowitz, who more than 20 years later would write the classic songs 'Because' and 'Always' with Fred C Bowers.

Harris saw no financial return for his early songwriting efforts. He certainly had talent, but he was also a hustler, in the best sense of the word, and an opportunist with enormous faith in his ability to succeed. Through the suggestion of a journalist friend, he landed himself the role of local correspondent for the *New York Dramatic News*, a position which not only guaranteed him entry to the theatres in the area but also gave him easy access to artists, to whom he could plug his songs.

Criticising one song in a show for not fitting the situation, he was asked to write one if he was so "cocksure". Harris went home that night and wrote 'Creep Baby Creep'. After its subsequent success, Harris was asked for another situation song for the same company. The song 'Alderman Michael O'Rourke' brought Harris the princely sum of $10, but its novel exploitation was the first instance of song-plugging: "I made up my mind that the song was going to be a success and so I conceived the idea that I would have someone in the gallery start the applause…This was the first time it was ever tried out in the history of modern song. That was the real beginning of song-plugging, which means exploiting or advertising a song by calling the public's attention to it either by singing or applauding it." However, the first night of this innovation was a disaster. Julius Caesar, the black expressman with "massive hands" to whom Harris had given a dollar, was clearly so taken with the song that he was meant to be applauding that he fell asleep.

Despite Harris' increasing popularity as a songwriter, royalties were few and far between. The first published song bearing his name, 'Thou Art Ever In My Thoughts', yielded only $16.75. He soon realised that in effect he was virtually giving his songs away to anybody willing to sing them. It might be good for the ego, but for Harris this attraction started to pall after a while, so the ever-inventive composer opened a songwriting shop! He rented premises at 207 Grand Avenue, Milwaukee, and took the same gamble as Stephen Foster in becoming a professional songwriter, but adopted a more audacious and zealous approach by displaying a sign which read: "Charles K Harris, Banjoist And Songwriter. Songs, Written To Order."

His luck began to turn in 1885, when he was asked to write songs for the show *Ali Baba* by the manger of the Chicago Opera House. Harris pawned his watch for $6 to pay his fare to the windy city, only for the manager David Henderson to almost renege on the deal due to the writer's tender years. Harris, still only 18, told Henderson: "The trick of the song business is this: fit your songs to the situation. Also, write songs that appeal to the imagination as well as point a moral. To keep your audience interested, give it a good popular tune, one that it can whistle, and you not only make a hit with the song, but also assure success for your show." Despite his initial misgivings, the boss of the opera house loved Harris' work, and paid him $400, which was considerably more money than the artist had earned in his life that far.

Getting songs published was still a major achievement for a young writer. It was almost impossible to simply approach a publisher with a manuscript; however good the song might be, if it wasn't being hummed or whistled by the public at large it was too much of a gamble. The writer was therefore responsible for a lot of his own legwork, and stood a much more realistic chance of his work being published if there was a known vocalist performing it in the theatres. Many publishers were reactive rather than proactive, much to the frustration of up-and-coming songwriters. If the song looked like being a success, they'd publish it. This was sound business sense, as far as the publishers were concerned, but aspiring young composers and lyricists felt circumvented by the lack of help that they felt was due to them and their material. Everyone knows that their own baby is greatly superior to everyone else's!

Harris felt this way when he decided to take a great financial risk and published one of his own songs, 'Hello, Central, Hello'. This meant having plates engraved, making up a title page, and working through all the other mysterious aspects of publishing sheet music. It wasn't cheap, and it was a decidedly risky venture, pitching in against the established and cash-rich publishing houses when the royalties for two of Harris' songs had brought in just $6.44 in six months.

Early in 1892, frustrated that publishers only passed on a small percentage of his potential earnings, Harris formed his own publishing company, soon realising that the mystique that publishers had been prone to weave around their profession was more smoke and mirrors than fact: "I felt very proud the next morning when arriving at my little studio. There were a few shelves lined against the walls containing copies of my songs. They were printed by Pollworth & Brother, two young men who had just opened a small establishment having only one press."

His first composition, after setting up his own concern, was a personal and professional triumph. The song features a singer relating the tale of how he lost the love of his life when he caught her kissing another man. The aggrieved lover's life-long intransigence on the subject is revealed as futile when, after her death, it emerges that the man was her brother. The inspiration for the song came during a ball in Chicago, where Harris first met his future wife.

> We danced together all evening, much to my delight. Gathered in our group that night was a charming young couple, engaged to be married. Suddenly we learned that the engagement was broken. Just a lover's quarrel, I presumed at the time; but they were both too proud to acknowledge that they were in the wrong. The ball lasted until early in the morning, and we were all leaving for our respective homes when I noticed, just ahead of our party, waiting for his carriage, this young man escorting, not his fiancée, but another charming miss. Lover-like he probably felt that, by causing his sweetheart a pang of jealousy, she would be more willing to forgive and forget. Of course, she did not know this. She simply knew that her Harry was easily consoled and that her place was usurped by another. Tears came to her eyes, though she tried to hide them behind a smile and a careless toss of the head. On witnessing this little drama the thought came to me like a flash, "Many a heart is aching after the ball…"

The verses, cloyingly sentimental and ideal for the late Victorian period, now read like misunderstandings reminiscent of a comedic farce, although the chorus has remained more enduring:

> After the ball is over, after the break of morn,
> After the dancers leaving; after the stars have gone,
> Many a heart is aching, if you could read them all;
> Many the hopes that have vanished, after the ball.

When it was first sung on stage, in 1892, the singer, Sam Doctor, forgot the words, and potential triumph turned into temporary disaster. Harris vowed never again to let an amateur be the first to introduce any new song of his. It was only when James Aldrich Libby performed it in the Broadway show *A Trip To Chinatown*, and received a five-minute standing ovation, that the song really took off.

Boy tenor and later major publisher Julius Witmark offered Harris $10,000 on the spot for the rights to 'After The Ball', but its writer correctly judged that, if somebody was willing to pay that much instant cash, it had to be more viable to publish the song himself.

It was a brave decision. At that moment, Harris could barely muster $5. However, within a short space of time, Harris had a cheque for $14,250 in his hand, and with the money continuing to pour in this grew quickly to $75,000. He was earning it faster than he could bank it. On average, he was earning $1,000 a day – no mean sum for the 1890s.

'After The Ball' would sell more than five million copies by the end of the century, demonstrating – as Stephen Foster had detected – that the ability to write a catchy song gave a composer enormous earning potential. Even US bandmaster John Philip Sousa included the composition in his concerts in 1893 at the Chicago World Fair, where the young ragtime pioneer Scott Joplin was also conducting. Sousa was still four years away from composing his patriotic march 'The Stars And Stripes Forever', and Joplin was six years away from introducing ragtime music to a wider audience. Harris' song was so popular with the public that, when he went to see Sousa conducting the song, the latter said: "Confound you, Harris, the playing of your song has tired me out! If you don't believe me, stand here for a few minutes and I will show you." Virtually every request was for 'After The Ball'.

Another of Harris' successes was 'For Old Time's Sake'. The idea for this song came to him while he was sitting in the Milwaukee Lodge Of Elks, of which he was the treasurer. One prominent lodge member was sporting a lapel button bearing the face of a beautiful girl, leading to Harris inquiring as to her identity.

> His face grew quite serious for a moment as he said that she was an old sweetheart of his, whom he had intended to marry. She came from a small farm in Wisconsin. The two were neighbours and had become sweethearts as youngsters; but one day a travelling salesman had come along, filled her ears with dreams of the city, and prevailed upon her to run away and be married in Chicago. When my friend returned from a trip, he heard that the girl had fled. The news broke his spirit for a time.
>
> A year later he had occasion to go to Chicago, and there he met her on the street. He was startled at her changed appearance. He greeted her kindly, as she looked so worn, weary and dejected. She returned his greeting by faintly crying his name, "Frank", and then almost collapsed in his arms. She told him the tragedy of her life: how the man had married her, but, soon tiring of her, deserted her in less that a year. All his old love for her returned instantly, and he took her in his arms, assuring her that, for old time's sake he wanted to be always near her, and that if she consented, he would marry her as soon as she was free. She replied that she was too fond of him to mar his life, as a doctor had told her that she could live only a few months at most. She said she had never known till then how much she loved him, and he kissed her, just for old time's sake.

Harris was immediately inspired, and lyrically followed the incident to the letter in the song 'For Old Time's Sake'.

His million-selling hit 'Break The News To Mother' was motivated by a line in the play *Secret Service*, starring William Gillette:

> There was a scene in the play where a young Southern boy, aged 15, was twitted by his little sweetheart because he did not join the army. He was willing to do so; but his father, an army man, and his brother John, an officer, insisted on his remaining at home. However, the youngster finally ran away and joined the army as a drummer boy. He was wounded, and his corporal carried him off the field. When they arrived at the boy's home he exclaimed to the person who met him at the door, "Break the news to Mother."

Harris was sitting in a barber's chair when the idea for the climax and how to resolve the drummer boy's plight came to him. He leapt up, crying "He's got to die...I'm going to kill him!"

There hadn't been a war in America for over 40 years, and so major sales of the song were not expected to be huge; but fate struck, and on the night of its first performance the US battleship *Maine* was blown up in Havana harbour. The ensuing Spanish–American war caused sales of the song to rocket.

Ideas for songs can turn up in many guises and in unusual circumstances. 'Always In The Way' was written after he'd overheard a young boy rebuke his sister for stepping on his foot as they looked in the window of a festively-decorated department store, while 'Just Behind The Times' was inspired by the impending demise of a well-known Milwaukee minister who was about to be replaced by a new, allegedly more forward-thinking incumbent. At one point, Harris was asked by the manager of the Western Book And Stationery Company to write a song that would help to boost their sheet music sales. Moved by an oil painting hanging on the wall of their offices, he wrote "Mid The Green Fields Of Virginia'. It was hoped that the song might sell 10,000 copies, but in the event it shifted 100,000 in a short space of time. When you're on a roll, every idea seems to work for you.

A close friend of Harris' and another of America's up-and-coming songwriters was Paul Dresser. Like Harris, Dresser wrote both words and music, and had written several successful songs, such as 'The Convict And The Bird' and 'The Curse'. He was convinced that 'Break The News To Mother' would be a million-seller, the same prediction that Harris had successfully made for Dresser's 'On The Banks Of The Wabash' a year earlier.

Not many people can instantly identify a potential hit song. It's a gift that can be worth more financially than just being able to write, sing or publish them. Independent record producer Joe Meek wasn't remotely musical, but he could spot a hit single, fly in the face of the major record companies and create hit after hit during the first half of the '60s. Singer-turned-producer Mickie Most also had a phenomenal run of success from the mid '60s, when he produced The Animals' 'House Of The Rising Sun', right through to the mid '80s, his talent of being able to sort the wheat from the chaff reaping him tens of millions of pounds.

Jonathan King is another producer with great ears, hearing possibilities in songs that no one else even remotely considered. Most of the acts he used, discovered or fronted were one-off successes, simply because the songs were commercially stronger than the artists. He also had the knack of seeing talent in, and getting involved with, several major acts early in their careers, such as Abba, 10cc and Genesis.

Another producer with the uncanny gift of being able to smell out a hit is Pete Waterman, of Stock, Aitken and Waterman fame. His adroitness brought their stable of stars dozens of hits and earned them millions. Now working independently, Waterman has continued to exercise his extraordinary intuition to great effect.

In the mid '20s, near the end of his career, Charles Harris identified this need in the business: "Few men are living today who can pick hits. I would be willing to pay $50,000 a year salary to any man who would work for me and do just that one thing…pick sure-fire hits." In the very late 1890s, Harris opened an office in Tin Pan Alley, New York's 28th Street, where all of the other music publishers were located.

As well as songs, Harris also devised scenarios for stage plays and for the silent movies, and also wrote a book entitled *How To Write A Popular Song*. Within its pages, he lays down four golden rules: "Look at a newspaper for your story line. Acquaint yourself with the style in vogue. Avoid slang. Know the copyright laws." He successfully followed the first of those rules when his wife called his attention to an item in that morning's newspaper, about a coal merchant who had recently become a widower, with only his seven-year-old daughter to comfort him. The story fired Harris' imagination and compassion: "As he was reading his evening paper, his little girl, who had been playing with some wooden blocks close by, suddenly threw them aside and climbed on a chair so as to reach a telephone hanging on the wall. Cranking the small handle of the old-fashioned telephone then in use, she said: 'Hello Central, give me Heaven, for my mamma's there.'"

Many writers have taken that same newspaper rule to heart, including John Lennon, when he began writing The Beatles' classic 'A Day In The Life': "I was writing the song with the *Daily Mail* propped up in front of me on the piano. I had it opened at their 'News In Brief' or 'Far And Near', or whatever they call it. There was a paragraph about 4,000 holes being found in Blackburn, Lancashire." Lennon even credits his inspiration in the song's lyrics:

> I read the news today, oh boy,
> Four thousand holes in Blackburn, Lancashire.
> And though the holes were rather small,
> Now they know how many holes it takes to fill the Albert Hall.

Fellow Beatle Paul McCartney was present when Donovan recorded 'Mellow Yellow', another song that had its origin from the same source. Don's ideas for it were triggered by press reports: "John Lennon, especially, would scan newspapers for clippings, bits, snippets, and in a collage sense he'd put songs together. Well, 'Mellow Yellow' is about many things gathered from newspaper articles and the back pages of magazines, like the reference to 'electrical banana'."

There were many who sought to make this song, written in a Swedish hotel room, an anthem for "banana smokers", who reckoned that you could get high through smoking dried banana skins. To that end, people marched in San Francisco carrying giant bananas and yelling slogans advocating the smoking of the fruit, all because of a piece in a newspaper that caught Donovan's eye.

Neil Sedaka, one of the most prolific songwriters of the '60s and '70s, was also occasionally inspired by a magazine: "'Calender Girl' was actually pinched from a TV guide. I was looking at the movies of the week and there was a Cary Grant film called 'Calender Girl'. The title intrigued me, so Howard Greenfield and I decided to do each month of the year, starting in January and ending with December. It was, I thought, one of his best lyrics; it was a very special piece of material."

Not only has the printed word inspired countless lyricists, but the wordsmiths in turn have often coined a phrase or a title which has passed into common usage. Neil Sedaka's collaborator Greenfield did just that in 1962, with the million-selling 'Breaking Up Is Hard To Do', although Neil had to convince Howie to write it: "I've seen that in print now for over three decades. Wherever I look...in newspapers, in magazine articles...it's become a phrase that's used everywhere." It appears that Harris' rule to use newspapers as inspiration has continued hold good down the decades.

Aside from his writing activities, Harris achieved one of his ambitions in working with and publishing fellow songwriter Victor Herbert. He also worked with and published work by his friend Oscar Hammerstein, who was extraordinarily ambitious: "Some day I will show them how to run grand opera, with new singing stars, new costumes and new theatres." He was as good as his word, building the Manhattan Opera House in New York and one in London, and encouraging and providing opportunities for budding American and European performers. His grandson would become one of the most successful lyricists and librettists of the '40s and '50s.

However, there was an increasing problem for successful composers and lyricists. For many years, the Music Publishers' Society and composers like Victor Herbert had been fighting for a copyright bill, to no avail. First the wax cylinders and then the flat discs could be sold by phonograph companies without them having to pay anything to the writer of the songs that they contained. At the behest of the society's president, Harris, a great champion of the cause, went to Washington to explore new possibilities of pushing for a new bill.

While he was there, he bumped into the manager of the Casino Theatre, New York, whose connections enabled him to arrange a meeting for Harris with President Roosevelt. So, on behalf of the songwriters of the world, Harris sat facing the president of the United States Of America: "Mr President, I am here on behalf of thousands of songwriters regarding the new copyright bill, which I hear has been pigeon-holed...We writers are working under the copyright law of 1701, which has never been changed, and the mechanical record is a device that has sprung up in the meantime and there is no clause in our copyright to cover it." Harris related his profession's side of the story, also pointing out to Roosevelt that it was possible for the president's own books to be exploited in the same manner.

Suitably impressed, Roosevelt concurred, agreeing that justice needed to be done. In 1905, he wrote: "Our copyright laws urgently need revision. They are imperfect in definition, confused and inconsistent in expression; they omit provision for many articles which, under modern reproductive processes, are entitled to protection; they impose hardships upon the copyright proprietor which are not essential to the fair protection of the public."

The ripples that spread from that meeting made an important contribution to the passing of the copyright bill that went into effect in 1909. Other writers had also worked like Trojans to further the cause, such as Victor Herbert and Harry Williams, who had written 'Under The Shade Of The Old Apple Tree' in tandem with the society's attorney, Nathan

Burkan. Nine years later, the American Society Of Composers, Authors And Publishers was formed by Victor Herbert and co, whose remit was to collect songwriting royalties from various areas, including the those of the fast-expanding technological world.

The first motion picture exposition, which was held at the Grand Central Palace in 1910, proved to be the vanguard of another new medium for songwriters. Producers and film stars, such as Mary Pickford, abounded at the various booths and stands that demonstrated the merits of the major film companies of the time, including Vitagraph, Biograph, Universal, Kalem and Lubin. Of course, it was all very new, and the industry was making up its own rules as it grew. Charles Harris was also present at this innovative exhibition, where it was suggested that he should write a scenario for a film based around his song 'After The Ball'. Following rejections from virtually every company, he eventually placed it with the William B Steiner Photoplay Company, and as soon as the picture hit the screens he was inspired to follow the same route with other songs of his that he felt were suitable. "I decided to use my other song hits and turn them into scenarios. I tackled 'Always In The Way', which was made into a five-reel photo-play by the Dyreda Picture Company...It went over with a bang."

Using this method, Harris had a string of successful films for a variety of production companies, proving that, if you're around at the infancy of a medium, you can get involved in helping to write its constitution to benefit your own particular area of expertise.

Of course, cinema brought more potential problems for songwriters, as did the radio revolution. Keeping tabs on where one's songs were being used (or, in most cases, misused) was becoming a nightmare. This called for more action, as the motion picture companies and the broadcasting corporations emphatically refused to pay for the right to use songs in their productions or radio programmes. To this end, a deputation of the songwriting hierarchy from ASCAP, including Charles Harris, Irving Berlin, Harry Von Tilzer, Jerome Kern, Victor Herbert, John Philip Sousa and Irving Caesar, went to Washington to add weight to the two bills being introduced and to meet with President Coolidge.

There was another unsavoury problem that was creating unrest among songwriters: the fact that publishers – increasingly aware of the large amount of money that it was now possible to make – were paying artists and the leaders of musical ensembles to record their material, as well as

The Songwriters Go To War

giving money to influential venues for exploitation rights. Publishers' earnings – which, of course, affected the writers – were thus being absorbed by having to fight their competitors in an increasingly commercial arena. Common sense at last prevailed, with the publishers forming the Music Publishers' Protective Association, and agreeing that there should be no further payments to artists by association members.

Harris, who with his fellow society members did so much to help protect the copyrights for generations of future songwriters, passed away in 1930, having denounced the new music. He mourned "the days of dancing before the great god jazz had cracked his whip".

A third songwriter whose successful world was to be dominated at one point by controversial rights issues was George M Cohan. He too fought for his beliefs, to such an extent that there are people in the business to whom his memory is still *persona non grata* – if indeed a memory can be described thus – even 60 years after his death. Cohan was an incredible man, and the change of attitude and look he brought to the musical stage cannot be underestimated.

Like Stephen Foster, Cohan was an Independence Day baby, born on 4 July 1878 in Providence, Rhode Island. His father, Jerry, was the son of Irish immigrants from County Cork, and the family's ancestral name, O'Caomhan, had been changed to Keohane and then to Cohan by the time they entered America.

Jerry Cohan loved the showbusiness life, and even took his young Irish wife, Nellie, with him when he toured. She soon joined him in his vaudeville routine, struggling through adversity to eke out a living, the pair eventually taking their children, Josie and George, on the road with them. As soon as they were old enough, the children joined the act, and the family toured as The Four Cohans or some permutation thereof that would bring in the most money.

Young George had no formal education, having lived out of a trunk from a very young age, although he did learn the violin and would often augment the family income by playing second violin in orchestras at venues where the Cohans were performing. They worked primarily for the rather unscrupulous but powerful vaudeville producer BF Keith.

At the age of ten, the prodigious George Cohan wrote his earliest song, 'First Floor Front', a song with a lyric that more than nodded to his Celtic roots, including names such as McCarthy, Clancy, Mike McGee, Jimmy Grogan, Pat O'Day, and even a man with the same name as an Irish-born Eurovision winner a century later, Johnny Logan.

North Brookfield was one of the few places where the family remained for any length of time, and it was there that George met his childhood friend Dennis F "Cap" O'Brien, whom he would later help financially when he wanted to attend law school. It was O'Brien who inspired Cohan to write what the young man considered to be his best song, 'Venus, My Shining Love', after answering George's question as to what star it was that shone so brightly in the evening sky:

> Venus, beautiful Venus, how bright you shine,
> None shall e'er come between us, sweet Venus mine.

As Cohan had had no formal schooling, O'Brien had to help him with the spelling and grammar for the song's lyric.

Another influence that made George want to write for the stage was the 19th-century Irish playwright Dion Boucicault, the man whom George Bernard Shaw would later claim to be as good as Molière, Goethe and Ibsen.

George's increasing love affair with the stage was matched only by his love of performing and writing songs. Even at a young age, he appeared to have an amazing amount of confidence in his creative abilities, sending two of his songs to a New York publisher. Their reply was brief and terminal: "Dear sir, your songs are not publishable. Please do not send any more." A response that would have deterred most aspiring songwriters, but it was like red rag to a bull for George, who wrote even more songs. He vowed to start his own publishing company when he eventually got to New York, where he was convinced everything happened.

He also had teenage dreams about building his own theatre and writing and starring in his own plays, and was frustrated by a lack of movement in these areas. Although still only 15, he decided to run away. He left a note for his mother: "Goodbye Mother, don't worry about me. I'm on my way to New York to sell my songs and plays and get a job in a Broadway show." As he pushed the note under his mother's door, his father appeared, who knew all about George's plan and with wonderful diplomacy announced that he'd decided to move the whole family to New York.

Once there, however, the family was forced to split up in order to get work. Much to George's chagrin, Josie made the most headway and earned the lion's share of the income. In 1893, though, he got his first break with one of his songs. He took five numbers to the publishers M Witmark And Sons, where he received a surprisingly warm welcome from Witmark himself, who it appeared had a great professional fondness for George's father, Jerry. Witmark offered George $10 for one of the songs, 'Why Did Nellie Leave Her Home?'.

Eager to be accepted as a professional songwriter, he had been hanging out with the song-pluggers and writers on 14th Street, singing 'Nellie' to them at every opportunity. On receiving the sheet music for his song, he was mortified to discover that his lyrics had been altered, and that the vaudevillian nature of the song had been changed so that it was now a rather maudlin ballad. George was mystified how this had happened, as no other writer was credited and the sheet proclaimed to the world that the words and music were by by Geoge M Cohan. The rewriting of the lyric, it was later revealed, had been undertaken at the behest of Witmark, and had been carried out by the uncredited Walter H Ford. However, this peculiar turn of events hardly mattered to the unwitting Cohan, who was just delighted at being accepted by the gang down on 14th Street.

During the winter of 1893, he wrote more songs, and finely honed 'Venus, My Shining Love', selling the latter and several others. It totally hooked him on songwriting: "I scribbled parodies and patter for comedians, comic songs and extra verses for serio-comics and even took a shot at after-pieces for burlesque shows…After a while, I got to writing sketches for variety teams and orders came in so fast that I found it impossible to supply the demand. With parodies in every pocket and sketch manuscripts under my arm, I was soon the envy of all the pencil pushers in the variety brand of the theatrical game."

By 1896, after a few turbulent episodes in their working life, The Four Cohans were earning an unprecedented $1,000 a week at Hyde And Behman's Theatre in New York. Working at that venue transformed their lives virtually overnight, with George – at his still tender age – managing the quartet, as well as performing and becoming increasingly in demand as a songwriter.

'Venus, My Shining Love' had become a standard in the repertoire of the Broadway café orchestras, while his 'Hot Tamale Baby' became a feature in the vaudeville act of the illustrious May Irwin. Both that song and 'You're The Warmest Baby In The Bunch' were "coon songs", although most of George's material at the time was in the novelty vein. Now self-confident and unswervingly optimistic, George broke The Four Cohans from the powerful agent Keith, setting his sights firmly on Broadway as a home for the family's act.

At the age of 20, he met the singer, dancer and comedienne Ethel Levey at an after-show party in Chicago. Born Ethelia Fowler, in San Francisco, to a Scottish father and Irish mother, she took her stage name from her Jewish stepfather, Sol Levey. Like Cohan, she'd also made herself sound more Jewish than she was, at a time when immigrants with genuinely Jewish names were frantically anglicising them. After a courtship conducted mainly by letter, George and Ethel were married in July 1899 in Atlantic City.

At the turn of the century, in New York, Cohan wrote his first full-length musical show, having had the experience of creating sixteen one-act plays and sketches between 1895 and 1899. Then, in 1904, after having been inspired by the exploits of the jockey Tod Sloan, he wrote one of his most famous musicals, *Little Johnny Jones*, with the enterprising New Yorker Sam H Harris. The two men were to become good friends and long-term partners.

It was a fervently patriotic production, and the first of many musicals in which Cohan would musically and lyrically wave the star-spangled banner. Although set in England, the show trumpeted the advantages of living in the USA, in particular through the song 'I'm A Yankee Doodle Dandy', which contained the line "born on the fourth of July", so apposite to its writer.

Another big song in the show was sung by Cohan as Johnny Jones, as he stood in the dock at Southampton, the same dock on which John Lennon would stand almost 65 years later, both literally and in his song 'The Ballad Of John And Yoko'. It was also Cohan, in character, who sang his own song 'Give My Regards To Broadway', the epic tearjerker that burst into a big, happy chorus. (Lennon's fellow Beatle and collaborator Paul McCartney made it a double Beatles/Cohan link when he parodied George's song title in his film *Give My Regards To Broad Street*, a now-defunct London railway terminus.)

Cohan rode out a roasting from the critics to establish himself on Broadway, and made a considerable sum of money into the bargain. At the behest of the powerful Theatrical Syndicate boss AL Erlanger, he came up with a blockbuster of a musical with 45 *Minutes From Broadway*, which was premièred in Ohio in 1905. As well as the title song, the show also contained soon-to-be-popular songs 'So Long Mary' and 'Mary's A Good Old Name'.

Cohan's other musical of that year, *George Washington, Jr*, was inspired by a song that he had written called 'You're A Grand Old Rag', which itself had been spawned during a funeral cortège for a Civil War veteran. One of the dead man's colleagues regaled Cohan with the story of the charge at Gettysburg as he stroked the flag and said, "It was all for this...she's a grand old rag." The critics, as usual looking for something to attack, homed in on the fact that Cohan referred to the nation's flag as a rag, thereby demoting its status, denigrating the country and generally being unacceptable.

In going for the jugular, they completely missed the point, which was that the flag had seen so much service that it was now a rag, and as such symbolised a cause dear to the men who'd followed it and served as a reminder of their long-dead colleagues. Deciding against such explanations and taking on the press, Cohan changed the title of the song to 'You're A Grand Old Flag'.

The show also featured the less contentious 'I Was Born In Virginia', a hit for George's wife, Ethel, and 'If Washington Should Come To Life', with lyrics imagining the USA's first president returning to the world at the beginning of the 20th century.

As many have discovered, success is a breeding ground for covetous vitriol, always perplexing to the recipient, who will often have ploughed a lonely and uphill furrow for a few moments of fame that never came with a guarantee. James Metcalfe, the drama critic for *Life* magazine, launched a scathing attack on the young George: "Mr Cohan is a sort of universal genius. He writes plays, he writes the words that are set to combinations of music to his words. These combinations of music are curious things, consisting mainly of several bars of well-known patriotic and sentimental songs strung together with connecting links of lively and more or less original organised trash. The words fitted to these curious contraptions are the kind of unmetrical stuff that children compose and call poetry, and are for the most part mawkish appeals to the cheapest kind of patriotism." Metcalfe also censured "the intelligence of a large part of the theatre-going public" for actually enjoying Cohan's musicals.

In the next 100 years, the culture of the critic would change little. Towards the end of the century, another popular and highly successful composer, Andrew Lloyd Webber, would also have to endure bitter invective from the critics whilst enjoying phenomenal commercial success.

With both Cohan and Webber, an absolute confidence in their own abilities has often been misconstrued as arrogance. Having the vision, determination and talent, and the wherewithal to successfully convert those three bedfellows, may infer a self-importance that, in reality, is no more than a creative human being trying to prove themselves through his respective talents.

Other critics soon jumped onto the bandwagon of denouncing Cohan's productions, leading him to respond by writing a front-page piece for the *Spot Light*: "I write my own songs because I write better songs than anyone else that I know of. I publish these songs because they bring greater royalties than any other class of music sold in this country." He also contested that he was the country's best playwright, best producer of plays, best singer, best actor and best dancer. He was confident, but not, he claimed, an egotist. His musicals spoke for themselves. They brought something quite new to musical theatre, in conception, delivery, pace and subject matter, without being influenced by either English theatre or German operetta.

By the time he was 28, he had produced his first non-musical Broadway play, *Popularity*, and his very real ambition was to own a part of Broadway. As he moved towards his goal, more musicals followed, including *The Honeymooners*, *The Talk Of New York*, *The Yankee Prince* and, in 1909, *The Man Who Owns Broadway*.

Due to the success of his musicals, Cohan and his partner, Sam Harris, were able to start buying and building theatres, but while that side of his life had been gathering momentum, his marriage to Ethel Levey had failed. Events soon turned out for the best, though, as George fell in love with and married Agnes Nolan, while Harris married her sister, Alice.

In 1910, at a function to honour Cohan, AL Erlanger's partner Marc Klaw made a speech in which he claimed that George "represents the spirit and energy of the country…a concentrated essence, four-cylinder power…a protest against and an apology for the palmy days of drama…I have sat in a restaurant in the Strand in London and in the boulevard cafes in Paris and felt my mind go lovingly across the sea as I heard the musicians playing 'Give My Regards To Broadway' and 'Mary Is A Good Old Name'. This youngster struck a universal chord in his songs and plays, and that is why we know and love him."

Present at that dinner were the young Samuel Goldfish (yet to change his name to Goldwyn), the 14-year-old Buster Keaton (engaged, with his parents, to perform vaudeville at the function) and Colonel William F Cody, aka Buffalo Bill, who referred to George as "one of the most remarkable young men this country has produced". The plaudits were welcome, but Cohan was happiest when he was indulging himself in his real passions, songwriting and the theatre, although he did expect everyone who worked for him to have the same high standards.

By 1910, Cohan and Harris had acquired interests in five major theatres, and also owned the Cohan And Harris Theatre and the George M Cohan Theatre.

Cohan's success as producer and writer continued unchecked during the second decade of the century, and when Woodrow Wilson announced that America was at war with Germany, Cohan shut himself in his study to pen something patriotic. Early the following morning, he sang his new song in front of his family. Wearing a large tin pan on his head and using a broom to replicate a gun, he marched up and down the room, treating them to his latest creation. The chorus was based on a popular bugle call. The song became America's favourite song of World War One:

> Over there, over there,
> Send the word, send the word over there
> That the yanks are coming, the yanks are coming,
> The drums rum-tumming everywhere.
> So prepare, say a prayer,
> Send the word, send the word to beware
> We'll be over, we're coming over,
> And we won't come back till
> It's over, over there.

Following the war, he reworked the script of a rather ordinary play called *Cherry Blossom* which had been brought to him by his first publisher, Isidore Witmark. He retitled it *The Royal Vagabond*, and it opened at the George M Cohan Theatre in New York early in 1919. Thanks to Cohan's Midas touch, it became a rip-roaring success.

Apart from the major stars, actors in musicals and plays were generally being paid badly by producers, and appeared to be getting the thin end of the wedge, while the theatre owners cleaned up. Having been in the same position himself as a struggling young teenage actor, Cohan had more sympathy than most with their plight, but assumed that the growing dissent would never be directed at him, as he'd always been a good payer and a considerate boss. The actors' petition for a fair wage continued to gather momentum, although it had met with nothing but contempt and disbelief from the theatre owners and producers.

On 7 August 1919, things came to a head. A new group calling itself the Actors Equity Association called a strike, bringing half of the shows on Broadway to a halt. Ironically, as Cohan had always been one of the most generous employees, the union parodied his song 'Over There', using it as a rallying call:

> Over fair, over fair
> We have been, we have been over fair...
> For we are striking, yes we are striking,
> And we won't come back till the managers are fair.

An anti-strike, pro-theatre managers' group, the Actors Fidelity League, known as "the Fidos", was also formed.

Feelings ran high on both sides, and after shots were fired on Cohan's home he became fiercely anti-equity, vowing to quit the business and work as an elevator operator if the equity supporters got their way.

As the strike continued, more theatres closed, resulting in 60 new shows and musicals being cancelled. Aggrieved at what he considered to be the wilful and aggressive actions of a bunch of renegades, whose attitude went against his personal philosophy and many of whom he'd personally helped, he accepted the presidency of the Fidos. At length, the theatre owners and producers conceded and signed an agreement with the Actors Equity Association, recognising them as the representative body for the acting profession.

For the rest of his life Cohan refused to join Equity, preferring to strike his own deal. Even in as late as the 1970s, Equity still displayed some animosity towards Cohan's memory and what they believed that his name still represented.

Although disgruntled at the outcome of the Equity situation, Cohan soon settled back into the old routine, having three more hit shows on Broadway by the autumn of 1920.

Over the next decade, many new songwriters would emerge to write the next generation of musicals, including Cole Porter, Rodgers and Hart, George and Ira Gershwin, Jerome Kern and Oscar Hammerstein II.

Every man has his time, and by the late '20s Cohan's style, although still popular, had become a little dated. The arrival of the new medium of moving pictures had given many actors and writers of musicals from the pre-movie generation a new lease of life, including George M Cohan. At the behest of Jesse M Lasky, he appeared in the 1932 Paramount film *The Phantom President*, acting, singing and dancing. The score had been written by Richard Rodgers and Lorenz Hart, even though Cohan had been promised that he could write some of the songs.

This snub was possibly still fresh in Cohan's memory when their paths crossed again five years later. The pair had written the songs for the new musical *I'd Rather Be Right*, in which George had been asked to portray the president, Franklin D Roosevelt. After Rodgers had played Cohan the entire score, Cohan rose, patted the young composer on the shoulder in a patronising manner and said, "Well, take care of yourself," and left the room. Rodgers was speechless, and never saw Cohan again, either at the rehearsals for the show or during the production. It was symptomatic of the old brigade finding it difficult to accept that a new generation could have as much or more talent than their own. Cohan sarcastically referred to Rodgers and Hart as "Gilbert and Sullivan", although they were great talents, both individually and as a team.

In 1940, Franklin D Roosevelt presented Cohan with a special Medal Of Honour, authorised by Congress, for writing the songs 'Over There' and 'It's A Grand Old Flag'. In that same year, Warner Bros hit upon the idea of portraying Cohan's life story in film, in Walter Kerr's *Yankee Doodle Boy*. A shooting script, playing down his personal life at his own insistence, was submitted in 1941. Cohan totally approved of the fact that he would be portrayed by James Cagney, and that the movie would contain many of his own own songs. He saw a print of the film in October 1941, and enjoyed it enormously. He wasn't the only one – Cagney would win an Oscar for Best Actor at the 1942 Academy Awards for his portrayal of Cohan.

In the summer of 1942, despite being terminally ill with cancer, he insisted on being driven down Broadway and watching at least a few minutes of *Yankee Doodle Dandy* at a picture house. As he left the building, the final number in the film, 'Over There', was playing. It was his final appearance on a Broadway that he'd once all but owned. George M Cohan died in November 1942.

Twelve years later, aware of Cohan's importance, Oscar Hammerstein II successfully spearheaded a movement to commemorate him with a statue in Times Square. In 1969, there was further commemoration, as Cohan's daughter, Mary – no mean songwriter herself – was brought in to revise her father's words and music for the musical *George M*. In the following year, she wrote several songs for his play *The Tavern*.

Cohan's input was put into perspective by Hammerstein, a great admirer of George's, in a piece he wrote for the *New York Times*: "Never was a plant more indigenous to a particular part of the Earth than was George M Cohan to the United States of his day. The whole nation was confident of it's superiority. Its moral virtue, its happy isolation from from the intrigues of the old country, from which many of our fathers and grandfathers had migrated...Cohan's genius was to say simply what everybody else was subconsciously feeling."

4 Rags To Riches

A new strain of music (to which jazz would become a blood brother) began to emerge during the 1890s and was to become a craze during the Edwardian period and up to and past the First World War. The music was called ragtime, and in a way it was America's first indigenous music, with its martial bass line and heavy syncopation, played in "ragged", or broken time.

In 1899, writer Robert Hughes explained its origins: "Negroes call their clog dancing 'ragging' and their dance a 'rag'…largely shuffling. The dance is a sort of frenzy, with frequent yelps of delight from the dancer and spectators and accompanied by the latter with hand-clapping and stomping of feet. Banjo figuration is very noticeable in ragtime music, and division of one of the beats into two short notes is traceable to the hand-clapping." It was almost a hybrid of African rhythms and the later introduction of the syncopation practised by some classical composers. Boogie-woogie, often referred to as *16* in the 1890s, was a first cousin of ragtime, but it was the latter that initially flew the commercial flag.

One of the earliest exponents of this new style was Scott Joplin, a young pianist from Texarkana, Texas. He was virtually self-taught, and began his career playing in low-life bars and clubs. In the 1880s, he formed a vocal group that toured the West and Midwest before playing cornet with The Queen City Negro Band Of Sedalia and attending college at the George R Smith College For Negroes. Joplin performed at the World Fair in Chicago in 1893, but for him the most important part of the event was hearing and getting to know the Chicago ragtime pianist Joseph Saunders, who was to have a great influence over the Texan's musical direction. If Joplin hadn't done the Chicago gig, would he have still pursued the ragtime route? Who can say?

In 1899, John Stark first published two of Joplin's rags, 'Original Rag' and 'Maple Leaf Rag'. The latter, together with his 1902 classic 'The Entertainer', became one of the most popular of his countless compositions, many of which used the rag tag: 'Fig Leaf Rag', 'Pine-Apple Rag', 'Palm Leaf Rag', 'Reflection Rag', etc. Like the twist dance craze 60 years later, when songwriters capitalised on the fad by adding the word "twist" to any title, in this case the appendage "rag" worked the same commercial magic.

Joplin followed his publisher to St Louis, and the composer and reporter Monroe Rosenfeld wrote an article for the *St Louis Democrat* that praised the talents of the young Texan, albeit with a journalistic nod to the racial tension that still persisted in many quarters: "St Louis boasts of a composer of music, who despite the ebony hue of his features and a retiring disposition, has written possibly more instrumental successes than any other local composer. His name is Scott Joplin, and he is better known as 'The King Of Rag Time Writers'."

In 1904, Stark moved to New York City, and although Joplin followed some three years later their relationship was dissolved in 1909, when the latter started his own publishing company. It was in New York, in 1911, that Joplin published the ragtime black opera *Treemonisha*, which comprised 27 musical numbers. It was felt by Joplin to be his *pièce de résistance*, although his all-consuming passion for this work, and its subsequent lack of success on stage, would break him. A second opera, *A Guest Of Honor*, was lost, and so was he. Joplin died in 1917, at the age of 49.

The inclusion of 'The Entertainer' in the 1973 Chicago gangster film *The Sting*, starring Robert Redford and Paul Newman, led to chart success on both sides of the Atlantic for the pianist and the arranger of the piece, Marvin Hamlisch. Following the renaissance of Joplin's music, Houston Grand Opera turned *Treemonisha* into the triumph for which its composer had desperately craved, just 55 years too late to save a broken heart. John Stark, meanwhile, not only published Joplin's works but also a wealth of ragtime material, including works by two other leading lights of the genre's formative years, Joseph Lamb and James Scott.

Lamb, born in Montclair, New Jersey, was 19 years younger than Joplin. He too had received no formal musical training, but began composing ragtime songs during his time at college. 'Sensation, A Rag' was published in 1908, and over the next twelve years was followed by a welter of tunes bearing the highly saleable rag suffix, including 'American Beauty Rag', 'Champagne Rag', 'Ethiopian Rag', 'Patricia Rag', 'Top Liner Rag' and 'Bohemian Rag'. Second only to Joplin in reputation, he stopped composing during the '20s, having never turned professional, choosing to work in the textile industry from 1901 until 1945. He was rediscovered in as late as 1959, bizarrely going into the studio to make the first recordings of his career. He died in Brooklyn in the following year.

James Scott, another self-taught pianist, was born in Missouri in 1886. He was a year younger than Lamb, and started his working life as a sheet-music demonstrator for Dumars Music in Carthage, Missouri. The company published his first song, 'A Summer Breeze', in 1903, although John Stark later became his publisher for material such as 'The Frog Legs Rag', 'The Ragtime Oriole', 'The Climax Rag' and 'Evergreen Rag'. In 1914, Scott became a music teacher in Kansas City before becoming a theatre organist and musical director from 1916 until around 1930. Like Lamb, his output dwindled to a trickle as the demand for ragtime slackened, and he had nothing published after 1922, although he did play in and lead bands during the '30s, until his death in 1938.

Not to be outdone by the new breed of American writers, the end of the century saw a renewed interest in the folk music of the British Isles. In the 1890s, 20 years after the State Education Act was passed, it was decreed that the country's musical heritage should be taught in schools, an idea that could not have come to fruition without the Herculean efforts of Cecil Sharp.

Born in London, Sharp practised law in Australia before returning to England and working as an organist. He became the principal of the Hampstead Conservatory in 1896, later founding the English Folk-Dance And Song society. He travelled the length and breadth of the British Isles collecting old songs, some of which were already beginning to fade in people's memories. (In this technological age, it's easy to forget that, before recording techniques were widespread, songs often died with their creators; people forgot them, they weren't sufficiently retentive to absorb them, or they simply failed to pass them on.) Sharp also trawled the rest of the English-speaking world for old songs that had travelled with British emigrants, even tracking down long-forgotten remnants of words and melodies from our native songs in such remote outposts as the Appalachian Mountains in America.

Sadly, we'll never know the names of the writers of many of these durable folk songs that have been passed down through the centuries, but they were all somebody's inspiration, and an invaluable contribution to our musical heritage. They sprang from a long period of history when credit for their creation wasn't of primary importance, and their conception would have been for pleasurable, romantic, patriotic or cathartic purposes. They were passed on freely, with no ground rules, concerns about plagiarism or commercial requirements incumbent upon their originators.

Cecil Sharp rescued countless chunks of our musical history in the nick of time, as many men of all ages who knew the old songs lost their lives in the Boer War and in the conflict of 1914-18. The timing was also perfect, considering the speed at which 20th-century human beings began to develop. We were fast becoming susceptible to rapidly-decreasing attention spans, showing less interest in the past, suffering from widespread cynicism and being bombarded with a myriad diversions to rival and outstrip the sedate pace of life that had been the nursery of our native music. If one set about to collect those songs today, who would have the memory to instantly recall the 17th-century melodies that accompanied 'Hunt The Squirrell', 'Broom, The Bonny, Bonny Broom' or 'Shepherd's Holiday'?

There had always been a market for novelty songs, especially in Britain. The music halls had been such a great shop window for them that it encouraged writers to come up with more and more ridiculous ideas. Rhymings became popular in song titles at around this time, which usually included the name of a person, leading to a spate of songs like 'Mollie (A Dainty Bit Of Jolly)', 'Mary's A Fairy', 'My Gal Sal' and Robert Coote's 'Master (Tommy) Wattle And His Big Blue Bottle'. It was all delightfuly contrived, of course, but it did inspire later writers to occasionally reheat the theme and thus become even more contrived. The 1910s brought 'What Ho, Mr Wateau', Lionel Monckton's 'Neville Was A Devil', 'My Honolulu Honey Lou' and 'I'm Through With Roaming Romeos'. In 1937 we had 'Walter! Walter! Lead Me To The Altar', and in 1949 Jule Styne's 'Keeping Cool With Coolidge'. Three years later, another great writer followed the presidential theme, when Irving Berlin wrote 'They Like Ike', after the man who became US president in that year, Dwight D Eisenhower.

The list is endless, and includes 'It's Nicer In Nice', 'Lazy Maisy Daisy', 'Rosy Posey', 'Paddlin' Madelaine Home', 'Gilbert The Filbert', 'Razzle Dazzle Basil', Wodehouse and Kern's 'Bongo On The Congo' and Flanders and Swann's 'Madeira M'Dear'. Christian names and suitable rhymes must have been a well-trawled area at one time, although would-be lyricists would have been limited by the smaller selection available.

Silly titles also found a place in people's hearts, albeit in a temporary capacity, and were often written to enlighten an otherwise gloomy period of 20th-century life.

Surely the master of the meaningless song title was Nat D Ayer, who during the First World War came up with 'Oh! How She Could Yacki Hacki Wicki Wacki Woo', and with all the expertise and commitment of a man warming to his theme wrote 'Yula Hicki Wicki Yacki Dula' in the following year. Nat was now unstoppable, delivering 'The Jabberab-Jee' in 1916 and 'Ninny Nonny No' in 1917. Was Ayer's bizarre burst of creativity influenced by the classic 'Ta-Ra-Ra-Boom-De-Ay', with all of its subsequent parodies? And did he have a blueprint in Vernon Harriett's 'Ting-A-Ling Ting-Tay' and 'Pong! Pinga! Pong!'? Did he in turn inspire such nonsense as the 1934 song 'Zip-Tee-Tootle-Te-Too-Pom-Pom' from *Yes Madam*, and The Versatile Three's 'Ooogie Ooogie Wa Wa'? Let's not judge him too harshly, though. After all he did write those lasting classics 'If You Were The Only Girl In The World' with F Clifford Grey, and 'Oh! You Beautiful Doll' with Seymour Brown.

Alliteration also carved a niche in popular music at one time, a late Victorian exponent of the art being Vesta Victoria, who was responsible for 'Look What Percy's Picked Up In The Park', 'Two-To-Two To Tooting' and 'Ching, Ching, Chinaman'. Not content with delicately crafting alliteration, she also had the occasional nonsense title in her canon, such as 'Wing Tee Wee'; rhyming titles, with songs like 'The Naughty Little Spider Spied Her'; and even risqué titles that the Carry On team would have been proud of, like 'I Want To Play With My Little Dick'. Again, she can be forgiven her sins for penning the children's favourite 'Daddy Wouldn't Buy Me A Bow Wow'.

The all-time Number One song in the alliteration chart, however, must be 'Sister Susie's Sewing Shirts For Soldiers', written in 1913 by Herman E Darewski Jr and RP Weston. Fun they might be, but these and all other genres of popular music were helping to create a major industry.

By 1910, annual sheet music sales were grossing $6 million a year, and the more potentially popular songs necessitated initial print runs of around 10,000 copies, with each copy selling at about 10¢. Combine this with the 25,000 songs that were entered for copyright in 1909, and the number of artists who agreed to perform a song only if they had a writing credit, and it becomes apparent that a system had to be set up to protect the songwriters and their works. An artist cutting themselves in on a song which they had no hand in writing is a deplorable business, but is one fraught with loopholes.

It's a tricky choice for a writer. If a major artist of the day insists – as both Elvis Presley (or, more likely, his manager), Al Jolson and countless others often did – on having a writing credit, do you capitulate and earn some money or refuse, earn none and lose the goodwill of a performer with enormous earning capacity? One trick employed by many artists who pursued this route – almost certainly at the behest of, or under the sway of, tough management – was to alter the odd phrase, changing a note here or there or even suggesting an amendment to the title. To put this in perspective, if a writer attempted to cut themselves in on the money an artist earned through live performance, on the grounds that it was their songs were being sung, it would be a different story. It remained to be seen whether any protection for songwriters would be able to assist in this respect and other danger areas.

In America, the music publishers and other participants in the songwriting business initially centred around Union Square and 14th Street, New York, before moving north to West 28th Street, between Sixth Avenue and Broadway. History relates that Tin Pan Alley was inadvertently christened so by Monroe Rosenfeld, a newspaper reporter and songwriter who heard a noise coming from the offices of a publisher friend, which he likened to the banging of tin pans. However, it seems more likely that it refers to the old, square, tin-pan pianos. It's said that the publisher was Harry von Tilzer, Judy Garland's cousin, who had written the phenomenally successful song 'Bird In A Gilded Cage' and had been part of the ASCAP deputation that had helped to bring about those important changes in the rights of composers and lyricists.

Whether fanciful, apocryphal or gospel, a plaque on the corner of 28th Street commemorates this location as being the inspiration for the name Tin Pan Alley. The corresponding area for British music publishers was London's Denmark Street, and that thoroughfare inherited the same nickname.

5 East Meets West

In an unexpected way, the unacceptable face of Russian politics also played a major role in shaping Western music. Many with anti-semitic views in positions of power blamed the 1881 assassination of Czar Alexander II in St Petersburg (actually carried out by terrorists) on the Jews. This view, given the nod of approval by the new Czar Alexander III, led to Jews being forbidden to settle in rural areas, forced into ghettos in Moscow and St Petersburg and in many cases massacred. Many fled the country to escape from the long shadow of persecution. By the turn of the century, almost two million Russian and eastern European Jewish people had set up home in the States, half of them settling in New York, where they had a greater chance of finding work.

The arrival of three families fleeing the pogroms being carried out against the Jews in Russia was of particular significance, not only to the songwriting fraternity but also to music as a whole. As well as the emigrants, there were also several other families who had recently arrived in America from eastern Europe whose offspring would also become major names on the world songwriting scene.

One of the thousands fleeing the situation in Russia was the six-year-old boy Israel Baline, who arrived in New York's Lower East Side in September 1893 with his parents and five of his seven brothers and sisters. "There were eight or nine of us living in four rooms, and in summer some of us slept on the fire escape or on the roof." The boy who was known as "Izzy" later became Irving Berlin.

Two other products of the Jewish exodus from Russia were George and Ira Gershwin, the sons of Moishe and Rosa Gershovitz, whose families had both arrived in New York during the 1890s and who both married in 1895. They opted for the new Christian names of Morris and Rose, westernising their surname to Gershwin.

Ira was born Israel in 1896 and George, his brother, was born Jacob two years later. Because of the peripatetic existence of their parents, the boys moved from area to area during their childhoods. The two young Gershwins went on to attend grammar school, where one of Ira's classmates was future songwriter YP "Yip" Harburg. Harburg would go on to collaborate with George, and later reflected that Ira "spoke in murmurs, hiding behind a pair of steel-rimmed spectacles...Ira had a kid brother who wore high stiff collars, shirts with cuffs and went out with girls." George not only went out with girls but he also acquired a tough street kid image, while Ira won a place at the highly esteemed Townsend Harris Hall High School. Ira clearly had a golden future ahead of him, but George...?

In 1910, the family bought their first piano, ostensibly for the academic Ira, but George, who had been secretly practising on the instrument of a friend, surprised the family with his accomplished playing. He started to take lessons in 1910, but began studying in earnest under Charles Hambitzer, a musician from Milwaukee, quickly displaying an extraordinary virtuosity and a not unreasonable passion for modern music, despite his teacher's insistence on teaching him the classics.

George's tutoring in harmony and composition came from his next teacher, Edward Kilyeni, while adding even more depth to his style and comprehension of classical music when he was briefly tutored by Rubin Goldmark, who had studied under Antonin Dvorak. After the First World War, the graph of his output, talent and commercial success would climb steeply, but in 1914 he was still only 16 years old, and his future collaborator, Ira, was not yet 18.

Many of the new Jewish arrivals from eastern Europe were attracted to the world of showbusiness, but in the songwriting arena it was Irving Berlin who was the first to taste success. In 1901, the year after his father's death, he ran away from home to alleviate the financial pressure on his mother. After spending some time singing in the streets, he was taken on by the publisher Harry von Tilzer, through whose window the "tin pans" were allegedly heard. He employed Berlin (who had no formal musical education) as a boomer. These were characters who would stand up in theatres during the interval and belt out the refrain of whichever song they were plugging, the plan being to familiarise the audience with it. As a boomer for both von Tilzer and another publisher, Tony Pastor, Berlin began to build up useful contacts. He was still only 16.

It was at his next job – working as a waiter for another Russian Jew, Mike Salter, at Pelham's Café – that he began writing snatches of ideas for songs. Salter, known as Nigger Mike, was rather envious that a rival establishment had its own song, composed especially for them by professional songwriter Al Piantadosi, so Berlin wrote a lyric called 'Marie From Sunny Italy', to which Mike Nicholson, the café's composer, wrote a melody. He allegedly made about the same amount from that song that Stephen Foster had in his pocket when he died: 38¢. In the life of Irving Berlin, it's sometimes difficult to separate the myth from the reality, but his new name is said to have come about when Israel Baline was misprinted on the song sheet and he decided to adopt it.

In May 1911, Berlin gave the first public performance of his latest song 'Alexander's Ragtime Band', with none other than George M Cohan in the audience. Although not essentially ragtime, compared with the complex and syncopated rhythms of Scott Joplin, Joseph Lamb or James Scott, it went down a storm when it was featured in a vaudeville show called *The Merry Whirl*, and was picked up by singer Emma Carus. She really put the song on the map. The sheet music sold over a million copies, and the song became the first in a litany of commercial successes for Berlin. The bandwagon of a bastardised and commercialised ragtime was rolling.

New styles of music frequently have to transmogrify in order to gain wider recognition. *Variety* magazine confirmed the song's enormous success, referring to it as the "musical sensation of the decade", a high accolade indeed in a growth period for songwriters.

'Alexander's Ragtime Band' was a number played by the orchestra on the White Star Line's *Titanic*, the "unsinkable" ship that went down after colliding with an iceberg near Cape Race *en route* to New York. The band's playlist also comprised Lincke's 'Glow Worm', with lyrics by Lilla Robinson; Jack Norworth and Nora Bayes-Norworth's 1908 hit 'Shine On, Harvest Moon'; Seymour Brown and Nat D Ayers' recent success 'Oh! You Beautiful Doll'; Gilbert and Muir's 'Waiting For The Robert E Lee'; and the popular Mississippi River song 'Frankie and Johnny'. The oldest – and, as it turned out, the most ironic – song that they played was a Lowell Mason song from 1859, 'Nearer My God To Thee'. Berlin was the only composer to have two songs featured by The Titanic Orchestra, which also performed his 'Mesmerizing Mendelssohn Tune'.

Louis Hirsch's big ragtime show *Hullo Ragtime* featured two of Berlin's songs, 'Ragtime Soldier Man' and 'Snooky Ookums', although neither of these were sung by the great Ethel Levey, who had previously turned down

'Alexander's Ragtime Band' because she deemed it as being unsuitable for her voice. Hirsch wrote the words and music for several of the show's songs, including 'How Do You Do, Miss Ragtime?', and Lewis Muir contributed 'Ragging The Baby To Sleep'. The show was a resounding success in New York and at the Hippodrome in London, where it ran and ran. The poet Rupert Brooke was an enormous fan of the show, attending the Hippodrome on every possible occasion and writing to the actress Cathleen Nesbitt in March 1913: "I see we shall scarcely know *Hello Ragtime* when we see it again: for Ethel Levey had introduced 'Waiting For The Robert E Lee' in her own version; and some new performers have appeared."

Ragtime fever not only hit London but also, when Brooke was on board ship just off Honolulu in October 1913, the pianist in the saloon was performing "...*Hello Ragtime*, in a piano score, right through!"

Hirsch followed the revue with a show based on a popular new dance. *Hullo Tango* came to the Hippodrome late in 1913, and featured one of the earliest automobile songs, Maurice Abrahams' 'Get Out And Get Under'. The motor car was still a comparatively rare sight on the roads of the UK and the USA at that time, but it had inspired some songwriters to put pen to paper, giving us 'Home-Made Motor Car' in 1904 and 'Taxi Meter Car' two years later.

Berlin wasn't big on the latest vehicular invention, but he did write about what was then a more conventional mode of travel, the railroad, in 'When The Midnight Choo-Choo Leaves For Alabam', complete with upbeat syncopation. That song – along with 'Snooky Ookums' – would be revived for the 1948 film *Easter Parade*. He shrewdly became a partner in the firm that published his material, lengthening the company name to Waterson, Berlin And Snyder, and rather grandly had the sheet music to all of his songs proclaim him as "The Song Genius Of The World".

Like Charles Harris before him, when he set up his own music-writing shop, "the king of ragtime" (as the press erroneously called him) announced a set of songwriting rules to the world. These included making sure that a song had a memorable lyric content and an undemanding musical range, was well within the grasp of most vocalists, and possessed lucidity – a similar idea to the premise "the simpler the song, the more people will understand it", under which many songwriters have earned success. However, achieving a natural and uncomplicated blend of words and music that also has a wide commercial appeal is no mean feat.

Attempts at such simplicity frequently result in banality and triteness. Simple is best, but simple is hard. As John Huss, the Bohemian priest condemned for heresy, commented as a peasant added a single faggot to his funeral pyre: "O holy simplicity!"

The press enjoyed simplicity, too. If somebody told them that Berlin was the originator of ragtime, who were they to doubt it? Even if it wasn't true, there was no reason why they couldn't use a little journalistic license and a modicum of suitably flowery prose, as the British press did: "Ragtime has swept like a whirlwind over the Earth and set civilisation humming. Mr Berlin started it." Mr Berlin, of course, didn't start it, but musical myths are often as unfair as they are intriguing, tacitly exacerbated by the feigned equanimity of the writer and trumpeted from the rooftops by other parties on a percentage. Possibly eager to justify the London newspaper's belief in him, he is said to have written 'That International Rag' at London's Savoy Hotel in an hour.

In 1914, Berlin wrote his first musical score, but by the time *Watch Your Step* opened at the New Amsterdam Theatre in December the First World War was already five months old.

Although he was born in New York in 1885, Jerome Kern's roots were Central European. His father was a German émigré from Wurttemberg, while his maternal grandfather was a Bohemian Jewish émigré. He had the advantage of growing up in a musical household. His mother taught him piano from an early age, and encouraged him to pursue his studies in that direction. As his father became increasingly successful, the family moved to Newark, where he attended the local high school and increasingly involved in music, writing a revue for his graduation class and his first song, 'At The Casino'.

Moving on to the New York College Of Music, he studied under Paolo Gallico before leaving to work for TB Harms' publishing house in the middle of 1903. His attempts to break into musical theatre were hampered by the predilection of Broadway producers for British and European works, and to that end he made the journey to London. It was there that he met the all-powerful American producer and theatrical impresario Charles Frohman, and became friendly with young composer and performer George Grossmith Jr, who helped Kern to obtain some good contacts: "I knew him as Jerry Kern and liked him immensely. He came often to my house and played to us. He played divinely like nearly all of his kind, with a tremendous gift for 'tune'. He was the only one I could detect in a barren field likely to fill the shoes of Monckton, Paul Rubens and Leslie Stuart."

George Edwardes had just opened the new Gaiety Theatre, where Lionel Monckton and Leslie Stuart were in full flow and impressing the aspiring New Yorker. His reputation began to grow modestly, and he started writing for various productions and working with different composers and lyricists, including PG Wodehouse. Pelham Grenville Wodehouse, yet to become world famous as the creator of the timeless English characters Jeeves and Wooster, wrote with the young Jerome at the time, but many years later would re-emerge to work with Kern on more successful projects. During Kern's juvenile period, they wrote songs such as 'Mr Chamberlain', and although Kern had had material published in as early as 1902 his first song to come to the public's attention was 'How'd You Like To Spoon With Me?'. The number was included in a British production in the States in 1905. Edward Laska, who wrote the lyrics to the song, gives us a thumbnail sketch of Kern from that period, describing that he had "a straw hat on, of which the top was knocked out, and a long black cigar in his mouth, being cold-smoked...I don't think I ever saw him really smoke one, but it seemed to inspire him, as he ground out melody after melody without ever bothering to jot them down."

For years, Kern's songs were interpolated into successful shows, an art at which he became adept, tailoring songs to dovetail with other writers' works, seemingly at the expense of developing his own style.

The turning point came in August 1914, when he was asked to write a love song for the British production *The Girl From Utah*, the music having been penned by Sidney Jones and Paul Rubens. He came up with his first major number, 'They Didn't Believe Me'.

All of the groundwork that he'd done had paid off. During the next few years, after moving back to America, he wrote five major musicals, and in 1915 formed a writing team with PG Wodehouse and Guy Bolton. The three writers came up with a series of musicals, most of which were produced at the 250-seater Princess Theatre. *Nobody Home* and *Very Good Eddie* came out in 1915, *Oh Boy* and *Leave It To Jerome* in 1917 and *Oh, Lady, Lady* a year later. *Oh Boy* featured the song 'Till The Clouds Roll By', which would become the title of the biopic of Kern's life and hit the big screen in 1946.

He later worked extensively with Oscar Hammerstein II, who revealed how Jerome got his songs heard before his career took off:

> He became a rehearsal pianist, and he used this job as a device for selling his own compositions. Here is how it would work: about the third week in rehearsal, when the director, producers and the whole company were pretty tired of the Viennese score they had been rehearsing all that time, Jerry would come back early after lunch and start to tinkle a little tune of his own on the piano. Everyone who came in would say "What's that?" "Oh, just a little thing of my own," Jerry would answer. Pretty soon, everyone thought he'd discovered a potential hit. Jerry's tune had a freshness for them that the over-rehearsed score couldn't possibly have, and the first thing you know he had interpolated a song into the foreign score!

Richard Rodgers was only twelve years old when war broke out in 1914. He was also of eastern European stock, although it would be some while before his songwriting star would ascend. Both of his parents were Russian, but his father changed the family name from Abrams to Rodgers on their arrival in New York. Encouraged by parents William and Mamie, Richard began to play the piano from the age of six, and by the time he was nine he was composing melodies. Among the first stage musicals he was taken to were *Little Nemo*, for which Victor Herbert had written the music, and *The Quaker Girl*, from the pen of Lionel Monckton.

At home, he was influenced by the music that his parents enjoyed playing, such as Lehar's wonderful score for his 1905 opera *Die Lustige Witwe* (*The Merry Widow*), which featured the haunting aria 'Vilja'. Later in life, Lehar would appear to become a devotee of Adolf Hitler, rewriting 'The Merry Widow Waltz' and dedicating it to the German leader. Had William and Mamie still been alive then, one wonders how would they would have squared their love of the work with its newly attached dedication.

It was at summer camp that Richard Rodgers wrote his first song, 'Camp Fire Days'. One of the onsite tutors at the camp was Arthur Loesser, the half-brother of Frank Loesser, who 40 years later would find success with the musicals *Guys And Dolls* and, later still, *The Most Happy Fella*. As Rodgers became a teenager, in 1915, he began to take in more shows, and fell under the spell of the compositions of Jerome Kern. However, Rodgers' time wouldn't come until the dust had settled on the 1914-18 conflict.

Apart from a dozen or so major composers and lyricists, many songwriters from the first half of the century remain unknown to the public at large, despite their enormous and often sustained success. Two other songwriting brothers of eastern European origin who are still going strong in the new millennium are Milton and Ervin Drake, the sons of Transylvanian émigré and furniture pioneer Max Druckman. A third brother, Arnold, found success in writing the text for Superman, Batman and Jerry Lewis comics.

Milton Drake, born in New York City in 1913, became enchanted with the early days of performance radio, when America became a nation entranced by the radio in the late '20s and early '30s. Inspired by songs that he had heard as a boy, such as Malvin and John Schonberger's 'Whispering' and Vincent Rose and Al Jolson's 'Avalon' (both written in 1920), he learned the ukelele, and by his own admission the "four-finger piano". He began to present shows on the radio while he was still at school, initially playing other people's songs on two 15-minute slots on the radio station WOV, based in a building on the corner of Fifth Avenue and 42nd Street in New York which was owned by the Bulova Watch Company.

He went on to develop another radio show, *The Night Watchman's Setting-up Exercise*, which resulted in him being dubbed "the joy boy" by the New York press. His broadcasting output increased as he was joined on air by his friend Walter Kent. Their programme became so popular that NBC hired them to host a weekly Saturday night show. Milton's songwriting break came when a guy called Abner Silver appeared in the radio studio during the show and asked him to write some songs for a Broadway show.

As a writer, Milton worked in the birthplace of thousands of great songs: the Brill building. "It was a big white structure that had been built in 1930. I began working there in '33. It was on Broadway, on the corner of 49th Street, midway to 50th Street, and Jack Dempsey, the boxer, had his restaurant at street level. He also had the second floor, but above that, from the third floor to the tenth, and the penthouse, it was all music industry."

Milton Drake not only had over 300 of his songs recorded, but he was also hired to write for motion pictures, including *My Little Chickadee*, starring Mae West and WC Fields. 'I was enchanted by her, and we became close friends, but I was not taken with him...The song I wrote for the film was a thing called 'Willie Of The Valley'."

Among the most enduring songs from his cannon are 'Java Jive', a classic that, in the hands of The Ink Spots, hasn't dated; Champagne Waltz; and 'Mairzy Doats', a clever novelty song recorded by The Three Stooges and The King Sisters, among others. The British group Sounds Incorporated rather bizarrely recorded an instrumental version of it, which rather obviously lacked the humour of the original! In keeping with the taste of the time for all things Liverpudlian, they rechristened it 'Mersey Doats'. In 1967, the song became a US hit once again, this time for Innocence, one of many names used by songwriters Vinnie Poncia and Pete Andreoli.

Milton recalled that he and his brother Ervin heard the "catch" of 'Mairzy Doats' from their sister. "Our sister came home from summer camp singing this nonsense lyric, which Ervin and I became quite taken with. We both had it going round our heads for years, and rather strangely both wrote songs about it quite independently, at the same time. Mine was accepted by a publisher but his wasn't!" Milton and Ervin wrote together on only a couple of occasions, but surprisingly nothing ever came of their efforts as a team.

British writers were frequently given to writing about places in America that sounded romantic but to which they'd never been. Examples of American writers being moved by British towns and villages, however, are far less common. In the mid '40s, however, Milton Drake was suitably intrigued by the sound of the Leicestershire village Ashby-De-La-Zouch. The song that he wrote about it was titled simply 'Ashby-De-La-Zouch', and had a lyric which ran, "Ashby-De-La-Zouch castle abbey, it's a little English town by the sea." The writer later confessed: "On visiting it during the '60s I was given a lovely dinner, but my hosts did point out that it was, in fact, many miles from the sea!"

Milton had many more of his songs covered by major artists, including 'Kiss Me Sweet' by Kitty Kallen and 'Hotta Chocolatta' by Ella Fitzgerald. He was also the early songwriting inspiration for his brother, Ervin, who was born in New York on 3 April 1919, seven years Milton's junior. "All my youth I had been drawing cartoons for my college humour magazine and for commercial magazines. But I was writing songs at the same time and, when it came time to opt for one, I went down the song trail. I've never regretted the choice."

Following in his brother's footsteps, Ervin also worked in the Brill building. He wrote songs there for eight years, having hung out around the place as a young man. "I was a very eager youngster hanging around the publishing offices of Southern Music in the Brill building. I had discovered that breaking into the big-time music business was like besieging an impregnable castle surrounded by an alligator-stocked moat. So I started devising a plan of attack. It had become apparent that anybody who played the piano was a putative composer. There were hordes of them. But a good word man was always in demand. So I decided to put my compositional ability on hold and try to break through exclusively as a lyricist. I put words to anything they would throw me."

Songs ready for adaptation would arrive at the publisher's from Mexico, Cuba and Brazil, and these were usually given to established wordsmiths already on the company's books. However, one song that arrived in 1942, which was regarded rather contemptuously as a novelty tune, was thrown without much expectation in the direction of the young Ervin. Hungry for success, and keen to demonstrate his talents, he completed it in a day. Much to the publisher's surprise, 'Tico-Tico' not only became a hit for organist Ethel Smith, Xavier Cugat and The Andrews Sisters but the song also featured in several MGM musicals.

Surprisingly, many songwriters have never met the artists who have performed their creations, let alone been present at the recording of their material. Ervin's first opportunity to witness one of his songs being laid down came about in 1946, when he and co-writer Irene Higgenbotham watched Billie Holiday record their song 'Good Morning Heartache'. "Irene and I stayed in a corner of the recording studio, not daring to introduce ourselves to Ms Holiday...She was one impressive lady, that Lady Day." It was through Holiday's move to Decca in 1944, and their plan for her to record an increasing number of mainstream tracks, that she began to record more songs by writers like Ervin Drake. It was during this period that she also recorded classics such as 'Lover Man', 'Crazy, He Calls Me' and 'That Old Devil Called Love'.

Getting a song to an artist had never been the easiest thing for a songwriter to do. To achieve it they sometimes had to give away a percentage of their creation to a facilitator. They often had to run the gamut of agent, manager, publisher, record label and people who seem to have that magic key to the artist, as happened on 'Good Morning

Heartache': "Irene Higginbotham had composed the music, and I the lyric. In order to get to Decca Records and Billie Holiday, we had to cut in a young man named Dan Fisher. Bing Crosby, Rudy Vallee, Al Jolson and many other stars have occasionally made the cut-in the price for recording a song. Of course, Ms Holiday was not aware of this. In the long run it was worth it, considering that her version led to scores of others over the years." It would be 26 years before 'Good Morning Heartache' would reach a more global audience, after featuring in the 1972 film *The Lady Sings The Blues*, starring Diana Ross as Billie Holiday.

Ideas for songs come to writers and composers at all sorts of inconvenient times, frequently whilst travelling or in the bath. It was during a soak in the tub, while shampooing his hair, that Ervin subconsciously began to whistle a little tune with anticipated notes which would eventually be recorded by singer/bandleader Eddy Howard and would become the million-seller 'The Rickety Rickshaw Man'. However, the "I wrote the song in the bath" story didn't seem to be newsworthy enough for the publisher's press agent: "The man asked me how I happened to write the song. I told him the bathtub story…the truth. He said 'Naah, that's no story. Here's how you wrote it. You were in a Chinese restaurant and you opened a fortune cookie and the message said 'He who runneth his rickshaw fastest shall win fair lady.' And that's what they put out."

One wonders how many great songs have been lost through bad judgement or bad timing. Ervin's multimillion-selling classic 'I Believe' was deemed to be non-commercial by Jane Froman, the singer for whom it was written, and singer May Howard roared with laughter when Charles Harris played her 'After The Ball', commenting that nobody could seriously sing the line "Down fell the glass, pet, broken, that's all." She assumed that all of the people drinking in the audience would see it as an excuse to smash their glasses on the floor, and that the line would kill the number, while Harris countered that such a dramatic line would greatly contribute to the song's success. Legendary ballad singer Dick Jose maintained that songwriters only write one good song in their lifetimes, and that 'After The Ball' wasn't Harris' best. The highly-rated artist Raymond Moore also turned it down. Like 'I Believe', however, it too went on to sell millions of copies.

So many songwriters (and here we're dealing with souls with a significant degree of sensitivity) must have become disillusioned by the indifferent comments of publishers or artists. Many potentially good composers and lyricists have given up in despair as their efforts have been dismissed out of hand by people in the industry who can make or break them.

Another of Ervin Drake's masterpieces that almost suffered this fate was 'It Was A Very Good Year'. In 1961, The Kingston Trio permitted one of it's members, Bobby Shane, to do some solo recording, and to that end a friend of Ervin's who was involved in the group's publishing asked him if he had any material. Ervin asked to borrow his piano room: "Once there, I pulled out a work diary with song ideas and found a possibility that I had jotted down months before: 'A man's life told in vintage wine terms.' Title: 'It Was A Very Good Year'. Bingo! An hour later I had a song and a topline lead sheet. I call the process 'target shooting'. The target himself showed up the next day. I played and sang...and I continued singing to what seemed like a very unresponsive listener. When I finished, I turned around to look for Bobby. He was leaving quietly and I had a sinking feeling. 'No,' said the publisher, 'Bobby likes me, so he'll record it, and you'll make big bucks on the LP, 'cause The Kingston Trio is hot. But let's face it,' said the expert, 'the song is a dog!'" Fortunately for Ervin, Frank Sinatra judged the song differently, turning it into a top ten hit five years later, in 1966. In that year, it won a Grammy award.

A writer's own belief in one of their songs is only vindicated publicly when it becomes a hit. When Anthony Newley covered Ervin's 'Father Of Girls' in 1963, very little happened. It wasn't until the release of Perry Como's version five years later that the song became a hit and gained much wider recognition.

It's often impossible to determine a reason for a song becoming successful at one moment in time and not another. One could cite the artist as being the variant that convinces the public to buy a particular song, but this doesn't always hold water. Think of the number of acts who have had comparative failures with songs only to succeed with them at another point in their careers. Conversely, a major artist might bring more media interest, marketing and promotion to a product simply because of their name.

Another factor is the production, which can bring an added dimension to a song that previously hadn't been presented in its best light. Did modern technology arrive too late to for the pre-rock era songwriters, or would so much gadgetry have swamped their creations? Several writers who were active during that period feel that the more carefully- and meticulously-crafted songs of their era would undoubtedly have benefited from employing more advanced techniques. Ervin Drake feels that "Now brilliant technology is lavished and squandered on the most boorish rap song."

From the 1600s to the 1900s, there have been many generations of successful songwriters that have actually been born in America, but by and large it was the émigrés from the East or their offspring who became the most successful writers of commercial songs in the Western world from the First World War onwards. Of course, there were exceptions, such as Cole Porter. Was the reason for their musical triumph a magical blend of European culture and a new-found freedom of expression in families that had been subjected to oppression in their own countries? Whatever the reason, they flourished, inspired and dominated the art form of the musical and the popular song.

6 The Golden Years

After the 1914-18 conflict was finally over, the English-speaking world felt justified in letting their hair down a little, and the songwriters rose to the occasion.

In 1919, Irving Berlin founded his own publishing company, and at the same time was commissioned to write the score for the Ziegfeld Follies, which yielded the perennial 'A Pretty Girl Is Like A Melody'. Two years later, he audaciously tried to rival Ziegfeld by opening his own theatre, the Music Box, with the help of veteran showman Joseph Schenk and George M Cohan's business partner, Sam Harris. Berlin even wrote a theme song for his new venture, 'Say It With Music'.

After falling in love with the beautiful socialite Ellin Mackay, he wrote many great waltzes, including 'Remember', 'What'll I Do?' and 'All Alone'. Despite violent objections from Ellin's father, the business magnate Clarence Mackay, who couldn't conceive of his daughter loving a songwriter, she married Berlin, who wrote 'Always' for her as a wedding present.

Ironically, after he'd written 'The Song Is Ended', in 1927, he believed that his songwriting talents had run dry, and that he would never write any more successful material. His output suffered not only because of his psychological condition but also because his finances had been heavily depleted by the Depression.

Thankfully, this mental state proved to be only a temporary aberration, and by 1932 he was back as sharp as ever with a new musical, *Face The Music*, which alluded to the Depression and appeared to be a rather cathartic piece of writing for Berlin. Proving that it wasn't a transitory return to form, he penned 'How Deep Is The Ocean?' and 'Say It Isn't So' in that same year. Later, for the topical revue *As Thousands Cheer*, he wrote 'Not For All The Tea In China' and 'Heat Wave', the latter extolling the torrid virtues of the French dance the Can Can:

> We're having a heat wave, a tropical heat wave,
> The temperature's rising, it isn't surprising
> She certainly can Can Can.
> She started the heat wave by letting her seat wave,
> And in such a way that the customers say that
> She certainly can Can Can.

The song was covered by many artists, including one who really did cause a "tropical heat wave" and let her "seat wave", Marilyn Monroe.

Other Berlin classics in *As Thousands Cheer* were 'Steppin' Out With My Baby' and a song that previously hadn't seen the light of day because of it's weak lyric, the number 'Smile And Show Your Dimple'. Reworked, it became the classic 'Easter Parade', and subsequently became America's official Easter song.

From 1935 until the end of the decade, Berlin worked in Hollywood, mainly composing for the movies and writing *Top Hat*, a vehicle tailored to the talents of Fred Astaire and Ginger Rogers. Berlin admired Astaire, believing that "He's a real inspiration for a writer." He confessed that he'd never have written songs like 'Top Hat, White Tie And Tails', 'Cheek To Cheek' and 'Isn't This A Lovely Day?' if he hadn't had Fred and Ginger to write for. Ginger Rogers was equally complimentary about Berlin: "I think he's the sort of 'apple-pie' composer that makes you want to stand up and bleat out a song, whether you can sing or not. He writes that type of song."

The 1936 film *Follow The Fleet*, starring Ginger, Lucille Ball, Betty Grable, Randolph Scott and Harriet Hilliard, featured the timeless 'Let's Face The Music And Dance'. Hilliard would later find fame as half of TV's *Ozzie And Harriet*, and her son Ricky Nelson would rival Elvis Presley in the teen appeal stakes during the latter half of the '50s.

In 1939, Berlin pulled out one of his old "trunk" songs, 'God Bless America', a number that would become a "second national anthem of the United States", and the royalties for which he generously handed over to the Boy Scouts and Girl Guides of America.

With a keen eye for marketing, each Berlin show was announced as being his best, and the 1937 20th Century Fox film *On The Avenue*, starring Dick Powell and Alice Faye, was no exception. The sheet music was used for the high-profile branding of the composer. His name on it is more pronounced than that of any of the artists who performed it. The score reads: "Irving Berlin's greatest musical score", and "Lyrics and music by Irving Berlin and Irving Berlin Inc, music publishers." He was certainly a canny businessman who had no compunctions against letting people know who he was, what he was and how good his songs were! One of the film's big songs was 'I've Got My Love To Keep Me Warm', which went on to become a million-seller for Les Brown and his orchestra when they recorded it nine years later, belatedly issuing it in 1949.

In the following year, his song 'Change Partners' was the stand-out number in the RKO movie *Carefree*, and in 1940 he was back on Broadway with *Louisiana Purchase*, which ran for 444 performances and featured 'It's A Lovely Day Tomorrow' as its main song.

Following the Japanese attack on Pearl Harbour, Berlin came up with another patriotic and morale-boosting show, just as he had during World War One, *This Is The Army*. The show's title song, 'This Is The Army, Mister Jones', was based around a "bunch of frightened rookies" being told by a sergeant how much tougher the army was than civilian life. "Mister Jones" is informed that there are "no private rooms or telephones", "Mister Green" that they "like the barracks nice and clean", while "Mister Brown" is reminded of the days now gone, when "you and your baby went to town". (As Berlin had used three of the most common surnames, it's impossible to imagine that he didn't also toy with the idea of using a Mister Smith, something along the lines of "This is the army, Mister Smith/Don't think it's cushy – that's a myth" would have been a rather obvious fourth verse.) The revue played at the London Palladium in the following year, after which it was turned into a film, starring future US president Ronald Reagan and the current world heavyweight boxing champion, Joe Louis. Berlin was again magnanimous with his royalties from the show, this time signing them over to the Army Emergency Relief. *This Is The Army* toured America, Britain, Australia, Italy and American bases in the South Pacific, and Irving himself worked as part of the company for three years.

For the 1942 Paramount film *Holiday Inn*, Berlin penned what was to become the biggest-selling single of all time, the Academy Award-winning 'White Christmas'. When it was released by Bing Crosby (who had performed it in the film), it sold a million copies and a staggering 30 million by the late '60s. Translated into seven different languages, there are almost 500 recorded versions, including other million-selling covers by

Freddy Martin and his orchestra and Frank Sinatra. Bing's version was recorded in Los Angeles in May 1942, when Berlin demonstrated the song to him and the normally imperturbable Crosby responded with "This is one you don't have to worry about."

Berlin's other successful movies from the '40s were *Blue Skies*, starring Crosby and Fred Astaire, and *Easter Parade*, in which Astaire and Judy Garland performed 'We're A Couple Of Swells'. Berlin's delightfully ironic lyric has two tramps revelling in a tongue-in-cheek pretence of being a lot higher in the social pecking order than they really are before admitting that, in reality, they haven't even got the fare for the trolley car.

In terms of full-score musicals, Berlin's finest hour of the '40s (and possibly his career) was *Annie Get Your Gun*. Jerome Kern had originally been commissioned to write the score, but after his death in 1945 the show's producers, Rodgers and Hammerstein, brought in Irving Berlin. The show premièred in 1947, with a cast headed by Ethel Merman, and was packed with hits, including the song that she made her own, 'There's No Business Like Show Business', which subsequently became the anthem of the entertainment industry. It truly was an exceptional score, producing such classics as 'Anything You Can Do', 'Doin' What Comes Natur'lly', 'You Can't Get A Man With A Gun', I Got The Sun In The Morning', 'They Say It's Wonderful' and 'The Girl That I Marry'.

Berlin's next musical score, *Miss Liberty*, was first produced on Broadway in 1949, and this was followed by *Call Me Madam*, which starred Ethel Merman and included 'It's A Lovely Day Today' and 'You're Just In Love'.

In 1954, Berlin received the Congressional Medal Of Honor from President Eisenhower, although eight years later his musical *Mr President* failed to set theatres alight. Although his output had slowed considerably, his amazing songwriting career brought him further accolades when President Ford presented him with the Medal Of Freedom and he received the French Legion d'Honneur.

In 1972, Berlin presented the Smithsonian Institute with one of his two specially doctored pianos. They had been adapted to accommodate his rather limited piano technique. (He played only the black notes, using the key of F sharp major.) An attached lever shifted the whole keyboard, enabling him to transpose his songs into any other key.

Berlin was able to enjoy his 50-acre farm in the Catskill Mountains, his

New York apartment and the financial benefits of a phenomenally successful career until he was in his second century. He died in 1989, ten years after Richard Rodgers.

In 1917, Richard Rodgers was taken to see *Home James* at Colombian College, whose students included Lorenz Hart and Oscar Hammerstein II, both then 22 years old. Backstage, the 14-year-old Rodgers met Hammerstein for the first time, resolving then and there to become a student at the establishment, an ambition that he was to fulfil two years later.

He began writing for amateur shows, and in 1919 was introduced to Larry Hart, who turned out to be a close neighbour. Despite being eight years Rodgers' senior, Hart began to collaborate with the talented young pianist, convinced that they could eclipse the "theatrical holy trinity of Kern, Bolton and Wodehouse". Their first song that met with some success was 'Any Old Place For You', a geographical list-song on which Hart could flex his lyrical muscles, penning lines like "I'll go to hell for ya/or Philadelphia".

Producer Lew Fields saw enough of their work to give them the opportunity of writing the complete Broadway score for *Poor Little Ritz Girl*, although when it eventually opened in the summer of 1920 much of their material had been replaced. This somewhat depressing launch into the big time didn't deter them from writing nine amateur shows between 1920 and 1924, while Rodgers – who had enrolled at the Institute For Musical Arts (which later became the Juilliard School Of Music) – studied harmony with Percy Goetschius.

Because of the lack of interest shown in the output of Rodgers and Hart, the young student began to contemplate a career selling children's clothes, but just in the nick of time he received a telephone call from family friend Benjamin Kaye, a lawyer and sometime theatrical agent. Kaye's offer wasn't exactly the dream ticket, but he did give Rodgers the chance to write a revue for the Theatre Guild.

It proved to be the turning point for Rodgers and Hart. The actors and Theatre Guild directors went overboard for their songs, especially, as Richard recalled, for 'Manhattan': "Its easy-going melody and ingeniously rhymed lyric related all of the everyday pleasures to be found in New York…the audience could see and feel everything the song conveyed…and they ate it up…If one song can be said to have 'made' Rodgers and Hart, it was surely 'Manhattan'."

Rodgers' delightfully lazy tune and Hart's dexterous internal rhyming were the perfect marriage: "We'll have Manhattan/the Bronx and Staten Island too", "We'll go to Greenwich/where modern men itch to be free", "And tell me what street/compares to Mott Street in July" – Hart's words are a never-fading snapshot of '20s New York. Reviewing *Garrick Gaieties*, the *New York Times* commented that "The lyrics were mature and intelligently contrived. Rodgers' music was tuneful and well adapted to the needs of the entertainment."

Another success from the show was 'Mountain Greenery', which would still be popular over 30 years later, when it became a Top Ten hit in Britain for Mel Torme, who had only just been born at the time of the first full production of the second *Garrick Gaieties*. These two shows – along with *The Girl Friend*, which had opened in March 1926 – meant that Rodgers and Hart now had three shows running simultaneously.

The pair visited London in December 1926 to see *Lido Lady*, which included their song 'Here In My Arms', while *Peggy-Ann* hit the stage in the States. Their show *Betsy* proved a disaster, however, in spite of Irving Berlin's 'Blue Skies' being subversively smuggled into the show by the producers.

One of their most successful songs from the early part of their careers was featured in both *One Damn Thing After Another* and *A Connecticut Yankee*. 'My Heart Stood Still' was conceived when Rodgers and Hart visited Paris and overheard a young girl talking about how an accident with a taxi had affected her emotionally, confessing that "my heart stood still". Hart spotted it as a good song title, although it was Rodgers who jotted it down, later wrote a melody inspired by the title and presented it to Hart. The pair were now on a roll, with more hits and shows following over the next few years, including 'With A Song In My Heart' from *Spring Is Here* and 'Ten Cents A Dance' from *Simple Simon*.

Like many other songwriters at the time, Rodgers and Hart were producing material that was almost exclusively for the stage, and conformed to the time-honoured method of composing the music first and adding the lyrics later. One of their songs not written specifically for a show was 'Blue Moon'.

Hart had made several attempts to write words to the melody; the now-famous opening line "Blue moon, you saw me standing alone" started life as "Oh Lord, what is the matter with me?" Those words had been written in 1934, when the song was called 'Prayer', and had been performed by

Jean Harlow in the film unproduced *Hollywood Revue Of 1933*. The song's second incarnation was 'The Bad In Every Man', which Shirley Ross sang in the film *Manhattan Melodrama*. At the third and final time of asking, Hart came up with another, entirely different set of lyrics, and as 'Blue Moon' it became their only big song not to be associated with either the stage, film or television. In 1948, Billy Eckstine had a million-seller with his version of it, and so did Pittsburgh vocal quintet The Marcels 13 years later, when they topped the charts on both sides of the Atlantic. By all accounts, Rodgers loathed their doo-wop version, but softened a little on hearing how many it was selling!

Whatever he thought about the variation that rock 'n' roll artists brought to the songs of Rodgers and Hart, it must have been heart-warming to feel that they had a timeless quality and that these new young musical idols actually wanted to record their material. 'Where Or When', from *Babes In Arms*, was another of several of their songs which travelled successfully through time, with Dion And The Belmonts taking their harmony-laden version into the US Top Three in 1960, 23 years after the song's conception.

They wrote more classics in the late '30s, including 'Falling In Love With Love', from *The Boys From Syracuse*, and 'Spring Is Here', for *I Married An Angel*.

At the beginning of the new decade, they wrote *Pal Joey*, which spawned the delightful 'I Could Write A Book', another song that would become popular with the next generation, especially with Liverpool beat groups of the early and mid '60s. One of the best versions from that period was by The Chants, who would transmogrify into The Real Thing by the '70s. The same musical also featured the timeless 'Bewitched', another much-covered song that achieved million-selling status at the hands of Illinois pianist Bill Snyder and his orchestra in 1950.

In 1942, the Theatre Guild planned to stage a new version of the play *Green Grow The Lilacs*, by Lynn Riggs, and Rodgers and Hart were approached with a view to them writing the songs. Hart, by now a heavy drinker and increasingly concerned and secretive about his homosexuality, told Rodgers that he wasn't interested in doing it, preferring instead to holiday in Mexico. Despite his partner's entreaties, Hart remained resolute. Consequently, Rodgers allegedly approached Jerome Kern, who was busy writing scores for Hollywood, and then a disinterested Ira Gershwin, before turning to the highly enthusiastic Oscar Hammerstein II.

Two things would become ground-breaking in this new relationship: firstly, Hammerstein wanted to write the words first; and secondly, he wanted to write the book. Rodgers acceded to these suggestions, as this brought an alternative way of collaborating into play. "Put the right components together and an explosion takes place. Oscar and I hit it off from the day we began discussing the show." Up until that time, lyricists had almost always had to take their cues for songs from a third party, who would have written the book, but Hammerstein changed the rules to allow future wordsmiths a greater freedom and improved integration.

Their first collaboration, initially titled *Away We Go* but later changed to *Oklahoma!*, was bursting with great songs, including 'Surrey With The Fringe On Top', '(Everything's Up To Date In) Kansas City', 'People Will Say We're In Love', 'I Cain't Say No', the title track 'Oklahoma!' and 'Oh! What A Beautiful Morning'. On the latter song, it took Rodgers just ten minutes to put a melody to Hammerstein's lyrics. The composer humbly professed, "I merely put the lyrics on the piano and it wrote itself." Hammerstein was equally unassuming when it came to his contribution to the partnership: "Words are easier to analyse. Everyone speaks or writes words. Few can write music...its creation is a mystery."

Rodgers' style was to compose at the piano, whistling his melody and then writing in the harmony and chord symbols before writing a lead sheet and finally a full arrangement.

Many songwriters profess that some of their greatest songs were written very quickly, and 'Oh! What A Beautiful Morning' was certainly equalled for speed by George Gershwin and Irving Caesar's 'Swanee', which apparently took them eleven minutes. Rodgers himself would do it again with 'Bali Ha'I', one of the classics from *South Pacific*, which he famously dashed off while his dinner guests were having coffee.

With hindsight, it seems amazing that the Theatre Guild had enormous problems trying to raise the necessary money to stage *Oklahoma!*, but they managed it in the end, the show opening in April 1943 and running on Broadway for a record-breaking five years and nine months. Lorenz Hart attended the opening night, hugging his old partner and friend and generously admitting that it was a great musical. Behind the mask of equanimity was a sad man who was soon to die from pneumonia after a drinking spree.

Oklahoma! was a landmark in popular musicals, becoming the first to have a Broadway cast album, transferring successfully to the big screen and paving the way for a second collaboration for Rodgers and Hart. *Carousel*, too, had its fair share of unforgettable songs, including 'If I Loved You', 'When The Children Are Asleep', 'June Is Bustin' Out All Over' and the timeless 'You'll Never Walk Alone'. The latter song became a UK Number One for Gerry And The Pacemakers in 1963, and was subsequently a popular song with football crowds. The album soundtrack of *Carousel* became a million-seller while the duo worked on their next project, *State Fair*.

In 1949, they came up with yet another winner in *South Pacific*, adapted from James A Michener's Pulitzer Prize-winning novel *Tales Of The South Pacific*. It was packed with remarkable songs, including 'Some Enchanted Evening', 'There Is Nothing Like A Dame', 'Bali Ha'I', 'I'm Gonna Wash That Man Right Outta My Hair', 'Younger Than Springtime' and 'This Nearly Was Mine'. The show opened at New York's Majestic Theatre in April 1949 and ran for 1,925 performances, with both the cast album and the film soundtrack of 1958 selling many millions of copies. The film received an Academy Award for the best sound recording.

Another Rodgers and Hammerstein stage show that followed the same pattern, also being translated into film, was *The King And I*, which included the songs 'Getting To Know You', 'Hello Young Lovers' and 'Shall We Dance?'.

Rodgers and Hammerstein didn't let up, despite their phenomenal success. They went on to write *Allegro*, *Flower Drum Song*, *Me And Juliet* and their final coup, *The Sound Of Music*, in 1959. Adapted from the novel *The Trapp Family Singers*, by Maria Augusta Trapp, the stage show was first produced at the Lunt-Fontanne Theatre in New York in November 1959 and ran for 1,443 performances. In London, it enjoyed a record-breaking run for an American musical, notching up 2,385 shows.

The pair had excelled themselves, writing a clutch of songs that would become standards, among them the title song, 'My Favourite Things', 'Climb Ev'ry Mountain', '16 Going On 17' and 'Edelweiss'. The show was an incredible success, and earned the pair a Grammy Award in 1960 for Best Original Cast Album, but sadly this was overshadowed by the death of Oscar Hammerstein II in that same year. The lights on Broadway were dimmed in his honour.

Five years later, the film soundtrack went gold faster than any other soundtrack in recording history, selling seven million copies in the first year alone. The film itself won five Academy Awards.

Richard Rodgers went on to work with other lyricists, such as Stephen Sondheim and Alan Jay Lerner, but was fortunate to have found two of the century's greatest wordsmiths in Hart and Hammerstein for the main body of his canon. Rodgers, the composer who had spend his pocket money going to see shows containing Jerome Kern scores, died in December 1979 at the age of 77.

Just as Rodgers was blessed with two great partners, so was Oscar Hammerstein. On many occasions from 1925 onwards, Oscar Hammerstein II collaborated with Kern, and would continue to do so right up until the composer's death.

Kern's 1920 musical *Sally* yielded the eternally optimistic 'Look For The Silver Lining', a song co-written with Buddy DeSylva. The number was sung in the musical by Marilyn Miller, and would later be performed in the MGM biopic on Kern, *Till The Clouds Roll By*, starring Judy Garland. The book for *Sally* had been written by Guy Bolton and PG Wodehouse, with Victor Herbert supplying the ballet music and Kern the melodies.

Marilyn Miller also starred in Kern's 1925 Broadway musical *Sunny*, the book and lyrics on this occasion having been written by Otto Harbach and Oscar Hammerstein II, the three of them collaborating on the writing of 'Who?', one of the show's main songs. Again, Garland would sing it in *Till The Clouds Roll By*. In 1923, Harbach had worked with Hammerstein on the musical *Wildflower*, and so the two of them had been initially brought in to work with Kern on *Sunny* as a team.

1927 was a good year for Kern and Hammerstein. They landed the musical *Show Boat*, after the composer had approached the lyricist with the idea. "One day Jerry called me up and said 'How would you like to do a show for Ziegfeld? It's got a million-dollar title: *Show Boat*.' I said 'Isn't that Edna Ferber's new book?'. Jerry said 'Yes. I haven't finished it yet, but I've already bought it from Ferber. Get a copy and read it right away.' 'Is Ziegfeld enthusiastic?'. I asked. 'He doesn't know anything about it yet!' said Jerry."

One of the show's big songs was 'Bill', performed in the show by Helen Morgan. The number had originally been written in 1918 by Wodehouse and Kern, and was dropped from their work *Oh Lady, Lady* before being interpolated into *Sally*. It was then dropped from that show, too, and finally resurfaced in *Show Boat*, after having been re-touched by Hammerstein. Despite his credit as a co-writer, he was modest about his input: "I am particularly anxious to point out that the lyric for the song

'Bill' was written by PG Wodehouse. Although he had always been given credit in the programme, it has frequently been assumed that, since I wrote all the other lyrics for *Show Boat*, I also wrote this one, and I have had praise for it which belongs to another man." His self-effacing disclaimer served up a sharp lesson in humility for those who go to the other extreme and claim songwriting credits where they should have none.

The film version followed the stage production in 1929, with yet another stage version appearing in 1932 and a second film in 1936, starring Paul Robeson. *Show Boat* revivals seemed to be under way every few years. Incredibly, in 1951, a third big-screen version appeared, produced by MGM and starring Kathryn Grayson, Ava Gardner, Howard Keel and Joe E Brown.

Another *Show Boat* song, 'Why Do I Love You?', had a humorous alternative lyric written by Hammerstein, going under the title 'Cupid Knows Why'. The word *cupid* was anathema to Kern, as it represented to him all that was old fashioned and melodramatic about the musical theatre. He saw the joke, though, and had the spoof lyric framed.

The show also contained such classics as 'Make Believe', 'You Are Love' and 'Can't Help Lovin' Dat Man', with its simple no-frills lyric:

> Fish got to swim and birds got to fly,
> I got to love one man till I die,
> Can't help lovin' dat man of mine.

Another of *Show Boat*'s durable classics is 'Ol' Man River', a song which rather got to Oscar's wife over the years. She heard people talk about "that wonderful song that Jerome Kern wrote" once too often, and on one occasion pulled up the offender: "Jerome Kern did *not* write 'Ol' Man River'. Mr Kern wrote 'Dum Dum Dum Dah'...My husband wrote 'Ol' Man River'."

With the money rolling in, Kern bought a yacht, which he named *The Show Boat*, and it was onboard that vessel that he first played Hammerstein the melody to 'Don't Ever Leave Me', which he dedicated to his new wife, Dorothy. The song was featured in the Kern/Hammerstein 1929 Broadway show *Sweet Adeline*.

For the 1931 show *Cat And The Fiddle*, Jerome collaborated again with Otto Harbach. The production later became a film starring Jeannette McDonald and Ramon Navarro.

Kern and Hammerstein were back together for *Music In The Air* in 1932.

The musical contained a song that is still played regularly on gold radio almost 70 years on, 'I've Told Ev'ry Little Star', and a version of the number became a big transatlantic hit in 1961 for American singer Linda Scott. Oscar Hammerstein recalled the unlikely source of Kern's inspiration for the melody: "Jerry got the melodic theme from a bird. He swears it!...He heard a finch outside his window singing the first line and he built a refrain on it...'Ev'ry Little Star' proved to be a stubborn tune, and for a whole summer I resisted my efforts to set words to it. There were times when I wish the finch had kept his big mouth shut!" Paul McCartney would later draw inspiration from birdsong in exactly the same way with 'Blackbird'.

Another link between Kern and McCartney was the latter's song 'Yesterday'. Paul was worried for some while that the melody he literally dreamed up might have already existed. Satisfied at last that it wasn't, he set lyrics to it, assuming that there'd never been a song called 'Yesterday'. However, it was pointed out to him that there had been the Jerome Kern/Otto Harbach song 'Yesterdays', from their show *Roberta*, although thankfully this didn't deter him from using the title. While McCartney didn't attempt to employ a perfect rhyme for the whole word of his title, Harbach did, using "sequestered days" to rhyme with 'Yesterdays'.

The musical *Roberta* featured one of Kern's most outstanding compositions, 'Smoke Gets In Your Eyes'. Originally composed by Jerome as a signature tune for a radio series that never got on the air, the song was then used for a tap routine during a scene change in *Show Boat*. Harbach discovered the music for it while they were working on *Roberta*, and asked Kern "Why not change the tempo?...If these short notes might be made long notes, might it not make an attractive ballad?" The song has had a long shelf life, with sales reaching a peak in 1958 when The Platters' version became a million-seller, topping the chart on both sides of the Atlantic.

Kern and Hammerstein's *Very Warm For May* was produced in 1939, the show featuring the song 'All The Things You Are', which at the time was highly unusual for its three changes of key. From 1935, Kern had begun to establish himself in Hollywood with RKO, for whom he made *Roberta*. The songs of the film used his music and the lyrics of Hammerstein, Harbach, Jimmy McHugh and Dorothy Fields, the daughter of Broadway actor/producer Lew Fields: "He knew my father and brothers...I was working at RKO and Paul Berman, who was producing *Roberta*, asked me if I'd take a couple of days and work on it. He said 'We have a seriously uneven melody of Jerry Kern's that he's given us to add to to the score; it needs a lyric.' So I wrote 'Lovely To Look At', which absolutely astounded Berman…Jerry loved it, and from then on asked for me." Fields and McHugh also provided the words for another song that appeared in the film, 'I Won't Dance', a title conceived by Hammerstein but without his original contribution.

This film was followed in 1935 by *I Dream Too Much* and *Swing Time* a year later, with Dorothy Fields providing all of the lyrics for the latter. The RKO release featured three classic songs by the duo: 'This Is A Fine Romance', 'Pick Yourself Up' and the Academy Award-winning 'The Way You Look Tonight'.

1937 saw the release of Paramount's *High, Wide And Handsome*, with Hammerstein providing the lyrics to Kern's music on the film's two big songs, 'Can I Forget You?' and 'The Folks Who Live On The Hill'. Then, in 1938, the Douglas Fairbanks film *Joy Of Living* appeared, containing the song 'You Couldn't Be Cuter', with a melody by Kern and with lyrics that were inspired by Dorothy Fields' young son, David. Fields also contributed lyrics to Kern's next score, the 1940 movie *One Night In The Tropics*, which also featured lyrics by Otto Harbach and Oscar Hammerstein, while the 1941 MGM picture *Lady Be Good* featured songs by George and Ira Gershwin, Arthur Freed and Roger Edens, and Kern and Hammerstein. Kern and Hammerstein's 'The Last Time I Saw Paris' wasn't actually written for the film.

> This was the only song that I've ever written under any kind of compulsion. The Germans had just taken Paris and I couldn't get my mind on anything else at all. I loved the city very much and hated the idea of it falling. I thought of the enemy tramping through the streets and taking all the gaiety and beauty out of the hearts of the people there…I thought of Chevalier in his straw hat. And not just the beauty of the parks or the loveliness in the musuems but everything that was Paris: good and bad and of high quality and of cheapness. And this was a kind of lament. When I called Jerry and asked him to write some music for it, he almost fell dead. In all the years we'd been working together, this was the first time I had completed a lyric that he would have to set to music. He always wrote the melody and then I would fit words to it.

Kern rose to the occasion, putting a melody to Oscar's lyric in just three days.

Proof that attitudes have changed considerably in the last 60 years is borne out in Kern's and Hammerstein's response to receiving an Academy Award for the song. They felt that, as it hadn't been specifically written for the picture, it shouldn't have been eligible for the award. This was not false modesty; the Academy actually changed the ruling at Kern's persistence. It's difficult to imagine a writer pressing home their personal beliefs these days almost to their own detriment.

Kern was to write the music for just three more films that would be released during his lifetime: *You Were Never Lovelier*, with Johnny Mercer providing the lyrics; the Deanne Durbin film *Can't Help Singing*, with words by YP "Yip" Harburg; and *Cover Girl* in 1944, starring Gene Kelly, Phil Silvers and Rita Hayworth, and with lyrics by Ira Gershwin. Gershwin later wrote:

> It was in 1939 that Kern was between assignments and I wrote nine or ten songs with him. Nothing ever happened to them, although both of us liked several. During this time he played me many other tunes I liked but just didn't get around to. Some four years later, in the *Cover Girl* period, I tried to remind him of a lovely tune of the earlier period by humming a snatch of it. But he had never put it on paper and couldn't recall it. I told him his daughter Betty had been very fond of this melody, so he called her in and between us and our snatches, it came to him. "Good tune," he said. "What about it?" I told him it had begun haunting me that morning, and if he could split the opening note into two notes I had a two-word on-the-nose title for the flashback number in the film...When he heard the title, 'Sure Thing', with its race-track background, he said, "Of course...nothing to it...in fact, the two notes make a better announcement."

The problems facing Kern for his 109th score – which would turn out to be his last – were twofold: firstly, the cast that Otto Preminger was using weren't really singers; and secondly, his collaborator on *Centennial Summer*, Leo Robin, wasn't at his best. "I was completely in awe of Kern from the minute we got together, and it cramped my style a little bit. He used to call me up every day, bugging me: 'You got anything yet?'. I wanted so much to please him and to measure up to his high standard that I didn't think I did my best work on that picture." Jerome eventually brought in Harburg, Hammerstein and Johnny Mercer to collaborate with him on a song each, with Robin in the end writing just two numbers for the movie, 'In Love In Vain' and 'Up With A Lark'.

Jerome Kern passed away in November 1945, not long after Rodgers and Hammerstein – now wearing producers' hats – had asked him to write the score for *Annie Get Your Gun*. Irving Berlin subsequently got the gig and did a brilliant job, but one can't help wondering how it would have fared in the hands of Kern had fate not intervened, just as one might ponder how *Oklahoma!* would have turned out with Lorenz Hart's lyrics instead of Hammerstein's.

Oscar Hammerstein delivered a moving eulogy at Kern's funeral, describing him as "alert and alive. He bounced. He stimulated everyone. He annoyed some. Never bored anyone at any time…Our real tribute will be paid over many years of remembering."

Kern's sometime partner Otto Harbach was born in Salt Lake City in August 1873 to Danish parents, and worked in advertising and as a journalist until turning to his great love: writing for Broadway shows.

His career as a lyricist began in earnest in 1901. Between 1910 and 1926, he penned lyrics for such musicals as *Madame Sherry*, on which he worked with the Bohemian-born composer Karl Hoschna; *The Fire-Fly*; *Rose-Marie*, with Rudolph Friml; and *The Desert Song*, with Sigmund Romberg. In 1923, he collaborated with Oscar Hammerstein on the musical *Wildflower*, with Herbert Stothart and Vincent Youmans providing the music. Following its opening in the States, the production came to London, early in 1926.

Yip Harburg, born in April 1896, not only collaborated with Kern also but worked with his college friend Ira Gershwin. He ran an electrical business until his early 30s, when the Depression enforced his to rethink his career. Harburg commented wryly: "I had my fill of that dreamy abstract thing called business. I decided to face up to reality by writing lyrics."

His old friend Ira helped to introduce him to various composers, including the immigrant Jay Gorney, born Daniel Jayson in Bialystok in 1896. The pair later wrote the song that virtually became the anthem for the Depression: 'Brother, Can You Spare A Dime?'. In that year, 1932, Harburg also teamed up with Vernon Duke to pen 'April In Paris' and with Harold Arlen to write 'It's Only A Paper Moon'.

Harburg's biggest successes came when collaborating with Arlen, who was born in Buffalo, New York, in April 1896. The two men came up with 'Happiness Is Just A Thing Called Joe', and worked together on the seminal film *The Wizard Of Oz*.

A passionate jazz fan, Arlen never intended to be a songwriter, but while working as a rehearsal pianist for Vincent Youmans he wrote a song that ended up as 'Get Happy', with words by Ted Koehler, and began to write numbers for Cotton Club revues. The writers he replaced were Dorothy Fields and Jimmy McHugh, who had just begun to find success on Broadway. Other big hits for Arlen and Koehler (born in Washington, DC, in July 1894) included 'I've Got The World On a String', 'Between The Devil And The Deep Blue Sea', 'Minnie The Moocher's Wedding Day' and the ever-popular 'Stormy Weather'.

Arlen also collaborated successfully with Ira Gershwin, and wrote 'Blues In The Night' and other songs with Johnny Mercer, including 'That Old Black Magic' for the Bing Crosby/Bob Hope film *Star-Spangled Rhythm*. Mercer's lyrics and Arlen's music for that song still sounded good enough to give Louis Prima and Keely Smith a million-seller with the song in 1958. Mercer and Arlen also penned 'Ac-cent-tchu-ate The Positive' for the 1944 movie *Here Come The Waves*.

Harold Arlen's musical score credits include *Bloomer Girl*, written in 1944 with Yip Harburg; *St Louis Woman*, written in 1946 with Johnny Mercer; *A Star Is Born*, written in 1953 with Ira Gershwin; *House Of Flowers*, from 1954; and *Jamaica*, from 1954.

Arlen's and Harburg's finest moment was surely writing the exceptional set of songs for the 1939 film *The Wizard Of Oz*, winning the Academy Award for the Best Film Song of the year with 'Over The Rainbow'. It not only sold a million copies for the film's star, Judy Garland, but it also appeared on her million-selling 1961 album *Judy At Carnegie Hall*, which also featured songs by George and Ira Gershwin, Irving Berlin and Rodgers and Hart. In the same year, the song featured on Mantovani's million-selling album *Italia Mia*. 'Over the Rainbow' was almost dropped from the film at one point, as the producers thought that the movie was too long, but fortunately it survived to become one of the best-loved songs of the century.

Among the other songs that the duo wrote for the film were 'Follow The Yellow Brick Road', 'If I Only Had A Heart' and 'We're Off To See The Wizard':

MAJOR TO MINOR

> We're off to see the Wizard
> The wonderful Wizard of Oz.
> We hear he is a whiz of a wiz
> If ever a wiz there was.
> If ever a wever a wiz there was
> The Wizard of Oz is one because
> Because, because, because, because, because
> Because of the wonderful things he does.

Arlen had previously been the rehearsal pianist for Vincent Youmans, and Youmans had previously undertaken the same role for Victor Herbert before becoming a full-time composer. Vincent Miller Youmans, known as "Millie", was born in New York City in September 1898. As a young man, he worked alongside George Gershwin, plugging songs.

He collaborated with more lyricists than most over the course of his career, initially having a big hit in 1925 with the musical *No, No Nanette*, for which Oscar Hammerstein II and Otto Harbach wrote the words, and which included such songs as 'I Want To Be Happy' and 'Tea For Two'. In 1926, he wrote 'I Know That You Know' with Harbach for *Oh, Please*, and came up with the score for *Hit The Deck* in the following year, songs for which included 'Sometimes I'm Happy' (co-written with Irving Caesar) and 'Halleluja'. He also wrote songs for musicals with Billy Rose, Harold Adamson and Mack Gordon, but after penning 'Rise 'n' Shine' for the 1932 show *Take A Chance*, he went to Hollywood to write with Gus Kahn for the film *Flying Down To Rio*, after which he contributed to less successful musicals.

Youmans' publishing company went broke in 1935, and he went bankrupt. Despite suffering from tuberculosis, in 1944 he threw himself into a major project, *The Vincent Youmans Ballet Revue*, which was unsuccessful. He died in April 1946.

Descended from English and Scottish stock, Howard Hoagland Carmichael was born in 1899 in the university town of Bloomington, Indiana. His grandmother hoped that giving him the name of a successful businessman would help him in later life, and insisted on calling him Hoagland after the president of a Midwest railroad.

Carmichael was educated at Bloomington High School and Indiana

University, after his family moved to Indianapolis. It soon became clear that the young Hoagy had inherited his early musical talent from his mother, a popular ragtime pianist. While he was at college, he wrote 'Washboard Blues', which he recorded with Hitch's Happy Harmonists, while another of his songs, 'Riverboat Shuffle', was recorded by The Wolverine Orchestra.

After leaving college, he formed Carmichael's Collegians, and later Hoagy Carmichael And His Pals (featuring Tommy and Jack Dorsey), and began to release records in 1927.

Although a published songwriter, he went on from college to become a lawyer, practising first in New York and then in Florida, until the idea of being a lawyer for the rest of his life wore a little thin. "I got fed up with it. Sitting in my office one day I heard a recording of one of my songs, 'Washboard Blues', and suddenly I decided songwriting was for me. I locked up the law office and caught the next train for New York."

During the late '20s and early '30s, he led his own band, playing with the likes of Benny Goodman, Gene Krupa, Bix Beiderbecke and the Dorseys. He was working in New York when a friend suggested that one of the tunes he'd written in 1927, after he'd left college, a quick ragtime number, would sound wonderful with a lyric and played at a slower speed. Carmichael took up the suggestion, and one of the century's most popular songs was born, 'Stardust', with words by Mitchell Parish. The number had been recorded as an up-tempo piece of music in 1928 by The Chocolate Dandies, with Lonnie Johnson on lead guitar, and had also been recorded by both Isham Jones and Louis Armstrong; but it was the new, slower version with words that became a million-seller for Artie Shaw in 1940. It was also a million-seller for Glenn Miller and his orchestra in the same year, which served to further underline its popularity. The song would spawn more than 1,000 cover versions in the States alone, one of them by R&B outfit Billy Ward And The Dominos, which also sold a million in 1957, the year in which Nat "King" Cole also released it.

In 1930, Carmichael wrote both the words and music to 'Rockin' Chair', and in the following year came up with 'Georgia On My Mind', which would become a big hit for Ray Charles in 1960. He then penned 'Lazy River', with Sidney Arodin providing the words, the song becoming a million-seller for the Piqua, Ohio, family group The Mills Brothers in 1948. It also became a hit for Bobby Darin in 1961.

The classic songs from the '30s and '40s seem to have a long shelf life for artists being primarily concerned with recording a good song rather than with its incubation period or perceived sell-by date.

In 1933, Carmichael and Johnny Mercer wrote 'Lazy Bones', and a version of this song by Jonathan King became a UK hit in 1971. Carmichael and Frank Loesser's 'Two Sleepy People', from the film *Thanks For The Memory*, also became a popular record for Philip And Vanessa, enjoying heavy airplay in the early '70s.

In 1946, Carmichael had two Number Two hits in the States as an artist in his own right, with his own 'Ole Buttermilk Sky' and 'Huggin' And Chalkin". The team of Carmichael and Mercer also wrote 'Skylark' and 'How Little We Know', the latter featuring in the Humphrey Bogart/Lauren Bacall film *To Have And Have Not*, the first movie to feature Carmichael as an actor, in which he sang 'Hong Kong Blues'. (His breakthrough into films as a character began when a film director neighbour became amused at his drolleries. He continued to play and philosophise in several films, including *The Best Years Of Our Lives*, *Young Man With A Horn* and *The Las Vegas Story*.)

Another collaboration with Mercer produced 'In The Cool, Cool, Cool Of The Evening', which was featured in the 1951 film *Here Comes The Groom* and won an Academy Award in the following year. At the time, European radio said of Carmichael: "Hoagy has always been the exception to the rule that you can't write commercial real jazz. From the first his tunes have held the real core of the negro spirit...'Rockin' Chair', 'Georgia' and even his obvious exploitation of this [as in 'Lazy Bones'] has an undeniable taste and charm."

A song on which he and Harold Adamson collaborated, 'My Resistance Is Low', has been recorded by countless artists, including The Shadows, as an instrumental on their debut album, and Robin Sarstedt, who took the song to Number Three in Britain in 1976. Hoagy's melodies certainly didn't gather dust.

He continued to write songs for films, such as *The Stork Club* and *Gentlemen Prefer Blondes*, as well as having an acting role in the TV series *Laramie* from 1959-62. He died at the end of December 1981.

Sammy Cahn was born Samuel Cohen on the East Side of New York City in June 1913, and was educated at Seward Park High School before becoming a violinist in a vaudeville orchestra. "I showed an aptitude for the violin that would never bother a Heifitz but certainly confuse a Kenny Youngman. This led me to play with small bands, and eventually to meeting my first collaborator, Saul Chaplin." After meeting Chaplin, a pianist just a few months his senior, the two organised a dance band and began to write songs together. Their first success came out in 1935, when The Jimmie Lunceford Band recorded 'Rhythm Is Our Business'.

Cahn changed his name because there was already an MGM comedian named Sammy Cohen, and so he became Sammy Kahn. "After some success, I discovered that one of the great lyricists was named Kahn...Gus, that is! The thought that I might get his royalties was embarrassing since they were not comparable, so I finally changed it to Cahn with a C."

Cahn and Chaplin wrote many songs together, including 'Shoe Shine Boy', recorded by Louis Armstrong, The Mills Brothers and Bing Crosby for the *Cotton Club Revue*; 'Dedicated To You'; and 'I Could Make You Care', from the film *Ladies Must Live*.

Cahn's adaptation of the Yiddish song 'Bei Mir Bist Du Schön' became one of the biggest hits of the 1930s, the number becoming not only the first million-seller for Minneapolis trio The Andrews Sisters but also the first million-seller ever for a female group. This success came about despite its awkward title, and there are stories of people apparently going into record stores asking for the song 'Buy A Beer Monsieur Shane', or 'My Mere Bits Of Shame'.

Chaplin was the first of Cahn's three main collaborators, and the pair of them worked with other writers on the popular song 'Until The Real Thing Comes Along', which was later recorded by several artists, including Andy Kirk, The Ink Spots and Fats Waller.

In 1940, Cahn moved to Hollywood to write for the movies, and became even more successful working with composer Jule Styne (born in London in 1905), who had previously collaborated with Frank Loesser. Styne, who moved to the States in 1913, was educated at the Chicago College Of Music, where he won the college's Mozart Award, before going on to Northwestern University. A child prodigy, he had played solo with the Chicago Symphony Orchestra at the age of nine. He later went on to lead dance bands and write material for recording artists.

Cahn and Styne wrote many hits together, including 'I've Heard That Song Before' for the film *Youth On Parade*, a song which become a million-seller for the Harry James Orchestra. With vocals by former Artie Shaw singer Helen Forrest, the song went to Number One in the States in 1942 and stayed at the top for an amazing 13 weeks. Among the other successful Cahn/Styne songs of the '40s were 'Five Minutes More'; 'Let It Snow, Let It Snow, Let It Snow', recorded by Vaughan Monroe and his orchestra; and 'It's Magic', written for the 1948 film *Romance On The High Seas*, Doris Day's first film and the one that made her an international star. 'It's Magic' became her third million-selling single, and the record reached Number Two in America.

The Cahn/Styne song 'Three Coins In The Fountain', from the 1954 20th Century Fox film of the same name, was first performed by Frank Sinatra, but was an even bigger hit for The Four Aces, who took it to Number Two in America, and the song became their third million-seller.

The Cahn/Styne song 'It Seems I Heard That Song Before' had been nominated for an Academy Award as far back as 1942, and between 1944 and 1953 they were nominated for another eight Academy Awards. It was 'Three Coins In A Fountain' that secured them their first actual award, however, in 1954. Sinatra later said of Cahn: "I will always be indebted for the words you put in my mouth…As long as I am singing for my supper, I pray you will be by my side gifting me with unforgettable words and memorable phrases. We are a good team, and you are the first among equals."

The third composer to work closely with Sammy was Jimmy Van Heuson, born Chester Edward Babcock in New York in January 1913, a former World War Two test pilot. Van Heuson had previously worked with bandleader/composer Eddie DeLange, and then with Johnny Burke, with whom he wrote for Frank Sinatra and Bing Crosby. Bing sang their million-selling 'Swinging On A Star' in his film *Going My Way*, taking it to Number One and winning them an Academy Award for it. Recorded in 1944, the song's backing vocalists, The Williams Brothers, featured the as-yet-unknown Andy Williams. One of the highlights of Johnny Burke's songwriting career was penning the lyrics for Errol Garner's 'Misty'.

Jimmy Van Heuson and Sammy Cahn also wrote many songs for Frank Sinatra, including the title track for the film *The Tender Trap*, 'Come Fly With Me', 'It's Nice To Go Trav'ling' and the Academy Award-winning 'All The Way', from the film *Joker's Wild*. 'High Hopes', from the film *A Hole In The Head*, and more Sinatra vocal magic gave the pair another Academy Award in 1959.

The Golden Years

Lyrically, Cahn was on fire, and working flat out. "I'd been churning out 'special lyrics' for special occasions for years, and this helped facilitate my tremendous speed with lyric writing...Lyric-writing has always been a thrilling adventure for me, and something I've done with the kind of ease that only comes with joy! From the beginning, the fates have conspired to help my career...I am one of those lyric writers who says 'a word is only as great as the note it sits under', and Jule Styne has given me and all the 'word-people' the greatest notes."

Styne went on to have further success as a composer, writing 'Diamonds Are A Girl's Best Friend' with Leo Robin in 1949, and collaborating with Betty Comden and Adolph Green on songs such as 'Just In Time' and 'The Party's Over' for the play and film *Bells Are Ringing*. He also worked with Stephen Sondheim, writing the songs for the Grammy Award-winning film *Gypsy* in 1959, one of the most successful numbers being 'Everything's Coming Up Roses'. Robbie Williams wasn't the first to have success with a song called 'Let Me Entertain You', as Sondheim and Styne beat him by some 40 years. Styne also wrote 'Don't Rain On My Parade' for the Barbra Streisand film *Funny Girl*, with lyrics supplied by Bob Merrill.

The only Emmy Award ever awarded for a song was awarded to Cahn and Van Heuson for their million-selling song 'Love And Marriage', sung by Frank Sinatra and featured by him in a televised musical version of Thornton Wilder's *Our Town*. They had further success with Sinatra with '(Chicago Is) My Kind Of Town', from the film *Robin And The Seven Hoods*, and also with the title song from *Pocketful Of Miracles*. A further Academy Award was given to Sammy and Jimmy for 'Call Me Irresponsible' performed by Jackie Gleason in the 1963 film *Papa's Delicate Condition*, which told the story of a drinking man in Texas at the turn of the century. In 1967 they wrote the songs for the Universal film *Thoroughly Modern Millie*, set in '20s New York and starring Julie Andrews.

Frank Sinatra was as generous in his praise of Styne as he was of Cahn: "Jule Styne is simply the bet there is at what he does...His song list reads like the history of American popular music...There's only one Jule Styne, and I love him."

Frank might possibly have agreed that there was only one Cole Porter, too. Born in June 1891 in Peru, Indiana, to Samuel Porter and Kate Cole, his closest link to the East was through a Scottish maternal great-grandfather.

His earliest lyrical influences came from reading *Alice In Wonderland*, *Treasure Island, Swiss Family Robinson* and the Victorian poets, including his personal passion Robert Browning. As a boy he loved village parades and the circuses that visited there, particularly the marching bands, and determined to become a circus performer one day. He studied piano from the age of six and also learned the violin, performing anything from Gilbert and Sullivan through to English folk songs and pieces by Mendelssohn. His showmanship made up for what he lacked in vocal ability.

At the age of 14, he enrolled at the Worcester Academy, and his childhood friend Desdemona Bearss helped him to improve his grasp of the English language by playing word games with him.

At college he was much in demand as a pianist, becoming a leading light in the Academy Glee Club, writing material for the academy's students and editing the school paper. On a more negative note, he also broke his leg in a fall and was constantly rebuked for writing risqué songs.

Always a snappy dresser, he went up to Yale in 1909, describing himself as a cross between "Eddie Cantor and the Duke Of Windsor". While there, he wrote songs such as 'When The Summer Moon Comes Along', and successfully submitted 'Bingo Eli Yale' for a football song competition. The number caught on, and was published late in 1910, inspiring him to write other football songs, including the highly popular 'Bulldog'.

Under William Lyon Phelps, Porter improved the scansion and metre of his lyrics. He was also inspired when the British poet Alfred Noyes paid a visit to Yale, and avidly devoured the works of Shelley, Keats, Byron and Coleridge.

In 1912, he collaborated with fellow student Almet Jenks, who wrote the libretto for the show *Pot Of Gold*, by which time Porter showed all the signs of becoming an excellent songwriter, as well as a highly-accomplished performer. His first show at Yale was *The Kaleidoscope*, with one of the songs, 'As I Love You', later becoming 'Esmeralda'. It was published by Irving Berlin and, in 1915, was interpolated into the Broadway show *Hands Up*.

After a very brief flirtation with Harvard Law School, he transferred to the Harvard School Of Music and wrote a new show, *Paranoia*, which opened at Newhaven's Hotel Taft in April 1914. As Porter's reputation grew, the theatre producer and one-time US agent for Oscar Wilde, Elizabeth Marbury, was quoted in the *New Haven Evening Register* as saying: "I am convinced that Mr Porter is the one man of many who can measure up to the standard set by the late Arthur Sullivan." She went on to produce Porter's *See America First*, on which he again collaborated with Riggs, the show opening in New York in March 1916. Due in part due to a hammering from the critics, the show closed after just 15 performances, and Riggs, although from a wealthy family, lost $35,000 on the project. Many years later, Porter commented on *The Ed Sullivan Show*: "As they dismantled the scenery and trucked it out of the stage alley, I honestly believed that I was disgraced for the rest of my life."

Porter was sent to France when America entered the First World War, taking with him a zither and a piano keyboard. There are various accounts of his wartime exploits, including one of his own, in which he says that he spent some time in the French Foreign Legion. After the war, he remained in Paris, where he met and fell in love with the wealthy socialite Linda Lee Thomas, whom he would subsequently marry, despite his continuing homosexual relationships.

In 1919, he was asked to write the score for a show called *Hitchy Koo*, which included the sentimental and highly popular 'Old-Fashioned Garden'. During the 1920s, however, he became unsure of his musical talents, although he had a life that was comfortable enough not to be hungry and seemed happy just enjoying an active social life.

Although based in Paris, he and his wife led a peripatetic existence. Cole only took time out to write some songs for a jazz ballet for English producer CB Cochran's *Mayfair And Montmartre*, among which was 'The Blue Boy Blues', inspired by the sale of Gainsborough's 1771 portrait 'Blue Boy' for $620,000.

In 1923, Porter became wealthy in his own right, after his mother gave him $1 million from the money she had received in the will of her father. Then, several years later, he received another million. "Altogether, I received over two million dollars...People always say that so much money spoils one's life, but it didn't spoil mine; it simply made it wonderful."

An impromptu meeting of four great writers took place in Venice in 1926. While they were holidaying there, Richard Rodgers and Lorenz Hart bumped into Noël Coward, with whom Rodgers was acquainted. Coward informed them that there was somebody that they should meet, and Rodgers was agreeable. "His name was Cole Porter, but at that time neither the name nor the face was the least familiar to me."

MAJOR TO MINOR

During their stay, Rodgers, Hart, Coward and Porter dined together at the famous Palazzo Rezzonica, and while they ate Cole pumped Rodgers with questions about the musical theatre scene on Broadway. The three pianists then took it in turns to play selections of their material at the piano. Although Porter gave the impression of being something of a social butterfly, Rodgers noted that "as soon as he touched the keyboard to play 'a few of my little things', I became aware that he was not merely a talented dilettante but a generally gifted theatre composer and lyricist". He asked Cole why he was wasting his time being a socialite, and why he wasn't writing for Broadway. Porter later confessed that his ideal scenario would be to write for Broadway while living in Europe.

At one point in 1928, Porter and Ira and George Gershwin met up in Paris to enjoy a long piano-playing session through the night. Cole was also close friends with Irving Berlin, who also regularly socialised there.

Porter's *La Revue Des Ambassadeurs* opened in May 1928 at the Café Des Ambassadeurs, and he was also engaged as composer and lyricist for a new show called *Paris*, for which he wrote what was to become one of his most famous songs: 'Let's Do It'. He changed the original lyric…

> Chinks do it, Japs do it,
> Up in Lapland little Lapps do it,
> Let's do it, let's fall in love.

…to the more acceptable

> Birds do it, bees do it,
> Even educated fleas do it,
> Let's do it, let's fall in love.

Paris was followed in 1929 by *50,000 Frenchmen*, the show which included the hit song 'You Do Something To Me'.

During the '30s, Porter's star was really in the ascendancy, and he had ten shows and films produced, including shows that later became films. These included *The New Yorkers* (1930), *Anything Goes* (1934), *Born To Dance* (1936), *Red Hot And Blue* (1936) and *Rosalie* (1937). His 1932 stage musical which became the film *The Gay Divorcee* two years later featured another Porter classic, 'Night And Day'. His show *Anything Goes* not only featured the excellent title track, but also 'I Get A Kick Out Of You', 'All Through The Night' and the Top Ten hit 'You're The Top'. *Red Hot And Blue* contained the wonderful 'It's De-Lovely', the number inspired by an early morning in Rio De Janeiro. "It was dawn...As we stood on the bow of the boat, my exclamation was 'It's delightful'...My wife followed with 'It's delicious', and Monty [Woolley, his friend] in his 'happy' state cried 'It's de-lovely!'"

In 1937, Porter fell while riding a particularly skittish horse, and the animal crushed his legs when it fell on top of him. (The ambulance driver that came to pick him up was a man called Bart Howard, a man who, while unknown at the time, would later write one of Frank Sinatra's big hits, 'Fly Me To The Moon'.) As well as multiple fractures, Porter suffered from infected bone marrow and had to undergo many operations in order to save his legs. He complicated matters further by falling down the stairs and breaking a leg again in the following year.

The '40s brought more films and stage musicals, including *Mexican Hayride* and *Seven Lively Arts*, the latter featuring 'Every Time We Say Goodbye', the song that including the line "how strange the change from major to minor". Using major and minor keys in the same song was something of a trademark of Porter's.

'Too Darn Hot', 'So In Love' and 'Always True To You In My Fashion' were all part of the music that he wrote for *Kiss Me, Kate*, while *High Society* – the 1956 film for which he wrote some of his most memorable songs, starring Grace Kelly, Frank Sinatra and Bing Crosby – included 'Now You Has Jazz', 'Well, Did You Evah!' and 'True Love'.

By the late '50s, his golden years were over. His right leg was amputated in 1958, he became a recluse, and was badly burned in 1963 after setting his bed alight while smoking. He died in Santa Monica in October 1964.

7 The Child Is Father To The Man

However serious and mysterious the business of writing songs might seem, there is always room to have some fun. It's an outlet that many writers have accorded themselves down the centuries. The English baroque composer Henry Purcell wrote bawdy ballads as well as sacred music and secular operas, while the prolific and multifaceted poet Hilaire Belloc penned delightful nonsense verses for children as well as a wealth of books on religion and travel.

Songwriters have often turned to children's verse and nursery rhymes for inspiration, as songwriter Sam Richards did in as early as 1901 with 'Rag-Time Nursery Rhymes'.

In 1935, Sammy Cahn and Don Raye wrote the lyric of '(If I Had) Rhythm In My Nursery Rhymes' to music by Jimmie Lunceford and Saul Chaplin, the words implying that it would be easier to learn the subjects that were taught if it were done through music, if they all had rhythm. Jack Horner is in there in all but name, "in the corner", along with "Simple Simon at the fair", who "met a pieman who was there".

The "catch" used by Milton Drake for 'Mairzy Doats' was part of an old linguistic children's riddle that inserted incorrect spacing in an otherwise obvious phrase, giving it the appearance of being in Latin:

> Infir taris,
> Inoak noneis,
> Inmud eelsare,
> Inclay noneare.
> Goatsea tivy;
> Maresea toats.

Children's rhymes have provided a springboard for countless songwriters seeking a different angle or wishing to expand upon or exploit a simple lyrical idea. Paul McCartney himself drew on 'Mary Had A Little Lamb', proving – as everybody had previously joked – that any of The Beatles could have a hit with a nursery rhyme. "My daughter Mary, who was three at the time, liked 'Mary Had A Little Lamb', but I didn't know a tune to it, so I made one up and I quite liked it. I thought that it was a nice little children's song, like 'Yellow Submarine'. For some reason I felt like it would make a good single. I like children very much, and I always expected that as my kids grew up they would get into new forms of rock and would criticise me, but they seem to like what I do."

Neil Sedaka had earlier felt that he could could have achieved the same success with a song that every single child in the western world has sung on countless occasions: "'Happy Birthday Sweet 16' was my smug period. I was on a roll and was having a lot of hits at RCA Victor, and I said to my writing partner Howard Greenfield 'Oh, I can even sing and write a song called 'Happy Birthday' and it would be a hit.' And it was."

One of Paul Simon's many classics, 'April Come She Will', was based on old children's rhyme: "When I was living in England in 1964, I worked in a club in a town called Swindon. I spent the night with a friend of mine in a village called Great Coxwell [two miles southwest of Faringdon]...We'd stayed up all night...We went out at dawn, and she recited an old English nursery rhyme: 'April, come she will; May she will stay; June, she'll change her tune; July, she will fly; August, die she must.'" Simon also reworked 'The Lover's Tasks' into 'Scarborough Fair', after hearing John Martyn's arrangement of the tune.

The Jaynetts had a US hit in 1963 with a variation on an old ring dance, during which children would hold hands in a circle, dancing around another child who was positioned in the middle. 'Sally Go Round The Roses', written by Zanders and Stevens, was in much the same vein of the original. That began:

> Sally go round the sun,
> Sally go round the moon,
> Sally go round the chimney-pots
> On a Saturday afternoon.

Children's bedtime prayers have also been woven into popular songs by lyricists, such as:

Major To Minor

> I see the moon,
> And the moon sees me;
> God bless the moon,
> And God bless me.

Those lines became the basis of 'I See The Moon', a song written by Meredith Willson which failed to become a hit in the States for producer Mitch Miller but which went to Number One for The Stargazers in Britain in 1954. Cliff Adams, The Stargazers' pianist and later leader of the legendary Cliff Adams Singers, remembers the situation with clarity: "We'd had a couple of hits – not real biggies, though – when our producer, Dick Rowe, brought us 'I See The Moon' as a serious song. It had been produced in the States by Mitch Miller, who'd had this idea to do it in the style of a barbershop quartet. We tried it in rehearsal, but really we thought it was monstrous and started taking the mickey out of it. In the middle of our send-up, Dick Rowe walked in and said 'This is a straight number!' We replied that we thought it would be a better comedy song." The Stargazers stuck to their guns, and the song with its roots in a child's prayer consequently shot to the top of the chart in Britain.

Another prayer from the confines of the nursery turned up in a slightly disguised manner in a 1971 transatlantic Motown classic:

> Now I lay me down to sleep,
> I pray the Lord my soul to keep.

These words crop up in the bridge section of The Temptations' 'Just My Imagination', written by Norman Whitfield and Barrett Strong, as:

> Every night on my knees I pray,
> Dear Lord please hear my plea.

Perhaps the most frequently-used bedtime verse, however, has been

> Star light, star bright,
> First star I see tonight,
> I wish I may, I wish I might,
> Have the wish I wish tonight.

Those lines were featured in 'Little Star', The Elegants' US Number One from 1958. The writers Arnold Venosa and Vito Picone incorporated words from both the above song and 'Twinkle, Twinkle, Little Star', while songwriters Weiss and Harmon used it in 'Starlight, Starbright', an American hit in 1961 for Linda Scott and covered in Britain by Welsh singer Maureen Evans. A variation on that theme was released by The Fleetwoods in an uncharacteristic bluebeat vein three years later, as 'Ska-Light, Ska-Bright' and credited to the partnership of Blagman and Meglin.

British comedian Charlie Drake gave the same theme a new twist in 1959 with a spoonerism-laden 'Starkle Starkle Little Twink', which he co-wrote. The number rather inevitably began with a singular version of his catchphrase "Hello, my darlings."

Lullabies have also served songwriters well. The Mystics' 1959 US hit 'Hushabye', written by Doc Pomus and Mort Shuman, is based on a traditional song that has lulled countless infants to sleep over the years, as had the original lines that were used in 'Cradle Of Love', Johnny Preston's bestselling single released a year later. The lyric turned "Hush-a-bye baby" into the more commercial jargon of the time, "Rock-a-bye baby", although some versions already used that term many years before rock 'n' roll.

Both 'Mockingbird', written and recorded by Charlie And Inez Foxx, and Bo Diddley's self-penned classic 'Bo Diddley', use the age-old rhyme that runs:

> Hush, little baby, don't say a word,
> Papa's going to buy you a mocking bird
> If the mocking bird won't sing,
> Papa's going to buy you a diamond ring.
> If the diamond ring turns to brass,
> Papa's going to buy you a looking-glass.
> If the looking-glass gets broke,
> Papa's going to buy you a billy goat.

Every child's favourite giant egg, Humpty Dumpty, made an appearance in 'Humpty Dumpty Heart', written and recorded by country and western singer Hank Thompson in 1947, the song selling a million by 1949. 15 years later, in 1964, Georgie Fame recorded the nursery rhyme in bluebeat tempo, calling it simply 'Humpty Dumpty'. The Migil Five did the same thing, with their version of the song also starring other nursery rhyme favourites Little Miss Muffet and the old woman who lived in a shoe. Despite claims made by the label to the contrary, the song appears to have its roots in Jamaican ska music; Eric Morris recorded it in 1961, and the song was written and produced by Prince Buster (Cecil Bustamente Campbell). The hapless egg also made an appearance in Cliff Richard's 'Dancing Shoes', a song written for the film *Summer Holiday* by Hank Marvin and Bruce Welch, which also featured Bo Peep and her sheep and Jack and Jill.

The latter couple were not only the title of Ray Parker Junior's hit with his group Raydio but they also appeared in the lyric, with a fleeting guest appearance from Little Red Riding Hood. That same little girl also provided Ronald Blackwell with the title for Sam The Sham And The Pharaohs' 1966 US hit 'Li'l Red Riding Hood', while Stan Freberg had already changed her into 'Little Blue Riding Hood' for his 1953 million-selling parody on the popular TV series *Dragnet*. Sam The Sham clearly favoured the nursery rhyme route, and also recorded and released a version of McDill's social commentary song 'Black Sheep', using the original chorus:

> Baa, baa, black sheep
> Have you any wool?

Ted Heath had previously led the same famous flock over the five-bar gate and up to Number Three in the UK chart in 1958 with 'Swinging Shepherd Blues'.

Sid Tepper and Roy Bennett, who wrote so many classics for Elvis Presley and Cliff Richard, also wrote many fun songs, including one which changed the porcine trio to anthropomorphous pigs on 'Three Little Peggies' for olympic swimming star turned singer Peter Elliot. Another Ronald Blackwell song, 'The Hair On My Chinny Chin Chin', also used the theme of the three little pigs. In a quiet moment, when not huffing and puffing and attempting to blow down the hogs' houses, Sam (Domingo Samudio) recorded a reworking of the children's favourite 'Old MacDonald Had A Farm', releasing it as 'Old MacDonald Had A Boogaloo Farm'.

Other jingles in the same vein as 'Humpty Dumpty' that have translated into popular songs include The Equals' 'Rub-A-Dub' and Wayne Blackwell's 'Hickory, Dick And Doc', a song inspired by both 'Hickory

The Child Is Father To The Man

Dickory Dock' and 'Three Blind Mice' and recorded by Bobby Vee. Hickory, Dick and Doc are three guys all in love with same girl: Hickory, the small-town hick, Doc, the singer of the song, and Dick, his best friend, are tormented by the object of their desire, who likens them to:

> Three blind mice, three blind mice.
> See how they run after me.

Johnny Dankworth had previously dabbled with rodent research on his Top Ten record of 1956, 'Experiments With Mice', giving 'Three Blind Mice' a jazz arrangement.

In 1965, fully-paid-up members of the US Arachnaphobia Society didn't exactly rush out to buy The Kids Next Door's hit 'Inky Dinky Spider', a variation on an old favourite which was recited whilst doing the appropriate actions with the fingers:

> Incey wincey spider,
> Climbed the water spout.
> Down came the rain,
> And washed the spider out.

During 1962, following his phenomenal success in spearheading the twist craze, Chubby Checker attempted to create the same demand for the limbo.

As a majority of potential converts were unable to perform this feat, apparently designed solely for contortionists, the craze failed to take off in a major way, although the Strange/Sheldon song 'Limbo Rock' soared to Number Two in the States in 1962. The lyric of the song's chorus only differs from the original children's jingle in the substitution of the word "limbo" for "candle" in the last line:

> Jack be nimble, Jack be quick,
> Jack jump over the candlestick.

Georgie Porgie, the nursery rhyme character who "kissed the girls and made them cry", enjoyed his moment of musical glory in Jewel Akens' 1965 song bearing the name of the boy himself, who ran away "when the boys came out to play".

Two other rascals, Tweedledum and Tweedledee, had their names at Number Two in the UK chart in 1971 courtesy of a song written by Lally Stott and G and M Capuano and recorded by Middle Of The Road, which reversed the credits of the two miscreants in the song's title, making it 'Tweedle Dee And Tweedle Dum'.

Music-and-movement favourite 'Here We Go Round The Mulberry Bush' became a Top Ten hit for Traffic late in 1967, which they recorded with a new melody as the theme for the film of the same name.

Rufus Thomas unashamedly used the first four lines of 'Mary, Mary, Quite Contrary' in his much-covered blues standard 'Walking The Dog':

> Mary, Mary quite contrary
> How does your garden grow?
> With silver bells and cockle shells
> And pretty maids all in a row.

Incredibly, when The Rolling Stones covered the song, Mick Jagger managed to give the rather twee nursery rhyme a cutting edge!

Goldilocks and the three bears appeared alongside Little Boy Blue in 'Jack In The Box', a Goodman/Ray/Keith collaboration that provided The Moments with a Top Ten British hit in 1977. This wasn't the first successful outing for the boy who was advised to blow his horn because "the sheep's in the meadow, the cow's in the corn"; he had also appeared in the title of Billy Vaughn's 1956 US hit, and came up trumps again three years later for Huelyn Duvall.

The penniless Simple Simon, who met the distrusting pieman on his way to the fair, had new life breathed into him in the 1910 Fruitgum Co's 1968 transatlantic Top Ten hit 'Simon Says'.

The lengthy poem 'The House That Jack Built', which adds a line to each of its twelve verses, lent its title to Alan Price's self-penned UK hit of 1967, Aretha Franklin's US hit a year later and Tracie's 1983 Top Ten British success.

Juvenile invocations of precipitation also crop up in modern popular song, via numbers such as Bruce Ruffin's 1971 Top 20 hit 'Rain', which includes the chant:

> It's raining, it's pouring,
> The old man is snoring.

Bobby Vee's 'Please Don't Ask About Barbara', written by Buchanan and Jack Keller, substitutes "tears" for "rain" in the lines:

> Rain, rain, go away,
> Come again another day.

The first line of the old ditty became the title of a 1962 hit, when writers Shayne and Regney used it as the chorus on what became a Top 20 hit in the US for Bobby Vinton.

The children's song 'Billy Boy' was adapted by J Courville, who retained the theme found in the old verses, although he reversed the role of the characters. The original tells of a girl being courted who is too young to leave her mother, while in the 1960 hit Johnny Preston claims that he is too young to sever his maternal ties.

In 1833, Charles Sloman put words to an existing melody to create the children's favourite 'Pop Goes The Weasel', which remains in many a musical repertoire to this day, thanks in part to Anthony Newley's success with his 1961 version, for which he retained the original lyric. A year earlier, Newley had had even more success with his interpretation of the old children's song 'Strawberry Fair', which he introduced with the old street cry "Strawberries, ripe strawberries."

Another street cry had a substantial amount of radio play in 1968, when The World Of Oz released their self-penned song 'The Muffin Man'. Harry King's 'The Muffin Man' was written in 1889, and was popularised at the time by comedian Dan Leno, who also performed a lot of King's other material.

The commercial possibilities in children's songs featuring colours have also been explored thoroughly. The Merseybeats, The Fleetwoods and Marillion, amongst others, have employed versions of 'Lavender Blue':

> Lavender blue, dilly, dilly,
> Lavender green.
> When you are king, dilly, dilly,
> I shall be queen.

Meanwhile, songwriters Evans and Byron made the old rhyme 'Roses Are Red' the chorus for their song of the same name, which became a transatlantic hit for Bobby Vinton in 1962 prior to his release 'Rain, Rain, Go Away'.

Time-old Robin Hood verses, which began

> Robin Hood, Robin Hood,
> Is in the mickle wood.

became the basis for 1956 success for both Dick James and Gary Miller: 'Robin Hood', the theme for the top-rated TV series of the same name. The man in Lincoln green was revisited in 1979, when Sham 69's writers Jimmy Pursey and Dave Parsons included the line "Robin Hood, Robin Hood, here we are again" in their Top Ten hit 'Hersham Boys'. (The TV series *Robin Hood* was made at Nettlefold Studios in Walton-On-Thames, Hersham's neighbouring town.

When creating a follow-up single for The Searchers' 'Sweets For My Sweet', Tony Hatch opted for the response to a familiar nursery rhyme question: what are little girls made of? This provided the title and lyrical springboard for the group's second big success, 'Sugar And Spice'. Alma Cogan underlined the pro-female sentiment of the same rhyme with 'Snakes, Snails And Puppy-Dog Tails', a variation on what little boys were made of, according to the first verse of the old chant.

The Beach Boys revisited the US children's song 'Ten Little Indians' on their debut album, while Jerry Leiber and Mike Stoller gave 'This Little Piggy' a more adult lyric as 'I'm A Hog For You, Baby', and achieved success for The Coasters, whose version spawned subsequent covers by several British artists, including Screaming Lord Sutch.

'Sing A Song Of Sixpence' isn't exactly over-used in popular songs, but it found its way into a 1967 hit for Chris Farlowe, written by Mike D'Abo, entitled 'Handbags And Gladrags', while the tongue-twisting 'Peter Piper Picked A Peck Of Pickled Pepper' – a most unlikely scenario – found its way into Shirley Ellis' 1965 single 'The Puzzle Song'.

In 1974, The Rockin' Berries decided to go the whole hog and released 'Rock-A-Bye Nursery Rhyme', which parodied artists such as Roxy Music, The Rubettes, Steve Harley, The Sweet and Status Quo, with versions of 'Higgledy Piggledy, My Black Hen', 'Little Miss Muffett', 'Ring-A-Ring Of Roses', 'Little Jack Horner' and 'Humpty Dumpty'.

8 I Write The Songs (US)

There are many great songwriters who tread a lone path when it comes to creating songs, but let's take a look at five mainstream pop writers. One was influenced by classical music, another by country, a third by R&B, a fourth by jazz, and a fifth who was enamoured of the songwriters of the '60s.

Two of the most influential songwriters of the rock 'n' roll era were Chuck Berry and Buddy Holly. Both perfected unique vocal and guitar styles that helped to give their songs their own distinctive character.

Berry, born Charles Berry in San Jose, California, in October 1926, turned to crime in his youth, which led to him serving three years in a reform school, after which he studied to become a hairdresser by day while performing at night.

In 1955, blues singer Muddy Waters introduced Berry to Chess Records, who released his song 'Ida Red', rewritten as 'Maybelline'. The style and sound that came together on that session – which included Willie Dixon on bass, Berry on guitar and vocals, Jerome Green on maracas, Jasper Thomas on drums and Johnnie Johnson on guitar – became the million-dollar blueprint for subsequent Berry records. Led by Chuck's driving guitar rhythm, it was a fusion of up-tempo blues and country rock that married so perfectly that it created a pulsing new sound that appealed to American youth.

Berry's lyrics were rebellious. Not for him the cloying angst of the teenager gazing dewy-eyed at the moon, lovesick and misunderstood; more the kid who couldn't wait to get out of school and get to "the juke joint", or to be riding the Greyhound bus. The object of his love affair was the car or the guitar as much as the girl, and the girls he sang about seemed dangerously young. His lyrics were often arrogant, chauvinistic and to the point. You felt that the relationships that he wrote about were transient and self-gratifying, while the material assets provided more thrills and were longer lasting.

Following his success with 'Maybelline', he scored again with 'Roll Over Beethoven' in 1956, and the song become one of the most covered numbers from the rock 'n' roll period, featuring on The Beatles' second album and in the stage sets of thousands of groups, from then to now. Whenever musicians of any standard or age suddenly find themselves with guitars in hands and staring blankly at each other, not sure what to play, it's a safe bet that someone will kick in with that famous opening guitar riff, and within seconds a voice will be singing:

> I'm gonna write a little letter,
> Gonna mail it to my local DJ.
> It's a rockin' little record
> I want my jockey to play.
> Roll over Beethoven,
> Gotta hear it again today.

1957 brought the Berry classics 'School Day', 'Rock And Roll Music' (covered by The Beatles) and 'Oh Baby Doll', while in 1958 he came up with 'Sweet Little 16' (also a hit for Jerry Lee Lewis), 'Sweet Little Rock 'n' Roller', 'Run Rudolph Run' (later covered by Rolling Stone Keith Richards), 'Reelin' And Rockin'' (a transatlantic hit in 1965 for The Dave Clark Five) and 'Joe Joe Gun', which would be the inspiration behind the name of '60s hit group Jo Jo Gunne. Two major Chuck Berry classics of that year were 'Carol' (which would spawn a brilliant cover by The Rolling Stones soon after their debut single in 1963, with another Berry song, 'Come On') and 'Johnny B Goode', another song much beloved, covered and performed by British groups. However, as UK radio – and therefore the record-buying public – failed to latch onto Berry while he was at his peak in the States, the song was never a British hit for him, although it has charted in the UK on three occasions for such diverse acts as The Jimi Hendrix Experience, Peter Tosh and Judas Priest.

At the tail end of the '50s, Berry came up with 'Almost Grown', 'Let It Rock' and 'Back In The USA', the latter song inspiring Paul McCartney to write The Beatles' song 'Back In The USSR' several years later.

In 1959, things went terribly wrong for Berry when he was convicted for transporting a minor across a state line for immoral purposes, fined $2,000 and sentenced to five years in jail. Although he was freed in

1962, pending a retrail, he was sent down for three years, of which he served two.

Meanwhile in Britain, the rhythm and blues boom created a phenomenal interest in the music of the likes of Chuck Berry, Bo Diddley Willie Dixon, Little Walter, Howlin' Wolf and Muddy Waters, which led to Berry scoring with another spate of highly coverable classics. 1963 and 1964 brought 'No Particular Place To Go', 'You Never Can Tell', 'Nadine (Is It You?)', 'Memphis, Tennessee', 'Come On', 'Our Little Rendezvous' and even a song called 'Brenda Lee'!

Lennon and McCartney were big Chuck Berry fans. As well as featuring their own versions of 'Roll Over Beethoven', 'Words Of Love' and 'Rock 'n' Roll Music' on their mainstream recordings, The Beatles regularly performed other Berry classics like 'Little Queenie' and 'Sweet Little 16' in their early stage set, and others such as 'Memphis, Tennessee', 'Johnny B Goode' and 'Too Much Monkey Business' on the BBC radio show *Pop Go The Beatles*.

During the '60s, Berry continued to play live, record and inspire up-and-coming musicians, and was still turning out classics like 'Tulane' as the '60s turned into the '70s. In 1972 he topped the UK chart with what was possibly the weakest and least typical song he has ever written, 'My Ding-A-Ling'. Moral campaigner Mary Whitehouse attempted to get it banned because of the innuendo in the lyric, but most R&B aficionados would have liked it banned simply because it wasn't classic Chuck Berry.

Berry's life has been a rollercoaster of ups and downs. In 1979, for example, he performed at the White House at the request of President Jimmy Carter, and was later jailed for tax evasion. In 1989, he became one of the first ten people to be inducted into the St Louis "Walk Of Fame", while a suit was filed against him alleging that he had filmed woman without their consent for his own gratification. In the following year, the sinner in Berry was still walking with the saint, when he was inducted into the NARAS Hall Of Fame at the 32nd Grammy Awards while also being busted for the possession of marijuana and child abuse. He was cleared of the latter count but was given a six-month jail sentence for the former. (It's curious to note an interesting social anomaly in collective perception in that, while Berry remains a legendary rock 'n' roll hero around the world, British singer and songwriter Gary Glitter, convicted of similar offences to Berry, is hounded and pursued by the media in every country in which he tries to hide.)

Major To Minor

The definitive version of Berry's most frenetic song, 'Brown-Eyed Handsome Man', was by Buddy Holly.

The songs of Buddy Holly were equally inspirational, although Holly – born Charles Hardin Holley in Lubbock, Texas, in September 1936 – wrote of teenage romance in the role of the boy next door. In his songs, love only whispered it's name, led directly to a life of unparalled bliss, or was a heartache searching for a simple solution.

Buddy's greatest and most durable songs came thick and fast in a short spell that lasted from the summer of 1956 to the first two months of 1959, just prior to his untimely death.

In 1949, while at high school, he teamed up with Bob Montgomery, and the pair worked as "Buddy and Bob", singing and writing songs with a distinctive country feel, which led to them getting their own show on local country radio station K-DAV four years later. In 1955, they enlisted drummer Jerry Allison, and, influenced by the music being made by Elvis Presley, they moved away from country into more mainstream pop. Their experience and musical transition paved the way for them to supporting both Bill Haley And The Comets and Elvis Presley in October of that year, when they were spotted by Nashville agent Eddie Crandall. Crandall instigated a demo session for Holly and co, and although Decca liked Holly they didn't appear to want Montgomery. Bob stood down, in gentlemanly manner, to allow Buddy to seize the opportunity of stardom, although he too would continue to be a successful songwriter and record company executive. Holly brought in guitarist Sonny Curtis and bassist Don Guess to play alongside Allison and himself, the line-up recording 'Blue Days, Black Nights', which was to become Holly's first single release with Decca.

As Holly's writing output increased, records were released as either Buddy Holly or The Crickets in order to get two bites at the chart, but the lead vocals were always Holly, whose style and voice were so distinctive that songs that he didn't personally write are totally synonymous with his name.

Dissatisfied with Decca, he signed to Brunswick after striking up a good working relationship with Clovis writer/producer/studio-owner Norman Petty. Retaining Allison but bringing in new bass player Joe B Mauldin and rhythm guitarist Niki Sullivan, Holly went on to record the definitive version of his song 'That'll Be The Day', which is still regarded as a classic in the new millenium. Inspired by a line spoken in the film *The*

Searchers, the song was co-written by Holly and Allison and topped the US chart in the summer of 1957. It opened the floodgates for a stream of million-sellers and big hits on both sides of the Atlantic, most of which were written or co-written by Holly and became targets for acts in search of good songs to record. The Beatles covered Holly's 'Words Of Love', and also featured that song and his 'Crying Waiting Hoping' on their radio show *Pop Go The Beatles*.

Just as Buddy Holly and Chuck Berry had influenced the young Lennon and McCartney, they were also encouraging their own fans to appreciate songs that they might otherwise have ignored. How many songwriters would have given their eye teeth to have written 'Maybe Baby', 'Listen To Me', 'Think It Over', 'It's So Easy', 'Wishing', or 'Learning The Game'? The two I always wished that I'd written were 'What To Do' and 'That's What They Say', just two more great pop songs from the Holly canon.

His songs have spawned countless covers, some of the best-known being 'Well All Right' (Blind Faith), 'Every Day' (Don McLean), 'Not Fade Away' (The Rolling Stones), 'Heartbeat' (Nick Berry), 'True Love Ways' (Cliff Richard/Peter And Gordon/David Essex And Catherine Zeta Jones), 'Stay Close To Me' (Mike Berry), 'That'll Be The Day' (The Everly Brothers) and 'Peggy Sue' (The Beach Boys).

This is just the tip of the iceberg. Other artists that have turned to Holly songs include The Searchers, Dave Berry, Bo Diddley and The Hollies. Other as-yet-unmentioned material from the pen of Holly includes 'Peggy Sue Got Married', 'That Makes It Tough', 'Tell Me How', 'You're The One', 'Look At Me' and 'Love's Made A Fool Of You'. There were also many songs that he didn't write but on which he put his own stamp in such a way that they are percieved as being Holly songs. These include 'Oh Boy!', 'Rave On', 'It Doesn't Matter Anymore', 'Raining In My Heart' and 'I'm Gonna Love You Too'.

Holly died in a plane crash on 2 February 1959, along with fellow singers Ritchie Valens and The Big Bopper, leaving behind a stunning musical legacy made more incredible for having been amassed in such a short amount of time. His passing has been best immortalised in song by Geoff Goddard's 'Tribute To Buddy Holly' and Don McLean's 'American Pie'.

John D Loudermilk, born in Durham, North Carolina, in March 1934, is a unique writer who doesn't appear to fit into any pigeonhole. He seemed as much at home penning songs that encompassed American folklore – such as 'Indian Reservation' and 'This Little Bird' – as he did idealising teenage love in 'Angela Jones' or angst in 'Then You Can Tell Me Goodbye'. He could equally turn his hand to a song about fishing ('Google Eye'), a young and untimely death ('Ebony Eyes') or nostalgia, which he wove into the homespun lyrics of his own 1968 single 'Sidewalks'. Love, in his songs, was always wholesome. There was love by implication, teenage ecstasy and innate sadness, all with marriage as the idealised end product. His songs have been recorded by a wide range of artists, from Chet Atkins to Lonnie Donegan, Anne Murray to Gram Parsons, The Everly Brothers to Eddie Cochran and Bobby Vee to George Hamilton IV.

His parents were hit hard by the Depression, which left more than 14 million Americans out of work and forced Roosevelt to reorganise the country. The Loudermilks' plight was eased thanks to the assistance of the Salvation Army, for whose band the young John began playing the bass drum and trombone. In fact, during the early '40s he was so enthusiastic that he made his own ukelele and started to play and sing in church, and by the age of ten had made his TV debut, appearing with Tex Ritter, "the singing cowboy".

The young Loudermilk was heavily influenced by R&B and *The Grand Ole Opry*, and a particular favourite of his was Eddy Arnold, "the Tennessee plowboy', who would record Loudermilk's 'Then You Can Tell Me Goodbye' 20 years later. As a boy, music and songs were an all-consuming passion for him, so it was fortunate that his parents – who were older than those of most of his contemporaries – allowed him to hang out with local musicians. By the time he was twelve, he hosted a daily radio programme as Johnny Dee and had mastered even more instruments, including the fiddle and the double bass.

The idea of becoming a songwriter appealed increasingly to Loudermilk. "I'd take a favourite song, write new words to it and then put a new melody to those words, so I had an entirely new song. By the time rock 'n' roll came along, my musical direction had been formed. As well as country and R&B, I was a great fan of The Four Freshmen, whose harmonies become another influence."

In 1956, he worked as a commercial artist, designing and painting sets for WTVD in Durham. During this time, his song 'A Rose And A Baby Ruth' was recorded by George Hamilton IV and went on to become a Top

I Write The Songs (US)

Ten hit in the States. In the following year, both Loudermilk and Eddie Cochran had American hits with his new song, 'Sittin' In The Balcony'. "I'd made quite a bit of money out of 'A Rose And A Baby Ruth', so I was able to buy my parents a house and buy myself the time to go to college. I had a little band called Johnny Dee And The Melodees, and we were doing a daily TV show, and I was still writing. During my time at the University Of North Carolina, I attended chapel every day and sat up in the balcony, which is where I got the inspiration for 'Sittin' In The Balcony'. Simple as that. I wrote it sitting in the balcony during chapel."

He later moved to Nashville, where he planned to work in his father-in-law's hardware store so that he would have a job to fall back on if a career in music failed to materialise.

He needn't have worried, his songs proved to be in great demand. In 1959, Stonewall Jackson's version of 'Waterloo' – influenced by the sound of the Salvation Army bass drum and with a melody like an old Victorian hymn – soared into the Top Ten, and Loudermilk was on his way to becoming one of Nashville's most sought-after songwriters. After 'Sittin' In The Balcony' appeared in 1957, he recorded and released many self-penned singles in the early '60s, including US hits 'Language Of Love' (also a hit in Britain), 'Thou Shalt Not Steal', 'Callin' Dr Casey' and 'Road Hog'. In 1962, he also released his version of 'Angela Jones', which had been a hit in 1960 in America for Johnny Ferguson and in Britain for Michael Cox. "Our family moved from North Carolina to Washington, DC, where we stayed for a year. While I was there I took a course in ballroom dancing to try to become a teacher, and there was a girl on the course with me called Angela Jones. We'd often be locked in a room together for hours on end, just practising, but I ended up having a little fling with her, and wrote a song using her name as the title. Early in my career, I saw the potential in capturing the pathos of the teenage love experience, and tried to write for kids. It was one of the first songs I ever recorded, but I didn't find out what she thought about it as I never saw her again from that day to this."

Several of his "teenage love experience" songs – 'James', 'Norman' and 'Sad Movies' – were Top Twenty hits in the States for Sue Thompson, with British covers by Carole Deene, while Bobby Vee recorded 'Stayin' In' and The Everly Brothers released 'Ebony Eyes', recorded in Nashville on 1 November 1960 as part of a double A-side, along with Sonny Curtis' 'Walk Right Back'.

Major To Minor

The tragic lyric of 'Ebony Eyes' ends with the "relatives and friends" of those on board the doomed flight 1203 being invited to report to the chapel across the street. The news clearly wasn't going to be good, but Loudermilk doesn't smack us in the face with the final grisly *dénouement* but instead increases the poignancy by leaving the obvious unsaid. He painted a very real picture with these lines:

> I watched the beacon light from the control tower
> As it whipped through the dark ebony skies,
> As if it were searching for my ebony eyes.

The song wasn't based on a real incident, although in the States many people believed that it was, as two aeroplanes were involved in an horrific mid-air collision over Brooklyn on the day after the record was released. Everybody imagined that it had been put out because of the accident. Nevertheless, both sides of the single reached the US Top Ten, and the song made Number One in Britain.

Seven years later, Don and Phil Everly recorded another Loudermilk classic, 'It's My Time'. The inspiration for this song came from the same passage in the book of Ecclesiastes from The Bible (that there is a time for everything and everything has it's season), as it did for The Byrds' song 'Turn! Turn! Turn! (For Everything There Is A Season)'. In Loudermilk's song, it's time to cry.

One of his best-known songs was the atmospheric '(The Lament Of The Cherokee) Reservation Indian', a US Top 20 hit for Don Fardon in 1968 and a Top Three record in Britain two years later. Surrey R&B outfit The Nashville Teens – who seemed to have a penchant for Loudermilk songs – also recorded the number, having already had success with John D's biographical 'Tobacco Road', 'This Little Bird' and 'Google Eye'. In 1971, Paul Revere And The Raiders topped both The Teens' and Fardon's versions by taking their offering to Number One in the States.

In 1999, a grateful Cherokee nation presented Loudermilk with their medal of honour, and many were keen to hear the story of the song's inspiration from the horse's mouth. One such person was American disc jockey Casey Kasem, who in an interview in 1980 asked John D Loudermilk about the song. John told him this story:

> I was going from Nashville to Durham, North Carolina, when I got stuck in a snowstorm on top of a mountain. I couldn't do anything but sit tight until it cleared. After two or three hours I heard a knock on the car window, and there were several Red Indians, all wearing coloured paint on their faces. Seeing that I was stuck, they took me down the mountain path to the place where they had a cave complete with decorations and everything, where I learned that their leader was a Cherokee called Bloody Bear Tooth. After a while, when the conditions improved, they escorted me back to my car. Back in Nashville, I got a letter from Bloody Bear Tooth informing me that they were Cherokee terrorists, and that the only reason they let me live was so I could write a song about their plight.

He repeated this story for 20 years, until a TV programme wanted him to tell it again for a show that they were making, and he was forced to come clean and admit that he'd made up the story. When the Cherokees presented him with his medal, he told them the story, which the tribe found highly amusing.

His plaintive story of a little bird that was born on the wind and lived its life entirely in the air was inspired by a film that apparently featured such a creature. The bird is supposed to come to earth only when it is time for it to die. The song became a transatlantic hit for Marianne Faithfull and a British hit for The Nashville Teens, enjoying a new lease of life 35 years later on when it featured on an album in the States by Jewel. Apparently, when she was a child, her mother used to sing it to her as a lullaby.

'Tobacco Road' was Loudermilk's only biographical song, but he was keen to show the pathos and desperation of the poor kids in the south who grew up with nothing but wanting to be something. He admits that "I can see it now better than when I wrote it. I'm very proud of that song."

There are also many other diverse classics in Loudermilk's canon, such as the positively catatonic 'Break My Mind', 'Talk Back Trembling Lips' and 'Then You Can Tell Me Goodbye', a Number One country song and Dick Clark's favourite, and a hit on both sides of the Atlantic in 1967.

Like Loudermilk, many other songwriters who released their own material had the potential to be successful recording artists in their own right but seemed content to assume a predominantly writing role, feeling that, if they had hits as well, then that would be a bonus. Otis Blackwell, born in Brooklyn, New York, in 1931, certainly had the voice to make it as a singer, winning a talent contest at Harlem's Apollo Theatre, which led to him signing a contract with Joe Davis' label. Influenced by Chuck Willis and Tex Ritter, like Loudermilk, his first release was his own song 'Daddy Rolling Stone', released in 1953, a powerful song that was a hit in Jamaica for Derek Martin and was later covered by The Who. During the mid '50s, he also recorded for RCA and Groove before deciding to concentrate on writing songs for other artists.

His first real success as a writer came in 1956, when Little Willie John took his 'Fever' to Number One in the US R&B chart. The song was a hit all over again two years later for Peggy Lee, and proved to be a durable classic when it was also a hit for Britain's Helen Shapiro and Stateside group The McCoys. It's said that Little Willie John continued to take the credit for writing the song, although on both of these versions the number is credited to Davenport and Cooley, who are apparently neither the blues singer Cow Cow Davenport nor C&W performer Spade Cooley.

Elvis Presley notched up his fifth and sixth gold discs with two songs that came out in the States as a double A-side in 1956, Jerry Leiber and Mike Stoller's 'Hound Dog' on one side and Blackwell's 'Don't Be Cruel' on the other.

On Christmas Eve 1955, Blackwell had sold six of his songs for $25 each, in a batch which included 'Don't Be Cruel', which he'd demo'd himself on piano, using a cardboard box as a drum. The record spent eleven weeks at Number One in America, and Presley recorded another of his songs in the following year. 'All Shook Up' was first recorded by Dave Hill for the Aladdin label, although Presley's version was later more famous. The singer adopted many of the Blackwell's vocal mannerisms as they were presented on the demo, and Mort Shuman's writing partner Doc Pomus attested that "There was an originality of phrasing and a strange little tense passion in Otis' voice."

'All Shook Up' was the most successful record of 1957, staying at Number One in the States for eight weeks and at Number One in Britain for seven, but Blackwell found that he had to share the writing credits with Elvis. It would be understandable for a songwriter to be bitter at an artist not only copying his style but also helping themselves to 50 per cent of a song that they had no hand in writing. Blackwell, however, remains suitably pragmatic about the situation: "People say 'He took a slice of your life and made millions.' Well, I'm happy someone took it, because I wasn't making anything with it. I'm happy as hell that he took my songs." In Presley's defence, as soon as he realised that he was being credited with songs that he didn't write, he insisted that the practice was stopped.

Among the other classic pop tunes that flowed from Blackwell's pen were 'Just Keep It Up', a Top 20 US hit for Dee Clark in 1959; Jimmy Jones' chart-topping 'Handy Man'; and 'Nine Times Out Of Ten', a British hit for Cliff Richard and covered in the States by Ral Donner.

After seeing the wild-haired Jerry Lee Lewis pounding the piano on *The Steve Allen Show*, Blackwell then offered the Louisiana pianist a song he'd written called 'Great Balls Of Fire.' With his seemingly characteristic egalitarian approach, Blackwell bought the title – which cost him 50 per cent of the royalties – from New York songwriter Jack Hammer, a title that Hammer had almost certainly picked up from the 1939 film *Gone With The Wind*, in which Vivien Leigh uses the phrase several times.

When it was announced that the new rock 'n' roll film *Disc Jockey Jamboree* was being produced, boss of Sun Records Sam Phillips got his singers Jerry Lee Lewis and Carl Perkins on board, with Lewis receiving top billing. Perkins had originally turned down 'Great Balls Of Fire', but Lewis was happy to record it, denying that its lyrics were near the knuckle. "They said 'Great Balls of Fire' was pure sex. Well, it is; it's sex in my way, and sex in my way is not dirty, it's pure…I never accepted that it was a vulgar record." The song sold an incredible one million copies in just ten days, causing Sam Phillips to proclaim, "How are you going to improve on perfection?…It's just a classic."

Lewis claims that Phillips never paid him any money for his recording of another Otis Blackwell song, 'Breathless', although the song sold in excess of three million copies. It was also the song that brought the 17-year-old Cliff Richard to the attention of record producer Norrie Paramor, after the would-be singer recorded it at a small studio in London's Oxford Street, along with Lloyd Price's 'Lawdy Miss Clawdy', for just £10.

In 1961, Jerry Lee Lewis again recorded material from the Otis Blackwell songbook when he waxed 'Livin' Lovin' Wreck' after emerging from a period of seclusion. Following this, Blackwell moved more into R&B, recording for Atlantic, MGM and Epic. He is now semi-retired, although he recorded his own tribute to Presley, 'The Number One King Of Rock 'n' Roll', and was in the process of writing a musical about him when the singer died.

It's interesting how some songwriters later reject songs that they don't feel have travelled well. Their work becomes an embarrassment to them, although the public still love the songs in question and can't understand the artists' unwillingness to perform them. The runts of the litter for Paul Simon are radio favourite 'I Am A Rock' and the wonderfully haunting 'The Dangling Conversation', two songs that he wishes that he'd never written. After completing 'I Am A Rock', he chastised himself, saying, "Oh man, I can't be this sick." On the other hand, he feels that '59th Street Bridge Song' is still worthy of gracing the Paul Simon canon.

> I came back from England to the United States in December of 1965. 'Sound Of Silence' had become a big hit, and when I returned I had to make the transition from being relatively unknown in England to being sort of semi-famous over here. I didn't adjust well. It was always slightly embarrassing to me, so I used to think all my sweets were gone. Good times gone, left over in England. All the songs I was writing were very down-type songs; nothing happy...I started to come out of it. I started to get in a good mood...I don't know why. So here I am, getting into this pleasant frame of mind, and I was coming home one morning about six o'clock...coming over the 59th Street Bridge in New York...and what a great day it was, a really good one...So I started writing a song which became the '59th Street Bridge Song', or 'Feelin' Groovy'.

Simon was born in Newark, New Jersey, in November 1941, and later sang at parties and social events and eventually professionally with his childhood friend, Art Garfunkel. Simon was always the writer, but Garfunkel's pure, clear voice contributed to many of the songs that they recorded as Simon And Garfunkel.

Starting out as the duo Tom And Jerry, named after the cartoon cat and mouse, they had a small hit with 'Hey Schoolgirl', which was very much in The Everly Brothers mould. Their debut album as Simon And Garfunkel was the 1964 album *Wednesday Morning 3am*, the first of a string of great LPs issued by the pair. Even as they were becoming successful, Simon toured the UK folk clubs as a solo act.

There's a plaque on Widnes railway station that proclaims that Paul Simon wrote 'Homeward Bound' there while waiting for a train. The inspiration, though, had its roots in Liverpool. "That was written in Liverpool, while I was travelling. What I like about it is that it has a very clear memory of Liverpool station and the streets of Liverpool, and the club I played at, and me at the age of 22. It's like a snapshot of a long time ago...If you know Widnes then you'll understand how I was desperately trying to get back to London as quickly as possible. 'Homeward Bound' came out of that feeling."

The duo broke America in a big way in 1966, with five Paul Simon songs charting in the States – 'The Sound Of Silence' (Number One), 'I Am A Rock' (Number Two), 'Homeward Bound' (Number Five), 'A Hazy Shade Of Winter' (Number 13) and 'The Dangling Conversation' (Number 25) – and 'Homeward Bound' and 'I Am A Rock' finding success in Britain.

In the same year, Irish trio The Bachelors took 'Sound Of Silence' to Number Three in Britain, while The Quiet Five crept into the bottom of the charts with their version of the song. It was written after the assassination of President John F Kennedy, an incident that also led to Bobby Hebb writing 'Sunny' and Brian Wilson and Mike Love writing 'Warmth Of The Sun' for The Beach Boys.

'A Hazy Shade Of Winter' would have to wait another 22 years to be a hit in Britain, courtesy of American girl group The Bangles. Simon And Garfunkel's version went into the Top 30 three years later.

In 1968, Simon supplied the songs for the Dustin Hoffman film *The Graduate*, and the main numbers – 'Mrs Robinson' and 'Scarborough Fair' – became extremely successful on both sides of the Atlantic, the former going to the top of the US chart.

For some, though, his finest hour as a composer was yet to come. In 1969, he put together what was to become one of the most popular albums in the history of music, *Bridge Over Troubled Water*. It spawned several hit singles, and the title track spent three weeks at Number One in Britain and six weeks at the top in America.

When Paul Simon's royalty cheques roll in, it's a fair bet that 'Bridge Over Troubled Water' is probably the song with the most zeros attached. It has remained firmly in the Top Ten of most popular music polls since its release over 30 years ago. The album of the same name topped the US chart for ten weeks and the UK chart for 35, selling millions of units in the process. During one five-week spell in the States, the single and album topped their respective charts for five weeks simultaneously before going on to win three Grammy Awards.

Simon recalled the birthplace of the song: "We were in California. We were all renting this house. Me and Artie and Peggy were living in this house with a bunch of other people during the summer." The house was in Blue Jay Way, which had been immortalised in a song by George Harrison on The Beatles' *Magical Mystery Tour* EP and was now the thoroughfare that would spawn 'Bridge Over Troubled Water'. Simon wrote it on his guitar, in the key of G, but needed it transposed to the key of E flat, and was keen to use gospel piano on it. The gospel idea came from having been inspired by a line from The Dixie Hummingbirds: "I'll be a bridge over deep water, if you trust in my name."

It took four days to get the piano part right, after which bassist Joe Osborn added two bass parts, one high and one low, and vibes were introduced during the second verse, in Simon's words "to make the thing ring a bit. Then we put the drum on, and we recorded the drum in an echo chamber…We did it with tape-reverb; that made the drum part sound different from what it actually was…Then we gave it out to have a string part written."

It was Art Garfunkel's suggestion to add a third verse, but Simon felt that it's glaringly obvious that this was added later, complaining that "It just doesn't sound like the first two verses…It was about Peggy, whom I was living with at the time. 'Sail on silver girl…Your time has come to shine' was half a joke, because she was upset one day when she found two or three grey hairs on her head!"

Simon summed up one of popular music's finest moments thus: "I think 'Bridge Over Troubled Water' was a very good song, and I think Artie sang it beautifully…He sang it white, but soulful. I don't feel that 'Bridge Over Troubled Water' even belongs to me…Walking down the street and having somebody sing a song of yours…that, I think, is the best feeling for a songwriter."

One of the most covered songs on the album, and a Top Ten US hit for Simon And Garfunkel, was 'Cecilia', which could almost have been a blueprint for some of his later solo material. "Cecilia was made in a living room on a Sony. We were all pounding away and playing things, so I said 'Let's make a record out of that.' So we copied it and extended it double the amount…so we now have three minutes of track…Now I pick up the guitar…The lyrics were virtually the first lines…'You've broken my heart, I'm down on my knees…' It was like a little piece of magical fluff."

Paul Simon's writing career may have reached a high point, but his writing continued unabated, with songs written in the '60s still being fresh enough to chart in the following decade. The timeless and dreamlike 'For Emily, Whenever I May Find Her', and the highly evocative 'America', had a chart renaissance during 1972, the year in which Simon began to have solo hits. By this time, his writing had become slightly raunchier and the productions gutsier. 'Mother And Child Reunion', with a title influenced by the name of a chicken-and-egg sandwich, and 'Me And Julio Down By The Schoolyard' paved the way for another stream of hit songs.

During the '70s, he wrote and had hits with a number of other songs, such as 'Take Me To The Mardi Gras', 'Loves Me Like A Rock', '50 Ways To Leave Your Lover' and 'Slip Slidin' Away', while the '80s brought numbers such as 'You Can Call Me Al' and 'The Boy In The Bubble'.

The grandson of a methodist minister, Will Jennings was born in Kilgore, Texas in June 1944, his father working for the Sun Oil Company there as a roughneck and roustabout. Jennings grew up in an oil company house just off Highway 31, between Tyler and Kilgore, and his family moved to another company house between Tyler and Overton when Will was seven or eight years old. While in junior high and high school, he was encouraged by the resident band directors to take up baritone horn and trombone, and continued to play them when he moved on to Tyler Junior College in 1961. He had already started writing songs of a fashion as a boy: "I wrote my first quatrain during a thunderstorm as I looked out of the high windows of Mrs Rozell's fourth-grade classroom at Chapel Hill and remember to this day the wonder that I felt when I rhymed the first and third and second and fourth lines and said something about the storm beating against the windows."

Gravitating to musical people around him, Will became interested in a wide variety of music, including classical, jazz, country, rhythm and blues and rock 'n' roll. He was also inspired and influenced linguistically by one of the Tyler Junior College teachers, Jerry Walsh, a Jesuit-educated Swedish-Russian polyglot. Oil money meant that the college could afford the best teachers, and Walsh was certainly one of them, inspiring the young Jennings with his own passion for the written and spoken language. "He had a dazzling style in the classroom...he started me in French and German, which I continued with at the University Of Texas at Austin and

Stephen F Austin University at Nacogdoches, Texas...Jerry gave me a love of language and an insight into it that has influenced my life...I knew that writing and music meant a lot to me, but I also knew that I had to figure out a way to make a living." He took a summer job to raise money for his university studies, working as a roustabout for the Sun Oil Company, as his father had done.

Jennings married his girlfriend Carole Thurman in 1965, got his MA two years later and taught at Eau Claire State University for three years before dropping out and heading off to Nashville. Whilst at Eau Claire, he formed a band, gigged in nightclubs and really started to write poetry and songs. In Nashville, he grew to know Kentucky guitarist/producer/songwriter Troy Seals, the cousin of Dan Seals, who would later become half of the duo England Dan And John Ford Coley. Seals had a good track record, having worked with many great artists, and through him Jennings got to know his musician backers, David Briggs and Norbert Putnam, and was able to hang out at their studio, Quadrophonic.

Seals helped Will with his songwriting, and this collaboration paid off when five of their songs were recorded by Dobie Gray, after mentor Williams came to record Gray at the studio. Jennings also got to co-write 'Feelin's', a US country Number One in 1975 for Conway Twitty and Loretta Lynn.

He subsequently moved to Los Angeles and signed a publishing deal with Irving/Almo Music, headed by Lance Freed, the son of pioneering rock 'n' roll disc jockey Alan Freed. Freed put him together with English composer Richard Kerr, the two writing together on and off for the next few years, penning such hit songs as 'Somewhere In The Night', 'I'll Never Love This Way Again' and 'Looks Like We Made It'. The two also collaborated on many other songs, such as 'I Can't Afford That Feeling Anymore'; Dionne Warwick's 'No Night So Long'; 'You Make Feel Me Crying', recorded by Roy Orbison and featured in the film *The End Of Violence*; and 'Blue Skies Forever', recorded by Frankie Miller, from the film *All The Right Moves*.

When Chuck Kaye – the son of legendary music publisher Lester Sill – took over the publishing company, he put Jennings with Joe Sample, the two of them writing The Crusaders' hit 'Street Life' as well as a stack of material for BB King, including 'Better Not Look Down' and 'The Blues Come Over Me'.

Their second album for King, *Take It Home*, brought them to the attention of Lionel Conway, who ran Island Music.

> They had an artist named Steve Winwood who had been in The Spencer Davis Group and Traffic and had started a solo career and had a second album that he was having trouble getting finished...They invited me to go to England to meet with him, which I did, and we wrote his comeback hit, 'While You See A Chance', and three other songs for the 1981 album Arc Of A Diver. A year later, we wrote all the songs on the *Talking Back To The Night* album, including 'Valerie'. The third album Steve and I wrote together, in 1984, was the biggest and best of all, Back In The High Life, with three hits, 'Higher Love', 'Back In The High Life Again' and 'The Finer Things'. We got a Grammy nomination for 'Higher Love', and Steve and co-producer Russ Titelman won Grammys for Album Of The Year and Record Of The Year for 'Higher Love'.

The hits continued on the fourth album, *Roll With It*, but Will Jennings himself admits that, by the fifth album, *Refugees Of The Heart*, "the boom was over". During the period in which he wrote with Winwood, Will was asked to write a song for the 1982 film *An Officer And A Gentleman*, starring Richard Gere and Debra Winger. He extracted various bits and pieces out of the film score, put together a melody from them, wrote a lyric and came up with the title 'Up Where We Belong'. The song went to Number One around the world and won Jennings and composers Jack Nitzche and Buffy Sainte-Marie Golden Globe and Oscar Awards for Best Film Song Of 1982.

During the '80s and '90s, Jennings was one of the most successful working songwriters, collaborating with writers such as Burt Bacharach, Roy Orbison, JD Souther, Frankie Miller, Simon Climie, Rodney Crowell and Peter Wolf. With Eric Clapton he wrote the Grammy Award-winning 'Tears In Heaven', and with James Horner wrote the theme song for the award-winning movie *Titanic*, Céline Dion's 'My Heart Will Go On'. That song went to Number One in the States and Britain and sold over a million copies in a relatively short space of time. Jennings has also had his songs recorded by dozens of other artists, including Johnny Cash, Bob Luman, Aaron Neville, Cilla Black, Diana Ross, Bill Withers, Placido Domingo,

Vera Lynn, Barry Manilow, Henry Mancini, Carly Simon, Dusty Springfield and The Bellamy Brothers.

The most successful independent songwriter operating in the US today is Diane Warren, who was born in 1956 in Van Nuys, California, and a confirmed pop music fan from an early age: "I grew up listening to Top 40 radio...I liked listening to my older sisters' records...people like Buddy Holly and The Beatles. But believe it or not, I was more fascinated by the songwriters Carole King, Leiber and Stoller and Burt Bacharach. Those were my idols." She grew up in the Valley, a suburb of California, and began writing as a child after her father, an insurance salesman, bought her a guitar. Despite the fact that he took her to various music publishers, she didn't begin to have any success until she was 24. In the last 20 years, however, she has had over 75 Top Ten hits and 55 songs in films. Her first step on that road was taken in 1983, when she was taken on as a staff writer by Laura Branigan's producer, Jack White. White asked her to write some English lyrics to a French song that he was keen on, and Warren produced 'Solitaire' in 24 hours.

She continued her slow but steady rise as a solo songwriter when she came up with DeBarge's big hit 'Rhythm Of The Night': "I've been writing by myself ever since I started out...It allows me to go within and live the song. It's a very intimate act, a vulnerable process, but it results in truer music and is so much more fulfilling to me."

In 1985, she formed her own publishing company, Realsongs. By this time, her compositions were being picked up by more and more artists, including Chicago, Milli Vanilli, Bad English, Taylor Dayne and Barbra Streisand. Starship had enormous success with her song 'Nothing's Gonna Stop Us Now', and Belinda Carlisle had a big hit with 'I Get Weak'.

Writing in her Hollywood office from 8.30am to 8.30pm every day whilst wearing her lucky socks, she pounded out hits for even more major artists, such as Whitney Houston, Ricky Martin, Tina Turner, Mariah Carey, Britney Spears and Aretha Franklin. Toni Braxton enjoyed massive success with Warren's 'Un-Break My Heart', while LeAnn Rimes' version of 'How Do I Live' stayed on the US chart for over 70 weeks – the longest run in the history of the *Billboard* chart – and went triple platinum. The number was first performed by Trisha Yearwood, and Warren wrote it for the Disney movie *Con Air*. The song won a Grammy for Yearwood, and received two Grammy nominations and an Oscar nomination.

I Write The Songs (US)

Trisha Yearwood loves the feel of Warren's songs. "Diane's songs appeal because she finds universal themes, everybody loves and loses. At the end of our lives, the people who have loved and who have loved us are what we will remember. Diane has tapped into this level of emotion."

Many artists want their material to be personal to them and are loath to cover a song if it's recently been a hit for another singer. Diane Warren's songs often prove the exception to this rule, with 'Don't Turn Around' being a prime example. This number has been covered by eight artists within a reasonably short period of time, including Aswad, Tina Turner and Ace Of Base.

Record executive David Geffen is a great admirer of her work: "There's a really good reason Diane is the most successful songwriter of the last decade. Her songs not only move us melodically; they also manage to capture the feelings and emotions that all of us experience during our lives, whether we're falling in or out of love, looking for inspiration, or celebrating life."

Songs for films became another creative stream. Diane wrote for many movies, including *Ghostbusters, James Bond: Licensed To Kill, White Men Can't Jump, The Golden Child, Neverending Story III* and *Armageddon*, the latter featuring 'I Don't Want To Miss A Thing', a monster hit in 1998 for Aerosmith and a country Number One for Mark Chestnutt. She also penned the title track for the film *Music Of My Heart*, the Oscar-nominated song being performed by N'Sync and Gloria Estefan. A multiple Academy Award winner and Golden Globe nominee, Warren added a Grammy to her trophies with 'Because You Loved Me', sung by Céline Dion, from the film *Up Close And Personal*. In 1999 alone, she wrote seven songs for seven motion pictures.

To help young songwriters, she set up the Diane Warren Foundation, working in tandem with ASCAP and VH1 to create a programme called 'Music In Schools', through which the Foundation provides folios, sheet music, band arrangements and method books for over 400 schools.

Not remotely complacent about her achievements, she still feels that she has to prove herself, and that drives her to keep putting in twelve-hour days. "I'm still so hungry to create…to succeed…to perfect my songwriting. I love the process…it's as though there is no finish line." The hunger and drive is understandable. While singers have the adulation and public acclaim that goes with their success, songwriters – whose names and faces remain unknown to the general public – continually feel that they have something to prove, and as such strive for a recognition that they may not achieve during their own lifetime.

9 I Write The Songs (UK)

Here come a clutch of British songwriters that started treading the Tin Pan Alley path in the '60s, when record company executives appeared to be more accessible, publishers were keen to find that next hit, good composers and lyricists were very much in demand and artists were desperate for songs in order to keep their career on a high. They wrote together and they wrote separately, but they wrote.

Mitch Murray's first hit song started life as two demonstration records, both recorded at Regent Sound Studios in London's Tin Pan Alley. Murray recorded one version while his friend Barry Mason, a singer but not yet an established songwriter, laid down the other. Barry's was the one that Mitch decided to use to play to people, so Mason invited Murray to accompany him to EMI, along with a few of his songs, where he had an appointment with record producer Ron Richards. Richards liked two of Murray's songs – 'How Do You Do It?' and 'The Beetroot Song' – enough to hang onto them. Mitch had already offered 'How Do You Do It?' to Adam Faith, who had turned it down, but despite that he still felt that it was a hit song, and didn't want to throw it away on an unknown act.

Richards played the two songs to publisher Dick James, with whom he was working quite closely at the time, who organised a meeting with the young writer, feeling that 'The Beetroot Song', especially, had big hit potential. James was starting to become involved as The Beatles publisher at the time, although the group had only had one hit record by then, 'Love Me Do'. The lyrics of the song aren't that impressive if seen on paper – "Love, love me do, you know I'll love you, I'll always be true..." – and so it was mooted that they should record 'How Do You Do It?', although Mitch remembers that the group wasn't that keen:

> The Beatles didn't want to record the song, and their producer, George Martin, who was an associate of Ron Richards at EMI,

did. George said to the boys "When you can write songs as good as this, I'll record them. Until then, this is what you'll do." Bloody embarrassing in hindsight, but on the other hand I had a bit of a track record as a songwriter, and at the time they didn't. Reluctantly, they recorded it, and a few days later Dick James played it to me in his office and I hated it. I hadn't signed a publishing contract – it was all done on trust – but I felt that it had been deliberately messed up, and Dick sort of agreed with me and respected my decision that I was not going to sign a publishing deal and let my song go out in that form. George Martin went along with the decision, admitting that Murray was right, and The Beatles could do a better job on it.

A session was arranged to re-record the song, but in the meantime Lennon and McCartney wrote 'Please, Please Me' and everything changed, although Paul recalls George Martin's enthusiasm: "He said 'I think this would be a great hit for you,' but we weren't sure that it was our style. He said 'It's fantastic. It'll be a hit – try it.' We rehearsed it in Liverpool, and the next time we went down we recorded it, but we dug our heels in over releasing it. I'm surprised we did – we must have been very cocky."

The Beatles' manager, Brian Epstein, was still very keen on the song, and thought that it might make a good single for another of his Liverpool groups, Gerry And The Pacemakers. He tried to persuade Murray to go up to Merseyside to see the outfit play live, and showed him their latest press photographs, selling Gerry as "a young British Bobby Darin" and convincing him that they were the biggest thing in Liverpool after The Beatles. Fed up with trying to find a star name to record the song, Murray replied that he didn't need to see the group. If they made a good record, he'd sign a contract. Epstein's judgement was shrewd; the song was absolutely right for Gerry, and Murray was delighted. "As soon as I heard Gerry And The Pacemakers' version, that was it – much better than my demo, Barry's demo or The Beatles' version, and better than my original conception!" In the spring of 1963, it knocked Cliff Richard And The Shadows' big hit 'Summer Holiday' off the Number One spot and stayed there for three weeks.

According to songwriter Barry Mason, however, the song might well have had a different history. "In the early days, I wrote a bit with Mitch Murray and this singer called Danny Angel, who was on the verge of possibly making it and had two songs to choose from. One was a song that I'd written with Mitch and the other was a song that Mitch had written alone. It was make or break time for the young guy, and he chose to record the song we'd written together, discarding Mitch's solo effort. Our song didn't mean a light. The song he turned down was a worldwide hit, 'How Do You Do It?'."

Naturally, Murray was asked to submit a follow-up, and was working on ideas when something came from one of his father's suggestions, much in the same way as Graham Gouldman's father would proffer ideas. He would scribble down title ideas and odd lines on scraps of paper and hand them to Mitch, hinting that he could work them into songs. Most of them, according to Murray were "total tosh", but while he was thinking of something that might work for Gerry And The Pacemakers, one of them caught his eye. "One title my father had written down was 'Do It Again', an idea that I started working on. That line in a way became the middle bit of 'I Like It', where I had the line "do that again". I made the demo of it and was looking forward to another hit, although you're never really sure; you think to yourself 'Maybe "How Do You Do It?" was a fluke, and I'm not really a good songwriter at all.' This goes on for years. You're never really confident, except when you come back after a dry period and you suddenly realise 'Yes, I am good at this.'"

Mitch Murray didn't exactly have the clear field he thought he'd have in writing the follow-up to Gerry's Number One. Although the group had recorded it, he hadn't heard about a release date and went into Dick James' office to find out what was happening. John Lennon was in there with a song that he and Paul McCartney had written for Gerry called 'Hello, Little Girl'. Lennon turned to Mitch and threatened, "If you get the follow-up for Gerry, I'll bloody thump you!" Murray replied that he thought that it was worth a thump. Although the group did release 'I Like It', the bashing never took place. As a consolation – as if the two Beatles needed it! – The Fourmost had a hit with the Lennon/McCartney song. Murray followed his two Number One songs with the Top 30 hit 'By The Way' for another Liverpool outfit, the highly acclaimed band The Big Three.

However good your songs are, it's usually the case that nobody specifically calls on your services until you have some sort of track record. Your talent doesn't change, but people's perception of it does. With three hits under your belt, your name starts to mean something and the telephone – so long silent – begins to ring for the right reasons.

I had a call from my publisher saying that Freddie Garrity of Freddie And The Dreamers had written the beginning of a song but couldn't quite get it together, as he wasn't really a songwriter, and would I go and see him. He was at Number Two in the chart at that time, and pretty busy, so I thought I'd go and see him backstage at a gig and listen to what he's got. He played me the main line, which was "I'm telling you now", but confessed that he wasn't sure what to do with it after that. I saw something in the song; after all, the chances were that it was going to make some money somewhere along the line with a big artist like that...which goes to show how sentimental I am about these things!

Murray wrote a middle section for the song, finished the rest of it off and gave it a structure. 'I'm Telling You Now' went to Number Two, but not before a degree of wrangling not entirely uncommon in the dividing up of a songwriting cake. Murray felt that it was traditional to go 50/50, but Garrity's management thought that the split should be 75/25 to them. Easing back on the gas a little, they then offered a 60/40 split, to which Murray replied, "If he's happy with forty, I'll take sixty." Although he had the phone slammed down on him for the cheeky remark, he knew that the song was in the can, scheduled for release, and nothing was going to stop it.

As with Gerry And The Pacemakers, he got to write the follow-up for this one as well, 'You Were Made For Me', which was another big hit. Murray had truly arrived as a songwriter.

On the heels of more success, he and fellow songwriter Peter Callander began working on songs together, one of which started life as an entry in the Eurovision Song Contest and made it to the last dozen or so. After the song got kicked out they rewrote it, and when the new version was recorded by The Tremeloes, as 'Even The Bad Times Are Good', it became a big hit. As Mitch remembers, a hit song in those days didn't restrict the song's life: "When you wrote a hit then, you usually got cover versions all over the world. Nowadays, most hits come from a production unit, and they want to have their own releases in other countries, so they effectively stop other people doing it. With our song 'Hitchin' A Ride', for instance, we had 160 covers around the world – Belgium, Scandinavia, Japan, Germany, Mexico and dozens of others – and that was not unusual for a successful hit song then. We even discovered the song on a piano roll in Disneyland!"

Major To Minor

After both writers had been to see the film *Bonnie And Clyde*, starring Warren Beatty and Faye Dunaway, they met up for a writing session and fell into discussing the fact that the only music in the movie was a piece of bluegrass: Lester Flatt and Earl Scruggs performing 'Foggy Mountain Breakdown'. Feeling that it was a wasted opportunity, and that the film would have been a great vehicle for a hit song, they decided to write one, even though the film had already been on the cinema circuit for a little while.

> Just after we'd written it, Peter had lunch with a guy called Ken Glancy from CBS, who was mourning the fact that they'd spent quite a lot of money signing Georgie Fame and he hadn't had a hit for some while. We didn't really know what to do with our song; we'd thought about Tommy Steele, or Lonnie Donegan, but hadn't considered Georgie Fame. Now we were re-addressing it with him in mind, I wrote a jazzier middle sequence. We made the demo with all the sound effects, complete with American police sirens and machine guns…it was a real symphony for the ear. The only problem was Georgie's lack of enthusiasm for the number, but his producer, Mike Smith, eventually persuaded him.

Fame's reticence wasn't the only problem. Television programmes, and *The Simon Dee Show* in particular, had a problem with the violence on the track, so its life almost came to as abrupt a halt as had the lives of Bonnie and Clyde themselves, and they were warned that they'd almost certainly get sued for the song's similarity to 'St Louis Blues'. Happily, though, the rulers of the small screen relented; there was no whiff of litigation in the air, and the song went to Number One in Britain and hit the Top Ten in the States. "We had one line that went 'Bonnie loaded dollars into the…something…bag. We knew there was a word we were looking for, and Peter came up with *dulap*. Bonnie loaded dollars into the dulap bag. I said that I'd never heard the word before, but he seemed absolutely certain, so we used it. He has the last word on lyrics; I have the last word on tunes. We made the demo complete with 'dulap bag'. Georgie Fame records it also with 'dulap bag', and it goes to Number One. Months later, Peter's reading a book and one passage says 'flesh hung on her like a burlap' and he says 'That was the word – burlap!'"

I Write The Songs (UK)

There were many more hits from the pens of Murray and Callander, including several for Tony Christie, the most successful being 'I Did What I Did For Maria', which climbed to Number Two in Britain. Mitch Murray came up with the tune while staying at a friend's château in Normandy. "I thought 'I want Peter here' because, before I progressed the tune, I wanted to work out the lyrics...I was mostly music, and he was mainly words, but we also used to react to one another. I was at a very crucial point in writing this song and I wanted Peter to be there so that, if I needed to change the tune around or change the structure, it was being done for the right reasons. I called him in Paris, where he was staying, and told him the problem. He abandoned his wife...I left my friends in Normandy and we wrote the song in Paris the next day."

During the early '70s, Murray and Callander formed their own label, Bus Stop. After some eight or nine releases, they had still met with little success and were understandably wary about throwing bad money after good – running a record label is an expensive business. However, they had just signed a group called Paper Lace, who Peter's wife had spotted on the television talent show *Opportunity Knocks* and who Peter felt would do a good job on their latest song, 'Billy, Don't Be A Hero'. Mitch wasn't convinced, feeling that the song needed a big name like Cliff Richard to help put them back in the chart.

In the end, Paper Lace recorded it and it went to Number One in Britain so quickly that the two writers couldn't get the deal done fast enough in the States, where it was covered by Bo Donaldson And The Heywoods and also went to Number One. The song sold several million and put a smile back on the faces of Murray and Callander.

The follow-up was another story song.

> If you look at Peter's lyric, it goes 'Daddy was a cop on the east side of Chicago'. Well, the east side of Chicago is the river – it doesn't really exist. It's the east side of New York that's the seamy side, and because of that and our tradition of watching American movies the east side has always seemed like the seamy side, so it was natural to write it that way. It caused great hilarity in America, as it's the south side of Chicago that's the real gangster area, and it was rubbish because Capone never shot cops – the cops were supported by Capone...he was paying them a lot of

money, but it made it a better story! We also had the mayor of Chicago complaining bitterly about the whole thing. It shows you what lousy researchers Peter and myself were.

Songwriter, arranger and producer Mike Batt, born in 1950, appears tirelessly creative, having been influenced by the melodic structures of the songs of Lennon and McCartney and the writing talents of Mick Jagger and Keith Richards.

His favourites from The Rolling Stones' catalogue, such as 'Under My Thumb' and 'Lady Jane', were among the songs that helped him to choose his musical path. While still at school, he played with Southampton R&B group Phase Four, who featured material like 'Mr Pitiful', 'Satisfaction', 'Watermelon Man' and 'You Can't Catch Me'. At that point, Batt wanted to be Mick Jagger, although after leaving school he worked as an organist with The Johnny Ralph Trio, travelling from Winchester to Southampton in his Morris 1100 to play at the strip nights at the local carnival club. When the strippers turned away from the audience at the climax of their act, the young Batt got to see everything that the punters didn't.

As the music scene began to change, however, so did Mike's aspirations. "On Radio Luxembourg one night, I heard Cat Stevens' 'Matthew And Son', which really inspired me to start writing seriously. I then got into psychedelic nonsensical lyrics. I loved the songs that Jimi Hendrix and Roy Wood of The Move were writing, and came up with one of my earliest efforts, 'The Man With The Purple Hand'. It was a useless song. I thought Pete Townshend of The Who was a terrific songwriter, too, but unlike many people I never rated Buddy Holly very much."

During the day, Mike Batt would go to London and try to get appointments with various people in the music business, often returning to haunt those on his list who seemed helpful and friendly. One of these was Dick Leahy, who was then assistant to Jack Baverstock at Philips Records, a man who later became head honcho at Bell.

In that less corporate and accountant-led era, it was easier to get to hobnob with people in the industry. There appeared to be more time to hang out, the characters in the business were friendlier, there was more opportunity to get to know who was who, and seemingly bottomless expense accounts had yet to be replaced by accountable budgets. It's now almost impossible to wait around at record or publishing companies on the off chance that they might have a drink with you, a complete stranger, and listen to your songs on spec.

Another person on Batt's hit list was Pete Shelley, a junior A&R man at Decca Records who worked under Dick Rowe, Noel Walker and Ivor Raymonde. "Pete was really one up from coffee boy, but he did a couple of demos for me at Decca. One song was 'Mr Poem', and the other was 'Gazing Through The Railings'. Both were a bit wistful, and tipping their hat to Cat Stevens. The real breakthrough came via an advertisement that Ray Williams at Liberty Records had placed in the music papers that said something like 'Liberty Wants Talent'. He signed me on the same day he signed Elton John and Bernie Taupin, who'd both applied individually."

Following Ray Williams' subsequent departure from the label to work with Elton and Bernie, Mike took over as A&R man for Liberty at the age of 18 and stayed there for two years before leaving to concentrate on his career as a writer and artist. He remained signed to the label as a performer, however, releasing Lennon and McCartney's 'Your Mother Should Know' as a single, backed with Barry Robin and Maurice Gibb's 'Suddenly'.

During the early '70s, he was earning a very healthy £30,000 a year as a jingle writer, although it wasn't really the direction that he wanted to pursue, and so, when an opportunity arose for him to become involved with writing music and songs for the TV series *The Wombles*, he took it. The Wombles were fictional furry animals who lived on Wimbledon Common, and were created by Elizabeth Beresford, formerly married to Wimbledon tennis commentator Max Robertson.

Writing songs for animated animals is a big gamble for someone who wants to be taken seriously as a composer and orchestrator, but Batt transcended this trap in part by writing some genuinely good commercial songs for this unlikely vehicle. The downside was appearing onstage in a Womble costume.

Not too many songs in this rarefied area of popular music stand the test of time, but many of the songs, such as 'The Wombling Song', 'Remember You're A Womble', 'Wombling Merry Christmas' and 'Minuetto Allegretto' – the first two of which charted again in 1998 – still sound quite fresh over 25 years on. Mike Batt first led The Wombles into the chart in 1974, racking up eight chart singles and four gold albums in a space of two years. "'Minuetto Allegretto' was fun. I had this silly idea about what one of the Wombles – Uncle Bulgaria, who was 300 years old – would be dancing to in his youth. It had to be a minuet. I used tongue-twisting lines like 'Forgetting to be minuetting was letting the other minuetters down.' I took big chunks of Mozart and wrote a whole new verse myself. I also did 'Hall Of The Mountain Womble', based on Grieg."

As well as producing Steeleye Span, The Kursaal Flyers and Elkie Brooks, he also wrote and released his own singles, including 'Summertime City', which climbed to Number Four in the UK chart, but only after he'd failed to find anybody else to front it. Swimming against the tide of being labelled a womble, Batt went on to release two solo albums, *Schizophonia* and *Tarot Suite*. These albums contained European hits like 'Lady Of The Dawn', 'The Winds Of Change', 'The Ride To Agadir', and a song that should have been a big hit in Britain when it was released in 1977, 'Railway Hotel'.

In the canon of many songwriters, there often lurks a little-heard number that, inexplicably, has never been a hit but is much loved by the showbusiness fraternity. In Mike Batt's case, that song is 'Railway Hotel'. "When I was a lad, I had this girlfriend, but I couldn't afford to take her anywhere decent. I was living in this flat in Chelsea, just off the King's Road, with damp on the walls where I had the worst room, having been the last to move in. I felt that she deserved something better, but I couldn't afford it and felt inadequate. In the song, the flat became the Railway Hotel, with me wishing we were at the equivalent of the Savoy."

Mike also wrote 'Caravan Song' for the film *Caravans*, and Barbara Dickson had a hit with it in 1980, two years after its release. He also kept his eye firmly fixed on a new project that interested him. He'd heard about a new film that was being made, which involved the animation of Richard Adams bestseller *Watership Down*, and he was keen to be given the opportunity to write the orchestral score. He submitted many demos in an effort to secure the gig, but realised that there was stiff competition when he overheard one of the bosses on the project being told, while he was listening to Mike's material, "Don't worry if you don't like any of these; we've plenty of other possible writers."

Eventually, he was asked to write three songs. "John Hubbly, the animator, who was going to direct, suggested I wrote a song about death, as one of the rabbits in the story is assumed at one point to be dead. I wondered how to write a song about death. What happens? I thought, well the spark goes, and the eyes are no longer bright. The song really asks what death is, rather than trying to explain what it is. The strange thing is that John died a little while later, and I've often wondered whether he knew that he was dying and that's why he asked me to write a song about death."

When asked which artist he thought would be ideal to record the song, he made a wish list with his name at the bottom and Art Garfunkel at the top, not imagining for one moment that the American star would even consider it. To his surprise, Garfunkel agreed to fly to England and record the song. It subsequently went to Number One in Britain in the spring of 1979, staying in the chart for 19 weeks.

In 1980, Batt opted out of the business for a period, and he and his family travelled around the world in a boat called the *Braemar*, taking in France, the West Indies, Central and South America, Mexico, Hawaii and Fiji. He returned to Britain in 1982, having fallen in love with an Australian girl called Julie-Ann. The ensuing angst and passion from this potential relationship spurred him on to write three more hit songs.

Mike and Tim Rice had often talked about writing together (they almost collaborated on *Chess*), so after his aquatic sojourn Tim ventured down to Wentworth with a view to working on an idea that Mike had had for a musical about the Aztecs. That seed failed to germinate, but Batt had other fish to fry. "I told Tim that David Essex had given me a call, and it might be an idea to try to write a song for him. I also mentioned that my marriage had fallen apart and I'd subsequently fallen in love with Julie-Ann. Because of this, I had a song burning inside me and wanted to put the message across to her, as she was still in Australia. I had this idea that, although I was depressed about it, why should anyone else be concerned or care? We were looking for titles when Tim came up with 'A Winter's Tale'. It became a very personal song to me, and was an open letter to her. It worked, because at least it got her to come over and see me."

David Essex had a hit with the song, which entered the UK chart at the end of 1982, peaking at Number Two, while the less-than-ideal romantic situation was causing the rumblings of another musical outpouring. "'Please Don't Fall In Love' was written in a terrible frenzy, as I'd heard that, back in Australia, she was not only going out with a guy but was living with him. I started to pour it all into a song, jumped on a plane and finished it during the flight. I was coming up with lines that were about the situation: 'I know that you're with him just now as I write.' When I got to Australia I spent the weekend with her, played her the song and flew back two days later." The outcome of the romance was still hanging in the balance, but at least the song had tangible success – Cliff Richard recorded it and had a Top Ten hit with it in late 1983.

Many songwriters claim that theirs is not an art but a trade, while others dredge their souls to come up with what they consider to be important musical and lyrical statements. The songs of the workman-like writer sit outside their lives, separate from them, but for a few writers their canon is almost an intimate diary of their personal life. The third song in Mike Batt's trilogy of love songs was released by Alvin Stardust in the spring of 1984, and it gave the songwriter another Top Ten hit. "The previous two songs had seemed to work, as Julie-Ann decided to come to England to see how our relationship went. At the last minute, though, the TV soap in which she was appearing was recommissioned, meaning that she had another six-month contract. I was sitting in my sister's house near Heathrow Airport on a drizzly day, watching the planes landing and knowing that she wasn't on any of them, when I started to write 'I Feel Like Buddy Holly', identifying with other writers and singers who'd put despair into their songs."

In the lyric of the song, Batt relates to epic 45s that epitomised teenage angst: "I feel like Buddy Holly/'cause it's raining in my heart", "Now I know how Paul McCartney felt/when he got up to say/I wish it were yesterday", and "Now I know what Paul Simon meant/ by the words he found/I wish I were homeward bound."

The song was initially released on a white label, thus retaining the anonymity of the singer and allowing the industry – and especially the DJs – to guess at his identity. By the time they rumbled that it was none other than Alvin Stardust, it was in the chart and climbing.

If there is no previously-accepted blueprint to a song, a corporate decision will almost certainly be sought, as few individuals in the industry have the courage of their own convictions when it comes to something that doesn't slot into a ready-made category. This is certainly true of Batt's musical interpretation of Lewis Carroll's *The Hunting Of The Snark*, which appeared to fall into this non-compartmentalised trap by virtue of its originality and the apparent lightness of the piece. "A sledgehammer to crack a nut," muttered several music business folk, convincing him to organise performances and audio-visuals to demonstrate to the industry how it would work. At great cost, but with unswerving belief, he also recorded the album himself. After putting up £60,000 of his own money (a not inconsiderable sum in 1983), he managed to get Art Garfunkel to record one of the numbers from the project.

However, he needed more than one heavyweight name, and so he approached John Gielgud's agent, offering the legendary actor £5,000 for a day's work reading Lewis Carrol. With Gielgud on board, he then approached artists as diverse as Cliff Richard, Roger Daltrey, Captain Sensible, Julian Lennon, Stephane Grappelli, George Harrison, John Hurt and Deneice Williams, all of whom agreed to be on the 1984 album.

When Batt staged the piece at the Barbican Theatre, in London, it was 40 minutes long, although by the time he put it on at the Royal Albert Hall the show had grown to being 60 minutes long. "Sony took the album, but after a while said that they needed to cut out the orchestral passages. I felt that, if they removed them, that the album would be all meat and no gravy, so I refused to edit it. They insisted that, if those bits didn't go, we didn't have a deal, so we didn't have a deal. I then had to go to litigation to get my album back.

A smaller company then offered to run with the project, promising a £500,000 investment, although in reality they only came up with £5,000 before going to the wall. It then took a year to recover the album. Surprisingly, this adverse activity didn't discourage Batt, and instead he tried to put it on with West End producer Cameron Mackintosh, who appeared to be extremely interested in staging the show. After many meetings, Mackintosh became increasingly involved in *Les Misérables*, and another opportunity disappeared. Batt doggedly battled on, drumming up finance in New Zealand and producing it at Sydney's State Theatre in 1990 with the Elizabethan Sinfonia before opening in London's West End in the following year.

He not only conducted the 60-piece orchestra on stage every night; he also directed and designed the show, and while it was running he could be seen pacing the pavement outside the theatre, trying to raise money to keep the production afloat. Even though the audiences were increasing, the money was running out fast, and the show closed before it could reach its full potential.

The new millennium sees the never-complacent Mike Batt still driving his *Snark* to the success he feels that it deserves, setting up a new label, Dramatico, and putting together a new album, *Bright Eyes And The*

Railway Hotel – basically the Mike Batt songbook – with the Royal Philharmonic Orchestra.

Another songwriter who, like Batt, wanted to sing like Cat Stevens was Scott English, who would collaborate with composer Richard Kerr on a future American Number One. Born in Bedford in 1945, Kerr was first inspired to write by the songs of Buddy Holly and Lennon and McCartney, and by the atmosphere that pervaded London at the time of The Beatles and The Rolling Stones.

A pianist and clarinettist, he began to write songs with his flatmate, Jonathan Peel, in their lodgings at 90 Cromwell Road West in London. Kerr was in the wine trade at the time, studying the finer points of the liquid, but made time to make some demonstration recordings of their songs at Regent Sound Studios in Tin Pan Alley. A third Cromwell Road inmate, future Sky percussionist Tristran Fry, played drums on the tracks. Kerr did the rounds of the record and publishing companies, desperately hoping to get a song published, or at least to get somebody to show some interest.

Getting a song published was a big deal in the '60s. Being a published writer was a useful thing to have on your CV, and it certainly helped to persuade people to listen to your product. At that time, publishers were still interested in the song that came in off the street – it could always be the next hit. In their optimistic way, songwriters always hoped to find the publisher that would be the one to spot the potential – not necessarily in the their whole canon of work, as would be the case today – but in one song. The big one. The one that would change their life. In the year 2000, a publisher wouldn't give the time of day to a young writer who came in unannounced off the street with one badly-recorded demo. That thrill for the new writers has gone, but back in the '60s excitement coursed through the veins of the young Richard Kerr as he trudged the streets, trying to convince the music world of his talent.

Luckily, he found the catalyst that he was looking for in publisher and former Viscounts member Don Paul, at Essex Music. With Paul as his mentor, he continued to write in his spare time while also working for the publishing house by day, as a gopher for producer Denny Cordell. While Cordell recorded Georgie Fame, The Move, Joe Cocker and Procol Harum, Kerr fetched the sandwiches and plotted sales graphs, much as Reg Dwight in his pre-Elton John days did at Leeds Music.

I Write The Songs (UK)

Decca later released Kerr's debut single, 'Concrete Jungle', but, despite the record company's promotion pushing Kerr's "dark good looks", his "composing talents", and emphasising that the song was "a disturbingly accurate view of big city life", he failed to break through as an artist.

His first songwriting break came when he was out one evening in 1968 with Don Paul. "Don and I were going to see the new James Bond film at the Odeon, Leicester Square, when we saw this guy busking on the pavement and he had fantastic co-ordination...all those instruments surrounding him. Don Paul took this guy, whose name was Don Partridge, into Regent Sound Studio and recorded one of the singer's own songs, 'Rosie', for just £4. The follow-up – 'Blue Eyes', which I co-wrote – cost twice as much, as we used a double bass on the session. Two big hit singles for just £12!"

Kerr co-wrote the third single, 'Top Man', but it failed to chart, and apart from the odd cover (such as 'Hard Lovin'', a hit for for Neil Christian), the going was still tough. In an attempt to make something happen, Kerr signed to Screen Gems Music at the behest of publisher Terry Oates, who ran it with Jack McGraw. 'Love Grows (Where My Rosemary Goes)' had just been a hit, and, sensing that this sort of song was selling well, McGraw pushed the reluctant young writer, asking him to "write like Tony MacCauley". It was the only time in his life that he attempted to write in someone else's style.

His main writing partner during his time at Screen Gems was Scott English. The pair normally wrote at the publishing company's offices, or at Richard Kerr's home.

> One time we went to Scott's flat off Curzon Street to write, but there was a problem with the piano, so we went next door to use his neighbour's upright. It was a totally new atmosphere, and a melody came into my head very quickly. Scott was equally speedy with a lyric idea, and so 'Brandy' was conceived. I really thought the song had something, but Scott knew that it was a hit...he was absolutely sure. During the next nine months it was turned down by so many people that he decided to record it himself. He invited me to the studio to listen to it, and it was OK, but to be honest – and Scott knows this – I'd always hated his voice so much! I had to admit, though, that he'd done a good

MAJOR TO MINOR

job. He always wanted to sing like Cat Stevens, and that was what he did on 'Brandy'.

The version by Scott English got to Number Twelve in Britain in 1971, climbing into the bottom of the US Top 100 in the following year. However, the song's life was far from over. Three or four years later, Kerr went to the States to write, after signing to Irving Music, the publishing arm of A&M Records, and acceded to a proposal forwarded by Derek Green and Bob Grace that he should move to America to work with The Carpenters' songwriter, John Bettis.

> I'm not a keen flyer at the best of times, and I hate talking to fellow passengers for that reason. I just like to be left alone. Suddenly a big woman sat down next to me and said, "Do you mind if I sit here?" She seemed very interested in my portable keyboard. I apologised and said that I'd prefer it if she didn't…that I couldn't hold a conversation while I was flying, at which point she went and sat somewhere else. After the plane had landed, she gave me her card as she walked past, saying, "I'm Hoyt's mother." It was only after she'd gone that I realised that the lady was Mae Boren Axton, who'd written 'Heartbreak Hotel' and songs for Hank Snow and Jim Reeves.
>
> When I arrived at A&M's parking lot, I heard a familiar song coming from the publisher's office, although it took me a minute to realise it. When I got inside, I said, "I think that's my song." I was told that it was a version by Barry Manilow, but I didn't know who the hell Barry Manilow was, and was livid to discover that the title had been changed, without permission, from 'Brandy' to 'Mandy'. I soon discovered that the boss of Arista, Clive Davis, had insisted on the change, as there had recently been a chart-topper in the States called 'Brandy' by the group Looking Glass. I was fuming at the change, but only until it went into the US chart and subsequently to Number One.

Although it was intended that Kerr and Bettis would write together, Bettis had such a hectic schedule that Kerr ended up writing with lyricist Will Jennings. This proved to be a fortuitous pairing, as they came up with material like 'Somewhere In The Night', which became a hit for both Helen Reddy and Barry Manilow and spawned over 100 cover versions. They also collaborated on Manilow's 1977 US Number One 'Looks Like We Made It', and Dionne Warwick's 1979 Top Five hit 'I'll Never Love This Way Again'. It was a far cry from traipsing around publishing houses in London, hoping for a break.

While he was writing in America, Kerr did eventually write with John Bettis, and also worked with Troy Seals in Nashville and wrote a follow-up to Jennifer Warnes' 1977 hit 'Right Time Of The Night' with English lyricist and Elton John collaborator Gary Osborne. Despite high hopes, however, 'I'm Dreaming' failed to chart.

The penultimate time that Jennings and Kerr wrote together was for Roy Orbison. The pair had already formed a good relationship with the Texan singer, and they wrote 'In The Real World' for what was to be his last album. The three of them were planning to write for the Big O's next album, but it wasn't to be. Orbison died in December 1988.

After 15 years in the States, with a lot of success, Kerr returned to Britain. "I knew when I got back just how difficult it would be...I just didn't realise how difficult. Nobody even knew I was back. I was so impressed with Roy Orbison, though, it was if he'd never had a hit record. He was so unpretentious...so normal."

One British songwriter who was happier when he wasn't collaborating was Chris Andrews. Born in Romford, Essex, in October 1938, he started playing guitar at the age of eleven, had six years of piano tuition, and began writing songs while he was still a schoolboy at Reden Park in Essex.

He made his professional debut in 1957 at the Ilford Palais De Dance before becoming a regular on Jack Good's TV show *Oh Boy!*. He formed his own group, Chris Ravel And The Ravers in 1963, releasing 'I Do' on Decca. "It was the first song I ever recorded and it got a few plays on Radio Luxembourg but didn't really make it. I worked out the tune at a cave in Hastings at a deb's coming-out party...The Rolling Stones were booked, too, but Brian Jones was unable to perform, so they couldn't play. Bill Wyman was there...it was the first time I met him, but he told me years and years later at his house in the South of France 'I really liked that song of yours, "I Do". I actually bought the record.' Although it didn't happen for me then, a style was forming."

So many songwriters end up without copies of their own songs that have been released, and Chris Andrews is no exception. His entire record collection disappeared during a house move, including 'I Do' and covers of his songs by The Mamas And Papas and Cher, who had recorded her version of 'Girl Don't Come'.

An introduction to Evelyn Taylor (the manager of Adam Faith and Sandie Shaw) really gave Andrews a boost as a songwriter when Adam Faith, impressed by his writing ability, revitalised his career in the second half of 1963 by recording 'The First Time'. The song reached the Top Ten in Britain.

> I played to to Adam at a club we rented for the afternoon, To run through some new songs. He fancied getting away from his old style with the pizziccato strings, which had just about run its course, and change direction. I was writing heavier stuff for the time, which is how we ended up with this song that wasn't as light as his previous material. He made a brilliant job of it, recording it in three minutes flat at Abbey Road Studios. We had Vic Flick on guitar, Kenny Clare on drums and two of the guys from The Roulettes. The control room at Abbey Road is upstairs, so he came up after he'd recorded it and the conversation went something along the lines of "What d'yer think, cock?"
>
> "It's really good."
>
> "Do you want me to do it again?"
>
> "No, it's great."
>
> "All right, then. I'll see you later."
>
> And he was off...didn't even listen to it. His thing was actually recording it...he didn't want to hear it!

Although the follow-up, 'We Are In Love', didn't quite get as high in the chart as 'The First Time', Chris always felt that it was a better song. He always enjoyed the question-and-answer way of writing, and employed it in that song:

> Is it love? I don't know.
> Is it real? I don't know.

I Write The Songs (UK)

Between 1964 and 1966, Chris Andrews wrote an amazing nine hits for Sandie Shaw, including five Top Ten hits and a Number One, 'Long Live Love'. The other four songs that reached the Top Ten were 'I'll Stop At Nothing', 'Message Understood', 'Tomorrow' and 'Girl Don't Come. "'Long Live Love' was written as a rock 'n' roll song at the time, when Adam first introduced me to Sandie and suggested I write something for her. It was only when we gave the song to the arranger that he came up with the idea of giving it the 'Always Something There To Remind Me' tempo. When I first heard it, I thought 'Oh, what have they done?' It was really scary, and it took me a little while to get into what he'd done with it." The association continued to flourish, and he provided songs for some of her later singles, including 'Today' and 'Don't Run Away'.

One song that Chris played to Sandie with a view to her recording it was just a melody to which he had no lyrics. He was convinced that she would snap it up straight away, but all that she did was keep singing her own words to it: "Please don't send me away/to the big USA." This alluded to the fact that she was having trouble getting a visa to enable her to promote 'Girl Don't Come' in the States, as the authorities thought that the lyric was rather risqué. Sandie eventually decided against recording the song, and so, with encouragement from record producer and Rolling Stones manager Andrew Loog Oldham, Andrews went to Eve Taylor to suggest that she should release the number. "'Oh, terrible idea,' she said. I told her that Andrew Loog Oldham thought I should do it. 'Oh, good idea,' she said! 'Go and do it.' I recorded it, played it to her and she said that she thought it was the biggest abortion that she'd ever heard in her life. Fortunately, Jackie Trent was in the office at the time and said 'Oh, it's absolutely brilliant!' After just two plays on Radio Luxembourg, there was this buzz about it. I got a call from Decca, who said that they really believed in the record and were going to make it a hit. They didn't realise that I knew that it was already selling 15,000 copies a day!"

A hit record meant that he found himself back on the road with a group, performing a set which included 'Long Live Love' and 'We Are In Love', as well as bluesier material like 'Just A Dream' and 'Sticks And Stones' and '50s classics '16 Candles' and 'Lucille'.

In 1965 and 1966, he had four more hits with 'Something On My Mind', 'Whatcha Gonna Do Now?', 'Stop That Girl' and 'To Whom It Concerns', the follow-up to 'Yesterday Man'. "I thought the idea of sticking with a slow intro and then going into a big brass interlude would work very well. The first bit I had of the song was the intro: 'Oh my friends please hear me do…' For me, the main part of the song was the instrumental bit…It's still used on *The Late Late Show*…It's been used now for about 30 years. After that hit, I thought that it was time to stop doing regimental-sounding stuff."

In 1998 Chris Andrews received the coveted Gold Badge Award.

Guy Fletcher and Doug Flett came together as a writing partnership, after being introduced by a mutual friend, both of their previous collaborators having gone off in different directions. Fletcher's musical training was mainly classical, trumpet and french horn, but by the early '60s he had begun singing with his sister Barbara and brother Edward in a harmony group called The Cameos. One of the trio's gigs impressed the group The Checkmates so much that their keyboard player, Alan Hawkshaw, introduced the group to record producer Joe Meek, who was looking for session singers. They joined Meek early in 1963, singing backing vocals on countless records churned out by the eccentric but brilliant producer, working with artists such as Heinz, The Tornados, Mike Berry, Michael Cox, The Saints, The Checkmates, *Coronation Street* star Jennifer Moss, Houston Wells And The Marksmen and Glenda Collins.

In 1963, Meek produced their first single under the name The Cameos, 'Powercut', and the follow-up, 'My Baby's Coming Home', early in the following year. However, despite reasonable airplay, no hits were forthcoming.

Following the demise of the group, Guy began to move more into writing, his first real success coming after teaming up with Doug Flett. "Things just clicked between us. Guy asked to have a look at what I'd done before, so I pulled a few lyrics out and he said 'Well, they're good English, at least!' We started writing at weekends and nights, as we both had other jobs. Guy was in the music business and I was in advertising. We wrote some quite good songs early on, which encouraged Guy's publisher to come up with some money to enable us to be full-time songwriters. It then became the daily job. We were songwriters, going to work. Every day for three and a half years we'd go to the office and start writing from ten in the morning, breaking for lunch, just as people would in other professions." In those days it was bespoke songwriting, a profession now long dead in Britain, with retainers often available to give composers and lyricists the time and freedom to be creative.

Like many other aspiring writers, Guy and Doug were being paid to learn and perfect their craft, and their most successful songs weren't necessarily the ones with which they were most happy. As with many writers, it would be a title, a snatch of a tune or a riff that would get them fired up and lead them (hopefully) into a fully-fledged song. As partners, they wrote songs that they felt were possible hits which were ignored, and others that they felt were a little ordinary which became major successes, proving that writers aren't always the best judges of their own material. Conversely, they can also get a bee in their bonnet about certain numbers, and subsequently be proved right, as in the case of Fletcher and Flett's 'Is There Anyone Out There?', which Guy was convinced was perfect for Ray Charles.

> We were very green. We took the song to Los Angeles, assuming that Ray Charles would record it simply because we'd written it for him! We hired a car and drove to Tangerine Records at Watts, not knowing that if you're white and inexperienced you shouldn't be driving to Watts under any circumstances. The political balance was very delicate. However, we drove down with our acetate, took it into Tangerine Records and discovered that Big Dee Irwin, who'd had a big hit with 'Swinging On A Star', was head of A&R for Ray Charles – ie selecting the songs he could record. He told us flatly 'Mr Charles will not record this song.' 6,000 miles and a ton of enthusiasm went down the drain simply because we were white. Our publishers in LA were amazed at out naïevety and audacity.

Their conviction undimmed, they submitted the song time and time again to the singer without success, until Shelley Weiss, an east coast Jewish song hustler, finally got 'Is There Anyone Out There?' directly to Ray himself with a lead sheet written in braille. It was a triumph of persistence over prejudice, and five years after their initial approach Charles not only recorded it but also stretched the song from its initial length of four and a half minutes, making the final cut some six minutes long. This was incredible, really, because at the time most AM pop records were on average three minutes in length.

Fletcher and Flett worked from 17 Savile Row, London, the same address as Cliff Richard's manager, Peter Gormley. Because of this, they came to his attention, and it became easy for them to submit songs for Cliff, for which Guy remains eternally grateful. "Initially, we had a very sad song called 'What's More (I Don't Need Him)' that our publishers thought we should play to Peter. He came upstairs, heard it and said 'I love this song.' He played it to Cliff, who recorded it, although that makes the process of songwriting sound ridiculously simple; you do need a degree of luck. The song had several lives, including being the B-side of his 1968 single 'Don't Forget To Catch Me' and featuring on the 1970 album *Live At The Talk Of The Town*. It opened the door to writing more songs for Cliff."

Like many writers, Fletcher and Flett found that, although they tried to avoid writing to a format, they often found themselves in a situation where it was necessary. If a singer or group is having hits with a certain style of song provided by a writer or writers, it makes financial sense to conform, to a certain degree. They wrote several songs for Cliff Richard, and although Cliff would never demand a particular type of song, Fletcher and Flett, like other writers who submitted material to him, would be aware of subjects that would suit him and others that were taboo. Sex, drugs and overtly suggestive lyrics were definitely out, but at that time – in the late '60s and early '70s – he would sing about love, feelings and rock 'n' roll in a melodic pop/rock style.

Like some other artists, though, he was always liable to break the mould and record a song that surprised everyone, singing lyrics that were more than a little unusual, as with Doug and Guy's 'Power To All Our Friends'. "Although Cliff had had hits with songs of ours like 'Through The Eyes Of A Child' and 'Sing A Song of Freedom', we had entered 'Power to All Our Friends' anonymously for the 1973 Song For Europe contest, so although we were part of the family nepotism played no part in the hit, as the writer's names are not known until the final eight are announced. The inspiration for the song was the ecology movement that was gathering pace and power, having grown from the 'peace and love' ethos of the second half of the 1960s. Doug came up with a bizarre lyric that included getting laid in Monte Carlo…which Cliff thankfully didn't spot!" Over the years, the song has become a healthy source of income, having been covered by over 100 artists around the world.

However, another of their successful songs has had no major cover at all. 'I Can't Tell The Bottom From The Top' was a Top Ten hit for The Hollies in 1970, and the group still feature it regularly in their act. The record has also picked up a reasonable amount of regular radio airplay over the last 30 years.

Songwriting is a great insurance policy, but you can never be sure what the rate of interest will be, or certain of the stream of revenue. "We're astounded that nobody else recorded 'I Can't Tell The Bottom From The Top'. The only other version we know of is by Elton John, who wasn't well known at the time, when he recorded it as a session singer for a *Top Of The Pops* budget album."

In keeping with other writers, Guy Fletcher and Doug Flett have unrecorded songs, especially ballads, that they believe to be potential hits, and are probably perceived to be in a better position than many writers to get these songs to major artists. However, that is no longer the way in which the business works. The big hit ballads are now more likely to come out of other areas, such as film and television, than from mainstream pop.

In the mid '80s, Fletcher and Flett wrote for the group Rogue, a group comprising Guy, Al Hodge and JW Hodkinson. The album *Fallen Angels* yielded the songs 'Dedication', which became a US hit for The Bay City Rollers, and 'Fallen Angel', which charted in both Britain and the States for Four Seasons singer Frankie Valli.

So why do writers like Fletcher and Flett continue to work in what must be a frustrating environment for independent creatives, having written many big hits in a period of pop music that was more condusive to professional songwriters? Doug admits that, "If you think about it in depth, you wonder why you do it...What still drives you to write songs in an era where the atmosphere and conditions are far from ideal? The simple answer is that I really enjoy writing songs."

Guy concurs. "Yes, there is a pleasure in writing, but I'm not motivated by the mainstream pop business, more by the idea of writing interesting songs for television, film or theatre. There now has to be a vehicle for your song and some sort of viability on the horizon...there has to be a focus. You can't just write material without an aim in mind."

Many of the big British songwriting teams have written for Cliff Richard, providing him with great melodies and well-constructed lyrics for over four decades and making him the most successful singles artist in the history of British popular music, his single sales alone topping 86 million. Of his 130 or so British hits, two have transcended their chart success to take their place in modern cultural life. One is Brian Bennett and Bruce Welch's 'Summer Holiday' and the other is 'Congratulations', written by Bill Martin and Phil Coulter. Bill admits that they were rather pushed into writing it:

> Phil and I had written a song for Cliff called 'My Magic Music Box', which had a cast of thousands and was meant as a potential Eurovision song. I thought it was one of our best songs, but the publisher, Jimmy Phillips, said that he thought we could write something better, so Phil began another number. The words to it went "I think I love you, I think I love you, I think the world is mine when you will say you're mine..." I thought that was awful. You can't say to sombody "I think I love you"; you either say "I love you" or "I don't love you". Phil knew that it wasn't quite right, so I worked around the five syllables of "I think I love you" and came up with "congratulations" and "celebrations", and really that was my only contribution to the song. Having such a catchy title, though, made all the difference. 'Congratulations' has become like a second national anthem, which has opened many doors for me. It's a great thrill, because it's played at weddings, for the queen and even when the British troops came back from the Falklands.

Bill Martin was born William Wylie MacPherson. He changed it in the early '60s as he thought that it sounded too Scottish for a songwriter, although he now wishes that he'd stuck with his original name. A footballer of some note, he played for Partick Thistle and Johannesbourg Rangers before turning to songwriting, informing interested parties that he used to "play for Rangers", hoping that they wouldn't ask him, "Which Rangers?" and assume that it was Glasgow Rangers!

In 1963, he wrote 'Kiss Me Now' for Brian Epstein's latest protégé, Tommy Quickly, but despite having the weight of The Beatles' manager behind him and the excellent Remo Four backing him the song refused to become a hit, much to Martin's dismay. Quickly was the only artist with whom Epstein failed to have commercial success.

Bill knew most people on the thriving group scene in Scotland, including Glasgow outfit The Beatstalkers (who were usually billed as "the Scottish Beatles") and fellow Glaswegian Tommy Scott (born Tommy Kilpatrick in 1940), who was designated to produce the group's singles for Decca.

Bill wrote 'Mr Disappointed', the B-side of The Beatstalkers' first record, 'Ev'rybody's Talking 'Bout My Baby', while Scott wrote the B-sides for their next two singles. Bill also wrote for Edinburgh group The Boston Dexters, penning both sides of their final single under that name, released early in 1966, 'Try Hard' and 'No More Tears', after which the group became The Buzz and were recorded by producer Joe Meek.

As a team, Martin and Scott wrote for The Bachelors ('Beneath The Willow Tree' and 'The Old Wishing Well') and also for Twinkle, the one-time girlfriend of Bachelor Dec Clusky. For her they penned the lyric of Serge Gainsbourg's Eurovision winner for Luxembourg 'Poupee De Cire, Poupee De Son', the song becoming 'Lonely Singing Doll'.

Scott, also a recording artist in his own right, wrote several songs for Twinkle by himself, whilst working with Martin on numbers for The Dubliners and Van Morrison.

In 1965, Bill met Phil Coulter, a composer from Northern Ireland, and the pair went on to have an incredible amount of success with many artists, including Ken Dodd, Dave Dee, Dozy, Beaky, Mick And Tich, Dick Emery, Tony Blackburn, Mirielle Mathieu and Los Bravos. Three of their biggest songs in the '60s were the 1968 Eurovision song 'Congratulations'; the 1967 Eurovision winner, 'Puppet On A String', a British and worldwide Number One hit for Sandie Shaw; and 'Surround Yourself With Sorrow', a Top Three record in the UK for Cilla Black. "When we were writing, Phil would come up with the melodies, but I would be the motivator...I'd start the ideas off, but didn't have the patience to sit there working on a song for ages like Phil was able to. He was very good in the studio...we mainly used Regent Sound and later Mayfair Studios. We were the last contracted writers to Tin Pan Alley publisher Jimmy Phillips. There'd been Jimmy Kennedy and Michael Carr, then Lionel Bart, Tommy Steele and Mike Pratt, and then us."

Bill Martin and Phil Coulter could almost be credited with assisting at the birth of the modern footballer, giving them pop-star status that has increased dramatically over the last three decades. Throughout the history of the game, footballers had neither attracted nor invited the public to focus on their personal lives. They got on with the job in hand, weren't paid inflated salaries, and wouln't have conceived of anything as distracting as making records. They were sportsmen, not singers. With players like George Best sporting fashionable Beatle haircuts and becoming pin-ups, however, things were changing, and two songwriters would help to create waves that would bring about a sea change in the way in which footballers were perceived, and in many cases the ways in which they would perceive themselves. Bill Martin tells the tale of the historic event:

> England had won the World Cup in 1966 and they had the bones of the remaining team left in 1970…Bobby Moore and all those guys. I knew Bill Cotton at the BBC and told him that we would have a go at writing the World Cup theme tune for Mexico. We came up with a song, but at the time we had to make the demo Phil had broken his arm, so there I was singing away and holding up his plastered arm while he was trying to play the piano!
>
> Eventually we finished the demo and I had to get it to a big BBC meeting where Bill Cotton was listening to material sent to him by other songwriters eager to get a shot at writing something. Apparently he said to the people at the meeting "I'm waiting on Martin and Coulter, the boys who wrote 'Congratulations' and 'Puppet On A String'. They've written a definitive song for Mexico, and I'm told that it's going to be great. I arrived with the demo whereupon it was played to the assembled company. Cotton's only comment was "Fuck me, that sounds like a man playing with a broken arm!'
>
> We later got a phone call telling us that it was a load of rubbish, so I resorted to using my salesman's brain and thought, why don't we get the England squad to record it. Football songs recorded by actual teams hadn't been done at that point. I went to see Alf Ramsay, the England manager, when England were playing Scotland at Wembley, but he wasn't interested. However, I remembered that Alf, who spoke very slowly and properly, had a twin brother who spoke cockney and said, "I met your brother last night", and Alf nearly died! He quickly said, "Why don't you go and discuss it with the boys?" I went upstairs to see Bobby Moore, Alan Ball, Jackie and Bobby Charlton and all those

phenomenal players. To get their attention, I said things like, "Bobby, you're holding the ball too long" and "Alan, why don't you run across the field a bit more?" They thought I was mad, but at least it got their attention so I could say "If we cut a record we can all make a bit of money, have a lot of laughs and appear on *Top Of The Pops*. I think we could have a Number One record." 'Back Home' was a typical war song, which is what we took as our inspiration...the troops are going away...they're thinking of us and we're thinking of them.

The song was recorded in Pye Studios in just one take, with the football team singing along to Martin and Coulter's guide vocals. Their appearance on *Top Of The Pops*, in which they all appeared in evening dress, helped to put the song at Number One in the UK chart, earn gold discs for all concerned, and establish a new image for the modern footballer. A precedent had been created in the face of initial opposition from the BBC, the England manager, Alf Ramsay, and the England team themselves, but no-one had taken into account the tenacity of Bill Martin.

Football songs have subsequently become a way of life and almost a part of the game, and the England team alone have charted on several occasions during the '80s and '90s with songs provided by the likes of Stock, Aitken and Waterman and New Order. The Lightning Seeds in collaboration with comedians David Baddiel and Frank Skinner took 'Three Lions' (the official song of the England Football Team) to Number One in 1996 and again in 1998, continuing a theme started by Bill Martin and Phil Coulter back in 1970.

Another of Martin and Coulter's great success stories were Edinburgh group The Bay City Rollers, who had originally called themselves The Saxons in 1967. After 'Keep On Dancing' had been a Top Ten hit for them in 1971, and they'd had a big hit in Israel, Belgium, France and Germany with 'Manana', it looked to the outside world as if the group had had their alloted five minutes of fame and would then be consigned to the history books as one-hit wonders. However, the group had a big following, especially in their native Scotland, and so Bill felt that he and Phil should write some material for them. Dick Leahy at Bell records was enthusiastic, but Phil Coulter wasn't too keen, although he was persuaded to sit down and work on something thet might be suitable.

They penned 'Saturday Night', which came out as a single in 1973 but failed to chart, despite Martin's conviction that it was a hit. He would later be proved right when it became the band's first US hit, topping the chart there early in 1976, becoming the first of the group's eight US hits.

In February 1974, both songwriters and group defied their critics by releasing 'Remember (Sha-La-La)', which reached the Top Ten, putting them in the teen idol bracket along with Donny Osmond and David Cassidy. As the songs poured out of Martin and Coulter and into the mouth of the group's lead singer, Les McKeown, "Rollermania" seized the female sub-teens and early teens of Britain, and the hits just took care of themselves. During 1974 Martin and Coulter supplied them with three more top ten hits: 'Shang-A-Lang', 'Summer Love Sensation' and 'All Of Me Loves All Of You'.

However, the group's peak came with their UK Number One 'Bye Bye Baby', originally a Four Seasons song written by another exceptional songwriting team, Bob Crewe and former Royal Teen turned Four Season Bob Gaudio (who famously wrote The Four Seasons' US Number One 'Sherry' in just 15 minutes!). Although Gaudio and Crewe wrote many classic songs together and with other collaborators, it's worth noting that three of their songs that they failed to pick out as potential UK hits went to Number One in Britain for other acts: 'The Sun Ain't Gonna Shine Anymore' for The Walker Brothers, 'Silence Is Golden' for The Tremeloes and 'Bye Bye Baby' for The Bay City Rollers.

During Martin's and Coulter's success with The Rollers, they concieved the idea of the group Kenny, which was basically just Bill and Phil in search of someone to front their songs and productions. At one point, Kenny was going to be TV presenter Keith Chegwin and his brother Jeff, but in the end the two writers went a different route, notching up four hits with the group, including the two big Top Ten records 'The Bump' and 'Fancy Pants'.

Slik was another of their creations, and the group's frontman, Midge Ure, went on to perform with several groups, including Rich Kids, Thin Lizzy, Band Aid and Ultravox, as well as having solo hits. Martin and Coulter wrote Slik's UK Number One 'Forever And Ever', and the group's subsequent singles 'Requiem', 'Don't Take Your Love Away', 'The Kid's A Punk' and 'The Boogiest Band In Town'.

In 1970, Bill and Phil started their own publishing company, immediately finding success with another Eurovision winner, this time for

I Write The Songs (UK)

Dana with 'All Kinds Of Everything', a song written by Dublin printers Derry Lindsay and Jackie Smith. This led to Martin and Coulter signing several singer/songwriters, including Van Morrison, Christie Moore, Billy Connolly, Midge Ure, Ian Curnow, Phil Harding and BA Robertson, as well as continuing to write not only pop songs but also material for films, such as *The Water Babies* and the Carry On films, and various TV themes.

Bill Martin and Phil Coulter now work apart, but in an incredible ten-year period they had Number One songs in every country in the world and won countless awards and gold discs.

In 1983 Bill Martin produced the musical *Jukebox*, which ran in the West End for six months and was chosen for that year's *Royal Variety Show*, and he has continued to write commercially. Coulter, meanwhile, has returned to his Celtic roots: "Phil will never write another hit without me because he's not into the chart thing any more...deep down he always wanted to be an Irish legend doing Irish songs."

A freeman of the cities of London and Glasgow, Bill has always been involved in the more workmanlike aspects of the songwriting community, including working with the British Academy Of Songwriters (now The British Academy of Composers and Songwriters) and the Performing Right Society, and was also a founder member of the Society Of Distinguished Songwriters (SODS). He has combined this work with a continued interest in writing – Garth Brooks and Shania Twain are amongst the current artists recording his material – and is currently engaged in penning new songs for Céline Dion with Brian Bennett, the former Shadows drummer turned composer who wrote the theme for *The Ruth Rendell Mysteries*, amongst many other fine pieces. Bill has also been working on songs for Tom Jones, collaborating with composer Les Reed.

One of the most successful partnerships of the '60s and '70s was that of Les Reed and Barry Mason, and one of their best-known songs was 'The Last Waltz'.

> It was pure luck that we wrote that song. Les and I were working in his house in Woking. It was a dull, rainy afternoon, and we were struggling with a song called 'Everybody Knows'. We were actually looking for something that wasn't there...a middle eight. Anyway, we stopped for a cup of tea and Les started talking about

his past. He said he always knew when his mum and dad were coming home from the village dance because, across the village, he could hear the music playing and eventually would hear the master of ceremonies say "Ladies and gentlemen, take your partners for the last waltz." He'd know then that his parents would be back in about ten minutes. Suddenly there was a pause and I said to Les 'Has there ever been a song called "The Last Waltz?"' As it happened, there hadn't been. In 20 minutes, the song wrote itself, and went on to become a Number One for Engelbert Humperdinck, and his third million-selling single. With other cover versions, it ended up selling something like ten million copies worldwide.

As a boy, Barry lived in Blackpool, where he heard music coming from every amusement arcade on the seafront. Another early influence was the sound of big bands, like those of Ted Heath and Johnny Dankworth, which played at the famous Winter Gardens. "One of my early heroes was trumpeter Duncan Campbell, who later played on 'Love Me Tonight', which Les and I wrote wrote for Tom Jones. Drummer Jack Parnell, another of my heroes from those days in Blackpool, also played sessions for me in the '60s, which was a great thrill."

Following the collapse of his parents' marriage, the young Barry went to live in America with his stepfather. After studying at Ohio State University, he became disillusioned and travelled across the States on the famous Route 66. "That was the first real respect I had for a lyric. The great thing was, because of the song, I knew which town was coming up next."

He ended up in Hollywood, where he earned money singing in clubs whilst toying with the idea of becoming an actor. The nearest he got was a bit part in the Carroll Baker/Roger Moore 1959 film *The Miracle*, set in Spain during the Peninsular War. He had more success working for the cosmetics company La Vie (with the natty slogan "Say La Vie") and at the Music City record store.

After three or four years, Mason returned to England to see his mother. With every intention of going back to the States, he found himself working as an actor at the Royal Court Theatre in London. While understudying for Albert Finney in *The Lilywhite Boys*, he realised that he hadn't really got what it took to be an actor and quit the job.

Fortune often approaches from different directions, and on this occasion it was through a poker school. He began to participate in poker sessions with showbusiness alumni that included singers Troy Dante and Leapy Lee and songwriters Les Reed, Gordon Mills and Gordon's wife, Jo. These connections would prove to be useful stepping stones on a career path that Barry had no idea that he would follow.

In the apartment below his was a guy called Tommy Bruce, whose gravel voice made Barry think that he could make him another Big Bopper. He found a trio to back him, made a demo of 'Ain't Misbehavin'' and sold it to EMI. "I suddenly find myself in the music business, but I didn't have a clue how to promote the guy. I was in the middle of Soho one day, and it was pouring with rain, and I still hadn't worked out how to make anyone notice the record. Just as I was thinking 'How do I manage an artist and how do I get him some publicity?', I saw a familiar figure walking towards me. It was the legendary bandleader Billy Cotton. I went up to him and said 'Excuse me, Mr Cotton, but I'm new to the business. How do I get publicity for my singer?' He was great. He said 'Go to my office and ask for Les Perrin. He's the number one publicist.'"

Les Perrin loved the fact that Tommy Bruce was an ex-Covent Garden porter, and subsequently helped to get his career off the ground. Mason soon realised that he now had to come up with more songs for his singer and thought that he might as well have a go at writing something himself. Along with the trio's guitarist, Peter Green (who was about to change his name to Peter Lee Stirling, and would later change it again to Daniel Boone), he wrote 'You're My Little Girl', although it was Stirling and his fellow musicians, and not Bruce, who actually recorded it. It was Mason's first song to be released, appearing on the other side of The Bruisers' 'Blue Girl' in 1963.

Flushed with this success, Mason and Stirling then came up with the twelve-string-laden 'Don't Turn Around' for The Merseybeats, for whom Stirling had already written a big hit with 'I Think Of You'.

It was publisher Stuart Reed who introduced Barry to pianist and composer Les Reed, and the budding songwriter Roger Greenaway, who helped him to have confidence in his own material. Les had already had some chart success with songs like 'Tell Me When', which he and Geoff Stephens had written for Birmingham band The Applejacks.

Two of Les and Barry's first songs together were 'You Came Along', for the Jon Anderson-fronted Accrington outfit The Warriors, and 'Here It

Comes Again' for The Fortunes. "We'd often write the words and melody at the same time, but with 'Here It Comes Again' Les had the melody done and I went away and wrote the lyrics. It wasn't all good, though. We had to go to Berlin to routine The Fortunes, and while we were there I got beaten up in a toilet by some German guys. Les drove me all over Berlin looking for them!"

The Reed/Mason team were responsible for many hit songs, especially for Engelbert Humperdinck and Tom Jones. "When 'Delilah' became a big hit for Tom, I felt on top of the world…I'd never felt so good. One day, I'm in a loo at one of the motorway service stations, and standing next to me at the urinal is a guy whistling 'Delilah'. It was so great hearing somebody whistling one of my hits that I couldn't resist telling him. I said 'You know that song you're whistling, "Delilah"? I wrote the lyrics for it. Totally unphased, and clearly unimpressed, he replied 'I'm not whistling the fucking lyrics!'"

Another of their big hits was 'Everybody Knows' for The Dave Clark Five, which reached Number Two in Britain and was a Top 50 hit in the States. "The words were really saying that it's bad enough if somebody blows you out and a relationship finishes, but it's even worse when they do it in front of your mates. That's really embarrassing. So we had 'Wish they hadn't seen you walk away and heard me beg you stay, please stay.' It's bad enough being told that it's over, but when your friends hear you pleading to be taken back…that's awful."

They both wrote with other people, as well as together as a team. Possibly Barry's most unusual collaboration was with Michael Carr, the writer of 'South Of The Border', 'Man Of Mystery', 'Kon-Tiki' and many other classics. The pair came up with one of Des O'Connor's big hits, '1-2-3 O'Leary'. Les teamed up with Geoff Stephens on several songs, including 'Tell Me When', Tom Jones' 'Daughter Of Darkness' and the 1972 football anthem 'Leeds United'.

Geoff was the first songwriting tax exile, and while he was living in Geneva he asked Barry to go over and write with him. They worked on an idea for a musical, which they realised that they would legitimately be able to avoid paying tax on if it were written outside Britain. The musical never saw the light of day, but they did come up with a song called 'Drive Safely, Darling', which became a hit in several countries for Tony Christie.

Musicals have never been lucky for Mason. In 1980, his then business manager Mark McCormack struck a deal with a major backer, who would put money into a musical that Barry was writing. It was all set to open on Broadway, with £500,000 spent on rewrites and rehearsals, when the financial backer was arrested. John DeLorien had been using government money to fund the project.

Barry continues to be enthusiastic about writing, often hosting evenings on stage where he tells anecdotes, plays some of his songs and chats with the audience. "I can't get over the fact that your songs touch people's lives. It sounds pompous, but I can't think of any other way of putting it."

During the '70s, Nicky Chinn and Mike Chapman had a phenomenal run of success as a team. The two met in early 1970 at the London club Tramp, where Mike was working as a waiter and Nicky was a customer. At the time, Mike was playing in a group called Tangerine Peel, who were not quite making the breakthrough they deserved, and Nicky had co-written a couple of songs with Mike D'Abo for the musical *There's A Girl In My Soup*. On the night that they met, Chinn had taken the songs in for the resident DJ to play, which is when Chapman introduced himself as a fellow songwriter. Chinn agreed to do some writing with him. "When we started writing, we were trying to write hits in the style that influenced us at the time, like the songs by writers like Tony Macauley and Roger Cook and Roger Greenaway. The idiom was very much the 'Sugar, Sugar' type of thing, which influenced us to write a song with two words that were the same, 'Funny, Funny'. We thought that, if 'Sugar, Sugar' could be Number One, then we might have a chance! A producer and writer called Phil Wainman said that he knew just the group to record it, and introduced us to Sweet."

Just prior to that meeting, Chinn and Chapman had been hawking their songs around London, playing them to publishers and looking for a break. With consummate belief in their material, they decided that they had to get to somebody who'd know a hit song when he heard one. They thought that record producer Mickie Most was the most obvious choice, but decided against the possibility of being turned away by a receptionist and took somebody from the business out to lunch, got them fairly inebriated and persuaded them to part with Mickie's home number. Nicky Chinn took the bull by the horns, phoned Most at home, and through blatant cheek managed to get a meeting with him the following day. "We played him five songs, including 'Funny, Funny', which he thought was OK but wasn't that crazy about, and in the end we had one song left which we hadn't recorded and that Mike had to play live on his guitar. The song was 'Tom Tom Turnaround', and thank goodness he liked it. It was the start of what would be a long relationship. I asked Mickie what made him see us, and he replied 'I learned a long time ago that you never know what's around the corner, and I wanted to meet the guy who phoned me at nine o'clock at night to tell me that he wrote hits!'"

Most didn't take 'Funny, Funny', although it did become the first of many hits for Sweet, charting in the spring of 1971, and the first of many hits that Chinn and Chapman would provide for them. Their second single, 'Co-Co', about a little boy in a Caribbean setting, unusually featured steel drums. Nevertheless, it set Sweet on course for stardom and moved Chinn and Chapman into a different style of writing.

Nicky felt that then they tried to get too smart too soon. "With the third single, 'Alexander Graham Bell', we tried to get too clever, lyrically. I think it's worth analysing why something doesn't make it so that it doesn't happen again. I think the bottom line was the subject matter. I'm not sure that record buyers were that interested in the story of the guy who invented the telephone! The whole record was a little too ambitious, and maybe slightly misguided."

To get back to a more commercial vein, they decided to be safe and come up with a song that would be close to 'Co-Co'. 'Poppa Joe' did the trick, and they followed it with the slightly rockier 'Little Willy', with which the group were certainly a lot happier. The record became their first US hit.

'Wig Wam Bam' was really the first Chinn and Chapman song for Sweet that allowed them to start getting into a real glam and glitter image, which would become increasingly outrageous visually. "Mike and I worked paid a lot of attention to titles, often using alliteration where possible. 'Wig Wam Bam' was in a way partly influenced by Johnny Preston's 1960 hit 'Running Bear'. The next single, 'Blockbuster', gave us our first Number One. We had the idea sitting in my flat, where we'd meet at ten o'clock every morning. We got this riff going, and then thought of using a siren, which turned out to be a winner, as it made so much impact. At first it apparently used to empty factories, as their workers would think it was a warning siren when it came over the radio via their tannoy systems!"

'Blockbuster' became the first of four big Chinn and Chapman songs for Sweet in the same vein. It was followed by 'Hellraiser', 'Ballroom Blitz' and 'Teenage Rampage'. "After 'Ballroom Blitz', we were really struggling to come up with a follow-up, but were going through a dry period when we couldn't think of anything. One night, we were watching television – in fact, *The Six O'Clock News* on the BBC – and they showed The Osmonds arriving at London Airport, and it was absolute chaos. There were thousands of kids on the roof, screaming and going nuts, and the reporter said 'It's absolutely crazy, here at Heathrow. It's like a teenage rampage.' Mike and I turned to each other and said 'That's it – "Teenage Rampage"!' Once we had the title, the whole song just happened.

In tandem with their success writing for Sweet, they wrote songs for Mud, a band produced by Mickie Most, starting them off with a song that had actually been written as a follow-up to Sweet's 'Little Willy'. That group hadn't liked it, so the song became Mud's first Top Ten single, 'Dyna-mite'.

They wrote the follow-up, 'Tiger Feet', in Regent Sound Studios in London's Tin Pan Alley, Denmark Street, in the half hour that they had left after recording a demo session for another song. Mickie was so enthusiastic about the title that he scheduled a release date on the strength of it, before he'd even heard the song. The song became the first of three Number Ones for Mud.

As with Sweet, Chinn and Chapman kept the hits coming for Mud, providing the group with 'The Cat Crept In', 'Rocket', 'The Secrets That You Keep' and 'Lonely This Christmas'. "It was the only Christmas song that we ever wrote, and Les Gray did a wonderful Elvis vocal on it. The philosophy behind it was that, although Christmas is portrayed as a happy time, for some people it's one of the loneliest times of the year. There's no worse feeling in the world than being alone at Christmas, so if you were alone you could relate to it, and if you weren't you could relate to how lucky you were."

Chapman and Chinn also wrote many of the hits for Smokie, including 'If You Think You Know How To Love Me', 'Oh, Carol', 'I'll Meet You At Midnight', 'Don't Play Your Rock 'n' Roll To Me' and 'Living Next Door To Alice'. For New World they penned 'Tom Tom Turnaround', 'Sister Jane' and 'Kara Kara', and for Racey 'Lay Your Love On Me' and 'Some Girls'.

The also wrote a third single for Racey, called 'Kitty'. "Mickie Most recorded it twice with them and said 'I can't get it right. I've put it on the album, but it doesn't feel like a hit.' I'd always fancied the song, so when someone came to see me looking for a number for Toni Basil, I suggested it. I said 'Obviously you can't call it "Kitty", because you've got a girl singing it. Why don't you record it as "Mickey"?' They did, and her version went to Number Two in Britain and Number One in America."

A girl in Mickie Most's stable for whom they also wrote hits was Suzi Quatro, who Mickie had brought over from the States, where he'd discovered her playing in a band with her sisters. Her first album hadn't done that well, so Mike and Nicky were brought in to write some songs for her. Again, they were successful, coming up with just the right type of material for her raunchy image. Among the hits were the 'Can The Can', 'Devil Gate Drive', 'Wild One' and '48 Crash'. "'48 Crash' is about the male menopause: '48 crash come like a lightening flash' and '48 crash is a silk sash bash'. The 'silk sash bash' is either a smoking jacket or a dressing gown with a silk sash around it. It was really, really obtuse, and I was absolutely certain that nobody knew at the time what '48 Crash' was about. Why we had Suzi singing about the male menopause I just don't know – we were quite a way off it. A lot closer now! I think that the thing about writing songs is quality control. It's knowing what to bin before you get to the recording studio, or very often knowing what not to finish. I think songwriters have got to have very good ears."

Bristol boys Roger Cook (born August 1940) and Roger Greenaway (born August 1942) became songwriting partners in the mid '60s and went on to have enormous success together over the years.

Cook was a time and motion study worker for a shoe manufacturer before he became a building apprentice, and finally started singing with various local groups. He also tried his hand at songwriting, and one of his early efforts, 'Parisienne', was recorded by the eminent bandleader Frank Weir.

Greenaway left grammar school at 15 to train as a representative, while at the same time playing football semi-professionally for Bristol City. After contracting the music bug, he went fully professional with local singing outfit The Kestrels, alongside Tony Burrows, and the group released their versions of The Rooftop Singers' hit 'Walk Right In' and Lennon and McCartney's 'There's A Place'. Roger was inspired to write songs after working with The Kestrels on the first Beatles tour, when Helen Shapiro was top of the bill. He heard the songs that The Beatles were playing and felt that he could do just as well, if not better.

I Write The Songs (UK)

As a singer, he had plenty of contact with Denmark Street and the publishers that had offices there, as they used to call up to try to get them to record their copyrights. Barry Mason wasn't a big writer at the time, but he was managing a singer called Tommy Bruce and stopped Roger Greenaway in the street (not on the same day that he stopped Billy Cotton) and said, "I've never written a song in my life. I sing them but I don't write them, and I need a B-side for a Tommy Bruce record." He said later: "It got me thinking, so I started to write some very bad songs! I'd had a couple of songs recorded before meeting Roger, one by Petula Clark, who did 'Everything In The Garden'."

Roger remembers their first collaboration with Roger Cook. "Both Roger and I had been writing songs separately, but it wasn't until then that either of us wrote a hit, which was 'You've Got Your Troubles' for The Fortunes. What makes a great partnership work is chemistry. I haven't had the same chemistry with other writers that I've worked with as I had with Roger Cook. Roger was a catalyst for me, as I was for him…It's a mind thing. When Roger was my partner, I'd always think 'Now what would Cookie do here? What would he think?', and vice versa."

Following their initial success as writers, they landed a recording contract as a duo with EMI's Columbia label, renaming themselves David And Jonathan for the deal. They released their first single, 'Laughing Fit To Cry', in October 1965, but it wasn't until early in the following year that they made the Top 20 with their version of Lennon and McCartney's 'Michelle'. In that summer, they had a Top Ten hit with one of their own numbers, 'Lovers Of The World Unite', and released 'Ten Storeys High', but after that there were no more hits for them as artists.

During the second half of the '60s, they began to really flex their muscles as writers, penning 'Something's Gotten Hold Of My Heart' and 'Love Grows' for Gene Pitney, the former song becoming a Number One in 1989 for Marc Almond And Gene Pitney, proving once again that a good song never dies.

They wrote another hit for The Fortunes in 1966, 'This Golden Ring', which gave them another Top 20 record. Among their other hits from the late '60s were 'Good Times (Better Times)' for Cliff Richard, written with Jerry Lordan; Family Dogg's 'Just A Way Of Life'; 'Conversations', with Jerry Lordan for Cilla Black; 'The Way It Used To Be' for Engelbert Humperdinck; and 'Melting Pot' for Blue Mink.

They went on to write more hits for Blue Mink with group member and top session bass player Herbie Flowers, including 'Randy', 'Stay With Me' and 'The Banner Man'. For another Blue Mink chart entry, 'Good Morning Freedom', they collaborated with sometime Family Dogg members Albert Hammond and Mike Hazlewood.

Although partners, Cook and Greenaway were wise enough to realise that not every song that they created was going to be a hit, and that they had to work with other songwriters when necessary. Greenaway admits that it could be a daunting process:

> When you work with someone new, it's a fearsome thing to do, because you're taking all your clothes off. Everybody loves to think that there's a mystery about them, but when you sit down to write a song with someone you've never written with before, you're both in the nude. I hope I got on well with all the people I've written with, but you don't necessarily have to like the person you're working with to make it happen. But you do have to respect them and their ability. A lot of partnerships have fallen apart because the writers stopped liking each other. At the very least you have to get on.
>
> You also have to have one person who's dominant, although it doesn't always have to be the same person that's dominant...that can change from one day to the next. It's ideal if the writers are of one mind because, if you have to compromise on something that you really believe in, then the song's damaged in your eyes. When you're working with another writer for the first time, you do want to impress them from the first moment, and to write hits with them you have to get to know them well.

Both men worked with a variety of other people, but it was easier when it was with someone that they knew well enough not to feel too much pressure. Roger Greenaway always felt comfortable working with Barry Mason. "Writing with Barry was always a day of fun for me. We didn't have to write a song. We'd often start something, and if we were stuck we'd just stop and have a cup of tea or go down to the park for a walk. But it would always be a joyful day, because we enjoyed each other's company and had a great laugh together.

During the early '70s, Cook and Greenaway wrote several songs for the group White Plains, including 'My Baby Loves Lovin'', 'Step Into A Dream' and 'When You Are A King', as well as 'Sunny Honey Girl' (the song that was to become a hit for Cliff Richard), 'Today I Killed A Man I Didn't Know', 'Lovin' You, Baby' and 'Every Little Move She Makes', with Tony Macauley.

The Hollies were another outfit to benefit from Cook and Greenaway numbers, the pair collaborating with the group's frontman Allan Clarke on 'Long Cool Woman In A Black Dress' and 'Hey Willy'.

There were many other hits, including 'Softly Whispering I Love You' for The Congregation, featuring the vocals of former Plastic Penny frontman Brian Keith, and also songs for The New Seekers, including the multimillion-selling worldwide hit 'I'd Like To Teach The World To Sing (In Perfect Harmony)'.

The song began life as 'True Love And Apple Pie', and the two Rogers later adapted it for a Coca Cola commercial, after which the song reached Number One in Britain and all around the world. In the States, the single got to Number Seven, with a version by The Hillside Singers reaching Number 13.

No partnership lasts forever, though, and the Greenaway/Cook team was no different. "Our split wasn't acrimonious. Cookie wanted to go and live in America and I didn't. We loved each other as people, and still do, but we're chalk and cheese. I was always the pessimist, assuming that our last hit would literally be our last hit, while Roger was the eternal optimist."

Between 1973 and 1976, Roger Greenaway wrote some ten hits for The Drifters, three of which were co-written with Roger Cook. Those songs – and others – were written with three other collaborators: Tony Macauley, Les Reed and Geoff Stephens. Among these hits were 'You're More Than A Number In My Little Red Book', 'Hello Happiness', 'Down On The Beach Tonight', 'Every Night's A Saturday Night With You', 'Kissing In The Back Row Of The Movies' and 'Like Sister And Brother'.

Roger Cook still lives in the States, and continues to write hit songs, while Roger Greenaway moved into the organisation side of songwriting and is currently running the British branch of ASCAP. "I don't write any more 'cause I do other things, and I think, if you're going to be a songwriter, you have to be totally focused and not have other distractions. It's bloody hard. You hear writers say 'Oh, I wrote that in ten or 15 minutes.' Yes, that can happen; but sitting down with a blank sheet of paper when you may not have an idea in your head…"

10 Change Partners

It's fascinating to see who wrote with whom during the golden periods of British and American songwriting. As well as also being a team for some years, both Barry Mason and Les Reed were part of a group of British writers who worked with each other, and Geoff Stephens successfully collaborated with both of them. He also wrote many hits by himself, such as 'Winchester Cathedral' and 'Peek-A-Boo' for The New Vaudeville Band, and 'The Crying Game' and 'One Heart Between Two' for Dave Berry.

He in turn worked with the teams of Mitch Murray and Peter Callander on Cliff Richard's hit 'Goodbye Sam, Hello Samantha', and with Roger Cook and Roger Greenaway on The Drifters' 'Like Sister And Brother'. Another of his co-writers was Tony Macauley, with whom he wrote 'Smile A Little Smile For Me', a US Top Ten hit for Flying Machine, and The Hollies' Top Three record 'Sorry Suzanne'. Stephens also penned 'Knock Knock, Who's There?' for Mary Hopkin and the Herman's Hermits hit 'My Sentimental Friend' with John Carter, another prolific writer.

Carter's main writing partner in the '60s was Ken Lewis. At the age of 21, the pair travelled down from Small Heath in Birmingham, hoping to interest publishers with their songs. One publisher, Terry Kennedy, saw something in their material, and introduced them to Bob Kingston at Southern Music, who signed them as writers. Tommy Steele was so impressed with one of their demos that he felt that they should be recording as well as writing.

Their first successes were the instrumental 'Checkpoint' for Denis Newey and 'Come Back Running' for Gerry Beckle, although their first big hit was Mike Sarne's 'Will I What?' Having by now changed their names from John Shakespeare and Ken Hawker, they also fronted the group Carter-Lewis And The Southerners, who built up a formidable reputation through regular appearances on BBC Radio's *Saturday Club* and *Easy Beat*.

On becoming The Flowerpot Men, they wrote several hits for the outfit, including 'Tossin' And Turnin'', 'Funny How Love Can Be' and 'That's Why I'm Crying' before joining the group and penning 'Let's Go To San Francisco' and 'Walk In The Sky'.

Two of the most successful songs they wrote for American artists were 'A Little Bit O' Soul', a million-seller in 1967 and a US Number One for the Ohio quintet The Music Explosion, and 'Is It True?', which was a hit on both sides of the Atlantic for Brenda Lee. "Record producer Micky Most rang us up and said 'Have you got a song for Brenda Lee? She's coming in next week, and I've been asked to record her.' We said 'Well, no we haven't, but we'll sit down and write one…If it's Brenda Lee, great.' We wrote 'Is It True?' in a couple of days. Micky liked it, and recorded it three days later with Brenda. We got invited onto the session to sing backing vocals. That was quite a thrilling experience, going into the studio and singing with Brenda Lee."

One of their biggest American hits was 'Can't You Hear My Heartbeat?' a million-seller for Herman's Hermits. On one occasion, they actually had to become the Hermits. "I played the song to Micky Most and he said 'Yeah, I love the song…but I really love the demo. Could you actually recreate that demo for me for Herman's Hermits?' I told him that I could get some musicians in, and he said 'That's what I want to do. I want you to come in the studio, re-record that demo, and I'll bring Peter Noone in and we'll call it Herman's Hermits. So I did, and the track of 'Sunshine Girl' included myself on guitar and Hudson and Ford, who went on to join The Strawbs and have hits as a duo, on bass and drums. I did the high harmonies, and it ended up as a duplicate of the demonstration record we'd taken to Micky."

Carter also wrote with Russell Alquist, who had been responsible for The Fourmost's big hit 'A Little Lovin''. The pair also came up with 'Sleepy Joe' for Herman's Hermits. With Roger Cook, he wrote the as-yet unreleased 'Democratic Working Man', and with Tony Macauley 'Hard Working Woman'.

Macauley's main writing partner was John Macleod, and the pair came up with several hits for The Foundations, including 'Baby, Now That I've Found You', 'In The Bad, Bad Old Days' and 'Back On My Feet Again'. Another Foundations hit, 'Build Me Up, Buttercup', was written by Macauley with Manfred Mann frontman Mike D'Abo, writer of such classics as 'Handbags And Gladrags'.

Macauley and Macleod penned the hit songs 'That Same Old Feeling' and '(It's Like A) Sad Old Kinda Movie' for Pickettywitch, as well as The Paper Dolls' hits 'Something Here In My Heart' and 'That Same Old Feeling'. They also wrote Long John Baldry's hits 'Let The Heartaches Begin' and 'Mexico', and penned 'The Lights Of Cincinatti', which was recorded by both Baldry and Scott Walker. Meanwhile, Macauley supplied 'Baby, Make It Soon', 'Walking A Tightope' and 'Falling Apart At The Seams' for Marmalade. Then, to bring us full circle, in 1970 Macauley wrote the Number One single 'Love Grows (Where My Rosemary Goes)' with Barry Mason.

It's also interesting to take a couple of examples of artists that have enjoyed a long career through taking the best songs from prolific writers.

The Drifters' longevity has been helped by material from many of the above, in such combinations as Macauley/Greenaway, Cook/Greenaway/Stephens, Reed/Greenaway and Greenaway/Stephens. The group also used Brill building material from Goffin/King, Mann/Weil, Mann/Weil/Leiber/Stoller, Pomus/Shuman and songs from Bacharach/Hilliard, Art Resnick And Kenny Young and Bert Berns.

Cliff Richard's career has spanned more than four decades, and he admits that he "has always chosen to sing the best and most commercial song by the best writers". Among the many composers and lyricists that have made Cliff the country's most successful singer are Hank Marvin, Bruce Welch, Brian Bennett, John Rostill, Ian Samwell, Alan Tarney, Guy Fletcher and Doug Flett, Sid Tepper and Roy Bennett, Bill Martin and Phil Coulter, Raymond Froggatt, Don Everly, Neil Diamond, BA Robertson, Terry Britten, Mort Shuman and Jerry Leiber, and Mike Stoller.

It's amazing that more artists don't use this rather obvious route to success. As Cliff says, "I know that I can sing well, but I'm not that great a songwriter, so it makes more sense for me to do what I do best and let the songwriters do what they do best."

As well as the songwriting partnerships well known to the music buyers of today, hundreds of successful earlier composers and lyricists also worked together in one-off situations, or in the hope that a particular liaison might yield that magic and enduring formula. Much like Dodie Smith's *Dear Octopus*, the tentacles of the professional songwriting family are far reaching, all being related, however distant. As with romance, some relationships work for a time, some terminate acrimoniously, others turn out to be an ideal marriage, and some people search in vain for the right person with whom to team up while others opt for the lone path. Some seek the best of both worlds, the wife and mistress. Here are just a few examples of how an earlier circle of composers and lyricists are musically related to each other.

Harry Carroll was born in New Jersey in 1892, playing the piano for silent films while he was still at school before becoming an arranger in Tin Pan Alley in the USA. By night he caressed the ivories at New Jersey's Garden Café. He later teamed up with Arthur Fields and lyricist Ballard MacDonald to write stage musicals, but it was the partnership of Carroll and MacDonald that came up with that durable classic 'The Trail Of The Lonesome Pine' in 1913, a song made popular by The Hedges Brothers And Jacobson and Edna Brown (Elsie Baker) And James Harrison. The song's life was extended thanks to it's inclusion in Hal Roach's 1937 film *Way Out West*, starring Laurel and Hardy, and became successful again in 1975 when the two stars took it to Number Two in Britain with The Avalon Boys, featuring Chill Wills.

Between 1914 and 1917, Carroll was a director of ASCAP, whose duties he handled in tandem with his songwriting, and he also appeared as half of a vaudeville act with his wife, Anna.

1918 saw him producing his own Broadway musical, *Oh Look*, and from it came another classic, this time written with Joseph McCarthy. Marrying the melody of the middle section of Chopin's Fantasie Impromptu in C sharp minor to their own lyric, they created the million-selling song 'I'm Always Chasing Rainbows', which was popularised by The Dolly Sisters (Jennie and Rosie) and Harry Fox. In the '90s, Neil Sedaka, one of the most successful songwriters of the '60s and '70s, featured the song on his gold album *Classically Sedaka*. It was also interpolated into the 1976 reworking of the 1920 musical *Irene*, for which McCarthy was also the original lyricist. Another song that travelled reasonably well from that musical was McCarthy and Henry Tierney's 'Alice Blue Gown', sung by 25-year-old Edith Day.

McCarthy, who in 1924 would write additional lyrics for Bud Flanagan's delightful slice of pathos 'Underneath The Arches', teamed up with another partner in 1913, James V Monaco, to write the classic 'You Made Me Love You'. In that year it notched up sheet music sales of a million copies, and two years later it was interpolated into the 1915 musical *Keep Smiling*. Recorded by many artists over the years, it became successful on disc during the '40s, when it became a million-seller for trumpeter Harry James and his orchestra, and featured in his two films *Syncopation* and *Private Buckaroo*. The song sold another million when Al Jolson had a hit with it in 1946.

In 1916, McCarthy and Monaco teamed up with Howard Johnson to write another blockbuster, 'What Do You Want To Make Those Eyes At Me For?', which featured in the stage show *Follow Me* and later in *A Better 'Ole*. In 1959 it became a UK Number One for Emile Ford.

Jimmie Monaco also worked with lyricist William Jerome, born in 1865 and 20 years Monaco's senior. The pair wrote 'Row, Row, Row', which was included in the London version of *Hullo Ragtime*, at one point being sung by two of the shows stars, Bonita and Shirley Kellog. It was also interpolated into the Ziegfeld Follies' act of 1912, and was included in the 1963 stage version of *Oh! What A Lovely War*, along with many other songs from World War One, including Jerome Kern's 'They Didn't Believe Me'.

Jerome worked successfully not only with Monaco but also with one of Kern's early co-writers, George Grossmith Junior, and more prolifically with the composer Jean Schwartz. The best-known song from the Schwartz/Jerome collaboration was 'Chinatown, My Chinatown', from the show *Up And Down Broadway*, which later appeared in the 1915 musical *Push And Go*.

Although Schwartz (born 1878) and Jerome were a regular writing team, Schwartz also worked with other authors, including Sam Lewis and Joe Young, the trio collaborating in 1918 on a song that was to be made famous by Al Jolson, 'Rock-A-Bye Your Baby With A Dixie Melody'. The number also later appearing in the stage musical *Sinbad*.

Lewis and Young in turn teamed up with George W Meyer to write the jocular 'Where Did Robinson Crusoe Go With Friday On Saturday Night?', and also with prolific composer Walter Donaldson for 'My Mammy' and 'How Ya Gonna Keep 'Em Down On The Farm?'. 'My Mammy' sold a million copies of sheet music when it came out in 1920, and Al Jolson's recording sold million records in 1946. In 1967, The Happenings' version shifted a million units of vinyl. Donaldson also wrote the multimillion-selling Gene Austin hit of 1927 'My Blue Heaven', with George Whiting, and 'Little White Lies', which became a million-seller for Dick Haymes in 1948, a year after the writer's death.

His most regular writing partner, however, was Gus Kahn. During the '20s, the pair wrote many songs, including 'Carolina In The Morning', 'Beside A Babbling Brook', 'Yes Sir! That's My Baby' and 'Love Me Or Leave Me', the latter song giving the 1950 Doris Day/James Cagney film its title. Kahn worked not only with Donaldson; he'd also previously co-written the 1916 Al Jolson smash 'Pretty Baby' with Buddy DeSylva. Jolson shrewdly cut himself in on the writing credit of that one.

Lyricist DeSylva wrote with a variety of composers, including Louis Silvers on 'April Showers', Victor Herbert on 'Kiss In The Dark', Joseph Meyer on 'California, Here I Come' and Jerome Kern for the 1920 classic 'Look For The Silver Lining'. Kern in turn wrote with a variety of talented lyricists, including Dorothy Fields, Jonny Mercer, Yip Harburg, Ira Gershwin, Otto Harbach, PG Wodehouse and Oscar Hammerstein II. Hammerstein was fortunate to have two of the most prolific composers as his main collaborators, Jerome Kern and Richard Rodgers, and he also worked with George Gershwin on occasion.

And so the list goes on, a network of talent working together to produce an incredible volume of wonderful and durable songs. One can see how the baton of experience can be passed down the line as songwriters cross-pollinate down through the years. Let's take as a random selection the songwriter who came near the end of the previous list, Jerome Kern, and move through famous songwriters who have worked with each other. (I've left out the words "worked with", or it would get like people in the bible begetting each other all over the place. Suffice to say that each person has collaborated with the person following.)

> Jerome Kern, Dorothy Fields, Sigmund Romburg, Gus Kahn, Nacio Herb Brown, Vincent Youmans, Irving Caesar, George Gershwin, Ira Gershwin, Jerome Kern, Oscar Hammerstein II, Richard Rodgers, Stephen Sondheim, Jule Styne, Don Black, Andrew Lloyd Webber, Tim Rice, Elton John, Gary Osborne, Michael Carr, Jimmy Kennedy.

I'll end there, as several of the above have won the coveted songwriting award named after Jimmy Kennedy, and that seems suitably appropriate. However, if you prefer the alternative happy ending:

> Gary Osborne, Albert Hammond, Diane Warren (the most successful songwriter working today).

As you can see, it's a family.

11 *Let's Work Together*

One of the most durable and consistent partnerships of the last few decades has been that of composer Burt Bacharach and lyricist Hal David. I believe that the first song that Burt and I wrote together was called 'I Cry More', which was sung by Alan Dale. It wasn't a hit, but it was the beginning of what turned out to be a happy and successful relationship.

Alan Dale, who had changed his name from the less commercial Aldo Sigismondi, later had two million-selling songs in 1956, one of which was 'Cherry Pink And Apple Blossom White', with English lyrics by Hal's older brother, Mack. The senior David had had success in the middle of the '40s with Johnny Mercer, who took his 'Candy' to Number One. He would go on to write more great songs in the '50s and '60s. Among other Mack David classics were 'It Must Be Him', 'I Don't Care If The Sun Don't Shine', 'The Ballad Of Cat Ballou' and '77 Sunset Strip'.

Born in Brooklyn in May 1921, Hal was constantly writing songs, stories and poems as a boy, as well as editing the high-school magazine, and working during the summer with his band when he was a little older. It was for these musicians and local night-club acts that Hal began writing songs in earnest, at the same time holding down a job on the *New York Post*, but in keeping with millions of other young Americans his plans were put on hold. The country became involved in the 1939-45 conflict, after the United States declared war on the Axis powers in 1941, and the hopes and aspirations of many young people were altered for ever. However, Hal David was luckier than most in that he was able to pursue his passion. "When I was in the army during World War II, I was assigned to the Special Services unit that wrote shows for the troops in the Pacific. I think songwriting really got into my blood then. When I got out of the army, I knew that was what I wanted to do for the rest of my life. After I was released, in 1949 I met a fellow called Don Rodney, who was in The Guy Lombardo Band, and I wrote a lyric for him, and he said he'd try to write a melody for it. When I went into Lombardo's office to sign the contract for the song, 'The Four Winds And The Seven Seas', I still hadn't heard the music for it! It turned out to be my first big hit."

Burt Bacharach was born in Kansas City in May 1928 but was raised in New York, where he studied music under the Czech composer Bohuslav Martinu, the innovative US composer Henry Cowell and the French composer Darius Milhaud, one of musical côterie in France known as Les Six. With tutelage from this incredible pedigree of teachers, he eventually gave up his ambition to be a professional sportsman. Any inroads he wanted to make into the music industry were put on hold as he undertook his two years of duty in the army in the early '50s. After his military sojourn, he became accompanist and arranger for several artists, including Steve Lawrence, Vic Damone and The Ames Brothers, and he also had his first song published, 'The Night Plane To Heaven'.

Between 1958 and 1963, he toured with the husky-voiced, German-born singer and actress Marlene Dietrich (who was already in her mid to late 50s), working as her musical director and arranger.

It was at the New York publishers Famous Paramount that Bacharach and David first met, the first fruits of their partnership being 'The Story Of My Life', a US hit for Marty Robbins and a British Number One for Michael Holliday, where it also charted for Alma Cogan and Dave King. They followed this with another British Number One, the million-selling song 'Magic Moments', sung by Perry Como, which stayed on top of the UK chart for nine weeks, backed with Lee Pockriss and Paul Vance's 'Catch A Falling Star'. In the States, it made the Top Ten.

Working from the Brill building, on occasion both writers teamed up with different partners. Pockriss and David had previously collaborated on a song called 'American Beauty Rose', and later Hal worked with Sherman Edwards to write Sarah Vaughan's 1959 American Top Ten hit 'Broken-Hearted Melody', and later still he provided the lyrics for Henry Mancini's 'Baby Elephant Walk'. Hal's brother Mack, an eight times Oscar nominee, wrote 'Baby It's You' with Bacharach in the early '60s, a song which became a hit for The Shirelles and was later successfully covered by The Beatles.

Bacharach didn't only write with the David brothers; he wrote 'Heavenly' and 'Faithfully' with Sidney Shaw for Johnny Mathis in 1959 and 1960 respectively, after which he teamed up with the prolific Bob Hilliard. The pair penned 'Tower Of Strength', a UK Number One for Frankie Vaughan and a US Top Ten hit for the very underrated Gene McDaniels, who also scored with Burt and Hal's 'Another Tear Falls'.

Bacharach and Hilliard had more success with 'Please Stay' for The Drifters, a much-covered song that undoubtedly received its best interpretation at the hands of Liverpool group The Cryin' Shames. Producer Joe Meek wrung the emotion out of lead singer Charlie Crane.

> We'd just finished a gig on Merseyside and had this mad idea to drive down to London to try to get an audition with Joe Meek, who was really the happening producer at the time. We were absolutely knackered when we arrived outside his studio in the Holloway Road, and slept in the van. Being parked where we were, and in a group wagon, it was rather obvious what we were there for, so in the morning one of Joe's assistants came down to tell us that Joe wasn't seeing anybody and to go away. Well, we hadn't come all that way to just turn around and go home again, so we persisted and eventually he reluctantly got us to haul our equipment up to the first floor. My voice was a bit shot, having just done a gig and having had hardly any sleep, which didn't impress him too much. I ended up on the receiving end of one of the volatile outbursts for which he famed, and being dog-tired I was virtually in tears. Joe appeared delighted, knowing that he would now get a really emotional performance of our version of Burt Bacharach and Hal David's 'Please Stay', which he did!

The Cryin' Shames' version went into the Top 30 in Britain in the spring of 1966, by which time Bacharach and David had written many hits, among them Chuck Jackson's 'Any Day Now', Jack Jones' 'Wives And Lovers', The Walker Brothers' 'Make It Easy On Yourself', Sandie Shaw's 'There's Always Something There To Remind Me', Dusty Springfield's 'I Just Don't Know What To Do With Myself' and Jackie DeShannon's 'What The World Needs Now'.

The latter number, and songs like 'Alfie' and 'I'll Never Fall In Love Again', proved to be occasions where the lyrics came before the music, although Hal confesses that he and Bacharach were able to work the other way around as well. "Sometimes the words came first and sometimes the music, as with 'Raindrops Keep Falling On My Head', 'Walk On By' and 'The Look Of Love'. Sometimes we'd sit in a room and just bang songs out together, as with 'I Say A Little Prayer', 'I Just Don't Know What To Do With Myself' and 'Wishin' And Hopin''. We worked hard in those years, getting together every day when we were in the same city at the same time, and when we weren't together we were constantly on the phone, conferring with each other."

After Gene Pitney's success with the title track from the film *Town Without Pity*, many songs were submitted for the next one he was asked to perform, including one from Bacharach and David. Pitney remembers:

> Along came 'The Man Who Shot Liberty Valence', from Burt Bacharach and Hal David, and I just had to record it. The film then had all the ingredients: a great songwriting team, John Ford directing, and Lee Marvin, James Stewart and John Wayne starring. Paramount Pictures paid me a bundle of money to record that song for the movie, as well as paying for the recording session in New York. I was in the studio with Burt Bacharach, putting the song down, when somebody came in, saw the title on the box and said, "I see that that movie has just been released." Due to an oversight, the song never got put in the film! The company tried to get around it by saying that they would instruct the cinemas to have it played in the projection booths prior to the film being shown, which is ridiculous. All credit to the song for being a hit without ever appearing in the movie for which it was intended. Even today, people watching the film as a late night TV movie say to me, "I stayed up until 3am but I didn't hear the song. Where was it?"

Another Bacharach and David classic recorded by Gene Pitney was his transatlantic hit '24 Hours From Tulsa'. "It was a great song for me because it allowed me to go outside the borders of the US for the first time in my life. I love travelling and going to other countries and hearing other languages, and 'Tulsa' gave me that opportunity. It brought me to Britain for the first time, where I sang it on shows like *Thank Your Lucky Stars*, and the song just jumped into the chart."

During the late '50s and early '60s, Bacharach became increasingly frustrated with some interpretations of his songs and rejection from artists like Connie Francis and Vic Damone, driving him to create a situation through which his material could be channelled and over which he had total artistic control. The artist he chose to use to achieve this was Dionne Warwick, a singer he'd heard in 1962 providing backing vocals on The Drifters' 'Mexican Divorce', itself a song that would later inspire Steely Dan founders Walter Becker and Donald Fagen to write 'Haitian Divorce'.

The liaison proved to be a complete success. Burt and Hal provided her with a string of hits from 1963 onwards, including 'Don't Make Me Over', 'Anyone Who Had A Heart', 'Walk On By', 'You'll Never Get To Heaven', 'I Say A Little Prayer', 'Alfie', 'Message To Michael', 'Promises, Promises', 'Trains And Boats And Planes', 'Do You Know The Way To San José?', 'I'll Never Fall In Love Again' and 'This Girl's In Love With You'.

Using vocal group and orchestra, Bacharach had some success with his own recordings of 'I'll Never Fall In Love Again', which was a small hit in the States, and 'Trains And Boats And Planes', which became a Top Ten hit in Britain. He also recorded several others, including 'What's New, Pussycat?', 'I'll Never Fall In Love Again' and 'All Kinds Of People'.

During the '60s, British covers of Bacharach and David songs were legion, from artists which included Cilla Black, The Swinging Blue Jeans, Dusty Springfield, Billy J Kramer, The Merseybeats, Adam Faith and Sandie Shaw. In the States, apart from the US artists previously mentioned, their songs were also recorded by dozens of other top acts, including Bobby Vinton, Bobby Goldsboro, Aretha Franklin, Lou Johnson Jerry Butler, Brook Benton and Timi Yuro.

Possibly one of their most underrated songs was the charming 'Me Japanese Boy', which was a minor hit in the States for Bobby Goldsboro and a single in Britain for Cork duo Patrick Carroll and John Daly, who recorded as The Dalys. Their version was a winner, and should have met with more success.

Several Bacharach and David songs came from films, including *What's New, Pussycat?*, *Alfie*, *Casino Royale* and *Butch Cassidy And The Sundance Kid*, the latter winning an Oscar and a Grammy for Best Musical Score and a further Best Song Oscar for 'Raindrops Keep Falling On My Head'. Surprisingly, however, they pair didn't explore the world of stage musicals as much as one might have imagined, although when Neil Simon adapted the book *Promises, Promises* into Billy Wilder's film *The*

Apartment Bacharach and David provided the songs. The movie opened at the Schubert Theatre, New York, in December 1968, and ran until 1971, collecting a Tony Award and a Grammy for Best Original Theatre Cast Album. In London, it opened at the Prince Of Wales Theatre in 1969, under the musical direction of Ian Macpherson.

In tandem with his success with David, as an orchestra leader Bacharach sold a vast quantity of easy listening albums that blended choral and orchestral, and collected even more Grammy awards in the early '70s. His early musical training with such influential and innovative teachers gave him the expertise to work in diverse areas of the industry – films, stage musicals, pop, orchestral, classical and choral – and he brought to each a distinctive musical sophistication, depth and structure that eluded those of his competitors who had received no formal training.

By the early '70s, Bacharach, had stopped working with both Hal David and Dionne Warwick, and didn't work with another permanent partner until the early '80s when he began to collaborate with his new wife, Carole Bayer Sager. The pair came up with a string of hits, including three American chart-toppers: 'Arthur's Theme (Best That You Can Do)' for Christopher Cross, 'That's What Friends Are For' for Dionne Warwick, and 'On My Own' for Patti LaBelle And Michael McDonald.

Songwriting is an exciting journey into the unknown, whether one decides to operate as a solo writer or works with a partner. Some paths are strewn with despair and frustration, with possibly a brief period of glory thrown in. Writers on these paths have their time, their King Midas moment, when the songs come with consummate ease; they can write for the current trend, and the charts seem to be at their fingertips. Bacharach and David transcended fads and fashions, being able to create quality and durable songs. Of course, however talented the team, success is never guaranteed. "Burt and I always felt that we worked well together and could create something exciting, but there's no real way to know that what you're going to come up with is going to work. If anyone had the formula for the magic ingredient, we'd all be at the top of the chart."

After the great partnership of Bacharach and David had written Perry Como's 16th million-seller, another team, who had been writing together even longer, provided the singer with his 17th. Sid Tepper and Roy Bennett were both born in the summer of 1918. The pair first meeting at the age of eleven, when the

Tepper family moved in across the road from the Bennetts in Brooklyn, New York. Roy Bennett remembers the early friendship: "We went to high school together, although we were not in the same class...we were good friends. In 1929, we wrote our first song together. I was mostly the words and he was the music, but later we both wrote the words and the music."

Their songwriting partnership would span an incredible 40 years and lead to them writing over 500 songs. They had over 300 of these published, and Elvis Presley recorded more than 50 of them. Their careers as songwriters began in earnest in 1939, when they wrote 'Jungle Jive' – recorded by trumpeter Tommy Reynolds and his orchestra – and 'Candle Burning Blue'.

Although their partnership and writing activities were suspended when the US entered World War Two, Bennett recorded 'Candle' for HMV in India in 1945, courtesy of the Air Corps, where they called him the Frank Sinatra of India. While Roy spent a year in India and two in China, Sid served in the US Cavalry. After the war, they continued in their songwriting activities with renewed vigour, and Bennett turned down the chance of studying singing despite having the vocal talents to be an opera singer.

In 1945, they worked as part of the team at Crest Music, which, in Roy Bennett's words, after six months became "Crestfallen Music...We all jumped out of the window and separated!" During their time at Crest, Sid Mills of Mills Music had heard about them and subsequently offered them a job as staff writers. Tepper and Bennett stayed there for four years. "While we were there we wrote two songs that made the Hit Parade: 'Say Something To Your Sweetheart', which was recorded in England by Sir Peter Pears and Vera Lynn; and 'Red Roses For A Blue Lady', recorded by Guy Lombardo and Vaughn Monroe in November 1948." A 1965 version by Bert Kaempfert and his orchestra would become a million-selling single in 1965, and would also appear on one of his best-selling albums, *Blue Midnight*. 'Red Roses' was the all-time favourite song of the mother of American president Bill Clinton.

In around 1950, the two songwriters found themselves released by Mills Music.

> We were pretty miserable because it's so hard to make a living out of writing songs, and while we'd been at Mills Music we'd been well paid. These were all advances against royalties, so we knew

where our next buck was coming from. When they let us go, the bottom fell out and we knew we'd have to go to the top of the Brill building again and start working our way down, and start writing independently. As it turned out, it was the best thing that could have happened to us. Not being tied to Mills, we could work for any publisher. We wrote 'It's A Long Way From Your House To My House' for Sinatra, which was the last recording he made for Columbia Records before he went to Capitol. The song was inspired by the distance I had to travel to be with my fiancée. We wrote 'Naughty Lady Of Shady Lane' in 1955, when Sid's wife was pregnant. Incidentally, the "naughty lady" turned out to be a boy! '20 Tiny Fingers' was written just after my wife gave birth to twins.

'Naughty Lady' became a Top Ten hit in Britain for Ohio family outfit The Ames Brothers, the group going on to record another eight Tepper and Bennett songs, including their fourth-biggest US hit, 'My Bonnie Lassie'. One of the reasons for the pair's success with this particular act was the fact that, like the group, the two writers were baritones and were therefore able to demonstrate the songs in such a manner that the Ames boys could easily visualise themselves singing them.

Perry Como took their million-selling song 'Kewpie Doll' to the Top Ten in Britain and the States in 1958, and the song was also covered in Britain by Frankie Vaughan, getting into the UK Top Ten.

By the time they began writing for films, they had once again become staff writers, this time for Aberbach Music, with whom they remained for two or three years. The Aberbach brothers' Elvis Presley connection was to prove highly beneficial for Roy and Sid, as they were in the front line for writing songs for rock 'n' roll's hottest property, even though they were primarily ballad writers. Freddy Bienstock was in charge of the Presley operation, and it was through him that the pair had to work, although they still had to pitch their material.

We were one of a dozen or 15 teams that Freddy gave scripts to before making the movies. These scripts had spots marked where the songs were supposed to go, so we knew what the situation was and we wrote for that situation…So what happened was that Freddy might get twelve songs for one spot. He would be the first screener, and then he would choose four of the songs to be made into demonstration records to be sent to the producer and to Elvis. They would then do the choosing of the one that would be used for the movie. Most of our demos were not in Elvis' style, nor did we try to imitate his voice...we did it straight. He'd simplify the melody sometimes, which was quite unexpected, and often it was difficult to understand the words he was singing. Elvis had a great ability to twist words to make them fit a melody. We never had a problem with the words, but he did change the melody on a couple of our songs...I think 'Angel' was one. Only one word change he made bothered me, and that was in our song 'Drums Of The Islands'. We'd written "anywhere I wander, anywhere I roam", but he sang "wonder"...I don't know why.

Tepper and Bennett had over 50 of their songs recorded by Presley, the film *Blue Hawaii* featuring no less than five of them, including the romantic 'Island Of Love' and 'Hawaiian Sunset'. Strangely, neither of the writers had been to Hawaii at the time, and just wrote intuitively.

Despite writing so many songs for Presley, it's surprising that neither writer ever actually met him, although they did meet his manager, Colonel Tom Parker, on one occasion while demoing a song live in a hotel room.

The pair rarely collaborated with other writers, although the Polynesian Cultural Centre received a third of the royalties from 'Drums Of The Island', despite the melody being in the public domain. They did write 'Shoppin' Around', however, and the title track for Elvis' album *GI Blues* with Aaron Schroeder. The trio also teamed up to write 'Glad All Over', a song that was later recorded live by The Beatles.

As well as the Elvis connection, Tepper and Bennett also wrote many songs that became hits for Britain's top singer, Cliff Richard. "We had many Cliff Richard recordings, like 'Travellin' Light', 'When The Girl In Your Arms Is The Girl In Your Heart', 'Outsider', 'D In Love', 'Somebody Loses', 'Don't Be Mad At Me' and 'Where Is My Heart?', but the biggest of all was 'The Young Ones'. The Leeds Music representative from London came over to meet with the Leeds guy in New York, Lou Levy, who asked us to write a title song for a movie called *The Young Ones*, which was a smash in many parts of the world, especially England."

They also wrote 'Wonderful World Of The Young', a small US hit for

Andy Williams in 1962 and a Top Ten British hit for Danny Williams in the same year, and also 'I'll Step Down', a UK Top 40 hit for Garry Mills in 1961.

The method of writing songs varies slightly from writer to writer and team to team, but Tepper and Bennett's way of writing certainly wasn't the norm. "It always started with a title. I had studied music, but neither of us played an instrument...we just talked and sang at each other. It was an unusual way of working. We created the words and music at the same time. There was a piano in the room, but I didn't go to it until after the song was finished. That's when I wrote the lead sheet. We'd sometimes write four or five songs in a day. 'Red Roses For A Blue Lady' was written in just half an hour."

In the late '60s, Sid Tepper suffered a heart attack and moved to Florida, where he still lives, thus ending an incredibly successful songwriting partnership which spanned four decades.

It seems that, in line with the old adage "where there's a hit there's a writ", many writer/publisher relationships that started life full of promise turn sour when the money starts rolling in. As John D Loudermilk admitted, "The Everly Brothers, Roy Orbison fellow-writers Felice and Boudleaux Bryant and I all signed contracts with publisher Wesley Rose that we regretted."

The Bryants, like Loudermilk, would also write for The Everly Brothers, and would become – along with Goffin and King, and Ellie Greenwich and Jeff Barry – one of the most successful husband-and-wife songwriting teams in musical history. Boudleaux, born in February 1920, studied music and played violin in the Atlanta Philharmonic Orchestra before moving into the field of country music. In 1945, while playing piano in a hotel in Milwaukee, he met Felice (born August 1925), who was working there as an elevator attendant. They married and moved to Moultrie, Georgia, a very small town. Felice admits:

> "There wasn't much to do...I continued doing what I'd done before I married Boudleaux – I wrote poetry and song lyrics and did a lot of reading while he ran a local radio band...he was a very accomplished musician. We didn't have any money, so I suggested that he wrote to a few people he knew...after all, he'd worked with just about everyone at one time or another. I didn't write music, but if I had a tune, he'd take it and polish it up, or I would try to put

words to some of his melodies. In this way, we amassed about 80 songs, which is why I got him to approach people in the business. One of our first bites came from radio and TV star Arthur Godfrey, who wanted one of our songs, 'Country Boy', but wanted to publish it and have a cut of the songwriting. He said, "To hell with it, let's forget him." He had tunnel vision as far as that was concerned. Boudleaux sometimes had to go along with a cut-in, as he was the breadwinner, but I never had to. He had to make exceptions.

Despite digging in their heels over the Arthur Godfrey offer, in 1949 'Country Boy' was their first commercial success. Published by Fred Rose, it became a Top Ten hit on the country chart for diminutive singer Little Jimmy Dickens. Moving to Nashville in 1950, they wrote country hits for Carl Smith, a Grand Ole Opry singer from Tennessee, including 'Just Wait Till I Get You Alone', 'Our Honeymoon' and 'It's A Lovely, Lovely World'. In 1953, the pair had their first success on the pop chart when Frankie Laine had a big hit with 'Hey Joe'. The singer also had a Top Ten country hit with their 'Back Up, Buddy'. A big influence on John D Loudermilk, Eddy Arnold, recorded two of Boudleaux and Felice's songs in 1955, 'The Richest Man In The World' and 'I've Been Thinking'.

However, the number that saw the Bryants break through internationally as songwriters was still waiting in the wings. Their classic 'Bye Bye, Love' was originally written with Louisiana Hayride and Grand Ole Opry stars Johnny And Jack in mind. That duo – comprising Johnny Wright, who was married to "queen of country music" Kitty Wells, and Jack Anglin, who would be killed in a car crash six years later on his way to Patsy Cline's funeral – had been country favourites since the '30s, and seemed to Boudleaux like an ideal vehicle for the song. However, fate decreed otherwise, as Felice recalls:

> When Boudleaux started 'Bye Bye Love', he called me and said, "I've got the best idea for a hit for Johnny And Jack." Well, he only had the chorus when he played it to me...the "Bye bye love, bye bye happiness" bit, all that section, and I didn't think much of it. It was only when he started putting it together on the guitar that it began to sound good. We worked on it and finished it off, and Boudleaux started showing it around, but nobody seemed to

like it much and several people in the business were rather critical of it. Suddenly, though, the sound found a champion in the boss of Cadence Records, Archie Bleyer, who put it on hold for five of his acts, including The Everly Brothers. Four of the acts turned it down as not being right or not commercial enough, but The Everlys said, "We'll do it."

Even if the song didn't end up being recorded by her husband Johnny, Kitty Wells did record one of the Bryants' songs, 'A Change Of Heart'.

Inspiration for songs can come from many strange sources, even household objects. Reg Presley of The Troggs was watching the Salvation Army group The Joy Strings performing on television when a certain phrase sparked off the beginnings of what was to become the multimillion-selling 'Love Is All Around'. Chris Difford of Squeeze was also inspired by his TV set; while watching *The Benny Hill Show* he heard a song which he realised had the metre he needed for the song 'Cool For Cats', which would become a big hit for the group. More unusually, Felice Bryant's vacuum cleaner inspired her to write another top song for The Everly Brothers.

> We had a chipped marble roof, and I was always picking up chipped marble in the vacuum cleaner, which made a *chink, chink, chink* sound. One day, as it was chinking, I started singing these words, "take a message to Mary", along with the chink of the bits of chipped marble rattling around. My tape machine wasn't working, so I couldn't trap my melody, so I called Boudleaux on the phone and said, "Honey can you put the notes down to this?" He'd scribble the notes or words down on anything that was handy. By the time he got home, I'd veered right away from my original tune…I hadn't held it at all…it was just as well I'd called him or I'd have lost the song. When we'd written it, I said, "Show it to The Everly Brothers, but he said, "Oh, it's not for Don and Phil," and I said, "Are you kidding? Those kids can sing anything." Anyway, he felt that the song hadn't got a set-up, and that it needed one. At the time he was really pushing the song 'Poor Jenny', and was reluctant to push this one to them as well, but I made him promise. It was always difficult to get him to promise, as he'd never go back on a promise.

Anyway, Archie Bleyer fell in love with the song, although Boudleaux was still going on about the song not having a set-up. "Damn it," said Bleyer, "then write one!" So we did. This is the story of a frontier lad who lost his love when he turned bad, etc. The weird thing was that, when Don and Phil were recording it, Archie was struck by an idea and suggested to Boudleaux that he tap an empty Coke bottle with a screwdriver, a sound which ended up on the track. So without Archie Bleyer being aware of my initial inspiration, he put the *chink chink* on the song.

Most songwriters and publishers in the second half of the '50s and first half of the '60s were acutely aware of the importance of getting songs to the Elvis Presley set-up. To be one of the writing teams for the singer brought kudos and a not inconsiderable pay cheque. With that in mind, at some time during 1960 the Bryants' publisher, Wesley Rose, suggested that they should try to write a song for Elvis using an old Italian melody, a route which seemed to be hot at that time. In 1960 Aaron Schroeder and Walter Gold put English lyrics to 'O Sole Mio', an Italian song dating from 1901, and the ensuing 'It's Now Or Never' sold in excess of 25 million copies. In the following year, Mort Shuman and Doc Pomus adapted the Italian ballad 'Torna A Sorrento', turning it into 'Surrender', another multimillion-seller for Presley. In the same year, George Weiss, Hugo Peretti and Luigi Creatore reworked Giovanni Martini's even older Italian melody, 'Plaisir D'Amour', retitling it 'Can't Help Falling In Love'.

It wasn't only Italian melodies that songwriters were anglicising for Elvis, either. Sid Wayne and Abner Silver turned the German composer Jacques Offenbach's 'Barcarolle' from *Tales Of Hoffman* into 'Tonight Is So Right For Love', the song being featured on Presley's album *GI Blues*.

Felice Bryant didn't think that Wesley Rose's idea was that bad, but Boudleaux appeared to be intransigent. "He was adamant that he wouldn't do that. He said: 'Hell, no. I don't want to ride on the back of somebody else's hit.'" He had strong principles, although he had to go along with things he didn't really like, as he was the head of the family. I told him that it would be wonderful to write a hit for Elvis, but he pointed out that there was no guarantee that it would be. I was adamant that we should give it a try, and suggested that we had a go at putting words to a Spanish song I knew. I started to write some ideas, but Boudleaux was dead against it…he didn't even want his name on that record!" The song became 'She Wears My Ring', a hit in 1967 in Britain for Solomon King – not *the* King, admittedly, but a King nonetheless. In America, it was recorded by top country singer Ray Price, who also cut Felice and Boudleaux's 'Raining In My Heart'.

Boudleaux's reticence is all the more strange considering that in 1959 he'd given the Italian song 'Meravigliosa Labbra' a set of English lyrics, giving it the English title of 'Completely'.

Boudleaux and Felice had some 500 songs published either as a team, or with Boudleaux writing solo, or from an earlier time in Boudleaux's career, when he collaborated with Chet Atkins. Boudleaux also provided a lyric for Floyd Cramer's 'Last Date' with Skeeter Davis, as well as writing several songs with Atkins between 1952 and 1955 and penning Bob Luman's big hit 'Let's Think About Living'. Boudleaux and Felice together wrote the follow-up, 'Why Why Bye Bye'.

Their songs have also been covered by a wide range of other artists, including Lynn Anderson, Jim Reeves, Sonny James, Tex Ritter, Nazareth, Buddy Holly, George Jones, Emmylou Harris, Roy Orbison, Dolly Parton, Chet Atkins, The Osborne Brothers and Leo Sayer.

Above all, the Bryants' songs, seemed to be tailor-made for The Everly Brothers. Don and Phil recorded 17 of their songs, including Boudleaux's 'All Have To Do Is Dream', 'Bird Dog', 'Devoted To You' and 'Love Hurts'. Songs which they cut that were written by both Felice and Boudleaux included 'Bye Bye Love', 'Like Strangers', 'Poor Jenny', 'Problems', 'Wake Up Little Susie', 'Sleepless Nights' and 'Raining In My Heart'.

Felice recalled Boudleaux teaching Phil Everly the harmony on 'Devoted To You', and his love of harmony in general. "He loved harmony…he could hear them all. In the beginning, with all the songs we wrote, Boudleaux sang the harmony and I sang the lead. He always said that we were waiting for someone like The Everlys to come along, and they were waiting for someone like us."

Neil Sedaka didn't have long to wait long for somebody to come along, only this was in the form of a collaborator, Howard Greenfield, whom he met when he was 13 and Greenfield 16.

Sedaka, of Turkish descent, was born in New York City in March 1939. His father drove a taxi for a living, and was also an accomplished pianist.

His mother and grandmother also played well, so it was hardly surprising that he began to play from an early age, having become interested in music through listening to the radio programme *The Make-Believe Ballroom*. From the age of eight he studied the piano for five hours a day in the hope of fulfilling his dream of getting a doctorate in classical music.

At the age of 13, while giving a performance at a hotel in the Catskill Mountains, he was approached by a lady called Ella Greenfield, who suggested that the young pianist collaborate with her son, Howard, who wrote poetry. Despite some misgivings, Abraham Lincoln High School student Sedaka and Howie Greenfield began writing together in October 1952, a partnership that was to last over 30 years. In 1955, they moved into rock 'n' roll, writing a song called 'Mr Moon', after being inspired by The Penguins' 'Earth Angel'.

At school, Sedaka formed and played with The Tokens, who would later be discovered by record producer Morty Craft and would have a string of hit records spanning the years 1961-70, including a Number One with 'The Lion Sleeps Tonight'. Sedaka went solo after the first couple of unsuccessful singles, but he didn't lose contact with Craft.

Neil and Howie wrote 'While I Dream' for the group, although they never recorded it. "I started The Tokens in maths class at Abraham Lincoln in Brooklyn, New York…we sang for parties, weddings and barmitzvahs. They went on to be very successful, and I was chosen to play as one of the top seven New York high-school classical pianists by the wonderful pianist Artur Rubinstein, and was subsequently awarded a scholarship at the Juilliard School Of Music." He also began to record as a pop singer, putting down tracks for both the Decca and Guyden labels. His first single as an artist, 'Snowtime', appeared on Decca.

Although he was one of the first artists to experiment with vocal multitracking, he had no chart success with either his debut single or with the follow-up, 'Ring-A-Rockin''.

The big songwriting break came for Sedaka and Greenfield when Morty Craft produced their song 'Stupid Cupid' for Connie Francis. Neil was impressed by "a great Howard Greenfield lyric about cupid being foolish and stupid and shooting the boy through the heart and picking on him so much that he carries the girl's books to school. The gender changed, of course, when Connie Francis recorded it. Howie's words were very good; they were like little novels…they told a wonderful story, from beginning to end."

In 1958, Sedaka and Greenfield began writing for Don Kirshner and Al Nevins at Aldon Music, and had songs recorded by such eminent artists as LaVern Baker, Clyde McPhatter and Connie Francis again, who did a version of their song 'Frankie'.

Always keen to record as well as to write, record producer Steve Sholes signed Sedaka to RCA as an artist late in 1958. It had been Sholes who had brought Elvis Presley to RCA, and this proved to be another shrewd move. Only Presley sold more records than Neil Sedaka during the period from 1959-63. During that period, the record company shifted some 25 million Sedaka records.

His debut single for RCA, 'The Diary', gave him a healthy enough start, climbing to Number 14 in the States, but the follow-up faltered, despite being one of the best double-sided singles of his career. 'You Gotta Learn Your Rhythm And Blues', with its 'Queen Of The Hop'-style tempo, should have been a big hit, while the flipside, 'Crying My Heart Out For You', was possibly Sedaka's finest and most powerful interpretations of one of his own songs. It would also have made been a winner in the hands of Roy Orbison.

It was his third single in the spring of 1959 that really put him on the map, especially in Britain, where it reached the Top Ten. "I was very upset because it wasn't bigger in America, but I must say that the English had good taste! Another interesting lyric from Howie…he loved his monkeys…I liked all of his things about the zoo…monkey shine and the gorillas and the ape thing. I thought his phrases were very amusing, but there was no really deep meaning to it."

Another Sedaka/Greenfield classic was written about his girlfriend, Carole King, who went on to become one of America's top songwriters. Neil's classical training was certainly helping his ideas for writing interesting chord progressions and melodies, while his love of pop songs was keeping him on a commercially musical course. The tune of 'Oh, Carol' was inspired by the music of Brazilian composer Heitor Villa-Lobos, who had died in that year at the age of 72.

Carole King is now in denial over the song. "I wrote it for Carole Klien, now Carole King," says Neil, "who was my girlfriend at the time. She now doesn't like to hear the story about it…and she's asked me to stop telling it…she doesn't want to hear about the old Brooklyn days. She responded by writing 'Oh, Neil' with lines like 'Oh, Neil, I've loved you for so long/I never dreamed you'd put me in a song.' It's awful!"

In 1960, George Wells' novel *Glendon Swarthout* was adapted as a screenplay and made into a film called *Where The Boys Are*, starring Dolores Hart and George Hamilton and featuring singer Connie Francis in her first film role. Sedaka and Greenfield were asked to write the music for the movie. Connie sang the beautiful title track to notch up her tenth million-seller.

Between 1960 and 1962, Greenfield and Sedaka wrote eleven more hits for Neil in Britain and America. "The original 'Stairway To Heaven' was ours, not Led Zeppelin's! We had very good luck writing about subjects like heaven, devils (as in 'Little Devil') and angels (as in 'Next Door To An Angel'). 'Calender Girl' was undoubtedly one of Howie's most inspired lyrics. It was a very special piece of material, certainly better than the bubblegum music of the '60s. 'Breaking Up Is Hard To Do' was fictitious; it wasn't about anyone in particular. It was a sad title but a happy tune. I was always very partial to it, especially as it went to Number One in America for two weeks. I love my songs. They're all my babies! In those days, writing was really was a labour of love."

As well as penning Neil's hits throughout this period, Sedaka and Greenfield also wrote the teen ballad 'Venus In Blue Jeans', which became a Top Ten hit in the States for Jimmy Clanton and in Britain for Mark Wynter.

Part of the melody that record producer Joe Meek wrote for The Tornados' 'Globetrotter' was so similar to the title phrase of 'Venus' that it was often referred to as 'Globetrotter In Blue Jeans'. However, litigation never appeared to be on the cards, as far as Neil and Howie were concerned.

By 1964, along with many other solo artists, Neil experienced a major sea change in musical taste, as The Beatles and the group scene in general swept aside dozens of top singers who'd been having very successful chart careers. There were no further UK hits for Sedaka during the remainder of the '60s, and there were only three very minor hits in the States. He recognised that it was time to move on, change his style and leave the *tra-la* songs behind. However, RCA weren't keen on him recording anything except what were perceived as typical Sedaka songs.

The record company's thought processes would be understandable if the artist in question had minimal talent, but here was somebody who was a gifted musician, a fine singer and a talented songwriter. It would have been comparatively easy to switch direction with an artist of that calibre.

One aspect of those years that would help him through the lean spell which followed was his recording of his material in Spanish, German,

Japanese, Hebrew and Italian. Two other assets were his gift for melody and Howard Greenfield's knack for delivering a strong lyric, which led to them writing for the likes of Peggy Lee, Nancy Wilson, Johnny Mathis, Fifth Dimension, Lesley Gore, Patti Drew and The Monkees. In 1971, Tom Jones covered their Fifth Dimension hit 'Puppet Man', and Tony Christie took 'Is This The Way To Amarillo?' into the UK chart in the same year.

Although chart success eluded him in both Britain and America during the latter half of the '60s, a Number One came from an unexpected quarter, Australia, where he'd had seven hits between 1958 and 1962. 'Star-Crossed Lovers', a demo that he had recorded in New York, soared to the top of the charts down under in 1968 and stayed on the listings for 21 weeks. Neil also recorded the song in French and Italian. During the '70s, he made the Top 30 in Australia another five times, with 'Wheeling West Virginia' and 'Standing On The Inside' making the Top Ten.

He wrote some of his new material with fellow songwriter Carole Bayer Sagar, and he continued to collaborate with Howard Greenfield.

Ironically, Sedaka's renaissance in the early '70s was due in no small way to his old girlfriend, Carole King. Her album *Tapestry* was one of the main triggers that brought singer/songwriters to the fore, and artists such as James Taylor, Neil Young and John Denver benefited from the trend. In Britain it paved the way for the likes of Al Stewart, a new-look Cat Stevens, Clifford T Ward and Nick Drake.

Neil moved his whole family to London, where he staged his comeback, signing to Don Kirshner's eponymous label and releasing the album *Emergence*. Now geographically estranged from Greenfield, Sedaka also began writing with lyricist Phil Cody in 1972.

Working with the members of what would soon become the group 10cc, he engineered the rebirth of his career, proving that a good writer can write in any climate, if they're given the opportunity.

The title of the resulting album, *The Tra-La Days Are Over*, encapsulated the new Neil. He wasn't denying his songwriting past, but he wasn't dwelling on it either, nor writing in that style. He had a clutch of strong, current material. "'Standing On The Inside' is autobiographical. It's about my life in rock 'n' roll, running the gamut of the back-slappers, back-stabbers and survivors. It's a little caustic, but it's true. My favourite from that period is 'Laughter In The Rain', which is about my optimism, my enthusiasm and my ability to get over what was a drastic time and look at the bright side of things. 'Solitaire', however, is an introspective song; it's a lonely song that really came from both Phil Cody and me. I wanted to write a classical tune in the style of Chopin that touched a little on the style of Roberta Flack. I felt very good about it, especially lines like 'the king of hearts is well concealed', and things like that." Although Neil's own release of 'Solitaire' failed to chart, there was more than adequate compensation when Andy Williams took the song to Number Four in Britain. The Carpenters' version went to Number 17 in the States and Number 32 in the UK.

In 1973, Sedaka and Greenfield's swan song, 'Our Last Song Together', was another autobiographical piece, a sentimental yet humorous journey through their writing partnership. They also wrote Sedaka's last UK hit together, 'Queen Of 1964', which was about Cousin Roberta, a resident groupie from the early '60s *Peppermint Lounge* days in New York.

In 1975, Neil not only received a wonderful offer from Elton John to release his American records on Elton's label, Rocket, but he also topped the American chart with both 'Laughter In The Rain' and 'Bad Blood', each song selling over a million copies. The icing on the cake that year, however, was Captain And Tenille taking his 'Love Will Keep Us Together' to Number One in America, staying there for four weeks.

Another successful song for Sedaka that year was a collaboration with Cody on 'The Immigrant Song'. "Phil and I wrote that for John Lennon, who was a friend of mine and who was having trouble being accepted in the United States and trying to get his green card. It was also about my immigrant grandparents, who came from Istanbul, Turkey...so many of us New Yorkers are a melting pot of various nationalities."

Neil also co-wrote hits during the '70s for artists such as Maria Muldaur, Bo Donaldson And The Heywoods and Helen Reddy, and had done more than enough to carry his name as a major songwriter through the '80s and '90s. In 1980, he had his last Top 20 hit in the States, duetting with his daughter Dara on another song written with Phil Cody, 'Should've Never Let You Go'.

Sedaka often played new compositions to his family in order to gauge whether he had written a winner or not. "I always bring family and friends into the living room and play my new song on the piano so that I can see their reaction. I then have a wonderful barometer, but if I start to wince or get a little squeamish while I'm performing it then I know that I'm not that proud of the song."

In 1994, Neil was crowned "King Of Brooklyn", cutting a ribbon on the "Walk Of Fame" and receiving a street sign with his name on it. The Broadwalk at Brighton Beach was then officially renamed Neil Sedaka Way. It's difficult to imagine Britain acknowledging our successful songwriters in this way.

In 1995, Neil proudly displayed his classical roots in all their glory when he released the album *Classically Sedaka*, with his lyrics wedded to music by several classical composers, including Chopin, Tchaikowsky, Schumann and Puccini. The album won him a gold disc.

After a lifetime of collaboration, he was finding new-found freedom in working alone. "I find that writing by myself is wonderful. I'm like a kid in a candy store, because I love the sound of words and putting them together, although I did use to like getting feedback from Howie or Phil about a particular chord, or a certain phrase. When you write by yourself, it's certainly more lonely…It's your own soul…you're speaking from your own soul."

Songwriters working solo or in pairs – like Sedaka and Greenfield, Bacharach and David, the Bryants and Tepper and Bennett – are common, while songwriters working mainly as a threesome are not so common. However, this arrangement worked for one of the writing teams within Berry Gordy's Tamla Motown label, who became almost as well known as the label itself during its heyday in the '60s and '70s.

Holland, Dozier and Holland certainly possessed the magic touch when it came to writing commercial songs. Eddie Holland (born in October 1939), his brother Brian (born in February 1941) and Lamont Dozier (born in June 1941) combined their respective talents to provide hits for many of the acts in the Motown stable.

Eddie Holland began his relationship with Motown as a singer, on the would-be Jackie Wilson recording of Gordy's song 'Jamie', which gave him a Top 30 hit in the States in the spring of 1962. He also had three smaller hits during 1964, but any aspirations to make it as a performer were hampered by his lack of enthusiasm for stage work. A bad experience while performing before a very vocal audience at the Apollo Theatre made him decide him against further ventures into live work.

His younger brother, Brian, had started writing songs at a young age, having met Berry Gordy backstage at one of Brian's gigs, and in his very early 20s was already earning big money, earning 1% per song per record sold, a not unreasonable royalty for a young lad in the early '60s. Gordy also gave him a Cadillac in which to ride around, demonstrating his faith in the young songwriter.

His faith was more that justified when Brian co-wrote The Marvelettes' debut hit and Number One US single 'Please, Mr Postman', revived successfully by The Beatles on their multimillion-selling albums *With The Beatles* and *Meet The Beatles* and sparking off global interest in the song. Robert Bateman, also a co-writer on the song, worked with Brian on the group's Top 40 hit 'Twistin' Postman' and their Top Ten record 'Playboy' before leaving Motown for pastures new. Freddie Gorman, who co-wrote The Marvelettes' next single with Brian, also departed.

They should have stayed, because things were destined to get even better at Motown. Brian, whose influences were the arrangements on the early Drifters singles and classical music, co-wrote the group's 'Locking Up My Heart', and very soon would be writing for them as one third of the most legendary songwriting teams in pop history. This left Brian working with one partner, Lamont Dozier, and Gorman's and Bateman's departures left a gap for Eddie to write with his brother and Dozier.

The trio's first collaboration was 'Come And Get These Memories' for Martha Reeves and The Vandellas, which was quickly followed by three more for the all-girl group: 'Heatwave', 'Quicksand' and 'Livewire'. Good US chart positions (the first two songs went into the Top Ten, the third into the Top 50) set them up for the great songwriting career that followed, and led to them writing more big hits for the group over the next four years: 'Nowhere To Run', 'I'm Ready For Love' and 'Jimmy Mack'.

There were so many good songs that classics often ended up on B-sides, like the excellent 'Third Finger, Left Hand', on the flipside of 'Jimmy Mack', that number becoming a hit in 1972, when it was covered by The Pearls in Britain.

Many Motown classics failed in Britain during the '60s only to chart belatedly in the '70s. 'Locking Up My Heart', written for The Marvelettes, was another of their very early songs, written at the same time as 'Come And Get These Memories'. In the following year, 1964, Eddie collaborated with Norman Whitfield on yet another Marvelettes hit, 'Too Many Fish In The Sea'.

In that year, at the behest of label boss Gordy, the trio began writing for another all-girl group, The Supremes, initially coming up with 'When The

Lovelight Starts Shining Through His Eyes'. From then until 1968, Holland, Dozier and Holland penned a further 16 big hits for the group, including 'Where Did Our Love Go?', 'Baby Love', 'Stop! In The Name Of Love', 'I Hear A Symphony', 'You Can't Hurry Love', 'You Keep Me Hanging On', 'Love Is Here And Now You're Gone', 'The Happening', 'Reflections' and 'In And Out Of Love'.

Group members Mary Wilson and Diana (or Diane, as she was then) Ross both wanted to sing lead vocal on 'Where Did Our Love Go?', and the three writers had to cast votes for the voice they thought the most suitable. Brian and Lamont went for Diana, while Eddie was keen to use Mary. "I wanted Mary because at the time Mary had a softer sound, and I'd never heard Diana sing soft before, so my natural instinct was to try Mary on it...but they said no, that Diana could sing it softer, just drop her keys...so Brian and Lamont dropped the keys, and she sounded good."

Over the years, the trio have picked up many profitable covers of the songs they wrote for The Supremes, including those recorded by The Hollies, Kim Wilde, The Jackson Five, Phil Collins, Soft Cell, The J Geils Band and Vanilla Fudge.

As songwriters, the compositions of Holland, Dozier and Holland are direct, simplistic and appealing. The three of them worked with the session musicians to achieve the effect and the sound that they wanted for each track, and insisted that the seasoned players – who could have embroidered considerably – stuck to basic patterns and riffs.

With the lucid Eddie as their mouthpiece, they were really tapped into the demands of the young record buyers. "We handled it in many ways just like a person would handle a nine-to-five job. Brian and Lamont would get together, work out the melodies...I would come over and stay in contact with the melodies and the ideas...I would take the basic melodies on tape, listen to them and jot down the ideas and each tune as they were rehearsing."

Holland, Dozier and Holland also provided Top Ten hits for The Four Tops, beginning with 'Baby I Need Your Loving' in 1964, which was successfully covered in the UK by The Fourmost. After the follow-up, 'I Can't Help Myself', had become a hit, Columbia Records – who owned some of The Four Tops' back catalogue – appeared to be about to cash in on the group's recent change of fortune. Berry Gordy wasn't going to be outdone, however, after all of the work that Motown had put into the group, and asked them to write a sure-fire hit in double-quick time, a great test of nerve, talent and confidence for any writer.

Brian, Eddie and Lamont rose to the occasion, writing 'I Can't Help Myself' in just two days. Lamont and Brian cut it with the group on the third day, and the record company released it on the following Monday. It's a pity that modern marketing methods and scheduling windows have all but eliminated the spontaneity afforded to many singles in the '50s and '60s.

The turnaround time for Motown records was often so tight that the guys were called on to write at all times of day and night, and in all situations. They would often still be writing the lyrics and finely honing ideas when the red light went on. Brian once called Eddie at 3am to tell him that Berry Gordy wanted 'I Hear A Symphony' recorded on the following day, prompting Eddie to launch himself out of bed and work on the number for eight hours so that he would have it ready in time.

In the future, they would be fortunate to pick up many cover versions from the material that they wrote specifically for The Four Tops, including those by artists such as Johnny Rivers, Dave Edmunds, Gloria Gaynor, Barbra Streisand, Donnie Elbert, Rod Stewart and The Weathermen.

The team's songwriting talents were by no means exclusive to The Four Tops and The Supremes. Between 1963 and 1965, they wrote four hits for Marvin Gaye, including 'Can I Get A Witness?', 'You're A Wonderful One' and 'How Sweet It Is', the latter song becoming a hit again for Gaye's stablemates Junior Walker And The All Stars in 1966.

During the same period, Eddie wrote The Velvelettes' 'He Was Really Saying Something' with fellow Motown writers Norman Whitfield and William "Mickey" Stevenson. Meanwhile, Eddie and Norman collaborated on three classics for The Temptations: 'Beauty Is Only Skin Deep', 'Ain't Too Proud To Beg' and 'Girl (Why You Wanna Make Me Blue)'.

Holland, Dozier and Holland had first written for The Miracles back in 1963, when they gave the group 'Mickey's Monkey', and wrote another three hits for the group between 1964 and 1966. They also wrote material for Kim Weston.

The trio appeared unstoppable in the mid '60s, writing 'Heaven Must Have Sent You' and 'Darling Baby' for The Elgins, and 'This Old Heart Of Mine' for The Isley Brothers. Eddie was also busy co-writing, and teamed up with Shorty Long in 1966 to write Long's discotheque favourite, 'Function At The Junction'.

By late 1967, Berry Gordy – who had been spending most of his time in Motown's Los Angeles office – was becoming increasingly out of touch, and imagined that Holland, Dozier and Holland were doing very little work because he couldn't get in touch with them. To the record-buying public, the trio appeared to be as busy as ever, as the songs that they had stockpiled were still all over the chart during 1967 and early 1968. Unbeknownst to Gordy, the three writers were disgruntled at getting a smaller piece of the action than they felt was due to them and were preparing to leave his Motown family. Gordy allegedly offered them $100,000 a year each against royalties to stay, but the carrot wasn't juicy enough and he was compelled to move some of his writers in Los Angeles up to Detroit to fill their shoes.

In April 1968, Motown sued the three writers for $4 million in damages, and tried to stop them writing or producing for any other company, as it was claimed that they had violated their writer's contracts. The claim pointed out that, between 1965 and 1967, the trio had earned $2,235,155 in royalties, a sum that was a far cry from Stephen Foster's pittance a century earlier. Holland, Dozier and Holland counter-sued Motown for conspiracy, fraud and deceit to the tune of $22 million. The case dragged on until the mid '70s, when it was finally settled out of court in complete privacy.

The process had initially restricted their songwriting activities, but by 1970 the trio had formed the Invictus label, and went on to have hits with Freda Payne ('Band Of Gold'), Chairmen Of The Board ('Give Me Just A Little More Time', 'Everything's Tuesday') and others.

The team broke up in the early '80s. Lamont signed to ABC Records as an artist, and Eddie and Brian virtually retired, apart from doing some work for Motown, with whom bridges had since been mended.

Billy Steinberg has written for numerous artists, with both long-term collaborator Tom Kelly and latterly with Rick Nowels. Among the dozens of artists that have benefited from their songs are Air Supply, Madonna, Little River Band, Mel C of The Spice Girls, Sly Stone, Cheap Trick, Belinda Carlisle, Chaka Khan, Bette Midler, The Pretenders, REO Speedwagon, Céline Dion, Ace Of Base, Linda Ronstadt, Whitney Houston, The Divinyls and Heart.

Steinberg was born in 1950 in Fresno, the capital of San Joaquin Valley, the agricultural heartland of California, where his father grew grapes.

Exposed to music from a young age, he eagerly lapped up the records owned by older friends in the neighbourhood, and was "blown away" by the music of Ricky Nelson, Elvis Presley, Buddy Holly and The Everly Brothers. A keen music fan, he drove his parents mad by playing his records over and over again, especially his real favourites, 'Poor Little Fool' and 'All I Have To Do Is Dream'.

Later, Steinberg's family moved to Palm Springs, where he began to sing in bands from the age of 13. His first group, The Fables, performed covers of songs by British groups The Kinks, The Animals, The Rolling Stones and The Beatles. By the age of 18, he had begun to write songs, mainly on acoustic guitar, and later formed a group called Billy Thermal. (His family's vineyard operation was based in Thermal, California.)

Success as a songwriter came relatively late for Steinberg, whose 'How Do I Make You' – a song originally written for Billy Thermal – was successfully covered by Pat Benatar in 1980. It was Planet Records boss Richard Perry who saw the potential in the song and thought that it would be ideal for the Brooklyn rocker, who was formerly known as Patricia Andrzejewski. She also recorded his 'I'm Gonna Follow You' and 'Precious Love', with the latter song becoming the title track for her 1981 US Number One album.

In 1984, Steinberg and his writing partner, Tom Kelly, came up with a classic that many people imagine to have been written for Madonna. "I know most songwriters get the tune first, but I always write the lyrics first, which most people find a bit of an oddity. I had this lyric that was basically the 'Like A Virgin' lyric, and brought in my partner, Tom Kelly. The verse was quite heartfelt, and very sincere, almost a ballad, but when it got to the chorus, it sounded ridiculous. We got together every day to work on it but kept giving up until, out of frustration, Tom started to play the bass line and sing falsetto, like a cross between Smokey Robinson and The Stylistics. I said 'That's it!' Then it came together."

Steinberg submitted their demo to various record companies and producers, only to be told that no one would sing a song called 'Like A Virgin', or that it was "too shocking". The song sat around for one and a half years, until Warner Bros executive Michael Austin heard it and thought that it would be idea for Madonna, who had just cut her first album. Austin's judgement was sound, and the song became a big hit for her on both sides of the Atlantic.

The fact that both Steiburg and Kelly were vocalists was a bonus when it came to them demoing their songs. Kelly had been a top Los Angeles session singer, performing for many top artists as diverse as Mötley Crüe and Barbra Streisand.

'Like A Virgin' is Steinberg and Kelly's second most financially rewarding song to date, after 'True Colours', a hit for Cyndi Lauper in 1986 and for Phil Collins in 1998. It was also covered by Aztec Camera, and featured in a major advertising campaign for Kodak. "It was one of the most difficult songs that Tom and I have written. The chorus on the record is exactly like our original, but the verse is quite different...we felt the lyric was too specific, and that it should be more universal. I spent a year trying to write new verses, which was really painful going. Many singers copy the feel of your demos, which Heart did with 'Alone', but Cyndi's quirky version of 'True Colours' was totally different to our gospel-influenced version featuring acoustic piano."

One of Steinberg and Kelly's mid '80s songs, 'Emotional', was heavily influenced by Prince, who was very much in vogue at the time, and Kelly even used Prince-style vocals on the demo. They submitted the song to Clive Davis, the president of Arista Records, who thought that the song would be good for Whitney Houston, as it was always difficult to find her a good up-tempo song. When it comes to sending in songs for Whitney, most writers tend to go for for the slower ballad rather than more pacy numbers. Davis decided that the song should be called 'So Emotional' (which was already part of the lyric, but he felt that it sat better than just 'Emotional'), and that Narada Michael Walden should produce it.

Many songs are triggered by a certain phrase, after which everything else falls into place. This was certainly the case with The Bangles' chart-topper 'Eternal Flame'. In fact, for Steinberg, it had a double trigger: "Susannah Hoffs had been on the road with her group, The Bangles, when they'd gone to Memphis to visit Elvis' home at Graceland, and when she came back she was talking about an eternal flame burning at the house. Her mention of this flame brought back memories of a similar thing I'd seen as a kid in Palm Springs. I used to go to Sunday school at the local synagogue, where I remember the teacher pointing to a glowing red light in the sanctuary and saying something about an eternal flame. As a child, that made a real impression on me, the thought that something could last forever. It made me aware of my own mortality." The two reference points inspired Steinberg to come up with a lyric, before bringing in Hoffs and Kelly to work on the melody with him. The song went to Number One in Britain in 1989, and, although not an eternal chart-topper, it stayed at pole position for four weeks.

One of Steinberg and Kelly's all-time favourite singers was Roy Orbison, himself no mean songwriter and the owner of a voice that could emerge from the soulful depths of loneliness and despair to soar to powerful and majestic heights. They often tried to write in the spirit of Orbison, as John Lennon had done when creating 'Please Please Me'. The end result of these songs is often quite removed in feel from the original intention, but the feel of the artist in the writer's head acts as a useful conduit.

> We loved all those classics that Roy Orbison sang, like 'Only The Lonely', 'Runnin' Scared' and 'Crying', and often demo'd songs in his style, as we did with 'I Drove All Night'. We went to see him perform in a little club in Orange County to an audience of middle-aged ladies, thinking, "Don't be disappointed if he can't sing like he does on record." Out came the band, followed by the girls singing the opening to 'Only The Lonely' – *dum dum dum dum dee oo wah* – and then Roy...and he sang better than the records. It was a rapturous experience...and he didn't even have a record contract at the time. After the show, we went back to his trailer, met his manager and fixed an appointment to see Roy himself a few months later to play him some songs.
>
> When he arrived at our studios, we were so excited...There he was, cruising down our street in his red Ferrari, all in black with the famous black sunglasses. We told him that we were big fans, to which he humbly replied, "It's good to meet you. I love your work." We taught him 'I Drove All Night', which he liked, and put down a couple of vocal tracks and a piano...Just basic stuff, with a view to working on it later.

In the meantime, Cyndi Lauper was looking for a new song, so Billy and Tom played her their demo of 'I Drove All Night', which she liked, recorded and had a hit with.

By this time, Roy Orbison had signed a new record contract, and was being produced by Jeff Lynne. Unfortunately, though, Orbison died before the track could be taken any further.

Jordan Holmes of Virgin Records then had the idea of doing an album of songs that the Big O had recorded in the time leading up to his death, and as such was keen to use 'I Drove All Night'. Steinberg and Kelly handed over the basic tracks they'd made with Roy, and a production was built up around it. The song came out as a single and reached Number Seven in Britain in 1993, the same position that Cyndi Lauper had reached with her version four years earlier.

When Billy Steinberg was in New York City in the mid '90s, Davitt Sigerson, an executive of Polygram Records and the man who had produced The Bangles' 'Eternal Flame' asked him to look at the video of a young London-based Argentinian singer called Marie Clair D'Ubaldo. Steinberg thought that she looked and sounded good, and agreed to write with her. The singer was flown out from London to LA in order to write with him and Rick Nowels, whom she had also met.

Richard Perry and Steinberg ended up producing her album, with Paul Buckmaster being brought in to organise the string section. The album didn't really see the light of day, but Billy eventually submitted one of the songs, 'Falling Into You', to Céline Dion. She fell so in love with Marie Clair's "demo" (which was really a master) that, in order to be able to use the existing track, they had to negotiate with Polygram, in much the same way that Leiber and Stoller had had to sign a deal for the original backing track of 'I (Who Have Nothing)'. After Céline's vocals were put on the track, it became a big hit for her in 1996.

One of Steinberg's favourites amongst his own songs is 'I Touch Myself', a Top Ten hit for The Divinyls in 1991. He feels that, "lyrically and musically, it's a very satisfying song".

In 2000, Steinberg and Nowels wrote for Spice Girl Melanie C's solo album *Northern Star*. "I think 'I Turn To You' will be her next single. You never know what artists are going to be like before you work with them, but I was pleasantly surprised by her musical ability."

12 *Absolutely Brill*

1650 Broadway was the address of the Brill building, an acknowleged centre of American pop songwriting from the late '50s to the mid '60s, although many great writers had successfully worked from there during the '40s. Those songwriters, referred to as "Brill building writers", wrote both in and in the vicinity of the place, which often worked as a co-operative, so that writers were able to collaborate with each other more easily.

Two of the buildings' inhabitants were the phenomenally successful partners Jerry Leiber (born in Baltimore in April 1937) and Mike Stoller (born in New York in May 1933). In yet another example of East meets West, Leiber was of Polish-Russian extraction. His mother ran a grocery store right in the middle of two cultural areas: a Polish Catholic community and a black ghetto. As Leiber's area was anti-semitic, he tended to identify more with the people from the black neighbourhood, imitating their speech patterns and attitudes until they became part of his own make-up. This cultural exposure led to him listening to the black music stations and being influenced by the songs that they were playing.

His lyrical style – writing scenarios – was also influenced by listening to radio shows like *Amos 'n' Andy*. "I don't know where ideas come from...a shard of an idea here and the odd phrase there...sometimes a piece of poetry or an advertisement. Then that one line will lead to other lines."

When Mike Stoller was in his early teens, he dreamed of being a jazz pianist. Although he loved the songs written by the great writers, his heart was more in the rhythm and blues genre.

The pair first came together in Los Angeles in 1948, when both of their families moved there after the war. Mike Stoller was approached by Jerry Leiber. "I got a call from Jerry, who I'd never met, who said he'd got my name from a friend of his and had heard that I could write notes...music on paper...and I agreed to meet him, although I wasn't enthusiastic about it." They discovered that they both had a passion for black music and the blues, and landed themselves a job working as producers to Johnny Otis. Like Leiber, Otis was white (of Greek extraction), but had lived a black lifestyle. Having got their break, they began to write in that style for artists like Amos Milburn, Floyd Dixon and Jimmy Witherspoon. Their first R&B hit came when Charles Brown recorded their song 'Hard Times'.

They followed this with 'Hound Dog', for Willie Mae "Big Mama" Thornton, who took the epic piece of writing to Number One in the R&B chart in 1953. After meeting Thornton at Otis' house, they sat down and wrote the song in just ten minutes, the words flowing from Jerry, while Mike hammered away at the piano. Johnny Otis, their mentor in those early days, later went to court to try and claim the writing credit for 'Hound Dog.' He lost.

Freddie Bell And The Bell Boys featured the song in their act, which is where Elvis heard it and decided to include it in his set, recording it in 1956.

Mike Stoller almost didn't get to hear Elvis version.

> I'd gone on my first ever trip to Europe just before Elvis did 'Hound Dog'. I'd flown from Los Angeles to Copenhagen, deciding to return home by ship three months later. I boarded the *Andrea Dorea* for what was to be my first ever boat trip, planning to meet up with Jerry and the guys from Atlantic Records – most of whom I'd never met – when I got back. Twelve hours out of New York, the boat started to sink at about eleven o'clock at night. I thought I'd had it...I thought "This is it." By two or three o'clock, I'd got into the lifeboat, but we were unable to steer it. We saw a ship, the *Île De France*, all lit up, but we couldn't direct ourselves towards it. Then we almost collided with a freighter from Massachusetts, the *Cape Ann*, who luckily picked us up. We arrived in New York on the *Cape Ann* and there was Jerry waiting for me with an Italian silk suit in his hand...He thought that I might be in my pyjamas and need some clothes!

Jerry Leiber greeted him at the quayside not only with fresh clothes but also with the good news that Presley had recorded 'Hound Dog'. When the singer performed it on *The Steve Allen Show* on TV, he was told to wear formal clothes and sing their song to the bust of a dog. The record shot to Number One in the States, staying on top for seven weeks, and climbed to Number Two in Britain.

The success of 'Hound Dog' led to their penning songs like 'Loving You', 'Don't', 'King Creole', 'She's Not You' (with Doc Pomus), 'Bossa Nova Baby' and 'Treat Me Nice' for Elvis. They also wrote the score for his film *Jailhouse Rock*, and provided more songs for the king of rock 'n' roll.

He was referred to in some quarters as "the hound dog", as people identified him with the title of the song. "After I recorded 'You Ain't Nothin' But A Hound Dog', a bunch of people turned up, among them a man who said he'd written a song called 'You Ain't Nothin' But A Bear Cat'. When he tried to make trouble, a Memphis newspaper said, "Bear Cat Sues Houn' Dog."

In the same year that 'Hound Dog' was so successful, Leiber and Stoller formed the Spark label with Lester Sill, who would later launch Jamie with writer/producer Lee Hazlewood and Dick Clark, of television's *Bandstand* fame. Using The Robins, who had previously backed the highly talented young Texan singer Little Esther (Phillips) on singles for Johnny Otis, they began to write what lyricist Jerry Leiber referred to as "playlets". Their songs did indeed have storylines, often humorous and sometimes with a twist in the tail. Songs that would surely have benefited from video technology, had it been available.

Among these were 'Framed', 'Smokey Joe's Café' (the latter becoming the title for the '90s musical based on their words and music) and 'Riot In Cell Block Number Nine', which pre-dated and was a blueprint for 'Jailhouse Rock'. The tommy gun effect on the front of the record was influenced by a TV series called *Gangbusters*, every episode of which began in that manner.

Mike and Jerry were asked to write for Elvis' 1957 MGM film *Jailhouse Rock*, although the title didn't come into play until they were on board. Jerry Leiber recalled the time with alacrity:

> We wrote the songs without seeing any footage. All that we got was the script and the place we put the song. 'Jailhouse Rock' was marked down for a ballad. They'd usually point out the places they thought a song should go, then we wrote the songs around the script, taking on board their suggestions. Although that scene – where Elvis slides down the pole from the upper walkway – was earmarked for a ballad, we looked at it and thought "This is dead meat for a slow song," and wrote the up-tempo 'Jailhouse Rock'. In

a way, it was inspired by doing a faster version of a slower and blacker song, 'Comeback' by Memphis Slim. Anyway, the song became the title of the film, which they'd originally called something innocuous like *She Loves Me*, or something equally awful.

In 1957, Leiber and Stoller moved permanently to New York, into 1650 Broadway, the building which would soon attract the songwriting talents of Carole King and Gerry Goffin, Barry Mann and Cynthia Weil and Neil Sedaka and Howard Greenfield. This team of writers would operate from that address, 1619 Broadway (which was also the Brill building) and the offices of nearby Atlantic Records.

The two writers advised and worked with Doc Pomus and Mort Shuman, as well as Goffin and King and Mann and Weil, commenting on songs, working on ideas and trading thoughts. They also encouraged the young Phil Spector, bringing him to New York from Los Angeles and signing him to a production and songwriting contract.

Success with The Robins on Spark prompted Atlantic records to buy the label, rechristen the group The Coasters and hire Leiber and Stoller as independent producers, which in those days was an innovative move. Bill Guy and Leon Hughes were brought in to be Coasters, along with former Robins lead singer Carl Gardner and bass Bobby Nunn.

The record-buying public were now treated to more classic Leiber and Stoller dialogue records ("We don't write songs, we write records"), including 'Little Egypt', 'Along Came Jones', 'Yakety Yak', 'Searchin'', 'Young Blood', 'I'm A Hog For You, Baby' and 'Charlie Brown', all of which would start off as demos, with Jerry doing the different voices as they came to him.

They worked hard but had enormous fun, especially with The Coasters. As Mike Stoller recalls: "They were our group...almost our voice. They were like a team of actors, or a vaudeville group. We had a lot of fun performing our songs for them...They'd be on the floor at our performance, but they'd always learn them as we taught them. When they were out on the road, they would work up a choreographed routine, putting steps and actions in, so that, by the time they came off a tour, they'd do their version of the songs for us, and it'd be our turn to be on the floor with laughter."

Another of their "playlet" records was 'Love Potion Number Nine', initially a hit for The Coasters in 1959 but also a hit for The Searchers in 1965, The Coasters again in 1967 and The Tygers Of Pan Tang in 1982. The durable classic was also recorded by The Ventures, The Surfaris, Wayne Fontana and Sam The Sham, amongst others.

While groups up and down the country – including The Rolling Stones – banged out versions of 'Poison Ivy', not many of them would have known what the lyric was about. "'Poison Ivy' was about venereal disease, which no one in Britain would have cottoned on to...It was a phrase that belonged to American black culture, but would have been accepted purely at face value in Britain. Later on, we Americans would be equally baffled by the lyrics in 'Penny Lane' and 'Strawberry Fields Forever'."

Many of the songs that Leiber and Stoller wrote for The Coasters, became standard fodder in the stage sets of hundreds of British beat groups that played the length and breadth of the country during the early '60s. This particular brand of Leiber and Stoller song seemed to lend itself to the guitar/drums/bass line-up of the white British groups, whose own culture was far removed from that of Jerry Leiber. The songs had a tough, no-nonsense, confident approach that British songwriters weren't even coming close to at the time.

As well as 'Yakety Yak' – which went to Number One in the States – they provided The Coasters with another five Top Ten hits there: 'Charlie Brown', 'Searchin'', 'Poison Ivy', 'Young Blood' and 'Along Came Jones', possibly the most jokey of them all. As Jerry explains, this was yet another song sparked off by the entertainment that they enjoyed as kids: "A lot of our ideas for The Coasters came from the radio. *The Shadow* was certainly one series we listened to, and the movie serial *The Perils Of Pauline*, which shows up in the song 'Along Came Jones'...all that stuff – '...and then he tied her up...and then? And then?' It came from *The Perils Of Pauline*."

Many groups and artists covered the songs. The durable and loveable (but hitless) Screaming Lord Sutch recorded 'I'm A Hog For You, Baby' in the early '60s, and continued to perform it onstage until the end of his life; The Fourmost took 'Girls, Girls, Girls' into the UK Top 40; and The Hollies had a hit with 'Searchin'' early in their illustrious career.

Mike Stoller was there at the original Coasters session for 'Searchin'':

> We did 'Searchin'' on a session in Los Angeles with four other songs, including 'Young Blood'. There was five minutes left at the

end of our studio time, so we ripped off 'Searchin'' in one take and then didn't pay much attention to it. A lot of our ideas came from early radio shows or films we'd heard or seen as kids, and we used situations that might have happened in them. Some of these certainly came out in the lyric of 'Searchin'', like Charlie Chan, the Chinese detective, and other detectives, like Bulldog Drummond and Boston Blackie. The radio series *Boston Blackie* had footsteps at the beginning of it, and you imagined a cold, dank street. The stuff we were using was all part of early American pop culture.

The song also played an important part in the life of the teenaged Paul McCartney: "We made a journey across Liverpool to track down 'Searchin'', by The Coasters. We sat in this guy's front parlour all afternoon, playing 'Searchin''…getting the words, learning how they did it, and that went into the act. That was a big Cavern number, 'Searchin''."

'Poison Ivy' became a hit in Britain for the pre-Procol Harum Paramounts in 1964 (who also covered 'Bad Blood'), and The Lambrettas in 1980, the latter at the suggestion of Pete Waterman, who could always spot a hit song, a talent that would bring him dozens of hits of his own in the years to come.

Another Leiber and Stoller song that was a favourite with British beat groups was a single for Barrett Strong. Best known for his sole US and UK hit 'Money (That's What I Want)', he also recorded a storming version of their 'Tricky Dickie'. But were Jerry's lyrics really about the young Richard Nixon? "We didn't really write pop songs with political points of view, but 'Tricky Dickie' was indirectly about Richard Nixon. Richard Barrett had come in to talk about material, and before we knew it we were on a forward roll and laying down the song with him. The only thing that bothered us was that he sounded like he was doing an impersonation of Ray Charles, and we weren't into trying to impersonate other artists."

As independents with Atlantic, Leiber and Stoller worked with Ruth Brown, Joe Turner and LaVern Baker, as well as The Robins, before moving to the east coast to team up with The Drifters. The pre-1958 line-up of the group had disbanded, with the New York group The Crowns becoming The Drifters, with Ben E King on lead vocals.

Leiber and Stoller's songs, King's voice, The Drifters' name and the engineering wizardry of their young assistant, Phil Spector, proved to be a winning combination. The group notched up hit after hit, including 'There Goes My Baby', 'Dance With Me', 'This Magic Moment' and 'Save The Last Dance For Me' before Ben E King left to pursue a solo career late in 1960.

King's first solo hit was 'Spanish Harlem', one of the first songs written by Phil Spector after his arrival in New York, which he penned with Jerry Leiber. King had previously written 'Stand By Me' for his former group, but it seems that manager George Treadwell felt that he didn't need King's material, and so the singer took it to Leiber and Stoller, who embellished it, became co-writers (using one of their pseudonyms, Elmo Glick) and had a Top Ten hit with it. (The pair sometimes also wrote under the assumed names of Joel and Chuck Kaye.)

In 1963, Cliff Richard gave them a surprise hit in Britain with his version of 'Lucky Lips', although they hadn't originally written it for him. "We wrote 'Lucky Lips' with the intention of it being recorded by a black artist, even though it was a bit of a corny pop tune. Atlantic thought it would be good for Ruth Brown, and it became her first pop hit."

In 1964, Leiber and Stoller left Atlantic records (where they were replaced by producer/writer Bert Berns) to form the Red Bird label with rock 'n' roll entrepreneur George Goldner, who had previously owned the Rama, End and Gone labels. Although fond of gambling, Goldner was a fine promotions man, with good commercial ears. It was Goldner who selected 'Chapel Of Love' as a single for The Dixie Cups, a group which had been brought to the new label by Leiber and Stoller staff writers Ellie Greenwich and Jeff Barry, who had written the song with Phil Spector. The front of the song was nearly lost forever, as Ellie Greenwich recalls: "An integral part of the recording of 'Chapel Of Love' was literally trashed. Engineer Brooks Arthur arrived home after a hard day's night of recording the song at Mira Sound Studios with an edited piece of recording tape absent-mindedly slung around his neck from the session and tossed it in the garbage. When he went back to the studio on the next day, he remembered why he'd saved the scrap in the first place. He frantically called his wife, Marilyn, who ran the discarded tape, wastebasket and all, back to the studio. The piece of tape contained the *a cappella* introduction to the record."

Spector had already produced a version of the song with The Ronettes, but appeared reluctant to release it. Ellie suggested calling the group Little

Miss And The Muffets, but in the end they settled on The Dixie Cups, as they were from the South.

Somewhat peeved at not having spotted that the song was a hit, the petulant Spector replaced Greenwich and Barry, his favoured writers, with Peter Andreoli (who wrote as Pete Anders) and Vincent (Vinnie) Poncia. The two New York writers had formerly been The Videls, a pairing who had had a 1960 US hit with 'Mr Lonely' and had been contracted to Hill And Range publishers. With Spector, they wrote The Ronettes' 'Do I Love You?' and '(The Best Part Of) Breaking Up', as well as material for Darlene Love and Cher, when the latter recorded as Bonnie Jo Mason.

Anders and Poncia – no mean songwriting team themselves – would go on to record as The Trade Winds, writing the excellent US hit 'New York's A Lonely Town' and having a hit with it on the Red Bird label before transmogrifying into The Innocence and charting in the States with 'There's Got To Be A Word' and a version of Ervin Drake's 'Mairzy Doats'.

Now that Spector had two new writers, this meant that Leiber and Stoller's publishing company, Trio, now worked more closely with Jeff Barry and Ellie Greenwich, although they already had first call on their songs. Ellie recalls:

> My mother knew somebody who knew John Gluck Jr, who co-wrote 'It's My Party'. I called him, and we agreed to meet at room 902, 1619 Broadway. I put on my sorority blazer, my Peter Pan collar shirt and went to that address, which happened to be the office of Jerry Leiber and Mike Stoller, whom I had never heard of. I played John some tunes and he left, saying that he had a demo to finish and would be back in an hour. So I sat there playing and Jerry Leiber came in and said, "Hi, Carole" [King]. I said, "No! I'm Ellie Greenwich." He asked me to play some tunes, and made a deal with me. I could use their office to work out of if I gave Leiber and Stoller the right of first refusal on my songs. That's how it began for me. I found Jerry very funny and outwardly passionate. Mike was more reserved. They became my mentors.

In early 1965, Leiber and Stoller launched Blue Cat, a sister label to Red Bird, charting with The Ad-Libs' 'The Boy From New York City' and the excellent but lowly-placed follow-up 'He Ain't No Angel', written by Jeff Barry and Ellie Greenwich.

Meanwhile, on the Red Bird front, Leiber and Stoller became involved in a dispute with The Dixie Cups' manager, Joe Jones, who himself had had a big hit in 1960 with 'You Talk Too Much', and who was now suing them over disputed royalties. It was a frequent problem area for publishers and writers, and one which has blighted more than one career. Getting entrenched in protracted legal wrangles has been known to rip the soul out of some songwriters, rendering them creatively impotent, either permanently or semi-permanently. Contention begets altercation, which in turn begets litigation. In reply to the gauntlet thrown down by Jones, Red Bird sued for breach of contract, claiming ownership of the name and demanding $7.5 million in damages.

As their ongoing dispute with Jones continued, they re-recorded The Dixie Cups' 'Iko Iko', an old New Orleans chant which had been adapted by the group, with The Ikettes. When the song became a hit again in the '80s for both The Belle Stars and Cyndi Lauper, it was discovered that, at some point, Jones had altered the composer credits with BMI, adding not only his own name but also those of members of his family!

In 1966, Leiber and Stoller sold up to George Goldner, as they returned to work with The Coasters again, who were recording for CBS's Date label. The songs, however, were more successful for other artists – The Monkees, for example, who enjoyed Top 20 success in Britain and the States with 'DW Washburn'.

By the mid '60s, their songwriting was beginning to mature. They had already contributed to the song that became 'I (Who Have Nothing)', initially a hit for Ben E King and later for many artists, including Tom Jones, Shirley Bassey and The Spectres (yet to become Status Quo). Mike Stoller explains the origins of the song:

> "Ben E King was on tour with Al, his manager, in Italy, when they heard this Italian song by a singer called Joe Sentieri. Ben brought it to our attention, and we were asked if we'd like to put an English lyric to it. The original meaning of the title was 'I, One Of Many', but we didn't do a literal translation. Their lyric was basically saying, "I'm an ordinary guy," while ours was somebody less than ordinary...somebody with nothing. We thought the

original Italian backing track was so beautiful that we shouldn't try to emulate it, so we did a deal with the Italian record company to enable us to use the track from the Sentieri version. The original was over five minutes long, and as that was pretty impractical for radio play at the time we shortened it. Even though it now faded out on the trumpet solo, it was still a hit for Ben E King and we got a lot of covers from it.

In 1966, they started song called 'Is That All There Is?', and it was only after many rewrites after and trying it with different singers that it finally worked, three years down the line, when Peggy Lee sang it.

Leiber and Stoller later freelanced with Elkie Brooks, Procol Harum, Stealer's Wheel, Peggy Lee and T Bone Walker, although by now were producing more than writing. They were songwriting giants of the rock 'n' roll era, and they had the thrill of getting their songs covered by several of rock's top singers and acts, including Buddy Holly ('Baby, I Don't Care'), The Beatles ('Kansas City') and Cliff Richard ('Lucky Lips'), and of course Elvis Presley.

Tim Rice reckons that "Jerry Leiber's lyrics were the wittiest in rock music, varying from the out-and-out comedy of 'Yakety Yak' and 'Love Potion Number Nine' to the wry humour of 'Jailhouse Rock', via the romance of 'Stand By Me' and 'Loving You', to the social comment of 'Is That All There Is?' and 'Spanish Harlem'."

Leiber and Stoller's nearest rivals as a successful rock 'n' roll writing team were Jerome "Doc" Pomus (born in June 1925) and Mort Shuman (born in 1938).

Despite contracting polio as a child, Pomus toured and worked as a blues singer, in the Mose Allison mode, while embarking on a career of writing songs. He penned 'Boogie Woogie Country Girl' for the great Californian blues shouter Big Joe Turner, 'Lonely Avenue' for Ray Charles (later revived by The Crickets), and The Coasters' 'Young Blood' with Leiber and Stoller. Like Leiber and Stoller, Pomus also used a pseudonym on occasion, his being Jerome Felder.

In 1958, Pomus and Shuman began to write together, soon coming up with their first hit, 'Teenager In Love', a US Top Ten hit for Dion And The Belmonts in 1959, the song also reaching the UK Top 30, with British covers by Craig Douglas and Marty Wilde making Numbers 13 and Two respectively. This was a flying start for a new songwriting team.

Working out of the Brill building and Leiber and Stoller's office, their strike rate increased. The pair initially worked on songs for Fabian (Fabiano Forte), a good-looking boy who was sold as a cross between Elvis Presley and Ricky Nelson. Although introduced to the Chancellor label by Frankie Avalon, Fabian was not a great singer, but with a none-too-subtle use of early technological chicanery (loads of echo!) to cover up his vocal paucities and a handful of Pomus and Shuman songs he became a chart regular for two years.

In 1959 and 1960, Doc and Morty supplied Fabian with US Top Ten hits with 'Tiger', 'Hound Dog Man' and 'Turn Me Loose'. Cliff Richard even snarled a live version of the latter song on early British rock 'n' roll television.

Doc Pomus had already worked with The Crowns before they became The Drifters, and following the name change he recommenced the relationship, and he and Shuman hit a rich seam of inspiration. The two came up with three Top 20 hits for the group, 'This Magic Moment', 'Sweets For My Sweet' and 'I Count The Tears', as well as penning their chart-topping 'Save The Last Dance For Me', which climbed to Number Two in Britain.

Proving that good songs never lie down, The Searchers also recorded 'Sweets For My Sweet', which went to Number One in Britain in 1963, while CJ Lewis took it to Number Three in the UK in 1994. In 1969, Jay And The Americans revived 'This Magic Moment', taking it into the US Top Ten.

Pomus and Shuman proved their versatility by writing such diverse hit songs as 'Hushabye' for The Mystics, 'Can't Get Used To Losing You' for Andy Williams, 'Plain Jane' for Bobby Darin, 'Go, Jimmy, Go' for Jimmy Clanton, and 'Spanish Lace' for Gene McDaniels. They also wrote for Ray Charles and Gary "US" Bonds.

Like Leiber and Stoller, they also had the knack of writing songs that suited Elvis Presley. The singer went on to have hits with several of the numbers that they sent him, including 'Surrender', 'His Latest Flame', 'Little Sister', 'A Mess Of Blues', 'Kiss Me Quick', 'Viva Las Vegas', 'Suspicion' and 'She's Not You', which was written by Pomus with Leiber and Stoller.

Pomus also co-wrote 'Little Children' for Billy J Kramer And The Dakotas, which became a Number One in Britain and a Top Ten hit in the States, and wrote Erma Franklin's 'Piece Of My Heart', with Bert Berns, as well as many others for artists like Chubby Checker and Dusty Springfield.

Apart from having a successful partnership with Doc Pomus, Mort Shuman also collaborated successfully with several other writers. He co-wrote Cliff Richard's 1961 hit 'Theme For A Dream', The Hollies' 1964 success 'Here I Go Again' with Clive Westlake, and 'What Good Am I' and 'Love's Just A Broken Heart' for Cilla Black with Westlake's sometime writing partner, Kenny Lynch. He also wrote with Mink DeVille and Mac Rebennack (Dr John).

Doc Pomus died of lung cancer in March 1991, and was inducted into the Rock 'n' Roll Hall Of Fame in the following year.

Another successful Brill building duo were husband-and-wife songwriting team Barry Mann (born in Brooklyn in February 1939) and Cynthia Weil (born in Manhattan in 1942).

Following up on contacts that he'd made, Mann went to see Lowell Music in the Brill building, where he bumped into writer Jack Heller, who gave him some sound advice on to whom he should play his songs. Inspired by the fact that Paul Anka had written a million-seller by the age of 16, Mann had written a song called 'Eileen', which he then plugged to publisher George Paxton. Although nothing came of it, he met Heller a year later, who was then earning $200 a week against royalties at Don Kirshner's publishing house and felt that he could do the same.

In 1959, Mann, a former Madison High School and Pratt architectural student, began writing songs seriously, coming up with 'She Say (Oom Dooby Doom)', a Top 20 US hit for The Diamonds. He also released a single, 'Dix-A-Billy', as Buddy Brooks, but clearly the country wasn't ready for what sounded like it should be a hybrid of Stephen Foster and Billy Lee Riley.

A year later, at the age of 21, he signed to Aldon Music, and co-wrote 'Footsteps', a 1960 Top Ten US hit for Steve Lawrence; 'I'll Never Dance Again' for Bobby Rydell; and The Lettermen's 'Come Back, Silly Girl'.

On one occasion, when going off to play a song for Teddy Randazzo, he briefly met Cynthia Weil, who was writing with the singer. She was curious about the young Mann, and on learning that he was signed to Don Kirshner she got herself in with the same publishing company.

In 1961, Mann consolidated his position as an excellent new writer, coming up with the US Top Ten song 'I Love How You Love Me' for The Paris Sisters, the number also going Top 20 in Britain with a cover version by Jimmy Crawford. The song would become a hit again in 1964 for Maureen Evans, and again in 1966 for Paul And Barry Ryan. Also in that year, he had a transatlantic hit as an artist with 'Who Put The Bomp (In The Bomp, Bomp, Bomp)', a song that he had co-written with Gerry Goffin.

Meanwhile, Cynthia Weil had been trained as an actress and dancer, and had been writing for Frank Loesser before signing to Aldon publishing. She married Mann in 1961, and the pair went on to write 'Patches' for Dickey Lee and songs for Paul Peterson and Shelley Fabares.

Also in 1961, they collaborated on Tony Orlando's big hit 'Bless You', and Weil also co-wrote another of his hits at that time with Carole King and Gerry Goffin, 'Happy Times', just one example of interaction between the writers in the Brill building. Taking just that one artist, there are more instances of this cross-fertilisation: Jack Keller and Gerry Goffin writing 'Thrills', Keller penning 'My Baby's A Stranger' with other co-writers, and Goffin and King writing the single 'Talkin' About You'. It really was an industrious hive, with writers often working outside their usual partnership, or bringing in an extra collaborator or two. Most of the company's 18 writers – all between 18 and 26 – weren't brought into Kirshner's Aldon Music as teams but instead tended to gravitate towards partners from within, although Goffin and King did arrive as a package.

From a distance, it appears so simple, with hits just pouring out. However, for every writer that made it there were many who fell by the wayside.

In many other areas, our lives have been simplified, but not, it seems, in the writing and making of records. If a song was needed for an artist, several writers arrived at work in the morning, cut a rough demo in the afternoon and were playing it to Kirshner or one of the artists that afternoon. If the song seemed hot, it could easily be out within the month. Now, almost 40 years on, release dates are now determined by long-term policy, marketing strategy and a company overview, and are dependant on and the nod from the accountant. Writing songs can be spontaneous, immediate and exciting, but if the rest of the team that are to issue it move at a much slower and ponderous speed then the shine is taken off. No wonder the Brill building days seem exciting – the quick turnaround time must have inspired the writers to greater and greater heights. An average of six records a week were released from this team of writers alone.

Mann and Weil's songs from this period have often been referred to as "urban protest", but whatever banner headline one gave them they were just a great bunch of songs, including The Vogues' 'Magic Town', Jay And The Americans' 'Only In America', The Animals' 'We Gotta Get Out Of This Place', and 'Looking Through The Eyes Of Love' and 'I'm Gonna Be Strong' for Gene Pitney.

Four decades on, most writers – in Britain, certainly – are not only part of the same basic songwriting squad, but in all probability they write for just one or maybe two acts. For writers such as Goffin and King, Mann and Weil, Sedaka and Greenfield, Leiber and Stoller, Greenwich and Barry and Phil Spector, however, they had access to a whole spectrum of chart artists.

As well as writing for The Crystals with Spector, Mann and Weil also wrote 'Born To Be Together' and 'Walking In The Rain' for another highly successful girl group, The Ronettes. The most commercially successful and durable of their collaborations with Spector was 'You've Lost That Lovin' Feeling', a song which has been recorded by and has been a hit for many artists, although the original by The Righteous Brothers, which went to Number One in Britain and the States, remains the definitive version. Their version has charted in Britain on four separate occasions between 1965 and 1990.

It's a daunting task for any writer to follow a song like that, but amazingly Mann and Weil came up with a number that stayed at the top of the US chart for a week longer: '(You're My) Soul And Inspiration'. The Shadows, Britain's most successful instrumental outfit of the century, also recorded Mann and Weil's song 'Don't Make My Baby Blue' as a vocal, and the number became a Top Ten hit for them in 1965.

The friendly rivalry between them and the other Brill building teams – Sedaka and Greenfield and Goffin and King – kept them all desperate to better each other and to keep coming up with great songs that would impress Kirshner.

Weil wrote lyrics and Mann wrote lyrics and music, with either of them bringing in the initial idea for a song, as Cynthia Weil did with 'Uptown'. While she was walking through the rag-trade area of New York, she saw a great-looking black guy pushing a hand truck. She got to thinking that downtown this guy was nothing, but when he went uptown he was really something.

It was that song that inspired Gene Pitney to write 'He's A Rebel'. "I'd heard 'Uptown' on the radio, and thought it was so good that I resolved to write the next Crystals hit. I'd had the idea of composing a song incorporating the word 'rebel' for a couple of years, after a friend told me that he'd written a song with that word in the title. Not wishing to offend him, I waited to see whether he'd release his song. He never did, so I put together a song for The Crystals called 'He's A Rebel', and it was their next single."

Again, the songwriting commune all wrote for The Crystals. Phil Spector co-write their debut hit, 'There's No Other Like My Baby'; Mann and Weil provided 'Uptown'; and Ellie Greenwich, Jeff Barry and Phil Spector collaborated on 'Then He Kissed Me', 'Da Doo Ron Ron' and 'Little Boy.'

Meanwhile, Mann and Weil teamed up with Leiber and Stoller to write The Drifters' 'On Broadway', and also penned other classics for the group by themselves, including 'Come On Over To My Place', 'Saturday Night At The Movies' and 'I'll Take You Home'. They underlined their talent by going on to write songs like 'I Just Can't Help Believing', 'Here I Go Again', 'How Much Love', and co-writing Dan Hill's big hit 'Sometimes When We Touch'.

Weil went on to work with The Pointer Sisters, Lionel Richie and many other artists, while Mann – whose ambition was to write a Broadway show – went into writing for film and television.

Ellie Greenwich was born in Brooklyn in 1940 before moving with her family to Levittown, Long Island, in 1951. She was a fanatical music fan from an early age, and played the accordion at home until her parents finally relented and bought her a piano. She taught herself to a certain standard before going to Queen's College as a music major and then to university to study Psychology, English and Education.

A local record dealer helped her to land a deal with RCA as an artist, but she only made one single for them, and then as Barbara Gaye.

On meeting Jeff Barry, a cousin of her aunt, she was delighted to discover that he was also an aspiring singer and songwriter, whose song 'Tell Laura I Love Her' was soon to become a big hit for Ray Peterson in the States and Ricky Valance in Britain.

Ellie was still studying when she began cutting demos for Jeff, earning herself $15 a song, performing numbers that he had co-written with various partners, such as Art Resnick, Tony Powers and Ben Raleigh, all excellent songwriters. However, music now appeared to be her calling. "The house was always full of music…we always had the radio on. I would write these songs for the cheerleading team and get my sister Laura to sing all the harmony lines. I remember hearing The Shirelles' 'Will You Love Me Tomorrow', which had a melody very similar to one of my songs, 'Come Spring', so I thought maybe I could become a songwriter. If I was happy or sad, or whatever, I'd write. Music was my escape, my buddy, and I spoke through it all the time."

Greenwich graduated in January 1961, but after just a few weeks of working as a teacher she left to pursue a full-time career in music.

By now, she and Jeff Barry were an item, although she was determined not to hang onto his coat-tails and use his success as a stepping stone. Instead, she approached one of her parents' contacts, John Gluck Jr, which led to her working for Leiber and Stoller.

Like Jeff, she also wrote with Ben Raleigh and Tony Powers, as well as with Mark Barkan and Gluck. It was a hectic round of coming up with ideas for songs, writing, making demos and plugging them, all of which could lead to an advance of anywhere between $30 and $100 if they sold a song.

With Powers, her main collaborator, she wrote the follow-up to The Exciters' hit 'Tell Him', penned by Bert Berns. The group cut the song at Bell Sound Studios with four other titles. Producers Leiber and Stoller deliberated until the early hours of the morning about which track should be the next single. Ellie was "almost in a stupor" when it was decreed that her song would be the group's next release.

Leiber and Stoller also introduced Powers and Greenwich to the young Phil Spector, with a view to them collaborating. The trio subsequently coming up with material for Bob B Soxx And The Blue Jeans and Darlene Love.

In 1963, Barry and Greenwich became partners, both romantically and musically. After their wedding, they excused themselves from their existing collaborators, Tony Powers and Art Resnick. The two newlyweds then collaborated with Spector to write a song for a girl group from Brooklyn that he had found in 1962, The Crystals. The girls had already had four hit singles, but this latest song, 'Da Doo Ron Ron', became their second-biggest hit, climbing to Number Three in the summer of 1963. This song inspired Barry and Greenwich to write another hit for The Exciters. "After 'Da Doo Ron Ron' was such a big hit, we figured that those little singalong things…like 'papa oom mow mow' seemed to do pretty well. So we really did 'Doo Wah Diddy' on purpose, and it worked. But one thing I won't take credit for is the Manfred Mann interpretation of one line on the bridge, 'I knew we was falling in love.' As an English major, I would never have written that."

One song that Jeff and Ellie wrote together led to her fronting a successful group.

> Jeff and I loved this group The Sensations, and we wanted to write a song for them. We'd booked a session for ten o'clock in

> the morning and the night before we were not coming up with a song. When we were first married, we lived in Queens and would come into the city on the E train, so on the E train the next morning, with pad and pencil, we started coming up with ideas, and 'What A Guy' was literally written on the train and finished in the studio. I played piano and Jeff played drums. That's all that's on the record, just the two of us. Jeff sang the bass part and I sang everything else. We took the demo back to Jerry Leiber, who said, "You've got something here." He struck a deal with Jubilee, and the next thing you know we have a record out.

The song, which was never meant to be a master recording, was released and went into the US Top 50 by "The Raindrops", the name chosen after one of Ellie's favourite songs, 'Raindrops' by Dee Clark. With Greenwich on lead vocals and Barry on bass vocals, the group then went on to release several singles, including Stateside Top 100 entries 'Book Of Love'; 'That Boy John', which came out at the time of Kennedy's assassination; 'One More Tear'; and their biggest hit, 'The Kind Of Boy You Can't Forget'. (Barry didn't perform live with the outfit; he was represented on stage by Bobby Bosco.)

The Ronettes were another group that benefited from the songs of Greenwich, Barry and Spector, the latter signing the three New Yorkers, one of whom, Veronica, would become Spector's wife. The first hit written for them by the trio of songwriters was 'Be My Baby', which was followed by another of their songs, 'Baby I Love You'. Ellie Greenwich's record collection still boasts the original demo:

> I still have the demo of 'Baby I Love You', with me playing the piano, Jeff and me singing back-up, with Phil playing the guitar and singing lead. It sounds like Buddy Holly in drag, really weird. We would usually meet at Phil's office on East 62nd Street. I'd play piano, Phil would play guitar. We'd play and sing. Jeff would be playing and coming up with parts. We'd throw ideas around...riffs...lyrical ideas. Stuff would just come out of our heads. I don't know why or how; it just did. With three people, you could bounce off each other, and then you could sing something with three-part harmony. If we got a couple of goosebumps in a writing session, we knew we had something and would record a demo.

It had come to the attention of an old acquaintance of Ellie's, George Morton, that she was writing hit records, so with an eye on the top of the charts he turned up at their offices claiming to be a songwriter. A disbelieving Jeff Barry told him that, if indeed he was what he claimed to be, he should back the following week with a hit record.

Bizarrely, Morton – who had never written a song in his life – called Barry's bluff. He borrowed a studio from a friend, Joe Monaco, procured a band of musicians from another person in the business and got hold of a group of female singers from Cambria Heights, Queens, whom he thought might be ideal to front his venture. The only stumbling blocks left in his path were a lack of musical ability and the fact that his song didn't actually exist, which is when the old proverb "necessity is the mother of invention" kicked in. He wrote a song that he claimed took him only 22 minutes, recorded a seven-minute version of it with girl group The Shangri-Las and re-appeared at Greenwich and Barry's office within the week.

The two songwriters were not unimpressed with the unusual 'Remember (Walkin' In The Sand)', despite the way in which the song rambled on a little, and after a a fair amount of reworking and rewriting they played it to a very interested Leiber and Stoller. The song became a huge hit in both Britain and the States for the four-piece girl group, which comprised two sisters and twins, as did the follow-up, another million-seller, which came out of a songwriting session: "Jeff and Shadow [Barry and Greenwich's name for Morton, who was never around when they wanted him and often couldn't be found at all] and practically everybody had a motorcycle back then. I suggested we write a song about a guy and his bike. At first we didn't really know what to call it...'The Head Of The Gang?'...'The Front Of The Fender?'...Jeff's motorcycle was out on the street, and we brought the wire down the steps from the studio and recorded the sound of the bike outside."

Morton had a rather different take on the origins of the song, claiming that he wrote the song in the shower with a bottle of champagne and two cigars, scribbling down the lyrics on the back of a cardboard shirt stiffener with his kids' crayons!

In various combinations, Morton, Barry and Greenwich continued to write for The Shangri-Las, who had several more successful singles and helped to push up the number of chart hits for Leiber, Stoller and

Goldman's Red Bird. Of the label's 30 releases, they had an incredible 18 hits, eleven of which went into the US Top 40.

'River Deep, Mountain High' was only a minor hit in the States for Ike And Tina Turner in 1966, but in Britain it soared to Number Three, bouncing back into the Top 40 just four years later. In addition to Ike and Tina's success with the song in the UK, The Supremes and The Four Tops also had Top 20 hits with it in both countries in 1970 and 1971, while Deep Purple also had a small hit with it in America in 1969. The song always meant more in Britain, which surprised Ellie Greenwich: "I didn't realise what impact that song had made in England until I did a promotional visit in the early '70s. Anyone I met talked to me in hushed tones when it came to this record. They consider anybody who was even in the vicinity when that song was written or recorded to be royalty. Ian Hunter literally got down on his knees and kissed my feet."

Possibly the best-known Brill building team are Carole King and Gerry Goffin, not only because of the amazing amount of hit songs that they wrote but also because of King's success as a recording artist.

Born Carole Klein in Brooklyn in 1942, King had started a girl group at high school, where she and three friends performed as The Co-Sines. She met Goffin (born in New York City in 1939) at Queen's College, New York, where they were both studying Chemistry, and discovered that they shared not only a love of their subject but also a love of music. It's not surprising, with these common interests, that they became boyfriend and girlfriend, and soon married.

At this time, fellow student and budding songwriter Paul Simon had already made some inroads into the music business, having had success with partner Art Garfunkel, singing as Tom And Jerry. King's pre-Goffin boyfriend Neil Sedaka was also just becoming known. It was Sedaka who introduced her to the Brill building set-up, which she later referred to as a "chicken coop" due to the lack of space in which the songwriting teams had to work.

One of the first Goffin and King songs was 'Will You Love Me Tomorrow?' an American Number One and a Top Ten hit in the UK. Later, in 1961, they followed this with 'Some Kind Of Wonderful' for The Drifters and another chart topper, 'Take Good Care Of My Baby', which was also a Top Ten hit in Britain. The artist this time was Bobby Vee, who went on to have more success with other Goffin and King songs, including 'How Many Tears?', 'Sharing You' and 'Walkin' With My Baby'. Gerry, who had teamed up with Barry Mann to pen Mann's big solo hit 'Who Put The Bomp (In The Bomp, Bomp, Bomp)', also worked with fellow writer Jack Keller on Vee's 'Run To Him', and the pair also wrote 'How Can I Meet Her?', a hit in Britain and the States for The Everly Brothers.

Carole King also co-wrote with others. She wrote 'Cryin' In The Rain' with Neil Sedaka's usual collaborator, Howard Greenfield (which also became a hit for The Everlys), and with Leiber and Stoller also wrote what became one of her biggest hits, 'Stand By Me'. Initially a hit on both sides of the Atlantic in 1961 for former Drifters singer Ben E King, it returned to the UK listings as a chart topper in 1987. A much-covered song, it has also been a British hit for Kenny Lynch, John Lennon and 4 The Cause, and a US hit for King, Lennon, Spyder Turner, Earl Grant and David And Jimmy Ruffin.

In the same week that 'Take Good Care Of My Baby' charted, 'Every Breath I Take' – another Goffin and King song – went into the Top 100, sung by Gene Pitney, who had already made his mark earlier in the year by having a hit with '(I Wanna) Love My Life Away'. He also recorded their song 'Yours Until Tomorrow'.

Goffin and King also wrote two big hits for Tony Orlando, 'Bless You' and 'Halfway To Paradise', although in Britain the chart honours for the latter song were stolen by Billy Fury, whose career it helped to cement.

In 1962 and 1963, Goffin and King provided many artists with hit songs, including 'One Fine Day' for The Chiffons, 'The Point Of No Return' for Gene McDaniels, 'Don't Say Nothin' Bad About My Baby' and 'Chains' for The Cookies (the latter also covered by The Beatles), 'Her Royal Majesty' for James Darren, 'Don't Ever Change' for The Crickets, 'I Can't Stay Mad At You' for Skeeter Davis, and two more hits for The Drifters: 'When My Little Girl Is Smiling' and 'Up On The Roof'. They also had another Number One with Steve Lawrence, who took their haunting song 'Go Away, Little Girl' to the top of the American chart.

British artists and record companies were by now fast catching on to the fact that a Goffin and King song often meant a hit single.

'When My Little Girl Is Smiling' became a bigger hit for home-grown artists Jimmy Justice and Craig Douglas in Britain than it did for The Drifters, although the American outfit came back for another bite of the cherry in 1979.

In 1962, Carole King charted for the first time as an artist, with their song 'It Might As Well Rain Until September', but just prior to that it had made the Goffin's babysitter a star. Eva Narcissus Boyd became Little Eva overnight, and proceeded to scale the chart with three of her employers' songs. Her first single, 'The Locomotion', went to Number One in the States and Number Two in Britain, with the follow-up, 'Keep Your Hands Off My Baby', also scoring well on both sides of the Atlantic. Her last two hits were 'Turkey Trot' and a reworking of the traditional 'Old Smokie', as 'Old Smokie Locomotion'.

In 1964, the husband-and-wife team came up with 'I'm Into Something Good' for Earl Jean McCree, a former member of The Cookies. As Earl Jean, she had a Top 40 hit with it in the States, but in Britain the sharp ears of producer Mickie Most spotted it as a potential song for Herman's Hermits. Recording it with the Manchester group proved to be a shrewd move for all concerned. Most had just produced a Number One for The Animals, and this new Number One confirmed his position as a top record producer, while it launched the group into eventual and unexpected stardom in both the States and Britain.

In that year, The Tokens had a US hit with Goffin and King's 'He's In Town', which became a Top Three record in Britain by The Rockin' Berries, and Maxine Brown's US hit version of their 'Oh No! Not My Baby' became a UK hit for Manfred Mann in the following year. The song later charted again in 1973 for both Rod Stewart and Merry Clayton.

British artists continued to lap up Goffin and King numbers. The Animals scored with 'Don't Bring Me Down' and Dusty Springfield had a Top Ten UK hit with 'Some Of Your Lovin''. Dusty also recorded their songs 'No Easy Way Down' and 'Goin' Back', a British Top Ten hit in 1966 and a US hit for The Byrds in the following year.

Adapting to the ever-changing music scene in the '60s, they teamed up with Atlantic Records producer Jerry Wexler to write 'A Natural Woman' for Aretha Franklin, and also wrote one of The Monkees' big hits, 'Pleasant Valley Sunday'.

Gerry Goffin and Carole King divorced in 1968, but both went on to write successful songs. Having previously had just one real hit single, Carole experienced phenomenal success as a singer/songwriter, with her second solo album, *Tapestry*, becoming one of the best-selling albums of all time and spawning a string of hit singles for both her and other artists.

'It's Too Late', one of the strongest songs on an album full of good songs, gave her an American Number One in her own right, having previously written for so many other people, while 'I Feel The Earth Move' was another popular track, as were her versions of her own songs 'Will You Love Me Tomorrow' and 'A Natural Woman'.

James Taylor covered another song from the album, which not only went to Number One in the States but also won a Grammy Award for Song Of The Year in 1971. Carole herself won three Grammy Awards, for Album Of The Year, Female Vocal Performance Of The Year and Single Of The Year, for 'It's Too Late'.

Fortune continued to smile on her. Out of the blue, Donny Osmond took his new version of 'Go Away, Little Girl' to Number One in America, making it the first US single to go to Number One by two different artists. This feat of two Number Ones by two different artists happened again with another Goffin and King song, 'The Locomotion', as Grand Funk Railroad, of all artists, took it to the top in America.

The new-look Carole King had a string of US hits and successful albums during the '70s, while Gerry Goffin repositioned himself in the songwriting world, proving that a good writer is a good writer, whatever the era. One of his biggest successes was 'Theme From Mahogany (Do You Know Where You're Going To?)', a US Number One for Diana Ross, which he wrote with Chicago composer and producer Michael Masser. The pair also penned two more big hits, coming up with Peabo Bryson And Roberta Flack's 'Tonight I Celebrate My Love' and Whitney Houston's 'Saving All My Love For You'.

The Brill building philosophy of the song being even more important than the singer or group has also worked in other situations, such as the Holland-Dozier-Holland songs for the Tamla Motown artists and the Stock-Aitken-Waterman songs for many '80s and '90s acts.

For the those who feel that these teams shouldn't be mentioned in the same breath, think again. Stock, Aitken and Waterman had an incredible run of highly commercial hits that any songwriter would be pleased to have written. They wrote big-selling songs for a wide variety of artists, appealed to very young record buyers – just as the Brill building writers did during the '60s – and brought many new young artists onto the music scene. They simply used the same policy that the Brill writers employed, which was to write great pop songs for young people. And there's nothing wrong with that.

13 Writing From Within

Alongside the dedicated independent songwriters – who might have dabbled in recording over the years but who are essentially and primarily providers of material – are the writers who have worked from within a group situation. They might have initially intended to write songs almost exclusively to purvey from their own platform, but their talents have often encouraged cover versions by other acts.

One could fill several books with the life and work of the many talented songwriters working in this situation. Mick Jagger and Keith Richards of The Rolling Stones, for example, who, apart from having their own phenomenal career as a group, have written so many classic songs that have been covered by a wide variety of performers. Their early material was recorded by such English acts as The Toggery Five ('I'd Much Rather Be With The Boys'), Twice As Much ('Sittin' On A Fence'), David Garrick ('Lady Jane'), Tommy Vance ('Off The Hook'), The Who ('Under My Thumb' and 'The Last Time'), Love Affair ('She Smiled Sweetly'), Cliff Richard ('Blue Turns To Grey'), Chris Farlowe ('Out Of Time' and 'Yesterday's Papers') and Marianne Faithfull ('As Tears Go By').

Americans, too, were queuing up to cover Jagger/Richards songs. Otis Redding and Aretha Franklin did versions '(I Can't Get No) Satisfaction', while Melanie recorded 'Ruby Tuesday'.

Another great writer who has been highly successful operating out of a group situation is Ray Davies, of The Kinks. As well as a long string of hits with The Kinks spanning the years from 1964-97, all of which were written by Davies, many artists have turned to his canon for inspiration, including The Honeycombs ('Something Better Beginning'), The Pretenders ('Stop Your Sobbing'), Kirsty MacColl ('Days'), Cathy Dennis ('Waterloo Sunset') and The Stranglers ('All Day And All Of The Night').

Two other great British songwriters who operated from a group base are Pete Towshend of The Who and Roy Wood of The Move and Wizzard.

Both men excel at turning out great pop songs and moving music into new areas. Townshend's songs really seemed best when handled by The Who, but British groups in the '60s also took a shine to some of them, such as The Untamed, who recorded 'It's Not True', and Fleur-De-Lys, who covered 'Circles'. Elton John also had a hit in the '70s with Townshend's 'Pinball Wizard'.

Roy Wood, founder of The Move, ELO and Wizzard, is a delightfully eccentric-looking chap who has written many great songs for all of the projects and outfits with which he has played. However, the individual sound of the material was usually so tailored to whichever band they were meant for that they rarely tempted other artists to cover them.

Hank Marvin and Bruce Welch began writing for both themselves and Cliff Richard after teaming up with him in 1958 as one half of his backing group, The Drifters. John Foster, Cliff's manager at the time, had gone to London's famous 2 I's coffee bar to ask guitarist Tony Sheridan if he'd like to join Cliff's group. Sheridan wasn't there, though, he was at the cinema, and one just hopes that the film was worth it because the man who first used The Beatles as his recording group missed out on becoming Cliff's lead guitarist. Hank was there instead, fresh from Newcastle-Upon-Tyne, and got the gig, insisting that his mate Bruce Welch came with him as rhythm guitarist.

Not only did they become a highly influential and successful instrumental unit; they carved out a career for themselves by backing Cliff for years, writing countless hits for him and The Shadows. Often collaborating with other members of The Shadows at different times (mainly with Jet Harris, Brian Bennett and later with John Rostill), the band enjoyed extraordinary success.

Among the songs that Bruce had a hand in writing for Cliff were 'Please Don't Tease', 'Summer Holiday', 'Wonderful Life', 'I Could Easily Fall In Love', 'Don't Talk To Him', 'We Say Yeah', 'Dancing Shoes', 'Thinking Of Our Love' and 'Bachelor Boy'. Solo, he penned such numbers as 'I Love You' and 'A Matter Of Moments'.

As well as having a hand in co-writing some of the above songs, Hank Marvin also has his name on many other Cliff tracks, including several songs that he wrote alone, such as 'The Day I Met Marie', 'Silvery Rain' and 'Throw Down A Line', the latter being a hit for Cliff and Hank as a duo.

As a team, Hank and Bruce wrote many tunes for The Shadows, including 'Foot Tapper', 'Midnight' and 'Shindig', also penning numbers like 'Nivram' and 'FBI' with original Shadows bass player Jet Harris. With later bass player John Rostill and drummer Brian Bennett, they came up with such tracks as 'Rhythm And Greens' and 'Theme From "The Boys"'.

Brian Wilson, the original leader, driving force and main songwriter for The Beach Boys', has written from within and without the group, and although his songs might not have yielded as many covers as Lennon and McCartney or Jagger and Richards, he is no less talented. In some ways, his creations are more difficult to cover, due to the intricate harmonic structures that he introduced as his writing became increasingly experimental. Unless one could emulate (unlikely), copy (not easy) or strip a song down to the bare bones (almost pointless), it was probably wise to leave well alone.

Fellow Americans working in the same area, such as Jan And Dean and The Rip Chords, were essentially part of the wider Beach Boys family, and would become involved at various stages rather than directly cover their songs. The finest British exponents of The Beach Boys' sound were Tony Rivers And The Castaways, a '60s group led by Rivers, who had – and still has – an incredible ear for harmony. Their 1966 versions of Wilson's 'Girl, Don't Tell Me' and 'God Only Knows' attest to this. Robb Storme And The Whispers also dabbled in Wilson's works, releasing their cover of 'Here Today'. Both of those acts were more than capable of reproducing the sound of Brian Wilson's songs, and among the others that could have made the grade in that area were The Summer Set, who released a commercial version of an early Brian Wilson song, 'Farmer's Daughter'. In the '70s, Adrian Baker and his group Gidea Park also had success in this area, and Baker later went on to work for a spell with The Beach Boys.

The Beach Boys began in 1961 when Brian, Dennis and Carl Wilson and their cousin Mike Love formed a group singing harmony songs in the style of The Four Freshmen and The Hi-Los. Led by Brian and encouraged by the Wilsons' father, Murry, himself an amateur songwriter, they initially called themselves Carl And The Passions, bringing in Brian's high-school friend Al Jardine to fill out the sound. At the time that Brian Wilson wrote 'Surfin", the group changed their name to The Beach Boys at the suggestion of Candix record label publicist Russ Regan, who went on to become president of 20th Century Records.

Brian began to craft songs with surfing themes, using phrases he'd picked up from Dennis, the group's only surfer until Bruce Johnston joined in 1965. In tandem with these songs, he also wrote about souped-up cars and hot-rods, thereby finding two rich themes on which to draw, neither as exhaustible as one might imagine. Brian's songs painted a world of everlasting summer, attractive sun-tanned girls, teenage thrills and eternal youth.

After 'Surfin' Surfari' in 1962, the group began to take off in the States. Three of Brian's songs – 'Surfin' USA,' 'Surfer Girl' and 'In My Room' – became successful in the following year.

In 1963 and 1964, Brian wrote an incredible number of songs, which radio stations still pump out as soon as the sun appears, including 'Girls On The Beach', 'All Summer Long' and 'I Get Around', the latter giving the group their first big hit in Britain. In 1964, he and Mike Love penned 'The Warmth Of The Sun', 'Fun Fun Fun' and 'Little Honda'.

In spite of a nervous breakdown in December 1964 and suffering from deafness in his right ear, Wilson continued to write, although he gave up travelling with the group for the sake of his health,

More classics followed, including 'Help Me, Rhonda', 'You're So Good To Me', 'The Little Girl I Once Knew' and 'California Girls', with the lyrics of the latter providing what was tantamount to a tourists' guide to the attributes of the females in different areas of America.

By this time, Wilson was becoming increasingly eccentric. At one point, he enlisted a carpenter to build him a large wooden box and filled it with eight tons of sand in order to place his piano on it, claiming that "I want to play in the sand...I want to feel like a little kid. When I'm writing these songs, I want to feel what I'm writing...all the happiness."

When Brian Wilson heard The Beatles' *Rubber Soul* album, he knew he had to equal it or better it, and set to work with a vengeance on writing and producing what he hoped would be a timeless work of art. It was success and recognition he craved, not the material gain, admitting that "I've never written one note or word of music simply because I think it will make money."

The album that Wilson created as an answer to *Rubber Soul* was *Pet Sounds*, which displayed yet more of his songwriting talents with 'Here Today', 'Wouldn't It Be Nice?' and 'God Only Knows'. Brian's role was to write, either alone or with a partner, and he put the next album together ready for the vocals while the rest of the group were out on the road. This left a gap in the band while they were on tour, which had been filled temporarily by Glen Campbell, and from April 1965 by Bruce Johnston, a former member of The Rip Chords: "We recorded that with so many voices that we just killed it, so finally Brian decided to use just three voices…When you listen to 'God Only Knows', the first voice is mine, then Carl, and then Brian. Carl also sang the lead that night, but he was tired and went home, so I stayed on and sang the answering phrases and continued on singing Carl's lead where he'd left off. It's my favourite Beach Boys track ever recorded. Brian spent a lot of time on the tracks; he'd really sweat over the stuff, and we'd come in and knock songs off in a night."

For Brian, 'God Only Knows' was one of the jewels in the crown of an album that he hoped would shake the world. "I think 'God Only Knows' explains a lot about me, in that I believe in God and I am humble enough to say 'God knows what I would be without…' whoever I was talking about, or say I was an imaginary person, which I was at the time…it just goes to show feelings. When you believe in something, you reflect it in your songs…you say how you feel, and songs don't lie. Songs are the most honest form of human being there is…there's nothing that lies about a song."

Although a success in Britain, Wilson was dismayed and bewildered when *Pet Sounds* received a lukewarm reception from the American record-buying public. He withdrew into the studio and continued working on a song that he had intended to put on the album, 'Good Vibrations', but which hadn't been ready in time for inclusion. Bruce Johnston remembers: "For six months, he recorded and re-recorded this song…he was doing it during *Pet Sounds* but didn't finish it in time, so he wound up taking a song he didn't intend to cut for the album, 'Sloop John B'. There is one part of 'Good Vibrations' where it got so big…the bridge, where it goes 'Got to keep those loving good vibrations…' I even over-dubbed a gong, which put the needles into the red…so finally we did this real gentle middle and that turned out to be the missing piece that was right for Brian."

The inspiration for the song had come from Brian's formative years.

> My mother used to tell me about vibrations, and I didn't really understand too much of what she meant when I was a boy. It scared me, the word "vibrations"…To think that invisible feelings – invisible vibrations – existed scared me to death. But she told me about dogs that would bark at people but wouldn't bark at

others...that a dog would pick up vibrations from some people that you can't see but you can feel, and the same thing happened with people. So we talked about good vibrations and experimented with the song and the idea and decided that on the one hand you could say "I love the colourful clothes she wears, and the way the sunlight plays upon her hair. I hear the sound of a gentle word On the wind that lifts her perfume through the air." Those are sensual things...and then you say "I'm pickin' up good vibrations", which is a contrast against the sensual, the extra-sensory perception that we have. That's what we're really talking about.

The finished, recorded version of the song allegedly cost $16,000, a not insubstantial sum in 1966, but this was justified when the single went to Number One in Britain and America. As Bruce Johnston remembered, Wilson put his heart and soul into the song and the recording. "It was one night of background vocal and one night of leads, and that was it. Brian did the other six months."

Brian's writing was maturing and moving into uncharted territory. He became increasingly experimental, used more and more intricate, layered harmonies, and more adventurous arrangements. Each song was taking longer and longer to construct, a total contrast to their recording methods of just three years earlier, when they stood and sang for 13 hours non-stop to record the entire *Surfin' USA* album.

Up until this point, Wilson had either written alone or with Mike Love or with other partners from The Beach Boys circle, like ad man Tony Asher, Gary Usher or Roger Christian, penning songs like 'Don't Worry Baby', 'Shut Down' and 'Deadman's Curve' with the latter, but now he began to look farther afield, his eyes alighting on '50s child actor and prodigal arranger Van Dyke Parks. "Brian sought me out, having heard about me from some mutual friends...at the time, people who were experimenting with psychedelics were viewed as enlightened people, and Brian sought out enlightened people."

Brian, in turn, virtually admitted that he needed a new injection of lyrical inspiration, and that Parks could be the person to bring something of that nature to the table. "Van Dyke is a very creative person, and it was a boost to me because he had a lot of energy and a lot of fresh ideas...so that energy helped me."

The collaboration temporarily moved Wilson into a different direction, culminating in the album *Smile*, which didn't see the light of day at the time. The reasons for its collapse are manifold. Brian Wilson once confessed that "the lyrics Van Dyke Parks had written were all Van Dyke Parks and nothing of The Beach Boys. The lyrics were so poetic and symbolic...they were abstract."

They did, however, write some excellent material together, including 'Heroes And Villains', an epic in the style of 'Good Vibrations'. Even back in 1967, Wilson appeared to need a guru-type figure to guide him, and on that occasion he consulted an astrologer to determine the right time to release the song. He was building himself up, allowing the world to draw breath before his latest epic, but even when he and the rest of the group drove to the popular Los Angeles radio station KHJ to let them have an exclusive the portents weren't good. The disc jockey initially refused to play it, as it wasn't on the station playlist, and had to phone his boss for permission – an inauspicious start.

Bruce Johnston felt that it was a confusing track. "It was brilliant, but the tempo changed. I came over to England and took it out to Radio Caroline and played it, and they were really excited, and that night I went to a club where The Bee Gees were playing, and the club disc-jockey put on 'Heroes And Villains'. Everybody just flipped out when they played it, and suddenly the tempo changed and everybody stopped dancing...and I thought 'Well, it's over...'"

The song still made it to Number Twelve in the States and Number Eight in Britain, but Brian Wilson was a perfectionist, and if The Beatles had made Number One with Lennon and McCartney's 'All You Need Is Love' then so should his latest epic.

Wilson continued to craft excellent songs, as did Bruce Johnston, who contributed the beautiful 'Disney Girls' to The Beach Boys' album *Surf's Up*:

> I know it sounds a little strange, but it's an anti-drug song. I noticed that kids coming to our concerts at 16 years old in the early '70s waited until we came on stage at Carnegie Hall and then they would light up and start smoking and whatever. I thought back to what I was doing at 14, 15 or 16, so I wrote 'Disney Girls', about a more innocent time. The second verse is 'Patti Page, summer days and "Old Cape Cod".' Well, I remember

holding my girlfriend's hand in the back of her parents' car when that song was a hit in 1957, hence the title…'Disney Girls, 1957', with lines like 'Clearing skies and drying eyes and I see your smile, sadness goes and your softness shows a changing style…' It's just like taking a backwards trip in time.

A composition that could be the songwriters' anthem is often wrongly credited to Barry Manilow, who took it to Number One in America in 1976 and is unable to leave the stage of any concert without performing it. Not a lot of people realise that 'I Write The Songs' was penned by Bruce Johnston, and it had also been a substantial British hit for David Cassidy a year earlier. "All musicians that play and write are asked where they get their inspiration from, so I thought it would be great to write a song about that. At the time, Gallery had a hit with 'I Believe In Music' and so did Lobo, with 'I'd Love You To Want Me', so I took the chord structure from the Lobo song and then thought 'Where does the music come from?' Well, it comes from a higher place, so I would write about the higher place without making it like a hymn. I made it so that it could be misconstrued as someone's terrible ego saying 'I write the songs', but of course that isn't the truth; it's the higher place saying that it writes music through human beings."

In 1988, The Beach Boys returned to the top of the American chart with 'Kokomo', a song written by four people with a little help from a hit song from the early '60s. The verses were written by Doris Day's son, Terry Melcher, who had produced hit songs for The Byrds, along with some help from Mike Love and Scott McKenzie of 'San Francisco' fame, while John Phillips of The Mamas And Papas wrote the chorus. The chorus tipped its hat more than a little to Little Peggy March's 1963 US Number One 'I Will Follow Him'. Norman Gimbel, the co-writer of that song and later responsible for 'Killing Me Softly With His Song', was also a neighbour of Bruce Johnston, who admitted that they'd "borrowed" the infectious chorus on 'I Will Follow Him' for 'Kokomo'. Gimbel replied courteously: "Well, I am very honoured, and…congratulations."

The accolades and awards heaped upon the most successful team of the second half of the century, John Lennon and Paul McCartney, are too numerous to mention, but it has to be said that they changed the face of popular music around the globe in 1963.

Major To Minor

They also unwittingly brought about a change in songwriting. Until that time, many artists had simply not contemplated the idea that they could possibly write their own material, but the success of Lennon and McCartney from within the framework of The Beatles gave many new confidence in their own abilities. From that point, some performers began to grow as songwriters, with an increasing number providing their own material over the years, until almost four decades on most recording and would-be recording artists write or co-write their own songs.

However, even Lennon and McCartney had to start somewhere, as Paul remembers: "I know that John and I, when we first started, sat around for a long time before we got the knack of how to write a song. It wasn't that we were doing anything wrong, it's just that we weren't good enough. We hadn't written many. We used to say we'd written 100 songs, but that was a fib…it was more like 20, but we didn't really like them. I don't know what makes one person write a hit and another not."

McCartney, born in Liverpool in 1942 to Mary and Jim, was exposed to music from a young age, as his dad and his Uncle Jack had a small band called Jim Mac's Band. Jim was the guy at the parties who knew all of the songs, and encouraged Paul to take up the piano so that he would always get invited to places. He refused to teach his son himself, as he wanted him to learn properly, which led to Paul having lessons locally from a little old lady. He wasn't too enamoured of this, as it seemed more like musical construction than fun, and the homework was fairly tedious. At the age of 16, he took more lessons, by which time he'd written his first song, on the guitar instead of the piano. "I wrote my first song at about 14, which was 'I Lost My Little Girl', which went 'I woke up late this morning/My head was in a whirl/And only then I realised/I lost my little girl./Her clothes were not expensive/Her hair it didn't curl/I don't know why I loved her/But I loved my little girl.' The thing that was interesting was that I had the chords going down and the melody going up…a little obvious musical trick, but there was a bit of jiggery pokery starting even on my first song."

The first profound musical influence on the young McCartney was hearing Bill Haley's 'Rock Around The Clock', after which there was no turning back.

As a boy, he played early Elvis songs and skiffle at scout camps, Liverpool always having a good supply of American records brought in by the merchant seamen who worked out of the port. He bought Gene

Vincent's 'Be Bop A Lula', after it had been recommended to him by a friend at school who played in one of the top local groups, Cass And The Casanovas. Whenever possible, Paul would also try to get to see well-known American acts that came to town, including The Crew-Cuts, who had had a big US hit with 'Earth Angel'.

McCartney's first public performance was with his brother, Michael, at Butlin's in Phwllheli, when they performed 'Bye Bye Love' and 'Long Tall Sally' as Mike And Paul.

McCarney's historic meeting with Lennon came about through a schoolfriend, Ivan Vaughan, who lived in Woolton, and took Paul to meet his friends from that area who were playing in a group at the local village fête. The group were called The Quarrymen, so called because John Lennon went to Quarry Bank High School, and were in the middle of playing The Del Vikings' 'Come Go With Me' as McCartney arrived. "He didn't know the words, so he was making them up. He knew the chorus, but he was making up his own words to the verses...Later we went backstage at the church, where there was a piano...By this time, John was tanked up a bit. The big thing was that I knew the words to Eddie Cochran's '20 Flight Rock'...it was very good currency."

A couple of weeks later Paul was asked to join the group. They would often rehearse in the McCartneys' back room at 20 Forthlin Road, trying out their repertoire on Paul's dad, Jim, and his brother, Michael, who nearly became the drummer at one point. As well as known material, John and Paul had also begun to write their own songs. "One of the earliest songs John and I did together was a thing called 'Just Fun', a kind of 'they say our love is just fun, but we know better' type of thing. There was a terrible line that we could never fix that went 'There's no blue moon that I can see/There's never been in history.' Terrible! I used to see George Harrison on the bus, and although he was a little younger I used to go to his house and we learned chords together from *The Bert Weedon Guitar Book*. I said to John 'I know this fella who can play "Raunchy", the Bill Justis number,' and it all came together."

Lennon and McCartney's early songs might not have been Rodgers and Hart material, but they were learning their craft. To quote a later number of theirs, they were "getting better all the time". They loved Buddy Holly's songs, because they felt that they could relate to them, and because they were based around only three or four chords, which made it easier to attempt to write in his style.

After being rejected for The Carroll Levis Discoveries, the trio of John, Paul and George brought in an art student friend of John's, Stuart Sutcliffe, to play bass, although he wasn't really a bass guitarist.

Having played at the Casbah, a local club run by Mona Best, her son Pete joined on drums after various other skin-bashers had failed to work out, and the group made their first trip to perform in Hamburg. It was in Germany that they made their first real recordings, both backing Tony Sheridan and as themselves. The German label Polydor later released their version of 'My Bonnie'.

Following a few variations on the group name, they eventually settled on The Beatles, signing a five-year contract with Liverpool music shop manager Brian Epstein in October 1962 and releasing their first single, 'Love Me Do'. By this time, Sutcliffe – who had stayed in Germany rather than continuing with the group – had died, and Ringo Starr had replaced Pete Best.

The group followed their first, rather modest hit with the song that John had originally intended to be in the style of Roy Orbison, 'Please Please Me', with harmonic lines that fell away from the note, which would become one of the group's musical characteristics. This second single went to Number One in some charts and Number Two in others.

Published by former singer Dick James, they went back to Liverpool, boasting, "We've met the bloke who sang 'Robin Hood'!" Despite this initial enthusiasm, however, they still felt that their publishing deal should have been renegotiated later in their career. As Paul mourns, "We were saddled with that deal forever."

Money was never going to be a problem for Lennon and McCartney, as they seemed to be able to turn out commercial songs at will. "People were saying '"Please Please Me" is really going to earn you money.'…It was like winning the pools. We were very excited, 'cause John and I were quite prolific, so at the time we used to say 'Let's write a swimming pool,' or 'Lets write a new extension,' or 'How about writing a new car?' Our fourth single, 'She Loves You', we wrote in a hotel room on the twin beds that they have. He sat on one and I sat on the other, and we started writing. We wrote a few like that."

The group's third single, 'From Me To You', had been inspired by the letters page of the most popular British music paper at that time, the *New Musical Express*, which went under the banner of "From You To Us".

During the early stages of their songwriting partnership, John and Paul worked mainly to formulae, using little tricks, such as the repetition of personal pronouns. The songs of this period were littered with them: you, I, he, she and it. Both writers felt that it helped young people to relate to their records.

This idea worked especially well in titles where they used two personal pronouns, such as 'I'll Get You', 'From Me To You', 'PS I Love You', 'She Loves You' and 'I Wanna Hold Your Hand'. The last two songs topped the UK chart and sold millions, setting the tone of the phenomenal global success that was to come. From that point on, most of the group's singles and albums topped the charts and became multimillion-sellers.

Their manager, Brian Epstein, stubbornly refused to let The Beatles go to the States until they had had a Number One there, and 'I Want To Hold Your Hand' was the song that opened the door for them. From 1964 on, they took America by storm, sweeping all before them and paving the way for a British musical invasion of the US and finishing off the chart careers of many established American acts.

Throughout the songwriting careers of Lennon and McCartney and beyond, hundreds of artists would cover their songs; but in the early days, when they were keen to be writing all the time, they provided numbers for several other artists in the Epstein stable. These included The Fourmost ('Hello Little Girl'), Cilla Black ('Love Of The Loved') and Billy J Kramer And The Dakotas, for whom they wrote four hits: 'Do You Want To Know A Secret?', 'Bad To Me', 'I'll Be On My Way' and 'From A Window'.

Other artists who benefited from Lennon and McCartney songs at some time include The Rolling Stones, Del Shannon, Peter And Gordon, David Cassidy, Peter Sellers, PJ Proby, Joe Cocker, The Overlanders, The Applejacks, Cliff Richard, Kenny Lynch, Tomorrow, David And Jonathan, The Truth, St Louis Union, Bryan Ferry and dozens more.

Meanwhile, for The Beatles they wrote songs that gave them many hit albums, including *Please Please Me*, *With The Beatles*, *A Hard Day's Night*, *Beatles For Sale*, *Help!*, *Rubber Soul* and *Revolver*.

One of the most unusual and experimental tracks on *Revolver* was 'Tomorrow Never Knows'. Paul recalls:

> It was about *The Tibetan Book Of The Dead*. It was Timothy Leary time. It was all in the key of C, and a real departure for

us…it was well far out. George Martin never freaked out, even when we took him the most crazy ideas. He was very supportive that way. For that album title, we thought, what does a record do? Answer: it revolves. So we got *Revolver*. 'Good Day Sunshine' was on the album…that was written out at John's house at Weybridge on a sunny day. 'For No One' I wrote in Switzerland, and like 'Another Day' much later on I was thinking of the working girl. I like those "she wakes up, she makes up, she walks around the flat in her slippers" type songs. If you were writing a musical, 'For No One' and 'Another Day' would be in the same show.

They also started to enhance some of their songs with odd instruments that happened to be lying around at Abbey Road Studios. On the later track 'Because' they used a spinet that was handy, while on 'We Can Work it Out' they incorporated an harmonium that was in the studio. On George Harrison's song 'Don't Bother Me', they used a loose-skinned African drum that appeared to live at the studio. It became known within the group as "the Don't Bother Me drum".

In 1965, Lennon and McCartney won their first two Ivor Novello Awards, while the group won a Grammy Award and received MBEs. They had not at that point been a chart act for three full years, but their worldwide success brought them accolades faster than any other songwriters. In the previous year, they had topped the US chart with 'I Want To Hold Your Hand', 'Can't Buy Me Love', 'I Feel Fine', 'She Loves You', 'A Hard Day's Night' and 'Love Me Do', all of which (apart from the latter song) also went to Number One in Britain.

In the following year, they topped the US chart with another four Lennon/McCartney classics: 'Help!', 'Ticket To Ride', 'Eight Days A Week' and 'Yesterday'. The first two were also UK Number Ones, while the others weren't released as singles. Paul explains the roots of 'Eight Days A Week': "I was being driven down to John's and I had this driver. He was a good lad, and we got chatting, and at some point I said 'What have you been doing?' 'Oh, working,' he said. 'I've been working eight days a week.' I'd never heard that expression before…I thought, that's great. The minute I got to John's, we started on it and had it finished in half an hour. It was just such a great title."

The fact that John's and Paul's names on the label as writers could contribute heavily towards a song being a hit led McCartney to write the song 'Woman' for Peter And Gordon under the pseudonym "Bernard Webb". It was still a hit.

By now regular US chart-toppers, their new single in the summer of 1966 was the unusual 'Paperback Writer'. It seemed that they could even write hits about writing! "I liked the word paperback, and I had this idea on the way out to John's house...we often used to write out there. I thought it would be great to have a song that's like a letter. So it developed from 'Dear sir or madam' through to 'gonna write a novel' and 'it's gonna make a million for you overnight'. We just wrote it like a letter."

In 1966 they won two more Ivor Novello Awards, and 'We Can Work It Out' had the highest certified sales of 1965. However, they then ran into trouble in the US when Lennon's remark "We're more popular than Jesus now" was taken out of context. They caused more controversy when their album *Yesterday And Today* was released, the cover featuring the group with dismembered dolls and cuts of raw, bloody meat. Nevertheless, it still topped the US chart. Lennon later publicly apologised for his comments, but not before former Beatle fans – especially in the southern states – made bonfires of the group's records and memorabilia.

In an already action-packed 1966, a clairvoyant who had previously predicted President Kennedy's assassination declared that The Beatles would die on their flight from Indianapolis to Detroit on 29 August. The flight turned out to be uneventful, but on that night at Candlestick Park, San Francisco, they played what was to be their final major public show. There was no conscious decision that it should be their last, but after nine years of performing live things seemed to come to a natural end. (Later, of course, they played an impromptu set on the roof of the Apple building in London's Savile Row.)

In the following year, they released the album *Yellow Submarine*, the concept for which had come from McCartney and which would also become the title of an animated full-length cartoon film. "I just thought up a bit of it in bed. You know when you're just drifting off and you've got that five or ten minutes before you go, there's that nice little netherworld...I like that...it sends me to sleep thinking of songs then. Somehow I got this idea of submarines; there were going to be blue ones and green ones, but in the end it all came down to this yellow one. I thought it'd be nice as a children's song."

When the idea was later turned into a film in 1968, The Beatles declined the offer of voicing their own characters, which would have meant devoting more time than they wished to the project. As it was, they weren't overly happy with actors trying to imitate their accents, as it sounded too "hammy".

The single of 'Yellow Submarine' was backed with 'Eleanor Rigby', which began with Paul tinkering with the melody on the piano.

> It started off with an E minor chord, and as I was working on the tune a line just appeared in my head: "Picks up the rice in the church where a wedding has been." I thought, where did that come from? So I had a little old lady. The rest of it was trying to explain that line. There was lots of imagery…"keeps her face in a jar by the door", and stuff. I didn't have a name for her, but I happened to be in Bristol one day and I saw this shop called Rigby's, and I thought, that's it. Names are very special in songs; if you try and put a made-up name in it usually sounds daft. The Christian name came as we'd been working in a film with the actress Eleanor Bron, and I just liked the name. It then sounded like a person who actually could be this little old lady. We then needed the vicar's name, and wanted Mac something, so we got the phone book and looked through all the Macs and came across McCartney. John thought that that was a good idea, but I said, "Oh no, it'll be like my dad, and everyone would be saying 'Is he a vicar, then, your dad?'" So we went for Father McKenzie.

1967 saw Lennon and McCartney win Song Of The Year at the ninth annual Grammy Awards ceremony for 'Michelle', with 'Eleanor Rigby' winning Best Contemporary (Rock 'n' Roll) Solo Performance. They also won two more Ivor Novello Awards, with 'Michelle' as the Most Performed Work of 1966 and 'Yellow Submarine' as having the Highest Certified British Sales for 1966.

The year also brought them another clutch of big hit singles in Britain and America, including 'All You Need Is Love', 'Hello, Goodbye', 'Magical Mystery Tour' and the double-sided 'Strawberry Fields Forever'/'Penny Lane'. The piccolo trumpets were added to 'Penny Lane' after Paul had seen someone playing one on the television. He didn't know what the instrument was, or who was playing it, but after some detective work from their producer, George Martin, that actual musician, David Mason, ended up playing his piccolo trumpet on the single.

Lennon wasn't happy with the first take of 'Strawberry Fields,' although he did like parts of it. A second take also proved to contain some acceptable passages and others that didn't come up to scratch, which prompted John to ask George if he could take the best bits of both and link them together.

The Beatles' album *Sergeant Pepper's Lonely Hearts Club Band*, released in the summer of 1967, proved to be a milestone in the history of popular music through its conception, execution, recording techniques and collection of excellent songs by Lennon and McCartney.

'Getting Better' was inspired by a favourite phrase of drummer Jimmy Nicol, who had deputised for the temporarily ill Ringo Starr, while 'Being For The Benefit Of Mr Kite' was created by John from an old piece of Victoriana. "It was from this old poster I'd bought at an antique shop. We'd been down to Surrey or somewhere, filming a TV piece to go with 'Strawberry Fields Forever'. There was a break and I went into this shop and bought an old poster advertising a variety show which starred Mr Kite. It said 'The Hendersons would all be there, late of Pablo Fanques Fair.' There were hoops and horses and someone going through a hogshead of real fire. Then there was Henry The Horse. The band would start at ten to six. All at Bishopsgate. I hardly made up a word, just connecting the lines together word for word, really."

With the drugs culture playing a part in the lives of some people in the music business, the press and public were eager to uncover double meanings or hidden messages in the lyrics of Lennon and McCartney. The surreal words in 'Mr Kite' were initially thought to have been drug induced until Lennon told the real story. Even then, no one really wanted to believe him, as the mystical possibility seemed to be much more romantic. There were connotations that apparently hadn't dawned on John, like the fact that "horse" was a common term amongst drug users for heroin, and so Henry The Horse, the innocent victorian equine performer, got it in the neck!

There were other songs on *Sergeant Pepper's* that were subjected to misinterpretation, including 'A Day In The Life' and 'Lucy In The Sky With Diamonds'. Paul dispels the rumours:

> 'A Day In The Life' wasn't – as many people thought – about the Guinness heir Tara Browne…it was just one of those surreal songs where the words were images that didn't mean anything. A lot of it was pulled out of newspapers…The most controversial thing we did, knowing what we were doing, was including the line "I'd love to turn you on." But that's what art's about; it doesn't stay in one mould. John sang the song beautifully.
>
> With 'Lucy In The Sky With Diamonds', somebody made the assumption that, because of the songs initials, LSD, that it was about the drug. It was written after Jon's son, Julian, had come back from school with a painting, like all little kids do, and showed it to his dad, and like all dads do he said, "That's nice. What is it?" Julian replied, "It's Lucy, in the sky with diamonds," Lucy being a friend of his at school.

The song featured a welter of images, some – like the "cellophane flowers" and "newspaper taxis" – being inspired by the books *Alice In Wonderland* and *Alice Through The Looking-Glass*, of which John and Paul were devotees. The Reverend Dodgson, who had written the books under the pseudonym Lewis Carroll in 1865 and 1872 respectively, was in effect dealing in psychedelia a century before Lennon and McCartney and some of their equally experimental musical peers.

In August 1967, The Beatles' manager, Brian Epstein, was found dead. After this, the group never seemed quite as cohesive.

During the late '60s, the songs of Lennon and McCartney – with increasing contributions from fellow Beatle George Harrison – led the group further and further into a seemingly impregnable position, releasing more classic singles, including 'Lady Madonna', 'Get Back', 'The Ballad Of John And Yoko', Harrison's 'Something' and McCartney's 'Hey Jude'.

> John was getting divorced, and I liked both him and Cynthia, so it was a tricky situation. I was going out to see them one day when I got half an idea of 'Hey Jules', with "Jules" being a nickname for Julian: "Hey Jules, don't make it bad, take a sad song and make it better," really saying, "Don't be too brought down by the divorce." I played John a little tape I'd made, and when it came to the line "The movement you need is on your shoulder," I said,

"I'll be fixing that line." He said, "You're kidding. It's probably the best line in it." At the time, I thought it was a stupid line. I thought it sounded like a parrot on somebody's shoulder!

Despite Paul's misgivings over that line, the song won another Ivor Novello Award to add to the countless trophies won by Lennon and McCartney over the years, with more Grammys and Novellos to come.

George's song 'Something' had been written during the making of the album that has always been referred to as *The White Album*. "When you write songs, everything in a way sounds familiar, and the catchier it is the more familiar it sounds. I wrote the main part of that and then put it on ice for six months because I thought, that's too easy. It sounds so simple. It must be something else. But it wasn't."

With business dealings turning increasingly acrimonious between the members of the group, The Beatles finally called it a day in 1970, although John Lennon, Paul McCartney, George Harrison and Ringo Starr would all remain successful in their own rights in the next decade.

Although both gifted in their own right, there is no doubt that on some occasions John and Paul missed the input or appraisal of the other. As the '60s had progressed, it became more of an open secret which songs were John's and which were Paul's, despite the continuing "Lennon/McCartney" label credit. It became apparent, though, that even the odd nudge from the other over structure, approach or the finely honing of content could make all the difference between a good song and a great song.

During the '70s, John had ten UK solo hits before his untimely death at the tail end of 1980. These included the evergreen 'Imagine', written at his new home at Tittenhurst Park, Ascot; 'Happy Xmas (War Is Over)', which has charted in Britain on four separate occasions; 'Power To The People'; and 'Give Peace A Chance', which was recorded in a bedroom in a Toronto hotel.

Paul McCartney also continued to write major hits both, for his group Wings and, later, under his own name. Early '70s successes included 'Another Day', 'Hi Hi Hi', 'Helen Wheels', 'My Love' and the title track for the 1973 James Bond film *Live And Let Die*. "I had to write the song before I'd seen anything of the film. I basically read the Ian Fleming book and wrote the song the next day. We recorded it with George Martin, who then took it out to where they were filming. One of the producers heard it and said 'Great demo, George. When are you gonna do the real one?' I thought it would be a hard job to write a Bond theme. I took it as a job because it was a big gig."

Many think that the album *Band On The Run* was McCartney's finest post-Beatle album, with its intriguing celebrity cover and litany of outstanding songs. Bored of recording in London, Paul asked EMI where else in the world they had studios. Their reply included Rio De Janeiro, China and Lagos. He chose the latter, imagining the inspiration that he might get from African drum sounds and their intricate rhythms.

He'd written some songs before they got there, but not long after their arrival Paul and his wife Linda were mugged and the tapes for the album stolen, and so he had to start again and try to recall some of his original ideas. Apart from the title track, the album included 'Jet', and the highly unusual 'Picasso's Last Words'.

> A few months before, I'd been on holiday and met Dustin Hoffman, who at the time was filming *Papillon* with Steve McQueen, and we were staying near them...so we went out to dinner together. Dustin was talking about songs and asked, "How do you write songs? How do you write them, man?' I replied, "Well, you sort of just do it...I pick them out of the air, and there they are." He said, "Tell you what, I'll get you something to write a song about...I saw something great today." So he went and got his copy of *Time* magazine, and it had "Pablo Picasso recently died, and on the night that he died he was having dinner with friends, and the last thing he said to them was 'Drink to me, drink to my health, you know I can't drink any more.'" Off he'd gone to bed...and he died. Dustin said, "I thought that was great...can you write a song about it?" I started thinking vaguely *Dylany* in my mind...I hit a G and started "Drink to me, drink to my health." Dustin was leaping up and down and screaming. He was just so amazed. It gave me the inspiration to go and finish it off.

'Blackbird', another track on the album, really harked back to Paul's roots in Liverpool. With his mother being a midwife, they were often moving house, invariably ending up at the edge of new estates and therefore close to the countryside. The love of nature and country ways that has always been inherent in him was to be increasingly revealed, as the global madness and mayhem that had accompanied The Beatles phenomenon became less intense. "I was sitting out in the sun, and there was this bird in a tree, and he's doing a succession of notes. Now, if you're a composer, you're listening thinking, that's a good riff. I'm thinking, isn't it incredible…there's me, the inflated writer that's incredibly well paid, and there's this little bird up there, doing exactly what I do. All you'd have to do is to take down his notes and you've got a song."

Paul's love for the countryside was re-awakened when he bought a farm in Scotland at the suggestion of Lennon, who had a deep love for the country. (The front door of John's house Kenwood, in Weybridge, was adorned with a small, wooden, heraldic shield inscribed with the words "Lennon" and "Hibernia", demonstrating his Celtic.) It was while Paul was staying at his farm in Cambeltown, Kintyre, that he pondered the idea of writing a new Scottish song. "I thought I'd write one, so I got my guitar out. I found out what key the bagpipes were in by asking piper Tony Wilson, who I wanted to play on the song. I found out what notes he could do, 'cause I couldn't write a note that wasn't on his instrument. Then I set about writing it." The resulting song, 'Mull Of Kintyre', went to Number One in Britain, and became a million-seller.

As the years go by and a new millennium is upon us, Paul continues to write. "I remember Dave Mason – who used to be with the group Traffic – telling me that he had 'dry periods', where he couldn't write songs, and asked if I got them too. I was worried earlier in my career about my songwriting abilities drying up, but if I stopped tomorrow I'd have done enough, really."

14 Pop Into The Theatre

The names of three innovative writers immediately spring to mind when examining the renaissance of the British theatre during the '60s: Lionel Bart, Tim Rice and Andrew Lloyd Webber.

Bart was born Lionel Begleiter in London's East End in August 1930. As a child, he had the knack of being able to make up alternative words to popular songs, but instead of opting for a writing career he won a scholarship to study at St Martin's School Of Art before going on to do his national service in the RAF.

After his demob in 1953, he worked at the Unity Theatre in London' Kings Cross as a scene painter. On one day, he spotted that the actor Alfie Bass, who was producing a revue at the venue, had put up a notice asking if anyone wanted to write songs for the show. The theme of the show was the topical subject of the coronation of Queen Elizabeth II, and was to be called *Turn It Up*. The songs that Lionel submitted prompted Alfie to pull him out of the scenery department, assuring him that he had a great future as a songwriter. "I guess it's all down to Alfie, really," Bart recalls. "It was he who made me realise I could write lyrics and tunes and put them together."

Lionel's beginnings as a songwriter coincided neatly with the dawn of rock 'n' roll. He was there as embryonic skiffle groups frantically bluffed their way through a handful of songs with basic melodies and lyrics that suited guitars, washboards and tea-chest basses. To many of the young musicians, playing was hard enough, and actually writing their own material was something that only the real professionals undertook. Lionel had no such problem writing for rock 'n' roll:

> Rock 'n' roll, you sinners!
> Sing to save your soul.
> There ain't no room for beginners
> When the world starts to rock 'n' roll.

Eager to be part of the new scene, Bart and his cronies formed their own skiffle group, The Cavemen, with Lionel himself on washboard, Mike Pratt on tea-chest bass and Thomas Hicks (yet to change his name to Tommy Steele) on guitar and vocals. They played at various small venues in London, such as the Cave at Waterloo, the place from which they took their name and a venue on which record company men would descend in search of new talent. When they were offered a recording contract (mainly because of Tommy), Bart left to concentrate on writing songs with the newly-named Tommy Steele and Mike Pratt.

The trio had their first hit as songwriters in the autumn of 1956, when Tommy charted with 'Rock With The Caveman'. The record not only established Steele as the first British rock 'n' roller but it also heralded the arrival of an important new songwriter who could neither play an instrument nor read music.

Over the next four years Bart wrote many hits for Tommy Steele, including 'Butterfingers', 'Water, Water', 'Handful Of Songs', 'Shiralee', 'Happy Guitar', 'Hey You' and 'Little White Bull'. Some of these and other Lionel Bart songs were included in Tommy's films *The Tommy Steele Story*, *The Duke Wore Jeans* and *Tommy The Toreador*, the latter starring Sidney James and Janet Munro.

As a proven writer of hit songs, in the summer of 1958 Bart was asked to go to Cheshunt, in Hertfordshire, to listen to a new group and their singer, Cliff Richard, who it was thought had potential in the pop field. "The group set up their gear in Cliff's front room and they tried out dozens of numbers. They were good, but in the end I had to advise them against continuing with their ideas of entering showbusiness. Tommy Steele was still touring, Marty Wilde had just got his first hit and Terry Dene was topping variety bills. I didn't think there was room for any more."

By the time Lionel returned from a break in Cornwall, Cliff had released a song that his bass player, Ian Samwell, had written between Cheshunt and London on a green line bus. 'Move It' was almost certainly the first real British rock 'n' roll song, as the songs written by the Bart/Steele/Pratt partnership had been in a much lighter, almost skiffle strain of the genre.

Although Lionel had originally felt that there wasn't room for any more stars in the field of rock 'n' roll, he had been impressed by Cliff's voice. "Publisher Jimmy Phillips told me that film producer Mickey Delamar wanted me to write three songs for the film *Serious Charge*, and would be glad if I could suggest someone to sing them. I had little hesitation in naming Cliff, and of course he subsequently got the part." Out of the three songs that he wrote for the film – 'Mad About You', 'No Turning Back' and 'Living Doll' – it was the latter which became a British Number One for Cliff in the summer of 1959, staying at the top of the chart for six weeks. The song also gave Cliff his first American hit, reaching Number 30 there.

As Steele moved away from the pop star star image in order to become an all-round entertainer, Bart returned to the theatre – not as a scene-painter, this time, but as a writer, having been invited to create some songs for a play being produced by Joan Littlewood at the Theatre Royal, Stratford East. Again, the timing was ideal: new, cutting-edge "angry young man" plays needed songs with more bite and streetwise input than establishment writers could offer. There was a considerable dearth of composers and lyricists in this field.

While the stars of the play were rehearsing, Lionel sat in the stalls writing the songs and teaching them to the cast on the spot as he came up with them. *Fings Ain't What They Used T'Be* opened in February 1959 and starred Richard Harris and Barbara Windsor, with cockneys unusually in the limelight and not relegated to the minor roles that they played in most existing British musicals.

As with a lot of shows, it was adored by the public but slated by the critics. *The Stage* stated that "It's not a good musical, but there are some effective songs". *Theatre World* followed suit: "Ten songs by Lionel Bart…not especially captivating in themselves, acted like explosive dumplings in the stew."

The show later transferred to the West End, and Lionel wrote a more acceptable set of words for the title song. One could hardly imagine Max Bygraves having a hit with the original lyrics, which made observations about "poofs in coffee houses" and sang the praises of murderous pimps:

> Once, in golden days of yore,
> Ponces killed a lazy whore.

The Lord Chamberlain kept such a tight rein on the show's language and provocative acting that success was guaranteed.

In 1959, Bart won an Ivor Novello for Outstanding Services To British

Music, and also provided the lyrics for another musical, *Lock Up Your Daughters*, for Bernard Miles' new Mermaid Theatre. As the cast album sold out within four days, the *Sunday Dispatch* called Bart "the most successful songwriter since Ivor Novello and Noël Coward". Bart rose to the accolade telling the papers that "Anything I do must be bigger and better than anything I've done before. That's my kick, mate." However, his greatest moment was undoubtedly in adapting Charles Dickens' novel *Oliver Twist* for both stage and film, and writing the songs for it.

The stage play of *Oliver* is and was magnificent, but the film was unbeatable. A cast headed by Ron Moody, Oliver Reed, Harry Secombe, Shani Wallis, Mark Lester and Jack Wild roared their way through one of the greatest collections of songs in any musical film. There were powerful ballads, such as 'As Long As He Needs Me' (a UK Number Two hit for Shirley Bassey) and 'Where Is Love?'; rumbustious romps such as 'Consider Yourself', 'You've Got To Pick A Pocket Or Two', 'Be Back Soon' and 'Food, Glorious Food'; and the gloriously uplifting 'Who Will Buy?'

Bart had by now well and truly arrived as a mainstream writer. The *Sunday Times* proclaimed that he was "the first composer to have emerged fully-fledged from the labyrinths of rock 'n' roll".

In the spring of 1960, Bart came up with another British Number One, when Anthony Newley took his song 'Why?' to the top. He was also voted Showbusiness Personality Of The Year, and picked up three more Ivor Novello Awards.

Having been likened to Novello and Noël Coward, in terms of success rather than style, it's interesting to note that Coward, an admirer of Lionel's work, invited him to his home in Geneva, where he gave him some sound advice: "Never put money into your own shows." The time would come when Bart would need to heed Coward's words but would, to his cost, ignore them.

It wasn't all awards and plaudits, though. The similarity in melody between 'Why?' and the song 'In A Little Spanish Town' gave Bart his fair share of litigation-induced headaches.

After the death of the great lyricist Oscar Hammerstein II, Richard Rodgers approached Lionel with a view to them working together. "We tossed around an idea about Moll Flanders for about a year. He came here and I went to New York, and then I said 'Look, man, I usually leave holes in my songs because, if they are going on stage, I like to be amazed by what's going to come off the stage and then write for the people.' 'Oh, I can't work like that,' he said. 'Oscar Hammerstein always used to bring me his lyrics engraved in concrete, as it were.' I said: 'You've worked with the best lyric writer of the century, Lorenz Hart...you need me like a hole in the head.'" Bart, who was staggered that Rodgers even wanted to write with him, convinced Rodgers that he would be better off writing his own words. It seems like an incredible opportunity to pass up. He must have either had amazing confidence in his own creativity or been terrified of having his musical shortcomings exposed.

It's difficult to equate the Lionel Bart who was asked to follow in the footsteps of Hart and Hammerstein with the Lionel Bart who in that year released the chirpy, lyrically banal cockney single 'Give Us A Kiss For Christmas'.

Bart's next musical had originally been penned under the working title of *Down The Shelter*, but by the time it opened in 1962 it had become *Blitz*. It failed to match up to his previous efforts, but the write-ups were charitable, if a little lukewarm. Now strangely perceived as a flop, the show broke even in just four months and became another Bart hit, as *Oliver* – which had become a firm favourite of the Queen's – played its thousandth performance.

Bart was also having more success in the charts. Both Matt Monro and John Barry had hits with his title song for the latest James Bond film, *From Russia With Love*.

Bart's next show, *Maggie May*, followed *Blitz* into the West End's Adelphi Theatre at a time when the composer was expanding in several directions, starting both a publishing and a film company. He splashed out on a £60,000 house in Chelsea, and was earning in excess of £8,000 a week, a colossal amount in the mid '60s. Seemingly unstoppable, he turned his attention to the legend of Robin Hood, a theme that has never really worked as a musical.

This attempt was no exception. From the start, the show was rife with problems, but despite being poorly received by the audience, backstage squabbles and concerned backers, Lionel seemed untroubled, certain that the problems could be resolved. The cost prior to opening in the West End was a staggering £100,000, and to take it into London would cost another £30,000. The backer, Bernard Delfont, pulled out, so Bart, determined to make it work, sold a large chunk of his future royalties in order to raise the money himself. If the sagacious words of Noël Coward had returned to haunt him, he chose to ignore them, and ploughed full steam ahead into the Sherwood Forest fiasco.

The musical folded after just eight days, and Bart's finances were in turmoil. His fall from grace was assisted by damning news stories, litigation and, in 1972, bankruptcy. Even so, the writer appeared to remain buoyant throughout, always looking for that next hit musical.

He always had a few ideas on the back burner, and obviously still loved the theatre. Although I knew Lionel well enough to chat with at various social and showbusiness gatherings, there were two occasions when he didn't speak to me, and on both of these occasions he slipped quietly in and out of two of my own musicals. I was thrilled that he'd bothered to attend, but never actually had the chance to ask him of his opinion. Maybe that's why he'd left as swiftly as he'd arrived! The next time I saw him in a theatre was in 1995, when Cameron Mackintosh not only revived *Oliver* but also magnanimously gave Lionel back a percentage of the rights that he had signed away years earlier. Lionel was sitting at the back, making notes, obviously thrilled to be back in the thick of it. The writer had already had a brief chart flurry in 1989 when his jingle for an advertisement for the Abbey National Building Society had charted, under the title 'Happy Endings (Give Yourself A Pinch)'.

The last time I spoke to Lionel was a month or two before his death, when he told me that he had been asked by a major producer to come up with a musical of Dickens' *A Christmas Carol*, but hadn't felt up to it and suggested that they might be interested in the one that I'd had produced at the Theatre Royal in Nottingham. Sadly, he never told me who the producer was.

We lost a colourful and wonderfully opinionated songwriter and character when Lionel Bart died of cancer in 1999.

Two people that really breathed new life into British theatre were Tim Rice (born in November 1944) and Andrew Lloyd Webber (born in March 1948). Educated at Lancing, Rice first became a music fan at school, playing with his own group, The Aardvarks, while Westminster-educated Lloyd Webber followed a more classical route, even as a youth. His father, William Lloyd Webber, was principal of the London College Of Music, and it was living in this environment that inspired Andrew to start composing at the age of six. He had his first work published at the age of nine.

After being a Queen's Scholar at Westminster, Lloyd Webber became a student at the Guildhall School Of Music And Drama and the Royal College Of Music. "My father was against formal training for me, and it was quite a family battle for me to go to the Royal College Of Music at all. My music is largely based on what I've heard, and my father felt that an instant gift of melody could easily be educated out of people."

Tim became a law student, although he remained an avid lover of pop music and was determined to break into the business somehow. Before starting as an assistant to record producer Norrie Paramor, he worked for a solicitor's offices in Baker Street, London, and while there he became aware of a young writer who was seeking to collaborate with a lyricist. In April 1965, he put pen to paper:

Dear Andrew,

I have been told that you were looking for a with-it writer of lyrics for your songs, and as I have been writing pop songs for a short while now, and particularly enjoy writing the lyrics, I wondered if you considered it worth your while meeting me. I may fall far short of your requirements, but anyway it would be interesting to meet up – I hope! Would you be able to get in touch with me shortly, either at FLA 1822 in the evenings, or at WEL 2261 in the daytime? (Pettit And Westlake, Solicitors, are the owners of the latter number.)

Hope to hear from you.
Yours,
Tim Rice.

The two got together, and, although nothing happened overnight, they began to collaborate.

Alan Doggett, the choirmaster at Westminster Underschool – the prep school section of the school that both Andrew and his brother, Julian, had attended – had been a fan of Tim's and Andrew's first attempt at a musical, *The Likes Of Us*, the story of Dr Barnardo. Doggett suggested that Rice and Lloyd Webber wrote something for his boys to perform at a school concert. There would be no payment, no theatre and no professional performers. The only carrot was the chance that some educational music concern might publish the work, and that therefore other schools might then perform it at some point. Initially, they planned to make a mini musical about James Bond, but they eventually settled on Tim's favourite story from the Bible, Joseph and his coat of many colours. Tim's main source of reference was *The Wonder Book Of Bible Stories*, and his inspiration was the style of Michael Flanders and Paddy Roberts.

Intriguingly, like Ira Gershwin and George Cohan had done before him, Tim used slang terminology and anachronisms. He was also not averse to impromptu augmentation. The list of colours at the end of 'Coat Of Many Colours' initially only ran to red, yellow, green, brown and blue, but the eventual list, containing 29 colours in all, was put together by Doggett and his class of boys. Rice thought that the tale had all the right ingredients: "...plausible, sympathetic characters, a flawed hero and redeemed villains. The storyline is both original and unpredictable, yet moves with unerring force towards a happy conclusion. We certainly obeyed rule number one by choosing a good storyline. Writing the words was great fun, all the more so because every time that a tune came off the Lloyd Webber conveyer belt it sounded like a winner. My initial task was simply to suggest to Andrew what aspect of the story each musical scene should convey. He then produced a tune to fit the mood and plot of each scene and I added the words."

Their unique approach helped the piece to progress from a school production to a global success. Its world première took place at Colet Court School on 1 March 1968.

Tim still feels that 'Any Dream Will Do' is by far the best song in *Joseph*, and one of the best four or five that they ever wrote together. The song had been written a year or two earlier as a potential number for Herman's Hermits, with the rather ghastly title of 'I Fancy You'. As time passes, Tim has become more acutely aware that some of his early lyrics didn't contain accurate rhymes. He stills questions his own rhyming of the word "biscuit" with "district", and "beginning" with "dimming". Despite this, however, he feels that, of all his works, *Joseph* is the one which is most likely to survive into the 22nd century. Ironically, although the work subsequently made them a fortune and launched successful careers for them both, they initially received advances from Novello of just £100 each for the publishing rights.

For their next project, *Jesus Christ, Superstar*, they were able to use a couple of existing songs, including 'I Don't Know How To Love Him'. Tim wrote the lyric in two or three hours at the dining table of his parents' house in Harpenden. "Normally, love songs are the hardest to write, taking weeks, primarily because everything has been said so many times before, but also because the choice of vocabulary is much more limited than it would be in a novelty, humorous or unromantic number. Slang, puns and smart-arse gags are usually unsuitable, too. By and large, the number of syllables a lyricist is given to express his passion is fewer when he is working with a potential ballad than with an up-tempo melody, so every word has got to get straight to the point. The lyricist has to be extremely concise."

Restrictions of this sort are made worse when the melody comes before the words, which was certainly the case with most of *Jesus Christ, Superstar*, and in fact with most things that Tim and Andrew wrote together. These self same restrictions can often push a wordsmith to come up with some of their best work, as Tim felt was the case with the *Superstar* song 'I Don't Know How To Love Him', which was called 'Kansas Morning' before its inclusion in *Superstar*.

Tim has always enjoyed writing songs from the feminine point of view, resulting in many of his successful lyrics being sung by women. This is clearly written from observation rather than direct personal experience: "I have never been (yet) a prostitute touched for the first time by true feeling for a man ('I Don't Know How To Love Him'), a wronged wife or distressed mistress ('I Know Him So Well'), a manipulative vamp ('I'd Be Surprisingly Good For You') or an old woman in love with a gay man ('Ziggy', from *Starmania*). These and other female-centred songs have been among those I am most proud of. Come to think of it, neither have I addressed a crowd of 100,000 from a balcony in Buenos Aires wearing an expensive dress and decked out in extravagant jewellery."

Before Tim and Andrew came up with the idea of *Superstar*, they seriously considered the story of King David as a possible follow-up to Joseph but abandoned the idea after working on one number. The song in question began, "Sam-u-el, Sam-u-el, this is the first book of Sam-u-el", the tune of which later became the hook line for 'Jesus Christ, Superstar': 'Jesus Christ, Jesus Christ. Who are you? What have you sacrificed?'

The idea for writing *Jesus Christ, Superstar* seems to have originally come from Tim, although he had apparently have forgotten that he ever conceived it. Then, one day, record producer Mike Leander was chatting to Tim at a Joe Brown session and he asked him whatever happened to his idea for doing this particular story from The Bible. A rather confused lyricist had forgotten that he'd ever thought about it, or even mentioned it to anybody. However, once Tim and Andrew had started to move down that line, they were determined to be as faithful as possible to the story, as described by Matthew, Mark, Luke and John. Although aware that they were entering sensitive territory, and might raise more than few eyebrows in religious circles, they tried to steer away from being controversial, even discussing their plans for the musical with the dean of St Paul's Cathedral, who assured them that what they were doing was totally acceptable to any Christian who welcomed an honest challenge to the faith.

The title song began with a deceptively simple three-chord verse, for which Tim found the lyrics came easily.

> I knew exactly the sort of questions I wanted Judas to ask by setting it in the 20th century, rather than in the first. The question struck a strong contemporary chord. The title was the last part of the lyric to fall into place. My first run at the chorus made no mention of Superstar…I had more or less settled on the rather dreary 'Judas' Song' as the title, until I saw a full-page advertisement in the *Melody Maker* proclaiming Tom Jones as the world's first superstar. I wrote a second new couplet: "Jesus Christ, Superstar/Do you think you're what they say you are?"…probably the most important lines I have ever written, as far as our careers were concerned. They were at once shocking, yet respectful and unforgettable.

Rice finished the lyrics at his parents' home, and he and Andrew began to write the rest of the songs over a four-day period at Stoke Edith Hotel in Herefordshire. The melody from one of their songs that ended up being rejected from the Eurovision Song Contest, 'Try It And See', became 'King Herod's Song', and that pop song they'd written back in 1966 as 'Kansas Morning' became 'I Don't Know How To Love Him'.

The opening phrase to the melody of that song bore a striking resemblance to the second movement of Mendelssohn's violin concerto in E minor before launching into its own melody. As the original song was owned by another publisher, Tim and Andrew's manager, David Land, had to buy it back for £100. However, he wasn't so lucky in trying to secure the rights to 'Try It And See', as Tim's former boss, Norrie Paramor, decided to hold onto the publishing rights. This turned out to be a wise move.

The main body of the musical *Jesus Christ, Superstar* was written in the first few months of 1970, and in more or less the right order, with the songs coming first and Andrew's tunes preceding Tim's lyrics. Before writing the melodies, Lloyd Webber had a fairly clear idea of what Tim wanted to say. This method of writing held good for *Joseph*, *Superstar* and *Evita*: plot first, music second and lyrics third. Had they only been writing for the stage, there would have been fewer time restrictions, but as they were contracted to provide an album as well, they had to fit the whole story into an hour and a half.

The inspiration for writing the musical *Evita* came after Rice caught the tail end of a radio programme on Eva Perón called *Legends Of Our Time*. He became fascinated with the subject matter, as in the following week the programme featured James Dean. Tim reasoned that, if she were in his league in terms of being an icon, she was worth pursuing.

There proved to be very little material available in Britain on the wife of the former Argentinian dictator Juan Perón, who was born Eva Duarte in 1919, the illegitimate daughter of a middle-class Argentinian family. To glean more information on this woman, who died in 1952 at the age of 33, Tim travelled to Buenos Aires.

Most of the musical was written at the Palace Hotel, Biarritz. "A piano was wheeled into our suite…We had a very productive few days, writing four or five important songs, including the Perez Prado/Dean Martin pastiche 'On This Night Of A Thousand Stars', 'Eva, Beware Of The City', 'Buenos Aires', 'I'd Be Surprisingly Good For You' and 'Another Suitcase In Another Hall'. This was a pretty good work rate, by any standards."

They resumed writing at Andrew's Berkshire house, Sydmonton Court, coming up with 'Rainbow High', 'The Money Kept Rolling In' and 'High Flying Adored'. The latter song was another one that had new life breathed into it, having started out five years earlier as 'Down On The Farm'. At this point, Tim still didn't have a complete lyric or title for the most important scene, which would include the main airing of the tune featured in various places as 'Oh What A Circus' and 'Don't Cry For Me, Argentina'.

> 'Don't Cry For Me, Argentina' was one of those songs that, once I heard it on the radio, I knew it was a big hit. It just had that

indefinable quality. When we wrote it, we had no idea that it was going to be a single, let alone a hit; it was just part of *Evita*. We thought a song about some strange lady on a balcony talking to 100,000 peasants about Argentina was not terribly commercial, but we were wrong. Originally, we'd debated various other titles. Originally, it had been called 'It's Only Your Lover Returning', then 'All Through My Wild Days'. I had most of the lyric, but didn't think we could call the song 'Don't Cry For Me, Argentina' because it didn't really make sense, even within the context of the musical. But the point of the whole scene is that it's a dishonest politician talking to a huge crowd and saying things that you hear from all politicians at party conferences. They say things that often don't make sense, and the crowd love it. It was Andrew that said to me, "You've used that line 'Don't Cry For Me, Argentina' earlier. Use it here, as well, because it sounds nice." So we put it there because it sounded nice. There are one or two songs that get played so often, like 'Whiter Shade Of Pale' and 'You've Lost That Loving Feeling', that you forget that they are actually rather good songs. I feel that way about 'Argentina'. I think "Oh no, not that again!', but actually it was a great tune.

After three phenomenally successful musicals, Tim and Andrew began to work with other people. During the next two decades, Andrew collaborated with several new partners, including Don Black, Richard Stilgoe, Charles Hart, Ben Elton and Jim Steinman, on such successful musicals as *The Phantom Of The Opera*, *Starlight Express*, *Cats*, *Aspects Of Love*, *Sunset Boulevard*, *The Beautiful Game* and *Whistle Down The Wind*. In the mid '90s, Andrew was knighted before being elevated to the peerage as Lord Lloyd Webber.

Tim had equally outstanding success with new partners, such as Benny and Björn from Abba, Elton John and John Farrer, on such projects as *Chess*, *The Lion King* and *Heathcliff*. He was also taken to the bosom of the Disney family in the capacity of lyricist. He, too, was knighted in the mid '90s.

Unlike Tim, Don Black was already a very successful writer by the time he started to work with Andrew. He first made his mark by writing for balladeer Matt Monro, who was produced by George Martin had considerable chart success during the first half of the '60s. Monro covered the song 'Walk Away' (originally a German song called 'Warum Nur Warum'), a hit in the UK in 1964, for which Black wrote the English lyrics.

Composer John Barry was so impressed that he tracked down the lyricist. "It turned out that it was one of John's favourite songs, so he came to Denmark Street, where I was working as a song-plugger, and we went for a drink in a local pub called the White Lion. He asked me if I'd like to have a go at writing the lyrics for the title track to *Thunderball*, the new James Bond movie starring Sean Connery."

The song became a Top 40 hit for Tom Jones. Barry and Black then repeated their success by collaborating on the title track for the film *Born Free*, the 1966 film set in Kenya and starring Virginia McKenna and Bill Travers. "Whenever there are hits, people expect incredible anecdotes to go along with them, but it's not always the case…more usually, stuff is written as part of a brief and one becomes amazed at what happens to them…I've always been a great lover of words…so, being a lyricist, my job is really a labour of love…With the theme song, 'Born Free', the producer, Carl Foreman, didn't like the lyrics…he thought it should relate more directly to lions roaming in the wild. However, I preferred to make it more of a social comment, and felt vindicated when the song went on to win an Academy Award."

Don and John Barry teamed up to write two more title tracks for Bond films. In 1972, Shirley Bassey took 'Diamonds Are Forever', the theme to another Connery-led action-packed movie, into the Top 40. Two years later, they penned the theme for *The Man With The Golden Gun*, which was recorded by Lulu. By that time, Roger Moore had taken over the role of Bond.

Seven years earlier, Don had had tremendous success with Lulu with the title song for the Sidney Poitier/Judy Geeson film *To Sir, With Love*, with the single going to Number One in America. It was the first time that a British disc had topped the American chart without being a British hit.

Don scored another US Number One in 1972, when 'Ben' was released as a single by Michael Jackson, which climbed to Number Seven in the UK. Although the song was about a rat, it is also about a friendship. "Sometimes there's often a lot of opposition to these songs, and there's a lot of struggling and trying to fight one's corner to try and get the songs recorded, or into a movie. I got to know Michael Jackson quite well during that period, and he actually painted a picture for my wife that I think is probably worth more than the song, now...If only I could get my wife's name off it!"

Don's first taste of writing lyrics for a musical was with *Billy*, in 1974. Based on the Keith Waterhouse novel *Billy Liar*, it starred Billy Boyle, Diane Quick, Michael Crawford and a young Elaine Paige. The collaboration between the composer John Barry and Black worked yet again, and the pair have gone on to write even more material together, in a partnership that has to date lasted 35 years. "John and I have written hundreds of songs together. It makes it easier, because he's very lyric minded, loves poetry, and unlike most composers is able to come up with great song titles. He's a very well-read man, and very likeable, although he does have that Yorkshire bluntness that some people can't take. John's very much a loner, and isn't a natural collaborator, and doesn't have many close friends. I'm probably one of the people closest to him...We talk every week, and still write together."

Don has recently been writing the lyrics for John's new project, *Anan Cara*, based on the best-selling book of the same name, about Celtic philosophy.

Apart from John Barry and Andrew Lloyd Webber, Don Black has also collaborated with many other eminent composers, including Charles Strouse, Henry Mancini and London-born Jules Styne, with whom Don once went to visit his birthplace in Bethnal Green before going to see where he himself had been born, in Hackney. "Another wonderful guy. Before he played you his latest composition, he'd always put his arm round you and say 'This is the best thing I've ever written!' He was so passionate about his music that, while he was playing, all the veins would stand out. I've never forgotten some strange words of wisdom he once gave me: 'You will add ten years to your life if you live within walking distance of a cinema and a Chinese restaurant.' Another one of his favourite sayings was 'If you forget where you came from, you'll never get where you're going.'"

As well as writing the lyrics for countless movies, including *Dove*, *The Italian Job* and the Bond films, Black also moved into the world of the stage musical. In 1980, he supplied the words to Andrew Lloyd Webber's *Tell Me On A Sunday*, from which came the title track and the Marti Webb hit 'Take That Look Off Your Face'.

Amongst many other projects, he also worked with hit songwriter Geoff Stephens on *Dear Anyone* in 1988, the album featuring Maggie Moone, Steve Harley, Elaine Stritch and Gemma Craven. One of the songs, 'I'll Put You Together Again', becoming a big seller for the group Hot Chocolate.

In the following year, he wrote lyrics for Lloyd Webber's musical *Aspects Of Love*, co-writing the song 'Love Changes Everything', which went to Number Two in the UK for the show's leading man, Michael Ball.

Don also co-wrote with Lloyd Webber and others, penning 'With One Look' for Barbra Streisand, 'As If We Never Said Goodbye' for Glenn Close, and 'Amigos Para Siempre' ('Friends For Life') for José Carreras and Sarah Brightman. "There's no logic in a partnership. If you look at most of the great collaborations, they have always been fiery, whether it's Gilbert and Sullivan, Rodgers and Hart or Rice and Lloyd Webber."

Although he started life as a stand-up comedian, Don Black has been one of the country's top lyricists for over 35 years. He has retained his passion for writing words and is proud of his contribution to the songwriting industry, and yet remains wonderfully matter-of-fact about his achievements. His latest projects include writing the lyrics for a new Andrew Lloyd Webber production, *Bombay Dreams*, showcasing the musical talent of the most successful songwriter that India has ever known, AR Rahmen.

Rahman changed his name after converting from Hinduism to Moslem, from which point, he says, "everything has gone right". Don began working with him after Lloyd Webber fell under Rahman's musical spell. "This guy has won countless awards for his songs…He really has a terrific sense of melody. He goes to the mosque every day and claims that he has no anger in him, or jealousy…although I do have to take my shoes off when I go to his place…I hope it doesn't give Andrew ideas…"

15 The Stories Behind The Songs

Do songwriters ever stop and think about the unusual profession that they're in? After all, there aren't many industries where you're creating something from nothing, without tangible raw materials.

Paul Simon, one of the most innovative and creative songwriters of the '60s and '70s, realised what a peculiar and lucky situation he was in during what he called a "hashish reverie": "I was thinking to myself 'I'm in a really weird position. I earn my living by writing songs and singing songs. It's only today that this could happen. If I were born 100 years ago, I wouldn't even be in this country. I'd probably be in Vienna, or wherever my ancestors come from...and I couldn't be a guitarist/songwriter. There were none. So what would I be?...Well, what would a Jewish guy be?...I would have been a tailor.' Then...talking to my father about my grandfather, who I never knew...I found out that he was a tailor in Vienna!"

Simon tips his hat to that thought in the spoken interlude on 'Fakin' It', on the *Bookends* album. In the vignette, guitarist John Martyn's future wife, Beverly, enters the shop of a tailor, the shopkeeper of which (Paul Simon) is referred to as "Mr Leitch", a reference to Beverly's friend, singer/songwriter Donovan.

Born in Glasgow, Donovan got his big break on the TV show *Ready, Steady, Go!*, after having been on the road hitch-hiking just a month before. He was down in Southend to see St Albans group Cops And Robbers, who never made it in the way that The Rolling Stones or The Yardbirds did but nevertheless were fairly potent at the time, and sang during the interval. In the audience was songwriter Geoff Stephens, who was interested in Cops And Robbers but became more interested in Donovan.

> They took me up to London's Tin Pan Alley and recorded me in this pokey little basement, where The Rolling Stones were working. Within weeks I was on television, and within months I'd

met Bob Dylan. He in turn introduced me to The Beatles, so that first year was a rollercoaster ride. I was lucky to go on to have many hit albums and hit singles, both in Britain and the States. 'Wear Your Love Like Heaven' and its constant references to colours came from art school, and I believe it was the art-school lifestyle which created a lot of the fashion in sound and colour in the '60s. I really wanted to paint, as so many musicians did...Woody, then with The Birds; Keith Richards, of The Stones; John Lennon; and Pete Townshend. Art school was certainly very influential, as I used some of the more obscure colours in the song, like "Prussian blue". It was a philosophical lyric, and leant on the interest I had in Eastern and Celtic mysticism; but the reference to colours comes directly from my art-school background. It's a painter's song.

Another Donovan classic was 'Epistle To Dippy', which left many of his fans wondering who the hell Dippy was. "He was an old school friend who I lost touch with. I heard he'd joined the army in Malaysia, but didn't have an address or a contact number for him. I had this crazy idea of writing a song for him, getting it played on the radio programme *Two-Way Family Favourites* – he'd hear it and get in touch! So I wrote this song about our schooldays, and in particular made some references as to what we used to get up to, and called it 'Epistle To Dippy'. I got a reply from him...He was still in the army, and signed up for nine years. I asked how much it would cost to buy him out...He told me, and I sent him the money. That's the story of the 'Epistle To Dippy'."

The most successful song of Ervin Drake's career came about through the commercial needs of a television producer. In 1952, Ervin was one of four writers on *The Jane Froman Show*, a musical variety show which had opened to good press but was suffering from poor ratings. In a desperate attempt to save the situation, the producer thought that they might turn the viewing figures around if his four writers, Ervin, Jimmy Shirl, Al Stillman and Irvin Graham, could come up with a hit song for his star.

Ervin was incredulous. "Jane wasn't pop. She was all pear-shaped tones. She's never had a hit record. But the boss said...so we dumped romance and took a shot at writing her a song of faith...The next morning, I sang it through for her. She said she loved it, and asked me to sing it again. I did. Then I asked if she intended to record it as well as to sing it on the TV show. No, she wouldn't. She felt it was excellent special material for TV, but not commercial! So I visited my old friend Mitch Miller and sang it for him, and he immediately assigned it to Frankie Laine."

Laine's multimillion-selling version of 'I Believe' reached Number Two in the States and Number One in the UK, where it stayed in the chart for 36 weeks and at the top for an incredible 18 weeks. Proof of the song's timelessness has been demonstrated through million-selling versions by The Bachelors in 1964 and by Robson And Jerome in 1995. The latter duo's four-week run at Number One was testimony to the song's incredible shelf life and its appeal to different generations. A good song is a good song! 'I Believe' currently holds the British record for one song being at Number One: 22 weeks. Although she had judged 'I Believe' as a song with no commercial appeal, Jane Froman never forgave Ervin, Jimmy, Al and Irvin for obtaining a successful recording of the song that she'd rejected. To date, it has sold over 20 million copies worldwide.

Another multimillion-selling song that was written because a number was needed urgently for a situation was 'I'll Never Fall In Love Again', by Burt Bacharach and co-written with lyricist Hal David: "Burt and I were in Boston for the tryouts of the show *Promises, Promises*. David Merrick, the producer, and Neil Simon, who wrote the book, decided that they needed a new song for the second act, but Burt was in hospital with pneumonia. In the meantime, I sat down and wrote the lyrics for the song and gave them to Burt the minute he was feeling better. My wife was convinced that the lyrics 'What do you get when you fall in love?/You get enough germs to catch pneumonia' came from my subconscious concern for Burt's illness, but where else do good songs come from?"

Promises, Promises opened in London in October 1969, and Bobby Gentry's version of 'I'll Never Fall In Love Again' went to Number One in the same month. Bacharach himself had a small hit with it in the States, and Dionne Warwick took it into the Top Ten there in the following year. The show that spawned it was based on the screenplay for Billy Wilder's *The Apartment*, and featured intriguingly-titled songs such as 'She Likes Basketball' and 'Grapes Of Wrath'.

As well as writing in the States, Bacharach and David also wrote several songs in London, as Hal remembers: "'The Look Of Love' was written while I was staying at the Dorchester Hotel. It was for the movie *Casino*

Royale, and had become a big US hit for Dusty Springfield, who sang it in the film, later becoming successful all over again for Sergio Mendes. We also wrote and recorded the songs for *What's New, Pussycat?* in London, including 'My Little Red Book', 'Here I Am' and the title song."

The Shadows were one of the most successful, innovative and influential musical units of the early '60s, and continued to enjoy continued success right up until their demise in the '90s. Hank Marvin and Bruce Welch were the group's initial songwriters, penning a string of hits for themselves as well as writing major hits for their frontman, singer Cliff Richard. Hank Marvin recalls the birth of their 15th Top 20 hit, 'The Rise And Fall Of Flingel Bunt', at Abbey Road Studios: "I was just messing around during a session and came up with the introductory figure. I think it was our drummer, Brian Bennett, who said 'Hey, that's great' and started the drums thing, and we thought, we've got something here. It sounded really good, and Norrie Paramor, our recording manager, liked it a lot, and felt that it was worthy of release as a single. That was 1964, when the blues boom was just beginning to get under way, and we felt that it would fit within that genre as it was a little more meaty than the things we'd done in recent years. We didn't have a title, though."

The title that they used in the end came from actor Richard O'Sullivan, with whom they'd worked on the films *The Young Ones* and *Summer Holiday*. He often used the phrase "Flingel Bunt" in films. Instead of real words, if something was to be overdubbed at a later point, he'd just mouth those two words over and over again, much like actors who mutter "rhubarb, rhubarb" when they're meant to be having a background conversation. However, Hank felt that the title needed fleshing out. "A couple of years before, we'd seen a film called *The Rise And Fall Of Legs Diamond*, and the thought of this ridiculous-sounding 'Flingel Bunt', coupled with 'The Rise And Fall Of...', we felt would at least interest people in asking questions about the record, even if they didn't like the music."

Shadows Bruce Welch and Brian Bennett wrote the title song for *Summer Holiday*, the 1962 film directed by Peter Yates, with the main score by Peter Myers and Ronnie Cass. The film starred Cliff Richard, Lauri Peters, Melvyn Hayes, Una Stubbs, Teddy Green, Ron Moody, Lionel Morton and David Kossoff, and the storyline revolves around four young London Transport mechanics who take a double-decker bus from London to Greece.

On the subject of a title song, Bruce Welch was called by manager Peter Gormley, who explained that the plot was about a European holiday. "I said 'What about a summer holiday?' [The Shadows] were playing in Stockton-On-Tees, at the Globe, where Brian Bennett and I were in the orchestra pit the afternoon I got the call, and we wrote the song 'Summer Holiday' there and then. I automatically went straight into the 'We're all going on a summer holiday' bit, and 'No more working for a week or two', the length of most people's summer holidays, and within a couple of minutes I'd got a couple of verses. Brian then immediately followed with the 'We're going where the sun shines brightly/We're going where the sea is blue' section. It literally only took us 20 minutes. Not bad for an afternoon's work!"

Released in February 1963, the song shot to Number One, making Cliff the first artist to have four songs from the same film in the chart at the same time, along with 'The Next Time', 'Dancing Shoes' and 'Bachelor Boy'. The latter was a collaboration between Bruce Welch and Cliff, who played down his songwriting abilities: "I've always enjoyed writing, but I've never considered myself a composer. Normally, I throw my numbers together very quickly. I get fed up with them after a while. I'm afraid I'm not like Bruce – he can churn 'em out by the dozen!"

Another summer classic that begins to invade the airwaves as soon as the sun comes out in Britain is 'Beach Baby', which was a hit for First Class in the summer of 1974. The number was written by John Carter and his wife. Carter had written many big hits during the '60s and '70s. "I'd come up with the tune and played it to my wife, who took the cassette out on to the lawn in the middle of the men's finals. She thought that, as it was such a wonderful day and glorious weather, that it should be a Beach Boys-type song. By the time Jan Kodes had disposed of Metreveli, to become the 1973 Wimbledon champion, she'd completed the lyric, and it was perfect."

While tennis might have helped to inspire that particular song, a seriously good squash player, Eddy Grant, had kick-started the chart career of his group The Equals six years earlier with a song that came to him while he was skipping. The Equals, so called because they comprised black and white members, had already built themselves a formidable reputation as a discotheque act, but hadn't really managed to break through in a major way. It was the songwriting talents of Grant, who would continue to prove his prowess as a writer well into the '80s, that opened the door:

MAJOR TO MINOR

> I'd been down to Selmer's music shop in Tottenham Court Road, 'cause I had a friend that used to work there, and I'd go in and practise on the instruments, as I couldn't afford to buy any of them. I tried out Les Pauls and Fender Stratocasters and other guitars, and then ran back to Kentish Town, where I lived, 'cause I hadn't got the bus fare. I started skipping, and as I skipped I got this little repetitive tune in my head, which just kept going round and round. When I arrived at 17 Anson Road, where I lived, I went next door where a friend of mine – a singer called Gene Latter – lived to see if he'd ever heard this piece of melody. I thought I'd check with him, as he'd been in the business a while and would certainly know if it was nicked from somewhere. "Nah," he said. "Doesn't sound like anything to me." So I went inside and wrote 'Baby Come Back'.

In the July of that year, the song that had come to Eddie while he had been skipping knocked The Rolling Stones' 'Jumping Jack Flash' off the Number One spot and held onto it for three weeks.

Skipping and children's games also played a part in a song that went to Number Two in America at the end of 1960 and to Number One in Britain early in 1961 and was successful also around the world. The song's singer, Johnny Tillotson, recalls the conception of the million-seller:

> It was written by Mike Anthony and Paul Kaufman, who had a writing studio next door to a girls' school, from where they could see the kids playing and running and skipping in the yard. On this particular day, they'd come up with nothing, so they took a break and were staring out of the window when they saw some of the older girls on their way home. Mike suddenly came out with "You know, it's great to see the young girls. That's poetry in motion." They said: "Well, we haven't written anything today. Lets write about the beauty of these young ladies." They finished the song in 15 minutes, and when they played it to me I knew it was going to be a hit.

In Britain, 'Poetry In Motion' pushed Cliff Richard's 'I Love You' off the top spot. As Tillotson is actually descended from Oliver Cromwell, it seemed only fitting that his reign at Number One meant him deposing Cliff, the British king, and was brought to an end by the king of rock 'n' roll: Elvis.

One of the biggest hits for Elvis' RCA labelmate Neil Sedaka was 'Oh, Carol', which was sufficiently well known that one would have thought that it would have prevented anyone else from attempting to write a song with the same title. Not so, however. Writers Nicky Chinn and Mike Chapman gave it a go. "I think one of the reasons we wrote a song called 'Oh, Carol', knowing that Neil Sedaka had written one, was that we loved his song! What a lot of people don't know is that there is no copyright on titles. You can copyright melody, but not titles. I think there was also a kind of desire to see if we could get away with it. It was a bit of a cheeky thing to do. People said 'Oh, you can't do that!', to which I replied 'It won't make any difference.' And it didn't; it was a hit for Smokie."

Chinn and Chapman also used a famous introduction to an Elvis song on another hit that they wrote for the group. "We used the same riff as the Presley record 'His Latest Flame', which of course every DJ on the radio brought to the public's attention. We never tried to disguise the fact that it was the same riff, but it's not out-and-out plagiarism; we were just borrowing something."

Not many writers are able to load their songs with humour and still enjoy continued success and a cult following, but not many writers were conveniently placed within the ranks of the Bonzo Dog Doo Dah Band. One of their most popular songs was 'The Intro And The Outro', still a favourite of writer Neil Innes:

> I still think it's one of the most lovely sound images. The characters keep arriving...the whole thing is building into this large and unfeasible group who are the most unlikely collection of characters to be in a group together. The massed ranks included Princess Anne on sousaphone, Val Doonican as himself, Adolf Hitler on vibes, Eric Clapton On ukelele, "swinging" General De Gaulle on accordian, and J Arthur Rank on gong. Quentin Hogg was there at one point, on "pig grunt", but he was very litigious in those days so we felt we should send a copy of the record to his office. We got a letter back saying that Mr Hogg hadn't had a chance to listen to it, but to be on the safe side we'd better not include him. We removed him but kept the pig grunt.

Another classic from the mind of Innes, and The Bonzo's most successful chart hit, was 'I'm The Urban Spaceman', which reached Number Five in 1968.

'[I'm] The Urban Spaceman' occurred to me as a title because in the '60s they were talking about urban spaces, as they now talk about brown field sites. Being on the road with The Bonzos, I'd never seen the UK in one go. Everywhere we went there were embryonic one-way systems, department stores that had all the same kettles and shirts as each other…and I thought "Well, here we are, in urban space, so what about creating an urban spaceman?" It all fell into place after I heard the two-tone siren of a police car, which gave me the start of the melody. It took me most of one afternoon to write, but our singer, Viv Stanshall, thought that I had two verses too many and that I should cut them…and he was right!

The single was produced by Paul McCartney, after Stanshall had complained to him about the small amount of studio time their producer allowed them for each track. McCartney volunteered to produce 'Spaceman', and the group credited him as Apollo C Vermouth on the record label so that they didn't appear to cashing in on the success of The Beatles. "He also played drums and ukelele on the track, and the other producer's wife went up to him and said 'What have you got there? A poor man's violin?' 'No,' replied Paul. 'It's a rich man's ukelele.' During the session, he was tinkering around with this mournful tune on the piano, which later became 'Hey Jude'."

One of lyricist Gary Osborne's first successes was a piece of music with no words, written with his partner Paul Vigrass for a commercial for Lego Toys. The tune was resurrected later when they needed a B-side for a record, and Gary added some lyrics and the pair recorded it as Vigrass And Osborne. The song, 'Forever Autumn', made the Top Three in Japan, but then sat in a drawer until producer Jeff Wayne asked Gary for a song for his project *The War Of The Worlds*. He said that he needed a song like 'Forever Autumn'. Gary said 'I know one that's just like 'Forever Autumn'!" The song made it to the multimillion-selling album and became a hit single for Justin Hayward.

Gary was also responsible for the lyrics of Kiki Dee's first hit in the '70s. "Warner Bros gave me an album and told me they needed a lyric for a French girl called Veronique Sanson. They told me I could pick any tune on the album, but it had to be done inside a week. I was listening through the album and came to the tune 'Amoreuse', and my girlfriend at the time, a very beautiful model called Barbara Miller, came into the room and said 'Urgh! What's that? It's horrible!' As it happened, the following day we split up, and so out of spite I chose the song she hated to put a lyric to. It turned out to be my first chart record, and a hit in Britain for Kiki Dee. I later told my ex-girlfriend, and she had the audacity to ask for a cut."

Gary also collaborated on songs with Elton John:

> Elton would give me a batch of songs at a time…He always gave me five or six songs, and there'd always be a couple that he would never come back and ask for. I'd do the lyric, and he'd say "No, I don't want to do that." He wouldn't even look at the words. So I had to try and guess which ones he wasn't going to like, as I didn't want to do a lot of writing for nothing. I figured that 'Blue Eyes' was definitely the slushy one of the six songs he gave me, and the one he wasn't going to do, so I did the other five; but he kept faxing me and phoning me from Montserrat, where he was recording, asking me to do a lyric for this tune. I still thought "No, he's never going to do that song. It's too corny." Eventually, he did the full backing track and sent it to me, and I wrote the words in two hours and had it straight back to him. I'm very glad I did, because it bought me a house by the sea.
>
> When I gave Elton a lyric, he would just go and do it…he never changed a word or asked for any kind of alteration…he was wonderful in that way. On the song 'Little Jeannie', though, there was a word which he didn't like. The word was "strikes"…He didn't like the word "strikes". He said, "Can you just change that one word?" To change the one word meant I had to change the whole line. If I changed the line then I had to change the line on either side because of the rhyming structure. It took me two months to replace that one word, and every now and then I'd ask Elton, "Are you sure you want me to this?" But he insisted. "I just can't sing that 'strikes' line." After two months, I finally had an alternative verse for him, and on the day of recording he said, "We're going to do 'Little Jeannie' today." I said, "Good…I've got the new lyric." He said, "No, it's OK, I've got used to the old one."

As well as being a highly successful singer in his own right, with a string of hits in Britain, America and the rest of the world, Leo Sayer also wrote or co-wrote several of his big records:

In the middle of one recording session, we just started jamming during a break in the proceedings with the musicians I was using, including Ray Parker Jr and Lee Ritenour. The guys started playing a riff and I started singing. I think I was trying to do 'Shame, Shame, Shame', the Shirley And Company hit. Richard Perry, the producer, was running the tape in the background, saying "It's a smash!", shouting at the engineer, Howard, "Keep recording! Keep recording!" We were recording over takes of an earlier song that we'd been trying to perfect.

Richard came to me a week later and said, "Listen to this." And there it was. I said, "Oh, God, that was that jam session we did in the middle of a take." He said, "This is a Number One record." So I got the legendary songwriter/producer Vinnie Poncia in to work on the track. In about five minutes, we'd found a chorus out of the jam session: "You make me feel like dancing" – it was one of those instant things.

Shel Silverstein wrote several classics for Dr Hook, invariably laden with his own brand of humour. One of the group's two frontmen, Denis Locorriere, remembers recording Silverstein's 'Sylvia's Mother', the song that was written as a mickey-take of country music but ended up being taken seriously:

We'd just finished our first album, which was ready to be released, when Shel sang me 'Sylvia's Mother'. We were in California at the time, and I said to our producer "We should cut this song for the album." Even though the album had been put to bed ready for release, everyone thought it was so good that we recorded it and squeezed it on. It was a lucky stroke, because it was our first big hit.

It was also kind of a true story, because there was actually a Sylvia! One day, at Christmastime, Shel said, "Would you like to speak to Mrs Avory, the lady who was Sylvia's mother on the record?" Her real name was Pandolfi, but he couldn't find anything to rhyme with it, so he changed it to Avory. We all got on extension phones And he called her. She came on the line and said, "Oh, Mr Silverstein. It's lovely to speak to you. Would you like to speak to Sylvia? She's here." Sylvia came on the phone...and we listened to her talking to Shel...It turned out

> she'd married a bullfighter! We said to Shel "Why didn't you put that in the song?" He said, "You have to beef down in a song." It was great, though, to hear the legendary Sylvia!

Among the other songs Silverstein wrote for the group were '(Freakin' At) The Freakers Ball', 'Roland The Roadie And Gertrude The Groupie' and 'The Cover Of Rolling Stone'.

> We were on the road when Shel called us and said, "How would you like to be on the cover of *Rolling Stone*?" He said all we had to do was to sing this song he's written. He gave us the words over the phone and we wrote them down on a piece of paper. At that time, we were travelling in a nine-passenger station wagon, with all of us and our luggage, so we would practise stuff on our guitars in the back. We did it onstage at the next show, and the audience loved it. We released it as a single and it went to Number Two in the States, and in the end *Rolling Stone* magazine couldn't ignore it...but when they did put us on the cover it just said, "What's-Their-Name Makes The Cover." It was as if they wanted to get us famous and get us over with. It was another great stroke by Shel...as in those days getting on the cover was a hard thing to do. The magazine later admitted that, up to that time, it was the biggest-selling issue it had ever had.

Other Silverstein songs for the group, 'Queen Of The Silver Dollar' and 'Ballad Of Lucy Jordan', were successfully covered by Emmylou Harris and Marianne Faithfull respectively.

One of the youngest songwriters to write and record what would become a million-seller was Paul Anka. Born in Ottawa in 1941, he become famous over night when his song 'Diana' – which he recorded at the age of 15 – rapidly turned into one of the hottest properties on the chart. "I wrote it about a girl I was at school with...a girl I really liked. She was older than me and really wasn't interested and I thought the song might make her like Me! It didn't work...she wasn't impressed at the time; but after the song became a national hit, she called me, but by then it was too late...it was bye bye Diana!"

Anka was not only becoming a wealthy young man but he had also begun to collect accolades and gold discs. The follow-up, 'I Love You Baby' went

Top Three in Britain, and even the B-side, 'Tell Me That You Love Me', reached the Top 30.

In the light of this, it seems odd that a rather parochial and old-fashioned presentation occurred when he collected his gold disc for 'Diana' on Sunday 22 December 1957 at the Regal Cinema in Edmonton. Rather quaintly, the Chairman of EMI, Sir Joseph Lockwood, solemnly presented America's coolest new singer, fast heading towards being a millionaire, with a pen and pencil companion set!

Paul Anka's reputation as a songwriter was spreading so fast that even major artists who wrote themselves approached him. "Buddy [Holly] came to me and said 'I like what you're doing. I can't write that type of thing, but I want to go with a big orchestra, so could you write something for me that's suitable?' We were good buddies, so I told him that I'd be honoured, although at the time I was having a run of hits and wasn't writing for other people. I was more worried about my next single. So I sat down and tried to capture what I thought Buddy Holly would do, if Buddy himself had written it, and came up with 'It Doesn't Matter Anymore', complete with string licks."

Another of Anka's friends who was to die tragically young was the highly talented Bobby Darin, who made the dramatic and successful leap from rock 'n' roll as well as writing many great songs, including 'Early In The Morning', which was also a hit for Holly.

Paul Anka had an exeptional run of hits in the States throughout the '50s and early '60s, and again in the '70s, notching up three Number Ones and twelve Top Ten hits, and became one of the most successful singers and solo songwriters in the history of American popular music.

Some songwriters have favourite places for writing, while some are wary about selling a house in which they've written a lot of their big hits and others are happy to write anywhere at any time. Paul Anka often holidays and performs in Italy, and it was there in 1961 that he wrote what would become his first major success in Italian, for RCA Italiana, which was a hit in Britain and America as 'Love Me Warm And Tender'. He had just signed a new deal with RCA Victor and wanted to come up with something really different to coincide with the move. "Late one night after a concert I knocked out 'Love Me Warm And Tender' on a piano in one of the hotel bars. It was conceived in Italy and recorded in the States." Still a major artist, in August 2000 he performed for President Clinton.

*

Graham Gouldman started out in Manchester group The Whirlwinds, before joining The Mockingbirds along with Kevin Godley. After the demise of the group, late in 1966, he continued to write great songs for a variety of artists. Among the most successful of his '60s compositions were 'Bus Stop' for The Hollies; 'No Milk Today', 'Listen People' and 'East West' for Herman's Hermits; 'Pamela, Pamela' for Wayne Fontana; and 'Evil-Hearted You', 'Heart Full Of Soul' and 'For Your Love' for The Yardbirds.

> In my early teens, American music started coming on the radio. I spent my formative years listening to people like Chuck Berry, Buddy Holly, Eddie Cochran and Elvis, and English acts like Cliff Richard And The Shadows and Lonnie Donegan. The Shadows were the biggest influence on me before The Beatles came along.
>
> A cousin gave me a guitar when I was eleven years old and that pretty well changed my life. I decided I was destined to play the guitar, and from the age of 15 I started forming groups at the local youth club. One group was called The Whirlwinds, and we recorded a Buddy Holly song, 'Look At Me', before I started writing songs myself. That group split up and I formed The Mockingbirds, with Kevin Godley on drums. This was the time when The Beatles had just broken. They had shown everyone that you could do it by writing your own material. But I really started writing out of necessity because everyone was desperate for material. We went around music publishers in London, but of course no one would give anything to ann unknown band from Manchester.
>
> I wrote two songs, that we recorded independently. One was 'That's How It's Gonna Stay', which eventually became our first single, and the other one was 'For Your Love', which EMI rejected. We all thought it was a great song, but the record company wouldn't put it out. My manager, Harvey Lisberg, took it to a publisher, Feldmans, and to a guy called Ronnie Beck, who was friendly with Giorgio Gornelsky, The Yardbirds' manager. He played them this song, and they liked it a lot. I have heard that Eric Clapton didn't like it, but it seems that he didn't like the idea of doing more commercial records, which the others wanted. This was a very commercial song, so maybe that's why he left the band, though I believe he played on the middle part of the song.

There are two direct influences on the song. I had heard The Animals' version of 'House Of The Rising Sun', which I learned to play on the guitar. The chords intrigued me, because they were different to anything I had heard. I t was a simple blues sequence of E minor, G and A minor. I used those chords on a lot of songs, and kept playing those chords over and over in my bedroom. As with lots of songs, 'For Your Love' just came out of the blue. It just seemed to fit.

The other influence was The Everly Brothers. The first record I ever bought was 'Cathy's Clown'. Part of that song goes "don't want your love anymore". The great this is that one guy sings "don't want your love" while the other sings "love anymore", so there's one note and another melody moving underneath it. 'For Your Love' has that same thing. I played it to Harvey, and he thought it was great, but he said it needed to go somewhere else. Why not change the beat and do it faster? So I came up with that change of tempo in the middle, which at the time was quite and original thing to do, and it worked really well, so we recorded it.

I was very young when I wrote the song. My father was a playwright, and he would help write the lyrics for all my songs. My lyrics were a bit naïve, I suppose, and he would smoothe them out. As well as being a good song, the production on The Yardbirds' recording was great, and very original, particularly the use of the bongos and the harpsichord. It all helped to make a highly memorable track.

After a spell in Hot Legs, in 1972 Gouldman and Godley, Lol Creme and Eric Stewart became 10cc. Gouldman wrote many of their classics, including 'Rubber Bullets', 'The Things We Do For Love', 'I'm Mandy, Fly Me', 'Dreadlock Holiday', 'I'm Not In Love' and 'The Wall Street Shuffle'.

There are so many songwriters with stories to tell about their creations. Some have no idea where their inspiration came from, while others were inspired by passion in its many guises and some have the whole scenario permanently etched in their memories. Long may the inspiration continue.

16 Personal Experiences

Writing with other people is rather like going a date with someone you hardly know, or on a date with someone you know well but have never been intimate with!

I'd known Andrew Lloyd Webber since the late '60s, and, despite the odd erroneous newspaper reporting that he'd advised or helped me with some of my stage musicals, I'd never approached him with a view to collaborating on anything creative. He had, after all, some great partners in Tim Rice, Don Black, Richard Stilgoe, Charles Hart and Jim Steinman, and with such a wealth of talent to draw upon he wasn't exactly desperate for lyricists.

One can never account for the whims and workings of the creative mind, however. While I was at his country pad one Saturday, having lunch and watching the young Venus Williams looking every inch a future tennis champion (on the television, that is, not on the manicured greensward of the Webber acres), Andrew asked if I'd like to have a go at some lyrics for a tune he'd written.

When the cassette arrived, I was surprised to discover not another *Phantom* but a reggae/ska number that he had recorded on one of those organs that pounds out the tempo behind you. Lines of melody always suggest phrases, and one or two started to appear immediately, including a title: 'No Smoke Without Fire'. I thought that this was a pretty reasonable title, which as far as I could ascertain hadn't been used before. The only problem was that, in order to make the lyric work, I needed to clip and change the length of the odd note and line, but wasn't sure how the Andrew would feel about me doing a bit of necessary fiddling.

Every composer is different, and has their own way of working. Some don't want you to touch their melody at all, while others have so much going on that you're not sure which is the melody and which is the counterpoint. Others are happy for you to rejig a little. Of course, this also holds good for lyricists – some feel that their words are cast in stone, while others are glad of any input from the composer if it makes for a better song. In this instance, Andrew very generously allowed me to tweak a little where I felt it necessary. When I gave him my demo of the song, he then suggested a slightly different feel for the middle part of the song, with which I was happy to go along.

The number, which I'd demo'd in a UB40 vein, was then performed at Andrew's Sydmonton Festival in 1997, alongside songs from the embryonic *Whistle Down The Wind*. It clearly went down well, which was a relief, and, although we felt that it was a potential single for somebody, to date it has remained on the shelf, waiting for either of its writers to have the time to do something with it.

At that same festival, The Rodolfus Choir performed my settings of the poet Rupert Brooke's 1914 *Sonnets*. Writing these took me into a different kind of working area, as the arrangements where written by my chum Ralph Allwood, head of music and precentor at Eton. The Chapel Choir had already recorded my setting of Sir John Betjeman's poems some years earlier.

Hearing the Brooke settings being recorded by The Kings College Chapel Choir, under the baton of Stephen Cleobury, was an exciting experience, as was hearing The Eton Choral Choir recording them in Eton Chapel for the BBC World Service.

The world of classical and choral music isn't always that far removed from the pop songwriting scene. Another writer with whom I had the pleasure of collaborating was Geoff Goddard, creator of Number One hits but trained at the Royal Academy Of Music.

As a kid, there was a certain type of song on the radio that I loved. These songs had a particular feel; their melodies sounded haunting and they were dominated by a sense of loneliness. I didn't realise that there was a link between them; I simply liked each one individually. It was only later that I realised that these were records made by producer Joe Meek, and it was later still that I discovered that they had invariably been written by a guy called Geoff Goddard.

When I began in radio in 1976, someone told me that he lived in the station's catchment area. I put a call out, and he rather reluctantly came in to do an interview. He was a delightful but very shy man, from whom I eventually learned that it was he who played the organ on one of the biggest-selling instrumentals in pop history, The Tornados' 'Telstar'. On our many subsequent meetings, he also discussed at length what it was like working with the legendary Joe Meek.

> He was a very clever man, Joe. He knew what he wanted, but he was very volatile and would lose his temper easily. He was a genius, but he had a very short fuse. He wasn't musical at all, so I would often have to translate his ideas into a melodic shape to make them work and to get them ready for recording. I wrote 'Johnny Remember Me' after I'd called him from a phone box to see what was happening. It was just a general call, but he said, "We've got this TV slot for John Leyton and we need a song for him to sing." The scenario was that he would appear as a pop singer called Johnny St Cyr in the record department of the TV series *Harpers, West One*, which was about a department store. I went home that night and wrote the song. I gave it a lonely, haunting feel. I loved all that.

The song became a UK Number One for John Leyton, resulting in Geoff writing other hits for him, including 'Wild Wind', 'Son, This Is She', 'Lone Rider' and 'Lonely City'. He also wrote many other classic hits, such as 'Just Like Eddie' for Heinz and 'Tribute To Buddy Holly' for Mike Berry, Geoff and Joe, who were both obsessed with Holly, often conducting séances to attempt to contact his spirit. "Joe and I were enormous fans of Buddy Holly, and I sometimes felt that he was around, guiding me to an extent. Some very strange things happened during one séance that made me realise that he was around. I've always been very interested in the spirit world, and the possibility of life on other planets…I sometimes leave my tape recorder running at night in case it picks up something unusual while I'm asleep, or in case someone is trying to communicate."

Why would someone as successful and as prolific as Goddard was at the time suddenly stop writing and take a job clearing away lunchtime plates at Reading University? This was no stop-gap job, either; it was a position for the rest of his life, until his untimely death in 2000.

I always found him a very sensitive, softly-spoken and genuine man, so when he told me of his reasons for ceasing to write while at the top of the songwriting tree I had no reason to doubt him.

> I believe in fairness and honesty, and had always been loyal to Joe, despite his funny little ways. I also think that, when you've written a song, you should at least get credit for writing it. There was a song I'd written for the group that became The

Honeycombs...They'd demo'd it but nothing much seemed to be happening...That's the way it was then, we did lots of songs...some happened and others didn't.

When I heard later that they'd released 'Have I The Right?', I asked Joe why my name wasn't on it. He was very evasive, but he knew very well that it was my song, even though it had a different title. He suggested that I forget about it, but I was upset that not only had my song been stolen but that Joe's loyalty to me was in question. We went to court in the end, and I lost because I couldn't afford to pursue it, but I was really upset that Joe didn't back me up when he knew full well that I'd written it. There was obviously something going on that I didn't know about...and still don't. The court ruled that I wasn't allowed to talk about it, or publicly claim that the song was mine, but I knew it was. It upset me so much that I stopped working with Joe and suffered from severe headaches for years. I was upset when he died, though; it was like the end of an era. We might have got together again one day. But suddenly that possibility was gone.

Geoff kept his hand in by writing the occasional song, but generally seemed content with working in the catering department at the university, among the people he considered to be his real friends. I always felt that he should also have been putting his very obvious songwriting talents to better use, and we talked about the possibility of collaborating at some point, but he didn't really collaborate, as he was a bit of a loner. I sensed that he had to feel comfortable with someone first, although by 1993 – by which time I'd known him for 17 years – our meetings had only been sporadic.

I'd had an idea that I was keen on that also appealed to him, about five US Navy Avenger torpedo bombers that disappeared in 1945 on a routine exercise from their Fort Lauderdale base. Although there was no satisfactory explanation for the swift and sudden simultaneous disappearance of all five aircraft, one of the rumours was possible abduction by UFOs. This was the route that we followed in the song lyric, with the airbase trying fruitlessly to make contact with the missing pilot, asking if they wanted to report a UFO.

We demo'd the song at Reading University, along with another song that we'd been working on, which had come from one of Geoff's ideas. The number, 'Yesterday's Heroes', had a retrospective lyric, and featured the line "Johnny, remember me", which to me was wonderful – co-writing a song with the composer of that original classic, with a lyric that included that famous title. It also included a line about the death of Buddy Holly.

Geoff worked on the demo at home, and the result was wonderful. It had that haunting feel that had moved me as a kid, and Geoff's swirling, almost Wurlitzer-sounding organ that almost sounded as if it came from another planet. Magic stuff! Both songs feature Geoff's unusual vocal style, and they still send a shiver down my spine when I hear them.

I was very saddened to hear of Geoff's death, in the early summer of 2000, especially as his songwriting career should have been much longer and more successful than it was, although he did tell me that the royalties from his hits in the early '60s remained fairly substantial over the years. Our two songs still sound good, and for Geoff's sake I'm determined that at some point they will see the light of day.

A great British songwriter who has been driven to working increasingly in the States, due to the continued lack of opportunity in his own country, is Chris Eaton. Chris, who has written many excellent songs, including two of Cliff Richard's big hits, 'Little Town' and 'Saviour's Day', is a prolific writer, and now works mainly in the area of Christian music, with incredible success. "In Nashville, where I work a lot of the time, you get calls most days from somebody wanting a song, or wanting to work on a song. I co-write with a lot of artists, especially gospel singers like Jaci Velasquez, who's only 21 but has gone multiplatinum with her albums. Fortunately, I've had a couple of songs on each of her albums. The good thing about writing Christian music is that I can explore new ways of saying old truths."

When I met Chris at a post-concert party of Cliff's, we thought it might be fun to try and write together, so we chose a weekend on which we were both free and agreed that I should go up to his house in the West Midlands.

Not being sure how somebody else likes to work, hardly knowing them and realising that this is meant to be a weekend dedicated to writing can put enormous strain on the situation, but we agreed to have a good weekend eating and playing tennis, and that if we wrote anything it would be a bonus.

We ate, played tennis *and* wrote. I woke up on the Sunday morning to the sound of Chris demoing a song that we had been working on the night before, 'Saturday Night And Sunday Morning' – quite appropriate, really! We were so pleased with it that we wrote another, 'Down On The Beach', and worked on some lyrics for a tune that seemed to be titled 'Heartland'.

Major To Minor

Chris is also aware that the atmosphere has to be condusive to collaborating.

> I'm used to working with all sorts of writers, from unknown people to big-selling artists, so I'm aware that I've got to relax both of us. There's no way you can write if you're not relaxed. I'm happy to take the musical lead, sitting at the piano, but I don't mind sitting with a guitarist while they take charge of the session. A writing session isn't about how much you can give; it's more about getting into each other's psyche. Some writers are concerned about their contribution to the final result, feeling that, unless they've written 50 per cent, they're not happy. My feeling is that, if you sit down to write together, the song belongs to both of you, whatever percentage you put in. Just the fact that that person is there will probably make me write a song that I otherwise wouldn't have written.

One of the most successful British born songwriters working in the States is Albert Hammond, whose hit strike rate is phenomenal. A Gibraltarian born in Paddington, London, he and his early writing partner, Mike Hazlewood, wrote hits like 'Little Arrows' and 'Gimme Dat Ding', and sang with the group Family Dogg. As a solo artist, Albert wrote and recorded the million-selling 'It Never Rains In Southern California', 'Free Electric Band', 'The Peacemaker' and 'I'm A Train' while writing songs such as 'The Air That I Breathe', '99 Miles From LA' and 'When I Need You' (the latter with Carole Bayer Sagar). Since then, he has written dozens of hits for many different artists.

A publisher friend of mine, Bob Grace, suggested that I should get together with Albert on one of his trips to London to see if we could work on some song ideas. I duly appeared at Albert's apartment at the prescribed time, guitar in hand and ready to bash out a hit or two, if not a US Number One! Clearly, Albert wasn't in the mood to write, which was actually OK with me, although I was a little disappointed, as I'd thought we'd be doing something. I think I probably feigned indifference, claiming that I wasn't really in the mood either, which seemed to perk him up a little. It soon became apparent that there was a football match on the television which he was keen to watch. Again, OK with me. At this point, he rallied considerably. The pressure was off!

After the match, he suggested a bite to eat, which I happily went along with, and we trundled out into the night. So much for writing a song. If you know someone well, it's easier to tell them you don't feel in the mood; but if a waif and stray is decanted onto your doorstep, you feel responsible for the poor creature's wellbeing. At least this poor creature was suitably compliant, happy to watch football, eat and generally hang out.

On getting back to Albert's apartment, I thought I'd grab my guitar, make my excuses and leave, with a jaunty "Maybe next time, then?"

"Got any ideas, then?" asked Albert.

"Yes. A couple of bits I've been tinkering around with."

Within an hour we'd written a fairly decent song called 'The Power Of Life', which I demo'd a few weeks later. Another song, another experience.

Simon May is one of the most successful composers of television themes, his music being heard over the titles of dozens of TV shows, including *EastEnders*, *Howards Way*, *Food And Drink*, *Trainer* and *El Dorado*. He also wrote such big hits as 'Always There', 'Every Loser Wins' and 'More Than In Love'. Simon and I have been mates since the mid '70s, but we had never really thought about collaborating until we had lunch together at the home of some mutual friends, our hostess being the girl who'd been the subject of my first recorded song.

It was during a conversation then that he discovered that I'd once owned the leg of a horse or two, and was moderately conversant with the terminology of the racing world. Certainly I had passed the odd pleasurable weekend in the village of Lambourn with the racing community. I also had an old friend, Bill Heath, with whom I'd shared the occasional house as a callow youth. Bill spoke the racing language so fluently that I picked it up, and could possibly have bluffed a non-habitual racegoer at a push. Why Simon was testing my racing knowledge over Sunday lunch was beyond me, but I was clearly performing well, and warmed to the theme.

It was only after I "ran on one-paced", as I believe they say in the results write-ups, that Simon revealed the plot. He'd been asked to write the music for a new TV series called *Trainer* and needed someone to write the words to the title song, and possibly one other.

As it turned out, I didn't use any turf terminology in the piece, but instead tried to capture the freedom, space and feelings experienced when riding a horse without actually referring to beast or rider by name. I used phrases like "acres of sky", "run like the wind on a summer's day" and "beyond the horizon" to convey the sense of freedom, and "heart worn like a ring around the moon" as a more romantic variation on wearing your heart on your sleeve. Ring Round The Moon was also the name of a horse once trained by John Dunlop at Arundel, in Sussex, so I thought that it would give the phrase an interesting double meaning.

The song was called 'More To Life' because, whether you're riding a horse, walking in the countryside or anything of a similar nature, you're getting right away from life's problems, and you realise that there is more to life than your four walls, be they real or imaginary.

With that and the other song for *Trainer*, 'Woman Of The World', Simon gave me the tape of the music with the basic shape, chord structure and melody and asked me to go away and work on it. He had so many contrapuntal ideas going on that I had to go back and ask "Which one of these tunes is the melody?" I swear that he could have got another three songs out of each of them.

Cliff Richard went on to record 'More To Life', which became a hit, while Kym Mazelle recorded 'Woman Of The World', which didn't. We said what all songwriters say: "It should have been a hit." However, we were delighted to win a TRIC Award for 'More To Life' in 1992 for TV Theme Music Of The Year.

We both had to get used to each other's way of writing. Simon likes to get the ideas structured on his computer, and I enjoy the spontaneity and freedom of playing on the guitar. He'd say "I don't mind you throwing in the odd 2/4 bar where you feel like it, but at least make it the same every time and don't change it back to a 4/4 bar in the next verse!" In Simon's case, a famous old songwriting adage really does hold true: "The line Sammy Cahn used, when asked 'Which came first? The lyrics or the melody?', and he said 'The phone call', really is true in my case. The phone call gives me a reason to write…In Mozart's day, they called it music for an occasion. I think that, when you come off the phone from the client, whether it's a group, an artist or a TV producer, the blood gets going…it creates an excitement. It makes you so much more creative than a producer coming on the phone and saying 'We're looking at 300 writers in all, but send me something in the next three weeks.' That doesn't really get your creative juices flowing. I find I work much better under pressure and with a deadline to meet."

Proof that songwriters have to be resilient was certainly borne out after he was nominated for an Ivor Novello Award and lost to Eric Clapton's 'Edge Of Darkness'. Confident of victory, he had to smile in the face of adversity and still manage to down a glass or two of celebratory champagne, even though the taste had soured! Simon vowed to be back for the trophy in the following year.

A couple of months later, a storyline in the soap *EastEnders* had one of the characters, Lofty, as a loser in love and another, Simon Wicks, playing in a group. The outcome was a song called 'Every Loser Wins', which Simon co-wrote with Stuart and Bradley James. Nick Berry, the actor who played Simon Wicks, took it to Number One in the UK, with the result that, in the following year, May finally received his Ivor Novello Award.

Highly successful in writing for television, he has worked very closely with Jerry Glaister, who produced *Trainer* and *Howards Way*, and with the late Julia Smith on *El Dorado* and *EastEnders*.

> I've always been honest with the producers that I've worked with, and when advising would-be writers when I give talks at schools I relate the following story to prove that honesty is the best policy. When Julia Smith asked me to write the music for the series *El Dorado*, I went back to a musical called *Mephisto* I'd written some while before and reworked it, as I genuinely thought that it would be ideal. I didn't pretend it was new, and told her that it was something I'd written for another show, but I felt that it would work for this one. She said, "Thank you for being honest and telling me." Some while later she was in conversation with a musician, who said, "Oh, Simon wrote that three years ago, didn't you know?" She was able to reply "Yes, I do know. He's already told me."

In the mid '90s, Simon was commissioned to write the score for a new film called *Caught In The Act*, and he asked me to write the lyrics for the title track. Somewhere along the line, it was decided that the opening would be a spoof operatic dream sequence, and that the lyrics would therefore sound much more authentic if sung in Italian! The nearest I could get to Italian was living close to a Roman road, but, determined not to let the side down, I reassured all parties that I would deliver the lyric in the language. At £6.99, I thought that Collins' Italian dictionary was a snip, and just as a back-up I also bought a Hodder And Stoughton "Teach Yourself" publication: *Beginner's Italian*. I looked up all the words of love that might come in useful, familiarised myself with the way the tenses were constructed, and got down to it.

I decided that 'Ci Vediamo' ('We'll Meet') would be a good title, and that, if it were to be a spoof opening, then there was no problem in going down an old-fashioned, over-the-top route lyrically. At least, that's the excuse I gave myself for following it with *"nella luce della luna"* ("in the moonlight") and for throwing in other typical lines straight out of Victorian melodrama. Lines like *"E in tutto il mondo/Tutto le stelle scintillio"* ("All over the world/All the stars will shine") and *"Non vedo viente solo te"* ("I won't see anything but you") would have sounded ghastly in English but sounded pretty smart in Italian.

I ran the whole thing past an Italian-speaking friend, who pointed out several errors that I really ought to correct or risk a personal war with Italy. It's funny how the odd letter or gender can make all the difference.

I think I got away with it. When I watched the video of the film, it sounded jolly professional, and nobody ever complained.

Another composer from the orchestral world with whom I've had the pleasure of writing is my phonetic but not actual namesake, Michael Reed. Michael has conducted over 20 West End shows, including *Phantom Of The Opera*, *Barnum*, and *Singing in the Rain*, and was also musical supervisor for the worldwide productions of Andrew Lloyd Webber's productions, including *Joseph And The Amazing Technicolour Dreamcoat*, *Whistle Down The Wind* and *Aspects Of Love*. A man of several parts, he has also orchestrated and arranged many successful shows, and has also conducted many top orchestras for television, the stage and radio, and has composed for both musicals and film, after Michael worked as musical supervisor and arranger for my musical *Great Expectations*. We started collaborating, on a musical version of *The Prince And The Pauper*, the millennium hymn '2,000 Years' and other projects, and now see a lot of each other socially but generally write apart, coming together to smoothe out any rough edges.

During our first session, I sensed that Michael wasn't too keen on having me leaning over his shoulder and making suggestions, and that he needed to be completely alone to write. This was fine by me. I feel that, in writing with somebody, you have to be aware of their needs and up to speed with their sensitivities, and that you need to work out when to pipe up and when to leave well alone.

On one session, I unwittingly drove him mad by stapling lyrics together while he was trying to make the computer accept a section of a song. It took me several minutes to work out why the music was getting louder and louder while he increasingly resembled a boiling kettle.

We both work quite happily in our own space and time, meeting up to demo or work through a song, and wishing that the other aspects of the industry allowed more time in which to be creative. On the whole, our writing relationship is clearly defined: I write the lyrics and Michael writes the music.

Guy Fletcher, on the other hand, has always worked as a songwriter. He has collaborated on many occasions, and is happy to do whatever it takes to make it work. For instance, he might be in charge of the melody and his partner responsible for the words, but both can wade into the other's territory if they think that they have something to offer. Meanwhile, I'm fairly flexible, and therefore genuinely happy with any situation which makes my collaborator feels the most comfortable.

Writing in the same room certainly keeps you on your toes. You can also hear the song taking shape, or not taking shape, which can be both inspirational and useful in weeding out musical or lyrical phrases that you might otherwise have left in. On the other hand, there can be the pressure – for better or worse – of feeling that you should finish off the song before the end of the session. Most of the musicals I've written have been solo affairs, so it's interesting working with Michael and Guy in completely different ways on two separate theatre projects.

Two lyricists for whom I can't speak, but with whose material I've worked very closely, are the two whose words I've set to music on several occasions: Sir John Betjeman and Rupert Brooke. I just hope that they would have liked the end result, and would have been pleased that their works have been given a new lease of life in a different area.

One rather peculiar collaboration came about after I'd had the idea of putting new words to Right Said Fred's hit 'I'm Too Sexy' as a single for British comedian Frankie Howard. Ever the master of the innuendo, I thought that it would be right up Frankie's street. The Fred boys very kindly allowed me to use the original backing track, and Frankie also thought it sounded like fun, so we were up and running with 'I'm To Sexy Too' It was great fun to record as he contorted his face in that familiar style to deliver the lines:

> I'm too sexy for myself, too sexy for myself…
> I often find myself saying "Nay, nay, and thrice nay…"
> Well, you've got to, haven't you?

Unfortunately, due to a few complications, the single didn't emerge, and then Frankie sadly passed away. He was a very funny man, and a British institution. I only hope that the project didn't cause him to wish himself into the next world!

Another great musician, also sadly no longer with us, was the songwriter Jerry Lordan. Jerry was the first person from the glamorous world of entertainment with whom I had my photograph taken. He was playing football locally for the Showbiz XI, and, although my friends were more excited about the various pop stars playing, I was more interested in seeing the guy who'd written big hits for Cliff Richard and The Shadows. Jerry wasn't the tallest of guys, but he still had a few inches on the young, blushing (yes, it even showed up in black and white) MR.

Born in Paddington, Lordan was educated at Finchley Grammar School, leaving at 16 to work in an ironmonger's shop before becoming a clerk in an advertising agency. At the age of 18, he went into the Royal Air Force as a radar operator, although he was desperate to get into showbusiness. While stationed at RAF West Kirby in 1952, 4107606 AC2, Lordon J, was approached by a burly, ex-Royal Marine drill instructor, who said to him, "I hear you make the lads laugh in the billet. Well, get up on the stage now and make us all laugh. That's an order!" He then added darkly: "And you'd better be funny, Lordan!"

"And that," said Jerry, "was how I started in showbusiness. I got up on the stage and cracked jokes ad lib for ten or 15 minutes, finishing off with a song. That memorable occasion in the NAAFI canteen really gave me a big kick. I then did two or three shows, miming to records, cracking jokes and singing. It was in 1955, when I came out of the RAF, that I decided to have a shot at showbusiness." He went for several auditions, most of them as a comedian, but became more and more dispirited, being forced to work in advertising agencies and for a spell as a London bus conductor.

However, it was while he was at another job, working as a projectionist at Piccadilly Circus, that he met another chap there who owned a guitar. Jerry suggested that they started to write songs together. The song that they came up with was good, but Jerry thought that they could do better. They did, coming up with 'A House, A Car And A Wedding Ring', and he and his partner also wrote 'So The Story Goes' and 'When You See Her', which they recorded under the names of Lee And Jay Elvin.

Not long after that, Jerry chalked up his second songwriting success, this time for Anthony Newley in the film *Idle On Parade*. The song 'I've Waited So Long' reached Number Three in Britain, giving Newley his first hit single. Within a year, Lordan was also having hit singles as an artist as well as a songwriter. "My own singing career started when the Parlophone office heard a few demonstration records I had made. They were quite favourably received, from a vocal point of view, and so I found myself in the recording studios." His first record, 'I'll Stay Single', made the UK Top 30 early in 1960, with the follow-up song, 'Who Could Be Bluer?', reaching the Top 20. His third single, 'Sing Like An Angel', was also a hit, making the lower reaches of the Top 40.

His songwriting career was soon to overtake his career as a singer. Another big break came after playing one of his tunes to Cliff Richard's backing group, The Shadows. Their lead guitarist, Hank Marvin, remembers talking to Jerry about songs:

> We weren't sure whether to trot out other people's songs, write our own, or whatever. We'd just come back from our first tour of the United States, and went straight into another string of British dates. On the tour with us was a young singer/songwriter called Jerry Lordan. In conversation, we got onto this problem we had, and he said, "Well, I have an instrumental which I've written." He proceeded to dig out of a small case a little ukulele, which he strummed, and sang this wonderful tune. We learned it straight away, and decided we'd like to record it. We did an arrangement of it, played it to our producer, Norrie Paramor, who thought it was terrific. ['Apache'] was initially going to be the B-side of our next single, but it got such an incredible response he agreed with us it should become the A-side. It became our first hit…went to Number One in Britain…and we've been forever in debt to Jerry Lordan and his little ukelele.

Jerry also wrote songs for Cliff, including the Top Three single 'A Girl Like You' in 1961, which was Cliff's father's all-time favourite. He continued to write for The Shadows, penning their 1962 chart topper 'Wonderful Land', which stayed at Number One for an incredible eight weeks, and co-writing another of their popular tracks, 'Mustang'. Another classic that he wrote for them was 'Atlantis', which Mark

Knopfler later referred to as "the greatest electric guitar sound you'd ever wish to get on a record...a great tune".

Hank was delighted to record yet another Jerry Lordan composition:

> 1963 was a tremendous year for us. According to *Cashbox*, we were the third biggest selling artists in the world, next to Cliff and Elvis. We'd already had two Number One hits that year, and followed them with another song that Jerry very kindly gave us, called 'Atlantis', which reached Number Two.
>
> From time to time, during the '60s, we recorded vocals. 'Mary Anne' was one of them, again written by Jerry. He brought us this beautiful ballad, which we recorded and had a Top 20 hit with. Listening to it now, I still realise how good the song is, and how it deserved better treatment. I think we approached it too simplistically. We tried to keep it too simple, and could maybe have structured it a little bit. One of these days, I think I'd like to re-record it and give it its full due.

Jerry Lordan continued to write great songs, despite the highs and lows that seem to affect many songwriters. In 1993, not long before his death, he appeared bemused and philosophical over a career of writing songs, and in particular a piece of music that he'd written in 1991: "It's a funny old business. You write and you put your heart and soul into a song. One, for example, was 'The Old Man And The Sea'...George Martin orchestrated it and we recorded it with a 32-piece orchestra in Studio One, Abbey Road. Ron Richards produced it, it went out on CBS, got two plays and sold 286 copies. It broke my heart. Then you do something like 'I'm Just A Baby' [a 1962 hit for Louise Cordet], which sells 150,000 copies...I don't know, it's a funny business."

In 1999, Jerry's widow, Claudine, sent me 'The Old Man And The Sea' with a view to me writing lyrics for it. Although I've come up with a few ideas, I want the words to be right and not rushed, as she hoped that, "Being a composer, you will undoubtedly sympathise towards Jerry's thoughts." It's strange to be asked to work on a piece of music written by the man who I stood beside in that photograph as a blushing boy.

17 Where Do We Go From Here?

Will independent songwriters ever return to claim their rightful places in popular music, or will the programmers and their technology become even more powerful? There is no doubt that the products of the computer age can improve sound quality, speed up processes that were once time consuming and laborious, generally enhance performances and create excellent patterns and rhythms. As we've heard from their own mouths, songwriters down the generations have railed against the "new music", whatever it may be.

The writers of early Victorian ballads thought Stephen Foster's songs contemptuous, while the late Victorian composers despised the onslaught of ragtime and jazz. Jazz purists loathed the commercialising of their brand of music, and many that wrote for the big bands of the '40s were disgusted at the increasing popularity of race music and rhythm and blues. Black writers were appalled at the watered-down white versions of their rock 'n' roll originals, whose proponents seized all of the credit, whereas pre-rock 'n' roll composers and lyricists dismissed the new music spearheaded by Bill Haley and Elvis Presley as puerile and inane. The arrival of The Beatles didn't suit everybody; many a writing and singing career came to a grinding halt under the onslaught of the fab four.

And so it goes, with '70s disco composers and format writers bewildered by punk, and punk writers in turn trying to hold out against the ensuing new romantic songs. The phenomenally successful partnership of Stock, Aitken and Waterman came in for much criticism from other writers in the '80s, and now it's the turn of independent songwriters to ask why barely adequate writers and their new technology have by and large supplanted them. (This, of course, doesn't apply to self-contained acts and artists, and there are many out there who still come up with durable goods.)

Unless you're also an artist, or you work as part of a production/songwriting team, your chances of getting someone to record your song in the time-honoured way – simply by sending it to them or to their company

– are virtually nil. If that route is blocked, committed writers who are not artists have to look for routes which *are* open to them, such as films, musicals, song contests, or even working in other countries.

One body that exists to help, advise and guide songwriters is the British Academy Of Composers And Songwriters, which came into existence on 1 January 1999 and is made up of three previous British writers' guilds. The oldest of the trinity was the Composers Guild Of Great Britain, which ran for over 50 years, it's members comprising only classical and concert composers. The other two were the Organisation Of Professional Composers, catering for film and television writers, and the British Academy Of Songwriters, Composers And Authors. The latter was the largest of the three, having a spread of members, from established writers to aspiring young composers and lyricists.

So what does Guy Fletcher – who, as chairman of the British Academy Of Songwriters And Composers, talks on a regular basis to fellow writers – feel about the current climate? "The future for the songwriter is quite bright, although I think it will be problematic for the independent writers. In a sense, they're dead in the water unless they align themselves with people who record, but that's always been the case, to an extent. In this day and age, they will often have to find an artist, possibly manage him and also get him a recording deal. The songwriter now has to be far more than just a composer and lyricist. Songwriters are like rivers, now, finding a different course as the old river bed dries up."

Ervin Drake admits that the situation has changed: "In an earlier era, I would fly to Columbia or Decca Records and show the latest hot-off-the-piano effort to Mitch Miller, Milt Gabler or Dave Kapp. That availability is now as dead as the Dodo bird, but we have a flourishing cabaret scene in New York, and just last year a song of mine, 'The Friendliest Thing Two People Can Do' from an old Broadway musical, was recorded by two female singers.

Despite the fact that Ervin's contemporaries stopped writing years ago, many young performers are only now discovering Ervin's songs. Recent covers of 'I Believe' by LeAnn Rimes on a quadruple-platinum album, and 'Good Morning Heartache' by Sheryl Crow on a million-selling album, prove that songwriters still have a role to fill. Leann and Sheryl are both young artists, but they haven't shied away from recording material by a senior songwriter in his 80s. In 1994, Leslie Uggams recorded a whole CD of Ervin Drake's songs.

As both songwriter and artist, Neil Sedaka is still in there, pitching, touring and re-inventing himself. "I like stepping outside myself...that always challenges me, and I like that. If you want to stay in the record business and the songwriting business, you have to be current and you have to try to appeal to young people. The '90s were the sensual years...I wanted to be politely perverse, if that makes sense. I had 'The Hungry Years', followed by the sensual years!"

Even top songwriters like Hal David have found placing songs increasingly difficult. "It seems to be getting harder and harder to encourage someone to listen to a demo of a song. In recent years, certainly in the United States, there seem to be more singer/songwriters who are more interested in just performing their own material rather than listening to someone else's creation. Having said that, time has not curtailed my enjoyment of writing, nor the feeling that I still have a lot more hits in me. I try to write a little every day. My ardour for songwriting...the art of songwriting...the creation of the popular song has never diminished."

Like Bacharach and David, Jerry Leiber and Mike Stoller might not write as many songs as they did in their heyday but the enthusiasm is still there, with several projects in the pipeline for the new century, including writing for the stage. "We're hoping to get our first musical on during the next year or year and a half. We've written 17 or 18 songs and demo'd them with a troupe of British actors and singers, as the location of the musical is London, and we want it to sound indigenous."

Leiber and Stoller are able to control and oversee their new project, but during the '50s, '60s and '70s there was a definite demarcation within the industry: there were record companies, artists, managers, publishers and songwriters, and each performed almost exclusively in their own fields of expertise. A writer would call a publisher or an artist's management company with a song that they thought suitable for a particular artist, and if it was deemed suitable then the singer would probably record it. This situation is sadly dead. Will it ever return?

Guy Fletcher thinks not. "Songwriters have become record producers and managers. Lawyers have become managers, because you're now required to be a man of the business. The partitions are down, and the divisions are no longer clearly defined. Songwriters have got to be prepared to throw in their lot with an established team, because you can no longer penetrate the business as an individual. Writers of substance are drafted in to be part of a creative team, some of whom – including the artist – may well take a share of the writing credits, and therefore a share of the royalties. That's the way it works now."

Chris Eaton is busier than ever, having written 48 songs between January and July 2000, 15 already having been recorded with more in the pipeline. "I couldn't make a living as a songwriter by staying in Britain the whole time. Nashville is full of people writing and making music on a daily basis. Everyone wants to write with you, and the whole thing is much more open."

Should the British Academy Of Composers And Songwriters be doing more to help the branding of and win more public recognition for composers and lyricists? Guy Fletcher: "We do believe that songwriters should be more recognised for their contributions to the music world. They're certainly more recognised in the States, where the top people in the profession are held in esteem and have gone down in the annals of American history...writers like Jerome Kern, Cole Porter, Richard Rodgers, Lorenz Hart, Oscar Hammerstein II and Irving Berlin."

There are now somewhere in the region of 30,000 members of the Performing Rights Society, of which just two per cent make 85 per cent of the money, so how can the academy help the struggling majority? Guy Fletcher:

> There is an extraordinary drive in your average person that leads them to believe that they can write a song, or a book, or a poem. They also believe that it's possible to be successful as a result of their creativity, and no matter how much you tell them how difficult or, sometimes, how impossible it is, they will still believe in their creation. They won't be dissuaded. So we do present an accurate picture to our members as to what the industry's about. Aspiring writers do, perhaps, expect more from being a member than the society is capable of giving them. We don't mislead songwriters into believing that we're going to help with their careers, other than in a community sense. The important thing now is that you have to do it from within the industry. You can't penetrate it from the outside. You can't stand beyond the city walls firing demos over the battlements, hoping that someone's going to pick one up. It doesn't happen any longer. Those day's have gone. The only way is from within, so we provide a songwriting and composing community with a strong political voice.

Where Do We Go From Here?

The future seems to point more to songs being written by committee. Certainly an increasing number of songs that are submitted for the annual Ivor Novello Awards appear to be assembled by a veritable football team of people. What do they all do? On the whole, a song has been traditionally regarded as the inspiration of one person, who may or may not bring in a partner to provide either words or music, but the current situation almost allows for anyone present in the room at the time of the song's conception to be credited.

On the subject of the Ivor Novello Awards, Jerry Leiber was delighted that he and Mike Stoller were recipients in 2000. "I found them very meaningful and touching...they really are about songs. To get an Ivor Novello and a Songwriter's Hall Of Fame Award in our 50th year of writing together is so wonderful."

Paul McCartney is a big fan of the songs of Leiber and Stoller and other classic material that goes back even further, to the '30s and '40s: "You go through trying to write songs, and you realise how clever some of those old songs really are. I love the thought that your songs might still be around in 200 years' time. That's one of the things that you're writing for: posterity."

Creations from almost every period have been scrutinised by the critics of the time, and the inevitable question asked: "Will this last?" In the year 2000, the media have already posed the questions "Who will be singing Spice Girls songs in 40 years' time?", "Will gold radio stations be pumping out Westlife hits every hour in 2040?", and "Isn't it highly improbable that Robbie Williams can sustain a career for the next four decades?"

All right, let's jump back 40 years to 1960. Wait a minute, that doesn't seem that long ago. Surely there can't be the same gap from 1960 to now as there is from now to 2040? 'Fraid so.

In 1960 the press was full of predictions: "No one will be singing 'Travellin' Light' and 'Oh, Carol' 30 years from now," and "It's unlikely that, in 1989, the world's teenagers will be singing Cliff Richard and Neil Sedaka." You would have got extremely good odds if you'd bet against Cliff sailing with ease past 1989, charting consistently throughout the '90s and still hitting the top of the chart as the next millennium dawned. And what would the odds have been on Neil Sedaka, notching up a gold album for his classical vocal album *Classically Sedaka* 35 years on?

Songs that are popular now will be played in 30 and 40 years' time, simply because teenagers who identify strongly with the music of any era will still have fond memories of it in their later years. Every era throws up songs that are durable, as well as those that were written for the current musical trends and others that haven't travelled well for one reason or another. It's human nature to put on the old rose-coloured glasses and just see the good ones.

Sticking with 1960 as an example, some record buyers from that period will, unsurprisingly, look back fondly on the music of the time. 'It's Now Or Never', 'Only The Lonely' and 'Cathy's Clown' get a healthy amount of radio play, and still sound good. They give 1960 a rosy glow, and a feeling that the whole year was packed with terrific music. However, apart from the thousands of records that weren't good enough to pick up airplay, let alone sell, the charts contained many records whose shelf lives was inevitably brief. When did you last hear or have a yearning to hear Top 20 hits from 1960 like 'Too Good', 'Happy Anniversary' or 'Fish Man'?

The same principle applies if we go back a further 40 years, to 1920. 'I'll Be With You In Apple Blossom Time' and 'Whispering' remained popular, and were hits again, the former in 1959 and the latter in 1963 and 1964. It follows that music lovers with fond memories of 1920 might well have perceived the writings of Von Tilzer and Malvin and John Schonberger as coming from a golden period of songwriting, but how many of them continued to hum other big hits from that year, such as 'Fill 'Em Up', 'Mr Gallagher And Mr Shean', or the lyrically demanding 'Who Put The Bricks In Brixton?' Again, there were hundreds of songs that didn't have a life outside that period, and others that were even too dire for the record buyers of the day.

With all of that said, however, in terms of songwriting the '50s, '60s and '70s will be perceived in the future (if they aren't already) as a golden age for the independent songwriter. In those decades, songwriters were very much creative artists, while studio engineers worked the desks and looked after the technical side. Now it pays for the writer to be up to speed with technology and to be aware of how it can help or hinder. It's now easier for young people – fresh out of school or college and knowing a lot about computers, but only a little about writing songs – to put a sound together that will get a deal with a record company. They may possibly have one or two things that the record company like, but if the first single doesn't go then they may well be dropped. If it's a hit, they'll get an album deal; but if that's a flop, again they'll be dropped. If that's a hit, however, they'll get another album, and so on. By and large, the days when record companies developed artists and acts and publishing companies worked on the careers of songwriters are gone.

Many songwriters, like Guy Fletcher at the British Academy Of Composers And Songwriters and Roger Greenaway at ASCAP, have moved successfully into influential positions on the business side of songwriting, and are now able to advise new composers and lyricists and fight the songwriters' quarter.

Roger has strong feelings about the difference in the current climate for songwriters and the way it was. "When we were successful, we used session musicians to make records, and they were the people that gave us that unique sound. That's why Anglo-American music ruled the world. It still does, to an extent, but not in the same way. Technology allows people from any country to sample the sounds of instruments from any record, which is why the Germans, the Dutch, the Swedes and the Japanese can produce stuff that sounds Anglo-American."

In the States, another useful organisation, the Songwriters' Guild, was formed in around 1920 by the likes of Irving Berlin and Richard Rodgers to assist writers in areas in which they needed help and to familiarise them with the legalities of what could be a complex business. However, bad deals still continued and continue to be done. The Everly Brothers, Roy Orbison and songwriters Felice and Boudleaux Bryant and John D Loudermilk all apparently signed deals with publisher Wesley Rose that proved to be less than satisfactory, which partly inspired Loudermilk to form a Nashville branch of the Songwriters' Guild, which still has a thriving thousand-strong membership.

Even though he has effectively retired (although does a writer ever really retire?), John D is keen to encourage new blood to become involved and keep the society flourishing. He has put unpleasant experiences from the past behind him, and now adopts a positive approach to life, although he still feels that "There are two types of people in the business: those who create and those who make money off those who create." This, however, doesn't check his enthusiasm in any way: "If you believe that we've been here before...then I'll be a songwriter in my next life, too. I just hope I learn some more chords!"

Songs written around basic chord structures either turn out to be the most trite or the most successful. It's becoming increasingly difficult to find natural melodies within the limitations of three or four chords, as songwriters used to do with apparent ease in the '50s and '60s.

Do songs even need as many as three chords, though? The Mavericks' 'Dance The Night Away', a huge hit in the late '90s, used only two! In fact, do modern writers need chords at all? It's often claimed that modern technology now allows anyone to become a songwriter, just as it allows anyone to become a singer. Paul Anka believes that the approach to writing has changed in many ways:

> The process in the early days was a simple one…you sat at a piano, with no tape machine as we know it today, and got the emotion down on paper. You'd structure something that had to have melody, with lyrics that could be understood, and you'd have to go into a studio with 20 or 25 people, depending on the size of the orchestra. You then had to capture that moment right there and then, and get it down on tape, as opposed to today, where the thought and the motivation is not overly concerned with quality. Now it's often a case of "Let's get the machine…Let's get the production…Let's get the vibe…and then we'll go and find two guys from McDonalds to sing it!" The song often comes last now. It's an interesting process, today.

For some of the great independent writers, like Felice Bryant, the enthusiasm has dimmed: "I really enjoyed writing when Boudleax and I started out…and we were together and writing for 42 years. I wrote a few things after he died in 1987, but I've basically given up…you get out of the habit. Anyway, many of today's artists want to do it all themselves…they want to be self-contained. But no man is an island."

So what of the future? As jazz, rock 'n' roll and punk stunned previous generations of songwriters into believing that music as they knew it was well and truly dead, will the shock value of today's lyrics become acceptable in the years to come?

At the present time, songs by 26-year-old Marshall Mathers have been denounced as "sickening", but how will they be viewed in 2030 or 2050? Recording as Eminem, his lyrics glorify rape, incest, drugs, violence and murder:

> Follow me and do exactly what the song says:
> Smoke weed, take pills, drop outta school,
> Kill people and drink.

Those words were from his 1999 release *The Slim Shady LP*, while these gems feature on his 2000 album *The Marshall Mathers LP*:

> I invented violence,
> You vile, venomous, volatile bitches.
> Knives, lives, wives, nuns, sluts.
> Bitch, im'a kill you.

Shudder you may, but there he is at the top of the chart. Disowned by his mother and on bail for assault and gun charges, he is on record as saying "I want to piss people off. I wanted people to think I was cool." One of his songs features his three-year-old daughter's voice, on a track about killing her mother, and he publicly supported the two boys who shot dead twelve of their classmates at Columbia High School in the USA.

Are these just shock tactics to appeal to a new generation, out-punking punk, or something more sinister that is beyond the realms of genuine songwriting?

Mathers isn't the only one peddling anti-social behaviour. Female pop duo Daphne And Celeste advocate bullying in their Number One single 'UGLY', at a time when authorities and parents are trying to find ways of eradicating it, with the pressures that it brings leading to more suicides. The head of policy for the support group Childline denounced the lyric as offensive: "The name-calling in 'UGLY' is just the sort of thing that young people call Childline about every day."

The sharp rise in female bullying is almost certainly due to the increased "laddish" behaviour of female role models, and the media-assisted erosion of traditional male and female roles. The lyrics to 'UGLY' that concern the authorities and those that are subjected to bullying include such lines as:

> You got eyes like a pig and your nose is big...
> You're so fat and ugly with a belly full of flab,
> When you wear a yellow coat people shout "Cab!"

Are these and Mather's songs bought for their shock value alone, or because young people really believe in the message? I suspect that there is an element of the former involved, because it's the current thing, although they are also bought for the music itself. Unnacceptable though the lyrics might be, most people aren't going to be acting on them, and will certainly grow through them as adolescence passes.

There was uproar of a similar nature in the '20s when Cole Porter brought a jazz band comprising all black musicians to Venice to play on his jazz boat. People were at each other's throats over this "threat to civilisation". The classical composer Sir Thomas Beecham became apoplectic over these outrageous musical antics of Porter, which subjected the local inhabitants to lyrics of an antisocial nature.

Rock 'n' roll, of course, was seen by many American preachers as the arrival of the devil in musical form. They felt that another Sodom and Gomorrah was upon them, and urged all right-thinking folk to smash records carrying this new and highly contagious disease. It was also thought that the type of dancing it encouraged would lead to a massive increase in teenage pregnancies.

If you're a budding songwriter, be warned: it's tough out there, but don't let that stop you; if you feel that you're bashing your head against a brick wall, don't just just think literally, think laterally. Discover your strengths and work on your weaknesses. Maybe you need to collaborate. You may need the support of the British Academy Of Songwriters And Composers. They can't write hits for you, or get them to artists, but they can offer advice and give you details of song competitions and the occasional writers' forum.

It would be wonderful to feel that the old Tin Pan Alley days could return, but the truth is that the industry has changed, and you're more likely to reach people in the music business via e-mail than by getting to know them over a drink down at the pub.

If you have a passion for songwriting, whether it be pop songs, material for musicals, film music or any other genre, there is no one to stop you. Do it. Unlike other industries, age is irrelevant in songwriting, as are tools of the trade. Thousands of songs have been written by people who can't play an instrument. As Samuel Johnson said, "A man may write at any time."

Bibliography

McCabe: *George M Cohan – The Man Who Owned Broadway* (Doubleday)
Staveacre: *The Songwriters* (BBC)
Hyland: *The Song Is Ended* (Oxford University Press)
Emerson: *Doo-Dah!* (Da Capo)
Kilgaroff: *Sing Us One Of The Old Songs* (Oxford University Press)
Ehrlick: *Harmonious Alliance* (Oxford University Press)
Cattell/Bowler: *ASCAP Biographical Dictionary*
Rice: *Oh, What A Circus* (Hodder And Stoughton)
Harris: *After The Ball* (Frank-Maurice, Inc)
McBrien: *Cole Porter* (HarperCollins)
Waters: *Victor Herbert – A Life In Music* (Macmillan)
Rice/Rice/Read/Gambaccini: *Guinness Book Of British Hit Singles*

Index

10cc 71, 300
1910 Fruitgum Co 136

Aardvarks, The 277
Abba 71, 283
Abrahams, Maurice 94
Ace Of Base 225
Ad-Libs, The 237
Adams, Cliff 132
Adams, Richard 166
Adamson, Harold 120, 122
Aerosmith 157
Air Supply 225
Akens, Jewel 135
Alexander II, Czar 91
Alexander III, Czar 91
Allison, Jerry 19, 142, 143
Allison, Mose 239
Allwood, Ralph 302
Almond, Marc 20, 193
Alquist, Russell 197
Ames Brothers, The 203, 209
Anderson, Jon 20
Anderson, Lynn 215
Andreoli, Peter 99, 237
Andrews Sisters, The 100, 123
Andrews, Barbara 13
Andrews, Chris 173-6
Andrews, Julie 13, 125
Angel, Danny 159-60
Animals, The 226, 242, 250, 300
Anka, Paul 241, 297-8, 322
Anne, Princess 293
Anthony, Mike 292
Applejacks, The 263
Arlen, Harold 118, 119, 120
Armstrong, Louis 121, 123
Arnold, Eddy 144, 212
Arodin, Sidney 121
Arthur, Brooks 236
Asher, Tony 257
Astaire, Fred 105, 107
Atkins, Chet 144, 215
Auntie Joan 13

Auric, Georges 15
Austin, Gene 200
Austin, Michael 226
Avalon Boys, The 199
Avalon, Frankie 240
Axton, Mae Boren 172
Ayers, Nat D 89, 93

Bacharach, Burt 90, 155, 156, 198, 202-7, 221, 289-30, 317
Bachelors, The 151, 181, 289
Bad English 156
Baddiel, David 183
Baker, Adrian 254
Baker, LaVern 217, 235
Baldry, Long John 198
Ball, Alan 182-3
Ball, Lucille 105
Band Aid 184
Bangles, The 151, 227-9
Barcels, The 110
Barkan, Mark 245
Barry, Jeff 211, 236-8, 243, 244-8, 276, 284, 285
Bart, Lionel 64, 181, 272-7
Bass, Alfie 272
Bassey, Shirley 238, 275, 284
Bateman, Robert 222
Batt, Mike 164-8, 239
Bay City Rollers, The 179, 183, 184
Bayer Sagar, Carole 207, 219, 306
Bayes-Norworth, Nora 93
Beach Boys, The 138, 143, 151, 254-59
Bearss, Desdemona 126
Beatles, The 21, 30, 48, 71-2, 78, 131, 140, 143, 152, 156, 158, 159, 160, 182, 192, 203, 210, 218, 226, 234, 239, 249, 253, 255, 258, 260, 262, 263, 265-9, 288 , 294, 299, 315
Beatstalkers, The 181

Beatty, Warren 162
Beck, Ronnie 299
Becker, Walter 206
Beckle, Gerry 196
Bee Gees, The 258
Beecham, Thomas 324
Beethoven, Ludvig van 22
Bell, Freddie And The Bell Boys 231
Bellamy Brothers, The 156
Belle Stars, The 238
Belloc, Hilaire 130
Benatar, Pat 226
Bennett, Brian 180, 185, 198, 253, 254, 290, 291
Bennett, Roy 134, 198, 207-11, 221
Benteen, FD 35
Benteen, Stephen 41
Benton, Brook 206
Beresford, Elizabeth 165
Berlin, Irving 59, 74, 88, 91-3, 94, 95, 104-8, 109, 118, 119, 126, 128, 318, 321
Berlioz, Hector 24
Berman, Paul 115
Berns, Bert 198, 236, 240, 245
Berry, Chuck 9, 22, 139-42, 299
Berry, Dave 143, 196
Berry, Mike 143, 176, 303
Berry, Nick 143, 309
Besley, Mr Edward QC 55
Best, George 182
Best, Pete 262
Betjeman, John 20, 302, 311
Bettis, John 172, 173
Biederbecke, Bix 121
Bienstock, Freddy 209
Big Bopper, The 143, 187
Big Three, The 160
Birds, The 288
Bishop, Henry Rowley 40
Black, Cilla 155, 181, 206, 241, 263

Black, Don 201, 301, 283-6
Blackburn 181
Blackwell, Otis 148-9
Blackwell, Ronald 134
Blagman and Meglin 133
Blake, Eubie 52
Blake, William 15
Bland, James 44, 46, 54, 56
Blann, Michael 36
Bleyer, Archie 213, 214
Blind Faith 143
Bloody Bear Tooth 147
Blossom, Henry 60
Blue Mink 193-4
Blumenburg, Marc A 59
Blunstone, Colin 20
Bob B Soxx And The Blue Jeans 245
Boer, Jay De 46
Bolan, Marc 37
Bolton, Guy 96, 113
Bonds, Gary "US" 240
Bonzo Dog Doo Dah Band, The 293-4
Boston Dexters, The 181
Bostonians, The 57
Boucicault, Dion 76
Bowers, Fred C 65
Boyd-Jones, Ernest 52
Boyle, Billy 285
Braxton, Toni 156
Briggs, David 154
Brightman, Sarah 286
Britten, Terry 198
Bron, Eleanor 266
Brooke, Rupert 20, 94, 311
Brookfield, Charles 53, 55
Brooks, Elkie 166, 239
Brooks, Garth 185
Brown, Charles 231
Brown, Edna 199
Brown, Joe E 114
Brown, John 39
Brown, Les 106
Brown, Maxine 250
Brown, Nacio Herb 201
Brown, Ruth 235, 236
Brown, Seymour 89, 93
Browne, Tara 268
Browning, Robert 126
Bruce, Tommy 187, 193
Bryant, Boudleaux 9, 211-5, 221, 321, 322
Bryant, Felice 9, 221, 211-5, 321, 322
Bryson, Peabo 251
Buchanan, James 38, 137

Buckmaster, Paul 229
Buddy Holly 168
Burkan, Nathan 62, 73-4
Burke, Johnny 124
Burns, Robert 25
Burrows, Tony 192
Buster, Prince 134
Butler, Jerry 206
Buzz, The 181
Byrds, The 17, 43, 146, 250
Byron, Lord 126

Caesar, Irving 74, 111, 201
Caesar, Julius 65
Cagney, James 83, 200
Cahn, Sammy 122-5, 130, 308
Callander, Peter 161, 162-4, 196
Callender's Original Georgia Minstrels 44
Cameos, The 176
Cameron, ST 61
Campbell, Duncan 186
Campbell, Glen 256
Cantor, Eddie 126
Capone, Al 163
Capuano, G and M 136
Carey, Mariah 156
Carlisle, Belinda 156, 225
Carlyle, Thomas 15
Carmichael, Hoagy 120-1, 122
Carpenters, The 172, 220
Carr, Michael 181, 188, 201
Carreras, José 286
Carroll, Harry 199
Carroll, Lewis 59, 168, 268
Carter, Bill 64
Carter, John 196-7, 291
Carter, President James 141
Carter-Lewis And The Southerners 196
Carus, Emma 93
Cash, Johnny 155
Cass And The Casanovas 261
Cass, Ronnie 290
Cassidy, David 184, 263
Castling, Harry 51
Cavemen 273
Chairmen Of The Board 225
Chants, The 110
Chaplin, Saul 123, 130
Chapman, Mike 189, 190-2, 293
Charles, Ray 121, 177, 235, 240

Charlton, Bobby 182-3
Charlton, Jackie 182
Cheap Trick 225
Checker, Chubby 135, 240
Checkmates, The 176
Chegwin, Keith 184
Cher 237, 174
Chesterton, GK 37-8
Chestnutt, Mark 157
Chicago 156, 251
Chiffons, The 249
Chinn, Nicky 189-92, 293
Chocolate Dandies, The 121
Chopin, Friedrich 199, 220
Christian, Neil 171
Christian, Roger 257
Christie, Tony 163, 188, 219
Christy, EP 36, 43
Christy Minstrels, The 43
Christy's Original Band Of Virginia Minstrels 30, 31
Clanton, Jimmy 218, 240
Clapton, Eric 155, 293, 299, 308
Clare, Kenny 174
Clark, Dee 246
Clark, Dick 147, 232
Clark, Petula 193
Clash, The 19
Clayland, Reverend James 23
Clayton, Merry 250
Cleobury, Stephen 302
Climie, Simon 155
Clinton, President Bill 208, 298
Close, Glenn 286
Clusky, Dec 181
Coasters, The 138, 233-5, 238, 239
Cochran, CB 127
Cochran, Eddie 144, 145, 261
Cocker, Joe 170, 263
Cody, Colonel William F ("Buffalo Bill") 81
Cody, Phil 219-20
Cogan, Alma 138, 203
Cohan, George M 38, 75-6, 77-4, 80, 81-4, 93, 104, 279
Cohan, Jerry (father) 75, 76
Cohan, Josie (sister) 75, 77
Cohan, Nellie (mother) 75
Cole, Nat "King" 121
Cole, Natalie 43
Coleridge, Samuel Taylor

126
Collins, Glenda 176
Collins, Lottie 51
Collins, Phil 223, 227
Comden, Betty 125
Como, Perry 102, 203, 207, 209
Congregation, The 195
Connolly, Billy 185
Conway, Lionel 155
Cook, Roger 189, 196, 192-3, 194-5, 197
Cookies, The 249, 250
Cooley, Spade 148
Coolidge, President Calvin 74, 88
Cooper, George 41
Coote, Robert 88
Cops And Robbers 287
Cordell, Denny 170
Cordet, Louise 314
Cossman, Bernhard 56
Cotton, Billy 182, 187, 193
Coulter, Phil 180, 182-5, 198
Courville, J 137
Coward, Noël 38, 127-8, 275, 277
Cowell, Henry 203
Cox, Michael 145, 176
Craft, Morty 216
Cramer, Floyd 215
Crandall, Eddie 142
Crane, Charlie 204
Craven, Gemma 285
Crawford, Jimmy 241
Crawford, Michael 285
Cream 17
Creatore, Luigi 214
Creme, Lol 300
Crew-Cuts, The 261
Crewe, Bob 184
Crickets, The 19, 142, 249
Crosby, Bing 42, 101, 106-7, 119, 123, 129
Cross, Christopher 207
Crow, Sheryl 316
Crowell, Rodney 155
Crusaders, The 154
Cryin' Shames, The 204
Crystals, The 243, 244, 245
Cugat, Xavier 100
Curnow, Ian 185
Curtis, Sonny 142, 145

Dale, Alan 202
Daltrey, Roger 169
Dalys, The 206

Damone, Vic 203, 206
Dana 185
Dankworth, Johnny 135, 186
Dante, Troy 187
Daphne And Celeste 323-4
Darewski, Herman E Jr 89
Darin, Bobby 121, 240, 298
Darren, James 249
Dave Clark Five, The 140, 188
Dave Dee, Dozy, Beaky, Mick And Tich 181
Davenport, Cow Cow 148
David And Jonathan 193, 263
David, Hal 202-3, 204-5, 206-7, 289-90, 317
David, Mack 202, 203
Davies, Marion 54
Davies, Ray 252
Davis, Clive 172, 227
Davis, Jefferson 39
Davis, Joe 148
Davis, Skeeter 215, 249
Day, Doris 124, 200, 259
Day, Terry 259
Dayne, Taylor 156
De Gaulle, General 293
Dean, James 282
DeBarge 156
Dee, Johnny 144
Dee, Kiki 294-5
Deene, Carole 145
Del Vikings, The 261
Delamar, Mickey 273-4
DeLange, Eddie 124
Delfont, Bernard 276
Delius, Frederick 46
DeLorien, John 189
Dempsey, Jack 98
Dene, Terry 273
Denver, John 219
DeShannon, Jackie 204
DeSylva, Buddy 113, 201
DeVille, Mink 241
D'Abo, Mike 138, 189, 190, 197
Diamond, Neil 198
Diamonds, The 241
Diana Ross 251
Dibden, Charles 25
Dickens, Charles 17, 275, 277
Dickens, Jimmy 212
Dickson, Barbara 166
Diddley, Bo 133, 141, 143

Dietrich, Marlene 203
Difford, Chris 213
Dion And The Belmonts 110
Dion, Céline 157, 155, 185, 225, 229
D'Ubaldo, Marie Clair 229
Divinyls, The 225, 229
Dixie Cups, The 236, 237, 238
Dixie Hummingbirds, The 152
Dixon, Floyd 231
Dixon, George Washington 29
Dixon, Willie 139, 141
Dobson, George C 64
Doctor, Sam 68
Dodd, Ken 181
Doggett, Alan 278-9
Dolly Sisters, The 199
Domingo, Placido 155
Donaldson, Bo And The Heywoods 163, 220
Donaldson, Walter 12, 200-1
Donegan, Lonnie 30, 144, 162, 299
Donner, Ral 149
Donovan 20, 287
Doonican, Val 293
Dorsey, Tommy and Jack 121
Douglas, Craig 239, 249
Douglas, Lord Alfred 55
Douglass, Frederick 35
Dozier, Lamont 221-5
Dr Hook 296-7
Drake, Arnold 98
Drake, Charlie 133
Drake, Ervin 98, 99, 100, 102, 103, 237, 288-9, 316
Drake, Milton 11, 98-9, 130
Drake, Nick 20, 219
Dresser, Paul 70
Drew, Patti 219
Drifters, The 196, 198, 204, 206, 222, 235-6, 240, 244, 248, 249, 249, 253
Dryden, John 23
Dubliners, The 181
Duke, Vernon 118
Dunaway, Faye 162
Dunlop, John 47, 308
Durbin, Deanne 117
Dvorak, Antonin 92
Dylan, Bob 17, 288

Earl Jean 250

Index

Eaton, Chris 20, 305-6, 318
Eckstine, Billy 110
Edens, Roger 116
Edge, Valerie 18
Edison, Thomas Alva 62
Edmunds, Dave 224
Edward, Prince Of Wales 44, 52
Edwardes, George 52, 54, 96
Edwards, Sherman 203
Egerton, Frank W 51
Eisenhower, President Dwight D 88, 107
Elbert, Donnie 224
Elegants, The 133
Elgar, Edward 19, 22
Elgins, The 224
Elizabeth II, Queen 272
Elliot, Peter 134
Ellis, Shirley 138
Ellis, Vivian 13
Elton, Ben 283
Emery, Dick 181
Eminem 322-4, 324
England Dan And John Ford Coley 154
English, Scott 170, 171-2
Epstein, Brian 159, 180, 262, 263, 268
Equals, The 134, 291-2
Erlanger, AL 78, 80
Essex, David 20, 143, 167
Estefan, Gloria 157
Eton College Choir, The 20, 302
Evans and Byron 137
Evans, Maureen 133, 241
Everly Brothers, The 17, 143, 144, 146, 150, 211, 213, 215, 226, 249, 300, 321
Everly, Don 198
Exciters, The 245

Fabares, Shelley 242
Fabian 240
Fagen, Donald 206
Fain, Sammy 42
Faith, Adam 158, 174, 206
Faithfull, Marianne 147, 252, 297
Fame, Georgie 133, 162, 170
Family Dogg 193, 194
Fardon, Don 146
Farlowe, Chris 138, 252
Farrer, John 283
Faye, Alice 105
Ferber, Edna 113

Ferguson, Johnny 145
Ferry, Bryan 263
Fields, Arthur 199
Fields, David 116
Fields, Dorothy 115, 116, 119, 201
Fields, Lew 108, 115
Fields, WC 98-9
Fifth Dimension 219
Finney, Albert 186
First Class 291
Fisher, Dan 101
Fitzgerald, Ella 99
Flack, Roberta 251
Flanagan, Bud 53, 199
Flatt, Lester 162
Fleetwoods, The 133, 137
Fleming, Ian 269
Fletcher, Guy 20, 176-8, 179, 198, 311, 316, 317-8, 321
Flett, Doug 176-8, 179, 198
Flick, Vic 174
Flowerpot Men, The 196
Flowers, Herbie 194
Flying Machine 196
Fontana, Wayne 234, 299
Ford, Emile 200
Ford, President John 107
Ford, Walter H 77
Foreman, Carl 284
Forrest, Helen 124
Forster, Therese 57
Fortunes, The 188, 193
Foster, Stephen 9, 12, 19, 23-26, 29, 31, 33-5, 36-7, 38, 40-1, 42-3, 46, 54, 56, 60, 64, 68, 75, 93, 225, 241, 315
Foster, Alexander (great-grandfather) 23
Foster, Ann (sister) 23, 38
Foster, Colonel William Barclay (father) 23, 33
Foster, John 253
Foster, Morrison (brother) 33, 34
Foundations, The 197
Four Aces, The 124
Four Freshmen, The 144, 254
Four Seasons, The 179, 184
4 The Cause 249
Four Tops, The 224, 248
Fourmost, The 160, 197, 263
Fox, Harry 199
Foxx, Charlie And Inez 133

Francis, Connie 206, 216, 217, 218
Franklin, Aretha 136, 156, 206, 250, 252
Franklin, Erma 240
Freddie And The Dreamers 161
Freed, Arthur 116
Freed, Lance 154
Froggatt, Raymond 198
Frohman, Charles 95
Froman, Jane 101, 289
Fry, Tristran 170
Fury, Billy 249

Gabler, Milt 316
Gainsbourg, Serge 181
Gallagher, Rory 20
Gallico, Paolo 95
Gardner, Ava 114
Garfunkel, Art 150, 151, 152, 167, 169, 248
Garland, Judy 90, 107, 113, 119
Garrick, David 252
Garrity, Freddie 161
Gaudio, Bob 184
Gaye, Marvin 224
Gaynor, Gloria 224
Geffen, David 157
Genesis 71
Gentry, Bobby 289
Gere, Richard 155
Gerry And The Pacemakers 112, 159, 160, 161
Gershwin, George 83, 91-2, 111, 116, 120 128, 201
Gershwin, Ira 37-8, 83, 91-2, 110, 116, 117, 118, 119, 128, 201, 279
Ghosts, The 19
Gibb, Ian 16
Gibb, Maurice 165
Gibbons, Carrol 20
Gidea Park 254
Gielgud, John 169
Gilbert, Ray 29
Gilbert, Willam 17, 53, 126, 286
Gilbert, Wolfe 39
Gillette, William 69
Gimbel, Norman 259
Glaister, Jerry 309
Glancy, Ken 162
Gleason, Jackie 125
Glitter, Gary 141
Gluck, John Jr 245

Goddard, Geoff 20, 143, 302-5
Godfrey, Arthur 212
Godley, Kevin 299, 300
Goethe, Johann Wolfgang von 76
Goetschius, Percy 108
Goffin, Gerry 198, 211, 233, 241, 242, 243, 248-9
Gold, Walter 214
Goldner, George 236, 238
Goldsboro, Bobby 206
Goldwyn (Goldfish), Samuel 81
Goodman, Benny 121
Gordon, Mack 120
Gordy, Berry 225, 221-2, 223-4
Gore, Lesley 219
Gorman, Freddie 222
Gormley, Peter 178, 291
Gornelsky, Giorgio 299
Gorney, Jay 118
Gouldman, Graham 160, 299
Gounod, Charles 24
Grable, Betty 105
Grace, Bob 172, 306
Graham, Irvin 288
Grand Funk Railroad 251
Grant, Cary 72
Grant, Earl 249
Grant, Eddy 291
Grappelli, Stephane 169
Grasshoppers, The 19
Gray, Dobie 154
Grayson, Kathryn 114
Green, Adolph 125
Green, Derek 172
Green, Jerome 139
Green, Teddy 290
Greenaway, Roger 187, 189, 196, 198, 192-3, 194-5, 321
Greenfield, Howard 72, 131, 215-20, 221, 233, 243, 249
Greenwich, Ellie 211, 236-8, 243, 244-8
Grey, F Clifford 89
Grieg, Edvard 166
Grossmith, George Jr 53, 95, 200
Guess, Don 142

Haley, Bill (And The Comets) 142, 260, 315

Hall, Owen 52
Hambitzer, Charles 92
Hamilton, George IV 144
Hamlin, Fred 59
Hamlisch, Marvin 86
Hamm, Charles 25
Hammer, Jack 149
Hammerstein, Oscar II 72-3, 83, 84, 97, 107, 108, 110-1, 112, 113, 114-5, 116, 117, 118, 120, 201, 275-6, 318
Hammond, Albert 20, 194, 201, 306-7
Hand, Judge Learned 63
Harbach, Otto 113, 115, 116, 118, 120, 201
Harburg, YP "Yip" 92, 117, 118, 119, 201
Hardin, Glen D 19
Harding, Phil 185
Harley, Steve 20, 138, 285
Harlow, Jean 110
Harris, Charles Kassell 63-9, 71, 72, 74, 75, 94, 101
Harris, Emmylou 215, 297
Harris, Jet 253
Harris, Richard 274
Harris, Sam H 78, 80, 81
Harrison, George 152, 169, 261-2, 264, 268, 269
Harrison, James 199
Hart, Charles 283, 301
Hart, Lorenz 83, 108, 109, 110, 111, 112, 119, 127-8, 276, 286, 318
Hatch, Tony 138
Hawker, Ken 196
Hawkins, Micah 29
Hawkshaw, Alan 176
Hawtrey, Charles 53
Hayes, Melvin 290
Haymes, Dick 200
Hayward, Justin 20, 294
Hayworth, Rita 117
Hazlewood, Lee 232
Hazlewood, Mike 194, 306
Hearst, Randolph 54
Heart 225, 227
Heath, Bill 307
Heath, Ted 134, 186
Hedges Brothers And Jacobson, The 199
Heinz 176, 302
Heller, Jack 241
Henderson, David 66
Hendrix, Jimi 140, 164

Herbert, Victor 56, 57-61, 62, 63, 73, 74, 97, 113, 120, 201
Herman's Hermits 17, 196, 197, 250, 279, 299
Herriett, Vernon 89
Hi-Los, The 254
Hicks, Thomas 273
Higgenbotham, Irene 100-1
Hill, Dan 244, 148
Hilliard, Bob 42, 204
Hilliard, Harriett 105
Hillside Singers, The 195
Hirsch, Louis 93, 94
Hitler, Adolf 97, 293
Hodge, Al 179
Hodkinson, JW 179
Hoffman, Dustin 151, 270
Hogg, Quentin 293
Holiday, Billie 100, 101
Holland, Brian 221-5
Holland, Eddie 221-5
Holliday, Michael 203
Hollies, The 143, 179, 195, 196, 223, 240-1, 299
Holly, Buddy 9, 17, 22, 139, 142-3, 156, 164, 170, 215, 226, 239, 261, 298, 299, 303
Holmes, Jordan 229
Holmes, Justice Oliver Wendell 63
Honeycombs, The 252, 303-4
Hooke, General Joseph 40
Hope, Bob 119
Hopkin, Mary 196
Horner, James 155
Horowitz, Charles 65
Hoschna, Karl 118
Hot Chocolate 285
Houston, Whitney 156, 225, 227, 251
Howard, Eddy 101
Howard, Frankie 311-2
Howard, May 101
Howlett Davis, G 61
Howlin' Wolf 141
Hubbly, John 166-7
Hughes, Robert 85
Humperdinck, Engelbert 186, 188, 193
Hurt, John 169
Huss, John 95

Ibsen, Henrik 76
Icicle Works, The 19

INDEX

Ikettes, The 238
Ink Spots, The 123
Innes, Neil 293
Irwin, Big Dee 177
Isley Brothers, The 224

J Geils Band, The 223
Jackson Five, The 223
Jackson, Chuck 204
Jackson, Michael 284-5
Jackson, Stonewall 145
Jagger, Mick 22, 136, 164, 252, 254
Jam, The 20
James, Dick 138, 158, 159, 160, 262
James, Edward 17
James, Harry 124, 199-200
James, Sidney 273
James, Sonny 215
James, Stuart and Bradley 309
Jan And Dean 254
Janks, Almet 126
Jay And The Americans 240, 242
Jaynetts 131
Jennings, Will 153-5, 172-3
Jimmie Lunceford Band, The 123
Jo Jo Gunne 140
John, Dr 241
John, Elton 165, 170, 173, 179, 201, 220, 253, 283, 295
Johnny And Jack 212
Johnny Ralph Trio, The 164
Johnson, Howard 200
Johnson, Johnnie 139
Johnson, Lonnie 121
Johnson, Lou 206
Johnson, Robert 19
Johnson, Samuel 324
Johnston, Bruce 255, 256, 257, 258, 259
Jolson, Al 43, 90, 98, 101, 200
Jones, Brian 173
Jones, Catherine Zeta 143
Jones, George 215
Jones, Isham 121
Jones, Jack 204
Jones, Joe 238
Jones, Sidney 96
Jones, Tom 185, 186, 188, 188, 219, 238, 284
Joplin, Scott 68, 85-6, 93

Jose, Dick 101
Judas Priest 140
Justice, Jimmy 249
Justis, Bill 261

Kaempfert, Bert 208
Kahn, Gus 120, 200-1
Kallen, Kitty 99
Kapp, Dave 316
Kaufman, Paul 292
Kaye, Benjamin 108
Kaye, Chuck 154
Keats, John 126
Keel, Howard 114
Keith, BF 75
Keith, Brian 195
Keller, Jack 137, 242
Kellog, Bonita and Shirley 200
Kelly, Gene 117
Kelly, Grace 129
Kelly, Tom 225, 226-9
Kennedy, Jimmy 181, 201
Kennedy, President John F 151, 246, 265
Kennedy, Terry 196
Kenny 184
Kent, Walter 98
Kern, Jerome 74, 83, 95-7, 98, 107, 113, 114-5, 116, 117-8, 200, 201, 201, 318
Kerr, Richard 154, 170-3
Kestrels, The 192
Khan, Chaka 225
Kids Next Door, The 135
Kilyeni, Edward 92
King 249
King, BB 154-5
King, Ben E 235-6, 238-9, 249
King, Carole 156, 198, 211, 217, 219, 233, 237, 242, 243, 248-9
King, Dave 203
King, Harry 137
King, Jonathan 55, 70-1, 122
King, Solomon 215
Kings College Chapel Choir, The 20, 302
Kingston Trio, The 102
Kingston, Bob 196
Kinks, The 226, 252
Kirk, Andy 123
Kirshner, Don 217, 219, 241, 242
Klaw, Marc 80-1
Kleber, Henry 30-Jan

Kneass, Nelson 33
Knopfler, Mark 313-4
Koehler, Ted 119
Kossoff, David 290
Kramer, Billy J (And The Dakotas) 43, 206 240, 263
Krupa, Gene 43, 121
Kursaal Flyers, The 166

LaBelle, Patti 207
Laine, Frankie 212, 289
Lamb, Joseph 86-7, 93
Lambrettas, The 235
Land, David 281
Laska, Edward 96
Lasky, Jesse M 83
Last, James 43
Lauper, Cyndi 227, 228, 229, 238
Laurel And Hardy 199
Lawrence, Steve 203, 241, 249
Leahy, Dick 164, 183
Leander, Mike 280-1
Lee And Jay Elvin 312
Lee, Brenda 196
Lee, Colonel Robert E 39
Lee, Dickey 242
Lee, Leapy 187
Lee, Peggy 148, 219, 239
Lehar, Franz 97
Leiber, Jerry 18, 138, 148, 156, 198, 230-9, 239-40, 243, 244, 245, 246, 247, 249, 317, 319,
Leigh, Vivien 149
Lennon, John 17, 19, 21, 22, 37, 71-2, 78, 141, 143, 160, 164, 165, 170, 192, 193, 220, 228, 249, 254, 258, 259-60, 261-69, 271, 288
Lennon, Julian 169, 268
Leno, Dan 137
Lerner, Alan Jay 113
Lester, Mark 275
Lettermen, The 241
Levey, Ethel 78, 80, 93-4
Levey, Sol 78
Levy, Lou 210
Lewis, Jerry Lee 140, 149
Lewis, Ken 196-7
Lewis, Sam 200
Leyton, John 303
Libby, James Aldrich 68
Lieber 9
Lightning Seeds, The 183

Lincoln, Abraham 39, 41-2
Lindsay, Derry 185
Lisberg, Harvey 299, 300
Liszt, Franz 24
Little Esther 232
Little Eva 250
Little River Band 225
Little Walter 141
Little Willie John 148
Littlewood, Joan 274
Lloyd Webber, Andrew 18, 80, 201, 272, 277-83, 285-6, 301-2, 310
Lloyd Webber, William 277
Lockwood, Joseph 298
Locorriere, Denis 296
Loesser, Arthur 97
Loesser, Frank 97, 122, 123, 242
Logan, Johnny 76
Lombardo, Guy 208
Long, Shorty 224
Lordan, Jerry 193, 312-4
Los Bravos 181
Loudermilk, John D 19, 143-7, 211, 212, 321
Louis, Joe 106
Louisiana Hayride 212
Love Affair 252
Love, Darlene 237, 245
Love, Mike 151, 254, 255, 257, 259
Lover, Samuel 56
Lovin' Spoonful, The 17
Lulu 284
Luman, Bob 155
Lunceford, Jimmie 130
Lynch, Kenny 241, 249, 263
Lynn, Loretta 154
Lynn, Vera 156, 208
Lynne, Jeff 228

Macauley, Tony 171, 189, 195, 196, 197-8
Macdonald, Ballard 199
MacDonough, Glen 59
Mackay, Clarence 104
Mackay, Ellin 104
Mackintosh, Cameron 169, 277
Macleod, John 197-8
Macpherson, Ian 207
Madonna 225, 226
Mamas And The Papas, The 174, 259
Mancini, Henry 156, 203, 285

Manfred Mann 245, 250
Manilow, Barry 156, 172, 173, 259
Mann, Barry 233, 241-4, 249
Marbury, Elizabeth 126-7
March, Little Peggy 259
Marillion 137
Marlin, Lena 19
Marmalade 198
Marquess Of Queensberry 53, 55
Marthyn, John 131
Martin, Bill 180, 181-3, 183-5, 198
Martin, Dean 282
Martin, Derek 148
Martin, Freddy 107
Martin, George 158, 159, 264, 267, 269-70, 314
Martin, Ricky 156
Martini, Giovanni 214
Martinu, Bohuslav 203
Martyn, Beverly 287
Marvelettes, The 222
Marvin, Hank 134, 198, 253-4, 290, 313
Mason, Barry 158, 159-60, 185-9, 193, 194, 196, 198
Mason, David 267, 271
Mason, Lowell 93
Masser, Michael 251
Mathieu, Mireille 181
Mathis, Johnny 219
Mötley Crüe 227
Mauldin, Joe B 142
Mavericks, The 322
May, Simon 20, 307-9
Mayall, John('s Bluesbreakers) 17
Maynard, Ambrose 49
Mazelle, Kym 308
McCarthy, Joseph 199-200
McCartney, Paul 9, 17, 21, 22, 37, 72, 78, 115, 131, 140, 141, 143, 159, 160, 164, 165, 170, 192, 193, 254, 258, 259-71, 294, 319
McCartney, Linda (wife) 270
McCartney, Michael (brother) 261
McCormack, Mark 188
McCoys, The 148
McDaniels, Gene 204, 240, 249
McDonald, Jeanette 114

McDonald, Michael 207
McDowell, Dr 41
McDowell, Jane 35, 42
McGraw, Jack 171
McHugh, Jimmy 115, 116, 119
McKenna, Virginia 284
McKenzie, Scott 259
McKeown, Les 184
McLean, Don 20, 143
McPhatter, Clyde 217
McQueen, Steve 270
Meek, Joe 64, 70, 176, 181, 204, 218, 302-3, 304
Melanie 252
Melanie C 225, 229
Mendelssohn, Felix 24, 126, 281
Mendes, Sergio 290
Mercer, Johnny 117, 118, 119, 122, 201, 202
Merman, Ethel 107
Merrick, David 289
Merrill, Bob 125
Merseybeats, The 137, 187, 206
Metcalfe, James 79
Meyer, Joseph 201
Michener, James A 112
Middle Of The Road 136
Midler, Bette 225
Migil Five, The 133-4
Milburn, Amos 231
Miles, Bernard 275
Milhaud, Darius 203
Millar, Gertie 54
Miller, Barbara 294-5
Miller, Frankie 154, 155
Miller, Gary 138
Miller, Glenn 43, 121
Miller, Marilyn 113
Miller, Mitch 132, 289, 316
Milli Vanilli 156
Mills Brothers, The 121, 123
Mills, Garry 211
Mills, Gordon 187
Mills, Jo 187
Mills, Sid 208
Miracles, The 224
Molière 76
Moments, The 136
Monaco, James V 199-200
Monaco, Joe 247
Monckton, Lionel 54-5, 88, 96, 97
Monckton, Sir John 54
Monkees, The 219, 238, 250

Monro, Matt 276, 284
Monroe, Marilyn 105
Monroe, Vaughan 124, 208
Montgomery, Bob 142
Moody, Ron 275, 290
Moore, Bobby 182
Moore, Christie 185
Moore, Raymond 101
Moore, Thomas 24, 25, 39, 60
Moretti, Guiseppe 42
Morgan, Helen 113
Morris, Eric 134
Morris, George P 25
Morrison, Van 181, 85
Morton, Charles 47
Morton, George 247
Morton, Lionel 290
Moss, Jennifer 176
Most, Dave 17
Most, Mickie 70, 189, 191, 197, 250
Move, The 164, 170, 252-3
Mozart, Wolfgang Amadeus 308
Mud 191
Muir, Lewis 39, 93, 94
Muldaur, Maria 220
Munro, Janet 273
Murray, Anne 144
Murray, Mitch 158, 159-65, 196
Musel, Bob 11
Music Explosion, The 196
Myers, Peter 290
Mystics, The 133, 240

Nashville Teens, The 146, 147
Navarro, Ramon 114
Nazareth 215
Nelson, Ricky 105, 226
Nesbitt, Cathleen 94
Neville, Aaron 155
Nevins, Al 217
New Order 183
New Seekers, The 195
New Vaudeville Band, The 196
New World 191
Newey, Denis 196
Newley, Anthony 102, 137, 275, 313
Newman, Paul 86
Newman, Randy 43
Nicol, Jimmy 267
N'Sync 157

Nitzche, Jack 155
Nixon, President Richard 235
Nolan, Agnes 80
Nolan, Alice 80
Noone, Peter 197
Norworth, Jack 93
Nowels, Rick 225, 229
Noyes, Alfred 126

Oates, Terry 171
Offenbach, Jacques 214
O'Brien, Dennis F "Cap" 76
O'Connell, John 61
O'Connor, Des 188
O'Sullivan, Richard 290
Oldham, Andrew Loog 175
Orbison, Roy 262, 43, 154, 155, 173, 211, 215, 217, 228-9, 321
Orioles, The 19
Orlando, Tony 242, 249
Osborn, Joe 152
Osborne Brothers, The 215
Osborne, Gary 173, 201, 294
Osmond, Donny 184, 251
Osmonds, The 191
Otis, Johnny 231, 232
Overlanders, The 263

Paige, Elaine 285
Paper Lace 163
Paramor, Norrie 149, 278, 282, 290, 313
Paramounts, The 235
Paris Sisters, The 241
Parish, Mitchell 121
Parker, Colonel Tom 210
Parker, Ray Junior 134, 296
Parks, Van Dyke 257-8
Parnell, Jack 186
Parry, Hubert 15
Parsons, Dave 138
Parsons, Gram 144
Parton, Dolly 215
Partridge, Don 171
Pastor, Tony 92
Paul, Don 170, 171
Paxton, George 241
Payne, Freda 225
Payne, John Howard 40
Pearce, Edwin 30
Pearls, The 222
Peel, Jonathan 170
Peretti, Hugo 214
Perkins, Carl 149

Perrin, Les 187
Perry, Richard 229
Perón, Eva 282
Perón, Juan 282
Peter And Gordon 143, 263, 265
Peter Pears, Sir 208
Peters, Lauri 290
Peters, WC 34
Peterson, Paul 242
Peterson, Ray 244
Petty, Norman 142
Phase Four 164
Phelps, William Lyon 126
Philip And Vanessa 122
Phillips, Jimmy 180, 181, 273-4
Phillips, John 259
Phillips, Sam 149
Piantadosi, Al 93
Picasso, Pablo 270
Pickettywitch 198
Pickford, Mary 74
Picone, Vito 133
Pinckard, George 27
Pitney, Gene 20, 193, 205, 242, 243, 249
Platters, The 115
Pockriss, Lee 203
Pointer Sisters, The 244
Poitier, Sidney 284
Pomus, Doc 9, 133, 148, 198, 214, 233, 239-41
Poncia, Vinnie 99, 237, 296
Porter, Cole 83, 103, 125-9, 318, 324
Pound, George W 61
Powell, Dick 105
Powers, Tony 244, 245
Prado, Perez 282
Pratt, Mike 181, 273
Preminger, Otto 117
Presley, Elvis 18, 29, 90, 105, 134, 142, 148-9, 208, 209, 210, 214, 226, 227, 231-2, 239, 240, 260, 292, 293, 299, 314, 315
Presley, Reg 213
Preston, Johnny 133, 137, 190
Pretenders, The 225
Price, Alan 136
Price, Lloyd 149
Prima, Louis 119
Prince 227
Proby, PJ 263
Proclaimers, The 19

333

Procol Harum 170, 239
Puccini, Giacomo 221
Pursey, Jimmy 138
Putnam, Norbert 154

Quarrymen, The 261
Quatro, Suzi 192
Quick, Diane 285
Quickly, Tommy 180
Quiet Five, The 151

Racey 191
Rachmaninov, Sergei 22
Rahmen, AR 286
Raleigh, Ben 244, 245
Ramsay, Alf 182, 183
Rank, J Arthur 293
Raydio 134
Raye, Don 130
Raymonde, Ivor 165
Reagan, President Ronald 106
Real Thing, The 110
Redding, Otis 252
Reddy, Helen 173, 220
Redford, Robert 86
Reed, Les 185-6, 187-8, 195, 196, 198
Reed, Michael 20, 310-1
Reed, Oliver 275
Reed, Stuart 187
Reese, Lizette 14
Reeves, Jim 172, 215
Reeves, Martha And The Vandellas 222
Regan, Russ 254
REO Speedwagon 225
Resnick, Art 198, 244, 245
Revere, Paul And The Raiders 146
Reynolds, Tommy 208
Rice, Dan 30, 31
Rice, Sir Tim 18
Rice, Thomas Dartmouth "Daddy" 29-30
Rice, Tim 9-10, 18, 167, 201, 239, 272, 277-83, 286, 301
Rich Kids 184
Richard, Cliff 20, 134, 143, 149, 159, 163, 168, 169, 178, 179-80, 195, 196, 198, 210, 236, 239, 240, 252, 253, 263, 273-4, 290, 291, 292, 299, 305, 308, 312, 313, 314, 319
Richards, Keith 22, 140, 164, 252, 254, 288
Richards, Ron 158
Richards, Sam 130
Richie, Lionel 244
Riggs, Lynn 110, 127
Right Said Fred 311
Righteous Brothers, The 243
Riley, Billy Lee 241
Rimes, LeAnn 156, 316
Rip Chords, The 254, 256
Ritenour, Lee 296
Ritter, Text 144, 148, 215
Rivers, Johnny 224
Rivers, Tony And The Castaways 254
Roach, Hal 199
Robbins, Marty 43, 203
Robertson, BA 185, 198
Robertson, Max 165
Robeson, Paul 114
Robin, Barry 165
Robin, Leo 117-8, 125
Robins, The 232, 233, 235
Robinson, Floyd 37
Robinson, Lilla 93
Rock-olas, The 19
Rockin' Berries, The 138, 250
Rodgers, Richard 97-8, 107, 108-9, 110, 111, 112, 113, 119, 127-8, 201, 201, 275-6, 286, 318, 321
Rodolfus Choir, The 302
Rogers, Ginger 105
Rolling Stones, The 136, 143, 164, 173, 175, 226, 234, 252, 263, 287, 292
Romberg, Sigmund 118, 201
Ronettes, The 236, 237, 243, 246
Ronstadt, Linda 225
Rooftop Singers, The 192
Roosevelt, President 73, 83, 144
Rose, Billy 120
Rose, Fred 212
Rose, Jessie Welsh 41
Rose, Vincent 98
Rose, Wesley 211, 214
Rosenfeld, Monroe 85, 90
Ross, Diana 101, 155, 223
Ross, Shirley 110
Rostill, John 198, 253, 254
Rowe, Dick 132, 165
Roxy Music 138
Royal Marines, HM Band Of 20

Rubens, Paul 52, 96
Rubettes, The 138
Rubinstein, Artur 216
Ruffin, Bruce 136
Ruffin, David And Jimmy 249
Russal, Thane 19
Russell, Henry 25-6
Ryan, Paul and Barry 241
Rydell, Bobby 241

Sainte-Marie, Buffy 155
Saints, The 176
Salter, Mike 92-3
Sam The Sham (And The Pharaohs) 134, 234
Samwell, Ian 198, 273
Sarne, Mike 196
Sarstedt, Robin 122
Sayer, Leo 20, 215, 295-6
Schenk, Joseph 104
Schmidt, Dr Wilhelm 56
Schonberger, John and Malvin 98, 320
Schroeder, Aaron 210, 214
Schumann, Robert 221
Schwartz, Jean 200
Scott, James 86, 87, 93
Scott, Linda 115, 133
Scott, Randolph 105
Scott, Tommy 181
Scott, Walter 25
Screaming Lord Sutch 138, 234
Scruggs, Earl 162
Seals, Dan 154
Seals, Troy 154
Searchers, The 138, 143, 234, 240
Secombe, Harry 275
Sedaka, Neil 22, 72, 131, 199, 215-21, 233, 243, 248, 249, 293, 317, 319
Sellers, Peter 263
Sensations, 245
Sensible, Captain 20, 169
Sentieri, Joe 238-9
Shadows, The 122, 159, 185, 243, 254, 290, 299, 312, 313
Shakespeare, John 196
Shane, Bobby 102
Shangri-Las, The 247
Shannon, Del 263
Shapiro, Helen 148, 192
Sharp, Cecil 87-8
Sharples, Tom 47

Shaw, Artie 121
Shaw, Geoffrey 14
Shaw, George Bernard 76
Shaw, Oliver 25
Shaw, Sandie 174, 175, 181, 204, 206
Shayne and Regney 137
Shelley, Percy 126
Shelley, Pete 165
Sheridan, Tony 253, 262
Sherwell, Michael 16
Sherwell, Robert 16
Shirelles, The 203, 244
Shirl, Jimmy 288
Shirley And Company 296
Sholes, Steve 217
Shuman, Mort 9, 148, 133, 198, 198, 214, 233, 239-40
Sigerson, Davitt 229
Sill, Lester 232
Silver, Abner 98, 214
Silvers, Louis 201
Silvers, Phil 117
Silverstein, Shel 296-7
Simon, Carly 156
Simon, Neil 206-7, 289
Simon, Paul 22, 131, 150-3, 248, 287
Sinatra, Frank 102, 107, 124, 125, 129, 183
Slik 184
Sloan, Tod 78
Sloman, Charles 137
Smith, Carl 212
Smith, Dodie 198
Smith, Ethel 100
Smith, Harry B 57, 58
Smith, Jackie 185
Smith, Julia 309
Smith, Keely 119
Smith, Mike 162
Smokie 191, 293
Snow, Hank 172
Snyder, Bill 110
Soft Cell 223
Soft Machine 19
Sondheim, Stephen 125, 201
Sousa, John Philip 60-1, 68, 74
Souther, JD 155
Spears, Britney 156
Spector, Phil 233, 236-7, 243, 244, 245, 246
Spencer Davis Group, The 155
Spice Girls, The 225, 229

Springfield, Dusty 156, 204, 206, 240, 250, 290
St Cyr, Johnny 303
St Louis Union 263
Stainer, Sir John 46
Stanford, Charles Villiers 46
Stanshall, Viv 294
Stardust, Alvin 20, 168
Stargazers, The 132
Stark, John 85, 86, 87
Starr, Ringo 262, 269
Starship 156
Status Quo 138, 238
Stealer's Wheel 239
Steele, Tommy 34, 162, 181, 196, 273, 273, 274
Steeleye Span 166
Steely Dan 206
Steinberg, Billy 225-8
Steinman, Jim 283, 301
Stephens, Geoff 188, 195, 196, 198, 285, 287
Stevens, Cat 164, 165, 170, 172, 219
Stevenson, John 25
Stevenson, Williami "Mickey" 224
Stewart, Al 219
Stewart, Eric 300
Stewart, Rod 224, 250
Stilgoe, Richard 283, 301
Stillman, Al 288
Stirling, Peter Lee 187
Stoller, Mike 9, 18, 138, 148, 156, 198, 230-9, 239-40, 243, 244, 245, 247, 249, 317, 319
Stone, Sly 225
Stones, Rolling 140
Storme, Robb And The Whispers 254
Stothart, Herbert 118
Stott, Lally 136
Strange and Sheldon 135
Stratton, Eugene 51, 52, 53
Strauss, Eduard 56
Strauss, Johann 56, 59
Strawbs, The 197
Streisand, Barbra 156, 224, 227, 286
Stritch, Elaine 285
Strong, Barrett 132, 235
Strouse, Charles 285
Stuart, Leslie 50-1, 52, 53-4, 55, 56, 96
Stubbs, Una 290
Styne, Jule 88, 123-4, 125,

201, 285
Sullivan, Arthur 17, 53, 58, 126, 127, 286
Sullivan, Niki 142
Summer Set, The 254
Suppé, Franz von 58
Supremes, Mike 248
Supremes, The 222-3, 224
Surfaris, The 234
Sutcliffe, Stuart "262, 263
Sweet, The 138, 189, 190, 191
Swinging Blue Jeans, The 206

T Rex 37
Tangerine Peel 189
Tarney, Alan 198
Taupin, Bernie 165
Taylor, Evelyn 174
Taylor, James 43, 219, 251
Tchaikowsky, Pyotr Ilich 221
Temptations, The 132, 224
Tepper, Sid 134, 198, 207-11, 221
Thin Lizzy 184
Thomas, Jasper 139
Thomas, Linda Lee 127
Thomas, Rufus 136
Thompson, Sue 145
Thornton, Willie Mae "Big Mamma" 231
Thurber, Jeanette 57
Thurman, Carole 154
Tierney, Henry 199
Tillotson, Johnny 292
Tilzer, Harry Von 74, 90, 92, 155, 320
Toggery Five, The 252
Tokens, The 250
Tomlinson, Eliza Clayland 23
Tomorrow 263
Torme, Mel 109
Tornados, The 176, 218, 302
Tosh, Peter 140
Townshend, Pete 164, 252, 288
Tracie 136
Trade Winds, The 237
Traffic 155
Trainspotters, The 19
Trapp, Maria Augusta 112
Travers, Bill 284
Travis 19
Treadwell, George 236
Tremeloes, The 161, 184
Trent, Jackie 175

335

Truth, The 263
Turner, Big Joe 239
Turner, Ike And Tina 248, 156
Turner, Joe 235
Turner, Spyder 249
Twain, Shania 185
Twice As Much 252
Twinkle 181
Twitty, Conway 154
Tygers Of Pan Tang, The 234

UB40 302
Uggams, Leslie 316
Ultravox 184
Untamed, The 253
Ure, Midge 184, 185
Usher, Gary 257

Valance, Ricky 244
Valens, Ritchie 143
Vallee, Rudy 101
Valli, Frankie 179
Van Heuson, Jimmy 124, 125
Vance, Paul 203
Vance, Tommy 252
Vanilla Fudge 223
Vaughan, Frankie 204, 209
Vaughan, Sarah 203
Vaughn, Billy 136
Vee, Bobby 135, 137, 144, 145, 248-9
Velasquez, Jaci 305
Velvelettes, The 224
Venosa, Arnold 133
Ventures, The 234
Verdi, Guiseppe 24
Versatile Three, The 89
Victoria, Queen 44, 50
Victoria, Vesta 89
Videls, The 237
Vigrass, Paul 294
Villa Lobos, Heitor 217
Vincent, Gene 260-1
Vinton, Bobby 137, 206, 137
Virginia Minstrels, The 30
Viscounts, The 170
Vogues, The 242

Wagner, Richard 24
Wainman, Phil 189
Walden, Narada Michael 227
Walker Brothers, The 184, 204
Walker, Junior And The All Stars 224
Walker, Noel 165
Walker, Scott 20, 198
Walker, T Bone 239
Wall, Thomas 49, 50
Waller, Fats 123
Wallis, Shani 275
Walsh, Jerry 153-4
Ward, Billy And The Dominoes 121
Ward, Clifford T 219
Warnes, Jennifer 173
Warren, Diane 9, 156-7, 201
Warwick, Dionne 154, 173, 206, 207, 289
Waterhouse, Keith 285
Waterman, Pete 71, 235
Waters, Muddy 139, 141
Watts, Dr Isaac 28
Wayne, Jeff 294
Wayne, Sid 214
Weathermen, The 224
Webb, Marti 285
Webber, AL 20
Weill, Cynthia 233, 241-4
Weiss and Harmon 133
Weiss, George 214
Weiss, Shelley 177
Welch, Bruce 134, 180, 198, 253-4, 290, 291
Welk, Lawrence 43
Wells, George 218
Wells, Houston And The Marksmen 176
Wells, Kitty 213
Wesley, Charles 28
West, Mae 98-9
Westlake, Clive 241
Weston, Kim 224
Weston, RP 89
Wexler, Jerry 250
White Plains 195
White, Jack 156
Whitehouse, Mary 141
Whitfield, Norman 132, 222, 224
Whiting, George 200
Who, The 148, 164, 252, 252
Wild, Jack 275
Wilde, Kim 223
Wilde, Marty 239, 273
Wilde, Oscar 53, 55, 126

Wilder, Billy 206-7, 289
Wilder, State Senator Doug 44
Williams Brothers, The 124
Williams, Andy 124, 211, 220, 240
Williams, Danny 211
Williams, Deneice 169
Williams, Harry 73
Williams, Ray 165
Williams, Robbie 125, 319
Willis, Chuck 148
Wills, Chill 199
Willson, Meredith 132
Wilson, Brian 151, 254-59
Wilson, Carl 254
Wilson, Dennis 254-5
Wilson, George 59
Wilson, Jackie 221
Wilson, Mary 223
Wilson, Nancy 219
Wilson, President Woodrow 81
Windsor, Barbara 274
Winger, Debra 155
Winwood, Steve 155
Withers, Bill 155
Witherspoon, Jimmy 231
Witmark, Isidore 77, 81
Witmark, Julius 68
Wizzard 252-3
Wodehouse, PG 96, 113, 114, 201
Wolf, Peter 155
Wombles, The 165
Wood, Roy 164, 252
World Of Oz, The 137
Wrubell, Allie 29
Wynter, Mark 218

Yardbirds, The 287, 299
Yates, Peter 290
Yearwood, Trisha 156-7
Youmans, Vincent 118, 119, 120, 201
Young, Joe 200
Young, Kenny 198
Young, Neil 219
Young, Paul 20
Yuro, Timi 206

Zanders and Stevens 131
Zanuck, Darryl 43
Zeppelin, Led 218
Ziegfeld Follies 104, 200